HOW RUSSIA VOTES

HOW RUSSIA VOTES

Stephen White
University of Glasgow

Richard Rose
University of Strathclyde

Ian McAllister
University of Manchester

CHATHAM HOUSE PUBLISHERS, INC.

CHATHAM, NEW JERSEY

How Russia Votes

Chatham House Publishers, Inc.
Box One, Chatham, New Jersey 07928

Copyright © 1997 by Chatham House Publishers, Inc.

Publisher: Edward Artinian
Production supervisor: Katharine F. Miller
Cover design: Lawrence Ratzkin
Composition: Bang, Motley, Olufsen
Printing and binding: R.R. Donnelley & Sons Co.

LIBRARY OF CONGRESS CATALOGING-IN-PUBLICATION DATA

White, Stephen, 1945–
    How Russia votes / Stephen White, Richard Rose, Ian McAllister.
        p.   cm.
    Includes bibliographical references (p.   ) and indexes.
    ISBN 1-56643-037-2
        1. Elections—Russia (Federation) 2. Voting—Russia (Federation)
    3. Representative government and representation—Russia (Federation)
    4. Representative government and representation—Soviet Union.
    5. Elections—Soviet Union. 6. Elections—Russia (Federation)—Sta-
    tistics. 7. Russia (Federation)—Politics and government—1991—
    Public Opinion. 8. Public opinion—Russia (Federation) 9. Public
    opinion—Russia (Federation)—Statistics. I. Rose, Richard, 1933– .
    II. McAllister, Ian, 1950– . III. Title.
    JN6699.A5W48   1997
    324.6'0947'0904—DC20   96-42449
                                                                            CIP

Manufactured in the United States of America
10   9   8   7   6   5   4   3   2   1

Contents

Tables and Figures

Tables

Figures

Introduction:
Coming Late to Free Elections

Free elections are central to twentieth-century politics. In the first half of the century governors faced demands to give every man and woman the right to vote for competing parties so that the government of the day would be accountable to the people. In the most fortunate parts of Europe, such as Britain and Scandinavia, the evolution of free elections occurred so peacefully that they are regarded as normal. But in Central Europe and the Mediterranean, the progress to democratic government was interrupted by detours into dictatorship. The fall of the Berlin Wall in 1989 opened up a new era, introducing free elections to countries where they were abnormal because for two generations or more they had been one-party Communist states.

Novelty makes the 1996 election of Boris Yeltsin as Russian president an international event, but it also means that Russia is a very late entrant to the world of free elections. Under the tsars, government was by despotic rule, occasionally enlightened but more often not. Following the abolition of serfdom in 1861, elections were introduced to regional and town councils advising tsarist officials; only a propertied minority was eligible to vote. Following defeat in the Russo-Japanese War and an uprising in Russia, in 1905 a *Duma* (parliament) was created, but neither the method of election nor the powers of the Duma were democratic as that term is used today. Terence Emmons (1983, vii) concludes from a study of that election that "the old regime survived longer in Russia than in any other European state" and adds: "when the end came the outcome was not only uncommonly violent but radically different in character from that of other European countries."

The Russian Revolution of 1917 was followed by the rise of the Communist Party of the Soviet Union, which preached and practiced the Marxist-Leninist dictatorship of the proletariat. In the last election to the Supreme Soviet held under normal Communist rules in 1984, a total of 99.99 percent of the electorate was officially said to have voted, and 99.95 percent voted for the Communist Party's slate of candidates. But official reports of virtual unanimity were literally "too good to be true"; the classic Soviet elections were institutions of *mis*representation.

Significance of Russian Elections

The median Russian elector was born in the last days of Josef Stalin, a totalitarian leader in the mold of Ivan the Terrible. She or he came of age politically under Leonid Brezhnev, who reduced the intrusive pressures of Stalinism—but only to the extent that this did not undermine the Communist Party's monopoly of power. Thus, a "normal" political system for a middle-aged Russian is not a democratic polity but an authoritarian, unresponsive, and corrupt bureaucratic party-state that mobilizes its subjects to endorse it unanimously in elections without choice. The Gorbachev initiatives begun in the late 1980s came long after the completion of the initial political socialization of most Russians.

The elections analyzed in this book are not just another vote, as would be the case in an established democracy. Instead, they are ballots held in the course of the collapse of the Soviet Union and the creation of a new state, the Russian Federation. This in turn has required the creation of a new constitutional regime. For the tens of millions of Russians who participated, the 1993 referendums and Duma election were evidence that the old authoritarian regime had gone; the second Duma election in 1995 confirmed this. But both ballots indicated significant electoral support for parties of dubious democratic commitment. The summer 1996 presidential election shows that the direction of change remains open.

The optimist can interpret the elections analyzed here as proof that Russia is now a democracy. But democratization is a lengthy process requiring fundamental changes in how a country is governed as well as in how governors are chosen. Many features of the relationship between the president and the Duma have yet to be resolved. The 1993 parliamentary challenge to the power of President Boris Yeltsin was resolved by the shelling of the parliament building. The big vote for Vladimir Zhirinovsky's slate of candidates in the December 1993 Duma election was a reminder that democratic parties are not the only parties competing for popular support in Russia. The vote in the 1995 Duma election for the Communist Party of the Russian Federation and Gennadii Zyuganov, its 1996 presidential candidate, raises fundamental questions about whether it is a party of reformed or old-style communists—or an unstable amalgam of both. A pessimistic interpretation of the record of Russian elections is that they show Western-style democracy is not, or at least not yet, suited to the country. When public opinion surveys ask Russian people this question, half say that they think democracy is incompatible with Russian traditions, a quarter disagree, and a quarter consider it difficult to answer (Levada 1995, table 2; cf. Neumann 1996).

The political system of the Russian Federation today meets two criteria for democratic elections: everyone has the right to vote, and there is free competition between and within parties. The two 1993 referendums showed that the era of coerced and unanimous voting has ended. When offered a choice between voting for and against government-endorsed policies, Russians have divided into three substantial but conflicting groups—pro, con, and abstainers. In the 1993 Duma election, no party won as many as one-sixth of the seats, and independents won the largest number of seats. In the 1995 Duma ballot, forty-three parties competed for votes, and an average of twelve candidates ran in each single-member parliamentary district. When the private opinions of the Russian people can be made public, the authorities can no longer pretend that "official" opinion defines public opinion, as it did in the days of the tsars and of the commissars (cf. Shlapentokh 1989; Noelle-Neumann 1993, 61 ff.).

Because democratization cannot be accomplished overnight, the Russian political system today is best described as transitional. It has yet to develop three characteristics necessary for a stable democracy. One condition is that no significant party favor an end to free elections (Higley and Gunther 1992). Yet each election has shown Russian politicians supplying a variety of alternatives to democracy—communist, nationalist, or some combination of both. Before an election, politicians debate not only who should win but also whether an election should be held at all.

A second condition for establishing democracy is acceptance of the rule of law. Political emergencies facing the new Russian Federation have been met by extraconstitutional acts, including the use of troops in Moscow as well as against a rebel movement challenging the state's authority in Chechnya. The transfer of valuable state assets into private hands as part of the introduction of the market has created a small number of dollar multimillionaires and an atmosphere of economic lawlessness in which a Russian-style *mafiya* has flourished (cf. Hedlund and Sundstrøm, 1996). Whatever their individual principles, the great mass of members of parliament are inexperienced in democratic politics. Those with most experience of party politics, starting with President Boris Yeltsin and his chief officials, learned their skills in the Communist Party of the Soviet Union. Yeltsin's former press secretary, Vyacheslav Kostikov, described the effect thus: "Boris Nikolaevich does not have democratic convictions.... His ideology—if you like, his friend, his concubine, his lover, his passion—is power. And everything that is outside the struggle for power is of much less concern to him" (quoted in Schmidt 1996, 62).

Third, the coexistence of a president, prime minister, and parliament chosen in different ways in different years creates confusion about accountability to the electorate and about who has the best claim to democratic legitimacy (cf. Linz and Valenzuela 1994). The first president, Boris Yeltsin, has responded by ruling through decrees as well as (or instead of) acts of parliament. Individually and collectively, members of the Duma are free to criticize the government in extravagant terms. But there are as yet no accepted conventions enabling the Duma to hold the prime minister and ministers accountable, as is the case in West European parliaments.

By comparison with postcommunist countries of Central and Eastern Europe, Russia is a laggard. The first free competitive elections were held in the Russian Federation in 1993; in Central and Eastern Europe, they were held in 1990 (White 1990). Postcommunist political systems from Estonia and Poland to Hungary have demonstrated a readiness to change governments in response to votes in parliament and at national elections (Rose and Mishler 1996b). When antidemocratic parties contest elections, they receive few votes, and there is widespread popular rejection of undemocratic alternatives. Russia lags behind its postcommunist neighbors because accountability to the electorate is weak and there is a significant supply and demand for undemocratic forms of government.

Objectives of the Book

To understand how Russians vote we must first examine elections as an integral part of the fundamental transformation of a Communist Party–state into a pluralistic political regime. This is not a matter of history but of current events. The Russian Federation only became an independent state in December 1991, when the Union of Soviet Socialist Republics (the USSR) collapsed. This occurred *after* Boris Yeltsin had been elected as the outsider candidate to the office of president of the Russian Republic in the old USSR. Initially, the government of the new Russian Federation was not elected; it was inherited from the days of the Soviet Union. Only after the July 1996 presidential election did Russia have a government elected under its current constitution.

The two opening chapters of this book focus on elections before and during what became the final months of the Soviet Union. Chapter 1 documents the monolithic ideology of the Soviet Union, which denied the essence of democratic politics, the idea that governance is about reconciling conflicting views. Marxist-Leninist doctrine required that the Communist Party win a unanimous vote when elections were held. Judged against this history, the elections of the 1990s are a much bigger leap in the dark than the first elections with a "one person, one vote" franchise in Britain or the enfranchisement of blacks in the American Deep South. The process of glasnost (openness) and perestroika (reconstruction) inaugurated after Mikhail Gorbachev took power in 1985 introduced cracks in this monolith. Chapter 2 shows what happened when elections were held in which Communists were able to run against each other or face challenges from nonparty candidates.

Second, this book examines what goes on in the minds of voters. Glasnost not only opened up Russian politics but also created opportunities for research based on asking Russian voters what they think. Notwithstanding the abnormal circumstances of Russia's experiment with free elections, it is possible to collect data through the normal social science method of nationwide sample surveys. As well as analyzing votes cast and aggregate election outcomes, we can draw on opinion surveys to see how firm popular support is for the winners and whether people are voting for or against democratic governance. By contrast with Soviet ideology, survey research assumes that the electorate is not of one mind about any issue of political importance, nor do voters necessarily endorse everything that their party stands for. The study of public opinion is about identifying and explaining the reasons why people differ in their political views.

The data in this book are drawn from the New Russia Barometer (NRB), an annual nationwide survey organized by the Centre for the Study of Public Policy at the University of Strathclyde, as part of an ongoing program started in 1991 under the leadership of Richard Rose, monitoring mass response to the transformation of fifteen postcommunist societies. The first Russian survey occurred in January 1992, the month in which the Russian Federation was launched. The surveys are described as barometers because trends are measured by repeating key measures of political and economic attitudes in different years (see Rose and Tikhomirov 1995, 11 ff.). New Russia Barometer II went in the field in June 1993, after the first Russian Federation referendum, and New Russia Barometer III in March 1994, after the second referendum and the first election of the federation's parliament. The account of the 1995 Duma election relies on the fifth New Russia Barometer, conducted weeks after that ballot.

The cumulative effect of decades of participation in elections manipulated on behalf of unpopular or corrupt officials has left a legacy of political distrust among many Russians. While the right to vote against the government of the day may be prized, a distrustful electorate is not positively committed to those for whom it votes. Chapter 3 draws on the New Russia Barometer to show in detail the political and economic attitudes of a demobilized electorate. Appendixes give technical details of the surveys, questions, and attitude scales.

Third, this book combines the analysis of voting behavior and the workings of electoral systems with the political context that shaped both. The Russian electoral system combines two contrasting methods of choosing members of parliament: half the Duma deputies are elected by single-member districts, as in the British House of Commons and the U.S. Congress, and half are elected by a party-list form of proportional representation, normal in parliamentary elections in Europe. Given such a hybrid electoral system, any headline flashed on television is not a fair summary of the votes of tens of millions of people, and even more, it misrepresents the complex procedure for allocating seats in the Duma.

Two elections for four different purposes were held in 1993. In April a referendum was held without parties or candidates; it was designed as an opinion poll for or against the person and policies of President Boris Yeltsin, who conspicuously refused to put his office at risk by seeking fresh confirmation of his position as president of the new federation or by becoming the leader of a party contesting parliamentary elections. Two additional referendum questions asked whether elections should be held soon for parliament and president, whose occupants had been chosen in the days of the USSR. The referendum was free, as people could and did vote against President Yeltsin's wishes, a fundamental change from what happened when elections simply endorsed the "objective" truth of Marxist-Leninist principles. Chapter 4 examines this referendum.

A referendum on a new constitution and the election of a new parliament were held on the same day in December 1993. The official referendum result narrowly endorsed a constitution designed to maximize the authority of President Boris Yeltsin. But a ballot is a blunt instrument that cannot express reservations in the minds of many who vote, on balance, in favor. The hesitancies of voters who supported the constitution are examined in chapter 5. In the election of the Duma, more than a dozen parties and hundreds of independents competed for votes. Chapter 6 sets out how members of parliament were elected. It shows that aggregating all MPs under nominal party names or ideological labels is a gross oversimplification; independents won the most seats. Parties varied in their approach to the electorate from the more academic emphasis on economics of Russia's Choice, led by former acting Prime Minister Yegor Gaidar, to the demagogic television presentations of Vladimir Zhirinovsky, whose previous political career was thought to have been sponsored by the KGB. Chapter 7 shows that the motives influencing voters differed substantially between parties. The chief influence was a sense of protest—some protesting against the old communist regime, others against the new system, and some against both.

Because the first free elections were a novelty for both politicians and voters, the fourth object of the book is to examine how politicians and voters have responded to the new regime. Even though many candidates had been active in the Communist Party, all were amateurs in listening to voters or learning from electoral defeat. Since President Yeltsin was preeminent in claiming the authority of popular election, chapter 8 examines the ups and downs of his popular support. The data emphasize that the narrow majority favoring President Yeltsin in the April 1993 referendum was not permanently committed to support him. Popular support for the president has fluctuated in Russia as in the United States. After starting as a popular challenger to Soviet authority, Boris Yeltsin saw his support drift downward for almost the whole of his first term in office.

Most of the business of government takes place between elections, under pressures that Marxists describe as historical necessity, such as what to do about enterprise that cannot survive in a market economy; whether to raise money to pay for social welfare services by printing it, borrowing it, or collecting it in taxes; what to do about crime in the streets or armed groups challenging the authority of the state in Chechnya; and finally, what rules were to govern the election of the Duma in 1995. Chapter 9 examines how politicians and personalities pursued their interests between the 1993 and 1995 parliamentary elections, while reacting to (or ignoring) major problems of governance.

The pursuit of power has led many political scientists to model politics as the rational pursuit of office by ambitious politicians. While Russian politicians say they are interested in power, chapter 10 shows that their behavior is often irrational or, at the very least, shows ignorance and inexperience in the attempt to create "democracy from scratch" (Fish 1995). Proportional representation rules for winning Duma seats make it imperative for politicians to combine in parties capable of winning at least 5 percent of the vote in order to gain any seats at all in the Duma. When dozens of parties contest elections, however, as occurred in December 1995, the arithmetic of the system condemns a majority of parties to total defeat. Chapter 10 describes the way in which politicians campaigned in the Duma election, even though for most of them the campaign was a prelude to electoral suicide.

The 1995 Duma election was normal, up to a point, for it gave the Russian people the democratic right to vote for or against the government of the day: upward of nine-tenths used the opportunity to vote against. Chapter 11 shows that the election was "normal" in Russian terms, for it was held in circumstances the electorate viewed as tense, critical, or explosive—and most Russians expected worse to come. The bulk of parties winning votes in the Duma ballot can be described as ambivalent in their commitment to government by free and fair elections. More voters favored the communists or nationalists than the party of the prime minister.

The concentration of power in the Russian presidency made the July 1996 election important: the reduction of the choice to Boris Yeltsin, the author of the new constitution, or Gennadii Zyuganov, his Communist opponent, presented the electorate with candidates representing very different political and economic regimes. In the June first round, almost a third of the voters had rejected both candidates in favor of one of nine other candidates; Yeltsin finished only three percentage points ahead of Zyuganov. In the second-round runoff between the two, Yeltsin was victorious. However, the victory was marred by evident disagreement within the Yeltsin camp about whether the election should be held or called off. The picture that emerges in chapter 12 is that of a rough-and-ready campaign rather than competition within the rules of an established democracy.

In the decade examined here, Russia has moved from manipulated elections unanimously endorsing an authoritarian regime to untrammeled competitive politics. Russia has shown that it can conduct free elections, which many traditional scholars of Soviet authoritarianism had doubted. But the same events have shown that Russia is not yet a stable democracy, for the "clans" that rule Russia today have yet to become fully accountable. The next decade will determine whether the behavior and institutions of the Yeltsin government have laid firm foundations for the creation of an elected government that is accountable to parliament under the rule of law.

Acknowledgments

The authors of this book bring to the subject almost a century of experience in studying politics, but in very different contexts. Stephen White's career has focused on the Communist Party of the Soviet Union, an extreme example of a party that allowed no competition in free elections. By contrast, Richard Rose has spent four decades systematically analyzing free elections throughout the Western world, and Ian McAllister has used multivariate statistical skills to examine voting behavior on three continents. This book is a joint product, in which each author has made a distinctive contribution to give readers an understanding of Russian elections based on a deep knowledge of Russian politics, concepts of elections, parties and voting, and multivariate statistical methods.

The book is organized around a sequence of elections that are historical facts. But the analysis is not descriptive in the journalistic sense. It is based on concepts and methods employed in the study of elections and democracy—including some that deal with issues so fundamental that they are ignored in the study of elections in established democracies. This study of how Russia votes is thus rooted in the political science literature about voting, elections, and democratization. A multiauthor book makes it possible to avoid the generalist's belief that theories developed in ignorance of life in the Soviet Union are equally applicable to postcommunist societies. It also avoids the complementary fallacy, the area specialist's belief that anything worth knowing about Russia is unique to that society and can be ascertained only by reading documents in Russian.

Financial support for this book has come, first of all, from the Research and Development Fund of the University of Strathclyde, which supports the CSPP's research program on postcommunist societies. Particular New Russia Barometer surveys have benefited from grants from the Centre for Research on Communist Economies, the British Foreign Office Know-How Fund, and the Paul Lazarsfeld Society's initiative for NRB III. The text and replies to all questions in NRB surveys can be found in the Studies in Public Policy series published by the Centre for the Study of Public Policy. Evgeny Tikhomirov of the CSPP undertook the task of translating ASCII files from Russia into machine-readable SPSS system files. Ian McAllister's contribution was funded by grants from the Research and Development Fund of the University of Strathclyde. Stephen White wishes to acknowledge the help of Tom Remington, Matthew Wyman, and Sarah Oates, and the financial support of the Leverhulme Trust. All three authors wish to thank the publisher, Ed Artinian, and all the staff of Chatham House who promptly and patiently dealt with this book as it kept taking longer and getting longer, as Russian elections kept getting more numerous.

A century and a half ago, a character in Nikolai Gogol's *Dead Souls* compared Russia to a speeding troika and asked: "Where are you off to, Russia? Give me your answer!" He found that Russia gave none. Here, we analyze the answers of more than ten thousand Russian people, who devoted much time to responding to the New Russia Barometer surveys. We share with them an appreciation of the importance of the events that made this possible, and we are grateful to the respondents for the time they freely gave. We also appreciate the work of the hundreds of interviewers who labored in the sometimes frozen or muddy ground of Russian cities and countryside to put the questions, and the hardworking, fast-moving, and professional staff of VTsIOM (the Russian Center for Public Opinion Research), led by Professor Yuri Levada, whose own lifetime has embodied some of the darkest and some of the most hopeful times in modern Russian history.

◖◗ 1 ◖◗

Elections Soviet Style

Elections are held in every continent and almost every country in the world. In democracies they involve a regular choice of representatives to national parliaments that hold the government of the day accountable. In the former Soviet Union, by contrast, there was no choice of party or even of candidate until the late 1980s, and often no choice about whether to vote at all. Levels of participation in elections without choice were high because undemocratic regimes used elections to mobilize a façade of popular support. Across ninety countries, the average turnout at national elections was 71.8 percent in the 1970s; among the communist-ruled nations it was 92.7, with six reporting an impossibly high 100 percent (Taylor and Jodice 1983, table 2.6).

Elections of this kind are undemocratic (cf. Hermet et al. 1978). Without at least two parties on the ballot, an election is nothing more than a plebiscite endorsing the party in power. A multiplicity of candidates, all belonging to the same party, may give voters a choice of representative, but there is normally no choice of policies. Moreover, a government so elected is not accountable to the electorate, and power will tend to remain in the hands of a ruling party or clique. A democratic election also requires respect for the rule of law, allowing parties to organize and solicit support free from censorship, suppression, or arrest. The majority of countries holding elections in fact show only partial respect for the rule of law, and some show none at all (Freedom House 1994).

The Soviet Union was a striking example of a country that proudly held undemocratic elections in this sense; it was the first to institute elections in which there were no more candidates than seats, and occa-

1

sionally there were even fewer. In the 1980s it was still holding elections without choice at a time when they were becoming uncommon even within the communist bloc. The Communist Party was the only organized party allowed to contest elections, and all other candidates were approved by the party authorities (cf. Pravda 1986).

Formally, the deputies elected to the Soviet parliament were a cross-section of the whole nation and were responsible as a Soviet parliament for electing and dismissing the Council of Ministers in charge of the executive branch of government. But the council was actually dominated by the Politburo of the Central Committee of the Communist Party of the Soviet Union, of which many leading ministers were members. Nor did the rule of law operate. Under Stalin, suspicion of holding dissenting thoughts was sufficient to result in deportation to Siberia or worse, and the state security police, the KGB, maintained its surveillance of what people said and thought long after the death of the dictator (Kryshtanovskaya and White 1993). State control of the press and broadcasting, for its part, allowed no opportunity for the direct criticism of government, still less for any attempt to replace it.

Why have elections at all when the result is a foregone conclusion? The official doctrine was that elections were a demonstration of popular support for the regime and an exercise in popular sovereignty. Dissidents, by contrast, saw elections as an instrument of repression, demoralizing critics by forcing them to make a demeaning and hypocritical show of compliance by casting a ballot for the communist authorities or else run the risk of being arrested for registering their opposition. Elections buttressed the regime, as Zaslavsky and Brym put it in the 1970s, "not by legitimizing it but by prompting the population to show that the *illegitimacy* of its 'democratic practice' has been accepted and that no action to undermine it will be forthcoming" (1978, 371).

In the light of Soviet experience, Russian elections in the 1990s were revolutionary in the literal sense. It was through partially free elections in 1989 and 1990 that power shifted from the party leadership to the wider society and in some cases to nationalists and oppositionists. It was an election, in 1991, that brought Boris Yeltsin to power as the president of Russia, the largest of the republics of the Soviet Union. And parliamentary elections now offer voters so wide a choice that fragmentation has replaced monopoly as the defining characteristic of the Russian party system. Elections in the postcommunist Russia of the 1990s produce a mixed picture of support, opposition to the government, and abstention, as they do in other countries; and Russian voters, for the first time, have begun to choose.

The Significance of Choice and Accountability

The denial of choice was central to the practice of elections in the Soviet Union. Even though everyone had the right to vote and by conventional standards electoral participation and party membership were high, Soviet elections were not democratic in the accepted sense because there was no choice between candidates and the government was not accountable to freely elected representatives. This did not mean there was an absence of politics. Instead, politics took place at the elite level, with very fierce struggles about who would hold positions of power and influence within the party itself and within the wider society. This was what Rigby described as "crypto" or secret politics (1964, 120) because it was a form of rule that dispensed almost entirely with the requirement that a government present and defend its policies in front of elected representatives: their function was simply to rubber-stamp the outcome of a factional struggle within the leadership.

Political differences, in these circumstances, were sometimes decided by caucus votes but more often by forms of competition and intrigue involving alliances between party factions and related groups in ministries, state enterprises, and the military-industrial complex. Losers could be not only deprived of office but also exiled, imprisoned, or, in Stalin's time, executed.

Soviet politics was described by a number of labels such as bureaucratic pluralism or, in recognition of the fact that its totalitarian ideal was in practice unattainable, as "imperfect monism," but there was little sign, before Gorbachev, of a widening of the boundaries of debate and political action that suggested any move toward more widely accepted definitions of democratic practice (for a review, see Almond and Roselle 1989, 170–224).

The evolution of established democracies is normally described as a process of the expansion of the right to vote (see, e.g., Rokkan 1970). In the nineteenth century the first steps were to move from a franchise based on traditional practices dating as far back as the Middle Ages to criteria for voting that could be justified in the context of a society in the course of modernization. The right to vote was often granted to owners of property, a sign that people had a stake in an emerging capitalist economy, and to persons with an educational qualification, assumed to understand issues of law and governance. It was denied on many grounds, including the immaturity of youth, the alleged incapacity of women, or the political unreliability of nationalities or religious adherents. The grounds for granting the right to vote were broadened in the twentieth century to give every adult male and subsequently every adult female the right to vote. The struggle for universal suffrage was completed in England in the 1920s and in some countries earlier still. The United States was a laggard in waiting until the enactment of the 1965 Voting Rights Act to guarantee the right to vote to every American regardless of race.

The rise to power of the Soviet communists introduced a new form of electoral politics to the European continent, a totalitarian system of electoral mobilization in which everyone not only had the right to vote but also was compelled to do so. Even though the ballot offered voters no choice and the government was not in any meaningful sense accountable to elected representatives, the party wanted to claim it had the unanimous support of the population, or at least of everyone except for "enemies of the people." In the 1920s the party was more concerned with suppressing opponents than with mobilizing the population in its support. But following the purges of the late 1930s, turnout at Soviet-style elections rose as high as 99.99 percent of the registered electorate, a higher level than any achieved by the other totalitarian regimes of the period, Hitler's Germany and Fascist Italy (see Linz 1978, 45).

In Western Europe predemocratic elections often offered the minority that was eligible to vote a choice between individual candidates. Hence, competing political parties were normally formed well before the achievement of universal suffrage. An individual casting his or her first ballot thus had a choice between a number of established parties representing different groups within society and making competing claims about how the country ought to be governed. Insofar as individuals identified with a particular religion, language group, or class, their choice of party was likely to be influenced by these basic loyalties. But inasmuch as class, religion, and language created divisions within society, this meant that the ballot offered a wide choice of alternative parties, and the introduction of proportional representation further increased the number of parties in parliament (cf. Lipset and Rokkan 1967).

In the Soviet Union, the leading role of the Communist Party meant that all candidates nominated were approved by the party, whose officials were responsible not only for campaigning but also for producing the results. The only way in which a candidate could be defeated was if a majority of electors who went to the polls voted against, rather than endorsed, the official candidate. This could happen—but it was a rare event. In elections for local soviets, more than 2 million councillors were usually elected and fewer than 100 defeated. As late as 1985, when Gorbachev took office, there were 2,304,830 seats to be filled in local soviets; 2,304,703 candidates were successfully elected, an overwhelming 99.994 percent of the total, and only 90 failed to win their seats (*Vedomosti,* no. 10, 1985, 126–27).

Throughout Europe, the campaign for universal suffrage occurred in parallel with efforts to make the government of the day accountable to a popularly elected parliament. Traditionally, the institutions of a European state insulated the work of the executive government from an assembly representing the nobility, the church, landed interests, and other major elites in society. The government depended on the monarch's confidence, not the confidence of parliament (see Anderson and Anderson 1967). In Britain the unelected House of Lords' veto over government legislation was not overcome until 1911. In the kaiser's Germany the Social Democratic Party was able to win the most votes in free elections, but the government of the day was not accountable to parliament. Democratic accountability in this sense was not introduced in Germany until after its defeat in World War I.

Logically, eight different types of elections could be held, varying in their degree of democratic authority by the extent to which the right to vote was granted to everyone, there was a free or limited choice between candidates, and the government was accountable to elected representatives. An evolutionary theory of democratization would see a country moving gradually from a system of elections in which the right to vote was restricted, government was not accountable, and there was little or no choice to an intermediate position in which a limited amount of choice between parties was available, more people were able to vote, and the government was increasingly subject to influence by a popularly elected parliament. The process would be complete when everyone had the right to vote with a free choice between parties that collectively held the government accountable. This was the course followed by Britain, Scandinavia, and the Benelux countries of Belgium, the Netherlands, and Luxembourg. Table 1.1 shows the wide variety of permutations found in political systems past and present. Central European countries such as Germany followed a more erratic course, swerving between democracy and dictatorship (Rose 1996c, chaps. 3–4).

Russia followed a very different course. Tsarist Russia was a classic authoritarian regime in which, until a very late stage, there was no parliament or right to vote. Democratic institutions were denounced by Slavophiles as threatening to deprive Russia of her unique traditions and replace them with alien institutions imported from the West. The 1905 revolution created a Duma (or parliament) whose members were

TABLE 1.1

ELECTIONS WITH AND WITHOUT CHOICE

	Right to vote	
	Everyone	Restricted
No choice		
Government not accountable	Mobilization: USSR	Classic authoritarian: Tsarist Russia
Government accountable	Mayoral recall: San Francisco	Estates general Netherlands
Limited choice		
Government not accountable	East Germany, 1949–89	Predemocratic Western Europe
Government accountable	Turkey, 1950–60	U.S. Deep South to 1964
Free choice		
Government not accountable	Russia today	Ireland, 1800–1880
Government accountable	Western Europe since 1945 Eastern Europe since 1990	Britain to 1918

chosen by electoral colleges in turn elected by most Russian males above the age of twenty-five. The division of voters into separate categories according to their landowning status or other criteria and their unequal representation in the Duma meant that the elections were not representative in the modern sense. In any event, the tsar's government was not accountable to the Duma. It remained a classic authoritarian regime in which royal advisers such as Rasputin had more influence than politicians accountable to the electorate (see Seymour and Frary 1918, 147ff.; Emmons 1983).

In the Soviet era the Communist Party preferred to debate issues within party congresses rather than in the national parliament, the Supreme Soviet of the USSR. The Supreme Soviet had formal responsibility for endorsing the names of holders of the highest offices of state; confirming the edicts of its Presidium, which was a kind of collective presidency; approving the budget and the economic plan; and endorsing legislation. The low status of the Supreme Soviet is shown by the fact that from the late 1930s to the 1980s it met for just five or six days a year, adopting an average of four laws and approving five decrees of its Presidium (Zlatopolsky 1982, 136). At the height of Soviet power, instead of progressing toward democratization, Russia had simply moved sideways, for while everyone had the right to vote, it was in elections without choice to a parliament to which the government was not accountable.

The Marxist-Leninist Inheritance

The only free elections held in Russia under communist rule were not of its design or choice. The Provisional Government that had replaced the tsar called elections for a Constituent Assembly in November 1917. Before a ballot could be held, the Bolsheviks seized power, but the elections were nonetheless conducted. The outcome was very unsatisfactory for the communist cause inasmuch as the moderate socialist bloc won more than half the seats and votes; the Bolsheviks and their allies won less than a third, although they had majority support in the largest cities and at the front (Radkey 1950). The newly elected assembly met once in January 1918 and was dispersed the next day by the Bolshevik Red Guards; it was the end of Russia's brief constitutional experiment.

The 1918 Russian constitution did not risk a repeat of such a counterrevolutionary outcome. The right to vote, first of all, was defined in class-war terms. Article 64 gave the vote to all men and women above the age of eighteen who earned their livelihood by "productive and socially useful work," including farmers who did not hire labor for profit, as well as to soldiers, sailors, and invalids. Article 65 denied the right to vote to those classified as exploiters (employers, people living on private wealth, and traders); to adherents of the old regime (monks, police officers, and members of the former ruling dynasty); and to others, such as those convicted of serious crime. About 2 to 3 percent of the electorate was thus disfranchised (Ponomarev 1982, 267). To make sure that everybody understood the importance of voting in the politically correct way, voting was by show of hands rather than secret. And in keeping with the idea of the communist revolution as an international movement, foreign residents were granted the right to vote on the same basis as Russians—provided they were not ineligible as exploiters under Article 65.

The class-war doctrine of elections was also evidenced in the apportionment of seats between urban and rural areas. Urban areas were considered to be the home of progressive workers, whereas rural areas were derided by Karl Marx and his followers as the ultimate in back-wardness. Hence, urban soviets elected one member to the All-Russian Congress of Soviets for each 25,000 electors, whereas in the more dispersed rural areas five times as many electors were required in order to elect a single representative.

As long as the correct candidates were elected, the party initially paid little attention to whether or not people voted. In the unsettled days of the early 1920s, turnout for elections to the urban and rural soviets was between a third and a half of the eligible electorate (table 1.2). By the beginning of the 1930s, turnout in elections had begun rising to West European levels, but the results showed anything from a twelfth to almost a third of the electorate not bothering to vote, and this was tolerated at that time. Following the adoption of the 1936 Soviet constitution and Stalin's purges, great emphasis was placed on everyone recording a positive vote for the regime; anyone failing to do so risked being considered an enemy of the people.

The 1936 Soviet constitution adopted a conventional franchise law; all Soviet citizens aged eighteen and above were given the right to vote, except for a small proportion who were ineligible because of mental incapacity or (until 1958) a criminal conviction involving the loss of electoral rights. Voting was to be by secret ballot rather than a show of hands. Stalin described the new electoral system as "general, equal, direct, and secret," and predicted a "very lively electoral struggle" in which "hundreds" of associations would be involved as well as the Communist Party (1967, 129–30). Another member of the leadership, Andrei Zhdanov, warned the Central Committee in 1937 that there might be "hostile agitation and hostile candidacies," particularly from religious organizations that were again becoming more active (*Voprosy istorii*, no. 5, 1993, 4).

In law, there was no limit to the number of candidates that could be nominated and no requirement that candidates represent the Communist Party, by this time the only party with a legal existence. In practice, no contests occurred under Stalin. The most important reason was that the right of nomination was reserved under the constitution to the Communist Party and a small number of other public organizations that it controlled. Public bodies of any kind had to register under a law of 1931 that required them to accept the principle of party dominance. Of those that did, the right to nominate was reserved for the trade unions, cooperatives, and other public associations, as well as for the Communist Party and its youth wing, the Komsomol.

Attempts were sometimes made to challenge this electoral monop-

TABLE 1.2
ELECTORAL PARTICIPATION, 1922–34

	1922	1923	1925	1926	1927	1929	1931	1934
Urban soviets	36.2%	38.5%	48.7%	52.0%	59.1%	70.8%	79.6%	91.6%
Rural soviets	22.3	35.8	47.3	48.9	48.4	61.8	70.4	83.3
Female participation								
Urban soviets	n.d.	n.d.	27.5	42.9	50.3	65.2	76.0	89.7
Rural soviets	n.d.	n.d.	19.9	28.0	33.5	48.5	63.4	80.3
CPSU members and candidates as percentage of deputies								
Urban soviets	60.6	58.4	51.6	n.d.	51.0	46.3	49.5	45.3
Rural soviets	6.1	7.8	5.7	n.d.	8.7	9.3	14.8	18.9

SOURCE: Gimpel'son 1971, cols. 199–201.

NOTE: Figures are percentages of the registered electorate.

oly. In 1979, for instance, historian Roy Medvedev was nominated by a
self-constituted body known as "Election 79," which also proposed the
wife of a prominent dissident. There was "jovial animation" at first
when Medvedev and his supporters took their proposal to the local
electoral commission: what country, the commission asked, did they
think they were living in? But Medvedev and his colleagues persisted
until the commission ruled that their sponsoring organization was not
registered under the 1931 law and had accordingly no formal right of
nomination (Medvedev 1979). Elections of this kind have been called
"elections Paradise-style": as God said to Adam, "Here is Eve, the
woman of your choice" (Ulc 1982, 116).

On election day, voters could in theory reject the party's choice.
But to do so required a voter to make use of a screened-off booth; a
vote in favor required no more than dropping the ballot paper, unmarked and even unread, into the box. After teething troubles in 1937,
when the reported number of invalid votes was above 1 percent, votes
cast for the official candidates for the two chambers of the Supreme Soviet ran consistently above 99 percent and as high as 99.95 percent in
1984, the last Soviet-style election (table 1.3). Invalid votes virtually disappeared at the same time, with only 35 recorded in an electorate of
more than 180 million (*Vedomosti*, no. 11, 1984, items 200–203).

The Stalinist and post-Stalinist eras were remarkable for the insistence that everyone ought to vote, reflecting a desire to mobilize the
masses in demonstrations of support for "their" regime. Official reports
showed that the campaign was successful. There were even occasions
when turnout exceeded 100 percent, as in the constituency in which the
"leader of leaders" (that is, Stalin) had stood in 1937 (Maynard 1942,
2:438). The extraordinarily high turnout owed a great deal to manipulation by election officials and to impersonation and other abuses. In the
whole of Turkmenia, for instance, there were 1.5 million voters at the
national elections in 1984, but only one was officially recorded as absent (*Pravda*, 7 March 1984, 1). The results were so predictable that
newspapers could be prepared in the 1950s with pictures of the successful candidates before the elections had taken place (*Pravda*, 5 March
1989, 1), and as late as the 1980s the Politburo could approve the final
communiqué with the election results two days before the polls had
opened (*Izvestiya*, 13 July 1992, 3).

Western scholars were generally—and rightly—skeptical of the
meaning of such exercises. But there were also attempts to calculate the
significance of the minor variations that occurred in turnout and in
support for the list of official candidates. Using local election data,

TABLE 1.3
ELECTORAL PARTICIPATION AND VOTES, 1937–84

Date of election	Turnout (%)	CPSU members (% of candi-dates)	Vote for official slate (%)	
			Council of the Union	Council of Nationalities
12 Dec 1937	96.79	76.1	98.61	97.75
10 Feb 1946	99.74	81.0	99.18	99.16
12 Mar 1950	99.98	83.5	99.73	99.72
14 Mar 1954	99.98	78.0	99.79	99.84
16 Mar 1958	99.97	76.1	99.57	99.73
18 Mar 1962	99.95	75.8	99.47	99.60
12 Jun 1966	99.94	75.2	99.76	99.80
14 Jun 1970	99.96	72.2	99.74	99.79
16 Jun 1974	99.98	72.2	99.79	99.85
4 Mar 1979	99.99	71.7	99.89	99.91
4 Mar 1984	99.99	71.4	99.94	99.95

SOURCES: Calculated from *Verkhovnyi Sovet SSSR devyatogo sozyva (statisticheskii sbornik)* (Moscow: Izvestiya, 1974), 46–51; *Vedomosti Verkhovnogo Soveta SSSR*, no. 11 (1979): 167–71, and no. 11 (1984): 199–203.

Gilison (1968) devised a measure of individual and group dissent that showed, for instance, that there was more dissent in Russia and Estonia than in the other Soviet republics, but that dissent of both kinds had been declining. Later studies devoted more attention to abstention, which was also a form of opposition. It was higher, surveys of émigrés suggested, in Moscow and Leningrad than elsewhere in the country (Karklins 1986). There was also some evidence that the electoral register was itself deficient because an increasing number of illegal urban residents were not included. By the mid-1980s, it was estimated that about 14 million potential voters—nearly 8 percent of the total—were excluded from the electoral process in this way (Roeder 1989).

The official view was that Soviet elections were all but unanimous because the USSR had none of the divisions that were characteristic of class-divided societies. As there was no private ownership, there was no exploitation and no basis for antagonisms. The working class, engaged in state-owned industry and agriculture, was the first of these classes, accounting in the early 1980s for about 60 percent of the population. Collective farmers made up a further 13 percent; the farms on which they worked were in theory a form of cooperative property, leased from the state for an indefinite period, and they were therefore held to constitute a separate class, although one that enjoyed a harmonious relationship with the proletariat. Finally, there was the "stratum" of intelligentsia, a quarter of the population engaged in predominantly nonmanual labor (*Narodnoe* 1983, 7).

Communist doctrine held that in a society without a social basis for conflicts of interest, Western ideas of democracy had no direct application. There was accordingly no basis for a multiparty system because the whole society shared the same objectives. In a society of the Soviet type the ruling party could express the interests of the working class and at the same time of the people as a whole. Not only was there a single party, there was also a single public opinion. Under socialism, it was held, there was "sociopolitical and ideological unity," and the views of workers, collective farmers, and members of the intelligentsia were "identical on the basic questions of social development" (Ilichev 1983, 449). Social consciousness reflected the forms of property in the society in which it existed; in a socialist society, based on public ownership, it was characterized by the "dominance of Marxist-Leninist ideology in all spheres of spiritual life" (Onikov and Shishlin 1978, 264).

There were no difficulties, for similar reasons, in holding elections throughout the fifteen republics of the Soviet Union because the interests of the working class were held to override distinctions of nationality. The vote for communist-sponsored candidates in the Baltic states of Estonia, Latvia, and Lithuania, for instance, which had been annexed as a consequence of the Nazi-Soviet Pact of 1939, was just as overwhelming as it was in Russia. In the Ukraine there were no nationalist or even independent candidates, and throughout the predominantly Muslim republics of Central Asia the vote in favor of officially approved and openly atheist candidates was usually the most enthusiastic of all. Nationalism, it was pointed out, was a "bourgeois ideology" that developed under capitalism; under Soviet conditions it was superseded by "socialist patriotism," which included a commitment to the motherland and to the cause of communism (Onikov and Shishlin 1989, 249–50, 289).

In a socialist society, communist doctrine held that there was no need for many of the familiar conventions of liberal democracy. For a start, who needed "parliamentarianism"? Why did a workers' state require a separate, parasitic group of full-time politicians when its purpose was to give ordinary people a chance to run their own affairs? In any case, what kind of people were represented in Western parliaments, and whose interests did they serve? A particularly scornful view was taken of the notion of pluralism and its application to Soviet societies. Pluralism, it was explained, obscured the existence under capitalism of "antagonistic class interests and the domination of monopoly capital in political life." The Marxist-Leninist approach was that different points of view could be freely expressed but that all were ultimately reconciled in the leadership of a broadly based Communist Party (Onikov and Shishlin 1989, 420).

Nor was there much scope for Soviet social scientists to explore the issues that divided their own society. Up to the 1980s, the existence of sociology was itself controversial; there were no university departments in the subject. Boris Grushin had pioneered the study of public opinion in the early 1960s through an inquiry based on questionnaires distributed through the youth paper *Komsomolskaya pravda* (Grushin 1967). The sociology institute attached to the Academy of Sciences came under continuous and heavy pressure, however, particularly in the late 1960s when a hard-line director was imposed in order to restore orthodoxy (Shlapentokh 1987; Pugacheva 1994). Yuri Levada, a popular Moscow University professor who had published a two-volume set of *Lectures on Sociology*, was attacked in the party's theoretical journal and forced to resign his academic position. One of the pioneers of Soviet public opinion research, Boris Grushin, found it impossible to publish the results of the surveys he had conducted in the Taganrog area in the late 1960s and had four manuscripts turned down by Soviet publishing houses between 1967 and 1981. When he took his study of *Soviet Society in Public Opinion Polls* to one of them, the response was "Are you crazy or what?" (*Ogonek,* no. 12, 1988, 20). The Centre for Public Opinion that Grushin had established in the Institute of Sociology was closed, and virtually all empirically oriented work was suspended. As late as 1987 sociology as a discipline was still "not completely recognized"; in the words of Tatyana Zaslavskaya, it was a "sociology without sociologists" (*Pravda,* 6 February 1987, 2–3).

Despite these difficulties, it was still possible for scholarly studies to appear that at least indirectly raised questions about official orthodoxies. Grushin's study of the Taganrog area, for instance, was finally published in 1980. Entitled *Mass Information in a Soviet Industrial Town,* it reflected the contribution of a coauthor from the Central Committee apparatus but was nonetheless able to point to a considerable disparity between the mostly negative letters that local newspapers received and the mostly positive letters they published (Grushin and Onikov 1980).

A legal scholar, Rafael Safarov, was able to undertake a parallel exploration of the relationship between citizens and local government, based on surveys in Moscow and Kalinin. Safarov found that the exist-

ing forms through which public opinion could influence public decisions were "not always effective"; members of the public were much
less likely than officials to suggest that local administrators took public
opinion into account, and 32 percent reported that the decisions taken
locally were often at odds with the views of local people (Safarov 1975,
145, 121, 159). For attentive readers, it was clear there could often be
tensions between official orthodoxies and the world in which they actually lived.

A Negotiated Relationship

Those who lived under the Soviet system were sometimes described as
"subject parochials," a term made popular in Almond and Verba's
work on political culture. Such people were aware of developments in
political life and had a view of the legitimacy of government, but had
no means of influencing the policymaking process. Their relationship
with government processes was "passive," in that they were expected
to carry out the decisions of government but were unable to influence
them (Almond and Verba 1963, 19).

The idea that Russians might lack political influence was dismissed out of hand by Soviet spokesmen. Within the framework of official orthodoxy, there could be wide-ranging debate. The Stalinist constitution of 1936, for instance, was considered for nearly six months in
draft, and changes were made in the final text (Wimberg 1992). The
constitution of 1977 was also subject to consultation. Leonid Brezhnev,
chairman of the commission responsible for its preparation, went so far
as to claim that more than four-fifths of the adult population—that is,
about 150 million people—had taken some part in the discussion by attendance at meetings or in other ways. The final text, approved in October 1977, incorporated 110 amendments and one new article. For
Brezhnev, the discussion had shown how "firm and creative was the
unity of all classes and social groups, all nations and nationalities, and
all generations of Soviet society, united around the Communist Party"
(1978, 518–19, 537). Only in 1990 was it disclosed that the letters that
reached the constitutional commission and press had actually raised all
kinds of awkward issues. Why, for instance, was there no choice of candidate at elections? Why had the CPSU been given a political monopoly in Article 6? And why had Brezhnev been given two Hero of the
Soviet Union awards thirteen years after World War II had formally
ended? (Zlokazov 1990, 73–77).

The use of the ballot to mobilize a ritual show of support for the regime did not deny Russians opportunities to participate in politics. The minority who became full-time party officials lived from as well as for politics, and the privileges of party membership were an incentive for seeking such posts. The majority of Russians were politically aware because of the dangers of inadvertently saying or doing things that invited sanctions in a police state. Political activity to advance individual goals tended to be covert rather than overt: the use of bribery, connections, or legal or semilegal means of influencing a government that could not be influenced through the ballot box.

Under Soviet conditions there was a big difference between the worlds of high politics, where decisions were made by the party elite, and low politics, which was much less closely regulated by the central authorities (Bialer 1980, 166–67). For many citizens, high politics was "none of my business—that's up to the Central Committee." But low politics gave individuals opportunities to pursue a variety of strategies in dealing with local authorities that involved invoking ethnic or family relations, the trading of favors, or straightforward corruption. Under democratic centralism, central directives could not be resisted; but interpersonal relations at the local level were normally of little interest to the regime, and individual citizens could negotiate their own forms of accommodation.

Local officials had other ways in which they could respond to the multiplicity of instructions that they received from the central government. Because instructions of this kind were often vague, belated, in conflict with each other, and short term in their application, officials outside the major centers of population were able in practice to choose their own priorities. Typically, they endorsed all the instructions they received from the center but took little notice of them in practice (this was known as "formalism"). And because central directives were based, in the last resort, on the information provided by local officials themselves, the way in which they reported their own performance had a considerable influence on the policies they would subsequently be invited to implement. The outcome was a negotiated relationship between regime and society, leaving the party's formal political monopoly untouched but modifying its practical effect.

There were many ways in which the exercise of political power could be mediated by individual or group pressures. One of the most important in the later stages of the regime was covert participation in the implementation of central policy directives, involving the "interaction between the citizen as client or supplicant looking for private benefit and the representative of the system interpreting and implementing policy for this individual" (DiFranceisco and Gitelman 1984, 604). Soviet citizens, on the basis of émigré interviews, had relatively high levels of political knowledge but were reluctant to discuss politics openly and had little faith in their ability to influence government decisions. Participation, it emerged, was "direct and personalized," and more likely to emphasize personal or family connections than regular forms of group action. Bribery was an important part of this pattern of interaction and was accepted as a "common way of handling difficult situations," particularly where employment, housing, or university admission was concerned (DiFranceisco and Gitelman 1984, 611).

Official mechanisms could also be adapted to local purposes. Voting, for instance, had little to do with the choice of an alternative government. But there were other ways in which it could be used to signify the preferences of electors. There was the threat not to vote, which was not illegal in itself but was a serious embarrassment to local officials responsible for ensuring the highest possible turnout. According to the testimony of émigrés who had worked as canvassers, the threat not to vote could ensure that housing repairs were carried out or that a local church was reopened (Zaslavsky and Brym 1978, 365, 367). Comments could also be written on the ballot paper itself, all of which were gathered up and analyzed after the exercise had been completed. Many could be accommodated with little difficulty. "Had I a hundred votes to cast," wrote a fervent Muscovite in 1970, "they would all be cast for the Party of Lenin which led a weak, illiterate Russia out of her darkness and made her a rich and mighty power." Remarks of this kind, the newspaper added, were "too many to list" (Friedgut 1979, 112–13).

In a rather different case quoted by Solzhenitsyn, an engineer just after the war had "given vent to his feelings and on his ballot paper had applied an obscene epithet to the Genius of Geniuses himself." Despite the shortage of labor, several detectives spent a month examining the handwriting of local residents before the offender was identified and imprisoned (1968, 51). In a still more disagreeable case the central authorities identified some "brown-colored matter ... giving off a strong smell" in an envelope delivered to Comrade Stalin in the mid-1930s, which was later checked out by the NKVD laboratories and confirmed as excrement "probably of animal origin" (*Istochnik*, no. 3, 1993, 126–27). It was more common in the later Soviet period for communications from the voters to be considered by the local party committee and then passed to appropriate administrative agencies. Comments were also considered by the police and KGB, which evidently found them a useful form of feedback (Hill 1976, 597).

It was easier and generally more effective to send a letter to a party committee or to the press. A tradition of this kind went back to early tsarist times, when a basket was lowered from a window in the Old Kremlin Palace in which petitioners could place their grievances (*The Times*, 12 July 1982, 1). Communications were discouraged during the Stalin years, but under Khrushchev and Brezhnev a new emphasis was placed on letters from ordinary citizens as well as other forms of conventional participation. More than half a million letters reached party headquarters every year during the 1970s; main newspapers such as *Pravda* and *Trud* received a similar flow of communications, and the total postbag of the central press was an estimated 60 to 70 million every year (White 1983, 51–52). About half the letters received contained complaints of various kinds; in *Izvestiya*, for instance, 19 percent of the letters were about housing, and 13 percent about social security (Vychub 1980, 8–9). Full analyses of newspaper postbags were sent to the party authorities, and ordinary members of the public often regarded letters as the best means at their disposal of influencing the direction of public policy (Mickiewicz 1981, 69); it was better still, others thought, to reach the press directly or to contact a deputy or local official (see table 1.4).

The combination of "formalism" and "informalism" reached its peak in strategies adopted by enterprises to fulfill the annual economic plan and by individuals seeking goods made scarce by the practices of a planned economy. It was important to meet plan targets on paper; this meant that factory managers were under great pressure to wheel and deal with suppliers and with recalcitrant employees in order to achieve production targets. It also meant that state officials turned a blind eye to the methods that factory managers used to achieve their goals, such as bartering commodities with suppliers, bribing individuals to release wanted supplies or equipment, or simply falsifying records of output (cf. Kornai 1992; Gregory 1990). Individuals could combine official employment with participation in a "rainbow"-colored variety of informal economies, involving cash-in-hand payments dealing in misappropriated goods, or accepting bribes or scarce consumer goods. Consumers, for their part, could turn to household production of food to escape the problems of a shortage economy (see, e.g., Grossman 1977; Katsenelinboigen 1978, chap. 7; Rose 1993).

Even in the years of political stagnation and strict official controls, Russians could also step outside the accepted boundaries of political action. A far from exhaustive study, counting only open, collective, and physical expressions of opposition, collected 592 examples of protest

TABLE 1.4

FORMS OF POLITICAL INFLUENCE IN THE EARLY 1970S

Q: What means of influence on local organs of govern-
ment do you consider the most appropriate and
effective?

Type of political influence

Publication in the newspapers, radio, or television	23%
Going to see a deputy	18
Making a speech at meetings	17
Going to see a local government official	12
Conducting local opinion survey	9
Going to see a local party official	9
Writing to a party or government body	5
Appealing to a civic body or association	2
Not sure	6

SOURCE: R.A. Safarov, *Obshchestvennoe mnenie i gosudarstvennoe upravlenie* (Moscow: Yuridicheskaya literatura, 1975), 172 (based on surveys conducted in the Kalinin region, 1970–72. $N = 1{,}500$).

demonstrations from 1965 to 1978. Over the period there was an increase in the frequency of demonstrations and in their geographic dispersion and social diversity (Kowalewski 1980). There was a particularly violent clash in the southern town of Novocherkassk in 1962, following an increase in the price of meat and dairy products. Patience ran out at the electric locomotive construction plant, where there was already considerable dissatisfaction with food and housing conditions. After a rally at the factory, workers marched on the city's party offices, carrying banners and portraits of Lenin. The workers' leaders were arrested, and troops were deployed; and then the demonstration was itself suppressed by machine-gun fire. As many as twenty-four demonstrators were killed and buried secretly the same day; two months later, fourteen of the "ringleaders" were put on trial, and seven were condemned to death (*Komsomolskaya pravda*, 2 June 1989, 4).

Jokes were a more peaceful form of accommodation, expressing what Hankiss (1990, 7) has described as the "ironic freedom" of communist subjects. Jokes could point up the gap between the claims of the regime and everyday realities. ("Doctor, I need an eye and ear hospital." "Why?" "I keep hearing one thing, but seeing something else.") And they could deflate official bombast. What, for instance, were the four main reasons for the failure of Soviet agriculture? "Summer, fall, winter, and spring." And what was the Moscow String Quartet? "The Moscow Symphony Orchestra just back from a Western tour." An entire category of jokes was attributed to an apocryphal Radio Armenia, which offered advice to anxious citizens ("Where should I go if the USSR's western borders are opened?" "To eastern Siberia, to avoid getting crushed in the rush") and explained why it could not reveal the results of the elections that would take place in ten years' time ("Yesterday they were stolen from the Central Committee offices").

Another form of accommodation was linguistic dualism: public encounters took place in officialese, while personal and private relations were much more openly and directly worded. The result was a certain ambivalence in personality—"two persons in one body," as a character in Dudintsev's celebrated novel *Not by Bread Alone* described it, with "two sides, the hidden one and the visible one." In this metaphor it was the "visible" person who repeated the phraseology of the authorities and took part in ritual demonstrations of unity. On the other hand, the "hidden" person retained a much older and more humanistic set of values and regarded the activities of the "visible" person with some skepticism (White 1979, 111). In this spirit party meetings could be unanimous in their resolutions, while members spent their time knitting (Unger 1981); or Central Asians who agreed to deplore the influence of religion could themselves take part in pilgrimages to the graves of local holy men (White 1979, 147).

The government of the Soviet Union was not democratic in the accepted sense of the word, but it was not a monolith. High politics, the articulation of competing views about what government ought to do, was "horizontal" rather than vertical. Differences of opinion regularly arose between ministries, between civilians and the military, between regions, and between groups that depended on different patrons within the party leadership. There was no vertical accountability through the ballot box, however, as occurs in democratic societies. Competition for high office was not decided by free elections, but by power struggles in which one Kremlin leader was deposed in favor of another (such as the replacement of Khrushchev by Brezhnev). And although there could be changes in policy, they reflected the priorities of a new general secretary rather than a popular mandate. It was not until the very end of the Soviet period that government became at least partly accountable to those who had elected it; it was a change that proved incompatible with communist rule itself.

◖◖ 2 ◗◗

Opening Pandora's Box:
The First Competitive
Elections

When Mikhail Gorbachev became general secretary of the CPSU in 1985, the electoral system of the Soviet Union was as it had been in the Stalin era. A new Supreme Soviet had been elected the previous year, but there were only 1,499 candidates for the 1,500 seats, as one had died on the eve of the poll. By noon, 89.4 percent of the electors had cast their votes; by 6:00 P.M., 99.6 percent. In the end there was a massive 99.99 percent turnout, with a vote in favor of the single list of candidates of 99.94 and 99.95 percent in each of the two chambers, the Council of the Union and the Council of Nationalities. Gorbachev himself was one of the successful candidates, for the Ipatovo district in his native Stavropol territory (White 1985). Electors had voted, but they had hardly chosen.

Gorbachev's own intentions at the outset of his general secretaryship were unclear. At the end of 1984 he had already agreed with Eduard Shevardnadze, the Georgian party leader who became his foreign minister, that "everything [wa]s rotten" (*Izvestiya*, 1 December 1990, 4). Talking to his wife on the eve of his nomination, Gorbachev was clear that—in a famous phrase—"we just can't go on like this" (Gorbacheva 1991, 14). Speaking to the Politburo that had agreed to nominate him, Gorbachev was nonetheless prepared to argue that "we don't need to change our policies" (Center 1985). And his acceptance speech to the Central Committee included a warm tribute to his predecessor, Konstantin Chernenko, as well as a promise that the strategy worked out by the 26th Party Congress—over which Brezhnev had presided—would continue unchanged, a policy of the "acceleration of the country's socioeconomic development and the perfection of all aspects of the life of the society" (Gorbachev 1987a, 129).

Gorbachev's first full address to the Central Committee, in April 1985, called for a "steady advance" rather than a clear break with earlier policies. He did call for a "qualitatively new state of society, in the broadest sense of the word," but it was changes in the economy that would play the "decisive role" in achieving their objectives (1987a, 153–54). The acceleration of economic growth, as he told the 26th Party Congress in 1986, was the "key to all our problems, immediate and long-term, economic and social, political and ideological, domestic and foreign," and the only way a new form of Soviet socialism could be built (1987b, 200; on the reforms more generally, see Sakwa 1990; Miller 1993; White 1994; Brown 1996).

From early in 1987 a rather different approach began to emerge. Speaking to the Central Committee in January, in a meeting that had been postponed three times because of resistance from party hardliners, Gorbachev explained that economic reform was conceivable only in association with a far-reaching "democratization" of the political system. The principle of collective leadership, he went on, had been violated by leaders who took no account of the views of their colleagues. Party officials had placed themselves beyond the reach of control or criticism, and some had become morally and criminally corrupt. All this argued the need for "truly revolutionary and comprehensive transformations in society," unleashing the "human factor" so that the energies of ordinary people could make a reality of the objectives of *perestroika*—the term for restructuring of the whole society that had already become the central focus of his reforms (1987c, 307–8, 317).

Electing the USSR Congress of Deputies in 1989

Gorbachev had spoken of the need for "corrections" in electoral procedures in his speech to the Party Congress in 1986. The first practical steps toward reform came the following year.

Voters, Gorbachev told the Central Committee in January, should be able to consider a "broader range of candidates," and he went on to propose a party conference—a meeting of a more consultative character than a congress, last held nearly fifty years earlier—to consider what was already a developing agenda of political change (1987c, 322, 354). Addressing the conference in June 1988, Gorbachev called for "radical reform" of the political system, not just "democratization," and went on to attack a "cumbersome managerial apparatus" that had now become the main obstacle to further advance (1989, 351, 370). Following the conference, a series of legislative changes was approved later in the year that included the first working parliament in Soviet history, a new electoral law, and a constitutional review commission intended to establish what Gorbachev, in a significant phrase, described as a "socialist system of checks and balances" (*Pravda*, 30 November 1988, 3).

There was a still larger agenda, the construction of what came to be described as a "law-based state" (*pravovoe gosudarstvo*, a Russian equivalent of the German *Rechtsstaat*). Gorbachev, a lawyer by training, told interviewers from *Der Spiegel* that perestroika was as much a "legal revolution" as a reform of the political system (*Pravda*, 24 October 1988, 2). As he explained, democracy "cannot exist and develop without the rule of law, because law is designed to protect society from abuses of power and guarantee citizens and their organizations and work collectives their rights and freedoms." As Russians knew from the Stalin period, violations of law could have "tragic consequences which [they could not] forget or forgive." And it was not only a matter of improving the laws and making the courts more independent. It was also important to reduce the state's totalitarian goal of controlling the lives of ordinary citizens and adopting the principle that "everything that is not prohibited by law is permitted" (Gorbachev 1987d, 105–9).

An outcome of these changes in official thinking was the introduction of elections with limited competition. There had already been a limited experiment with electoral choice in the local government elections that took place in June 1987 (Hahn 1988; White 1988). Now, for the first time at the national level, voters were to be offered a choice between candidates who differed on issues, if not in party affiliation—the Communist Party still enjoyed a political monopoly under Article 6 of the constitution, and other parties had not yet been legalized. The new electoral law, reflecting this principle of limited choice, was adopted by the Supreme Soviet on 1 December 1988. Under its provisions, the right to nominate candidates was extended to voters' meetings of 500 or more, and an unlimited number of candidates could be nominated. Deputies were not allowed to hold governmental posts at the same time as they exercised ministerial responsibilities—how, it was asked, could they be expected to hold themselves to account?—and they should "normally" live or work in the constituency for which they had been nominated. Candidates, moreover, were required to present "programs" to the electorate—in practice, their choice of personal priorities, such as the environment or housing. All were supposed to stay within the framework of the constitution, existing legislation, and CPSU guidelines.

The new electoral law also had consequences for how voters cast their ballots. In the past it had been enough for voters to cast their papers, unmarked and even unread, into the box to endorse the single slate of candidates. Now they had to enter a booth before casting their votes and make a positive indication of their preferences unless (exceptionally) only a single candidate was standing (*Vedomosti*, no. 49, 1988, item 729; more general discussions are available in Brunner 1990 and in White, Gill, and Slider 1993, 20–38). The new law was to apply to all future elections, beginning with the national elections that were due in March 1989; they would, the Central Committee promised, be "unlike all those that had preceded them" (*Pravda*, 29 November 1988, 1).

Under the new law the campaign was to proceed in two stages. In the first stage, nominations to the Congress of People's Deputies were to be made and then approved by a selection conference in the constituency or social organization for which the candidate was seeking election. In the second stage, approved candidates were to compete for election to the Congress of People's Deputies. There were 750 *single-member constituencies* around the country based upon equal numbers of electors; the great majority of these were in the Russian Republic. In addition, there were 750 *national-territorial seats* representing the various ethnic groups by the administrative units in which they lived (32 from each of the fifteen republics, 11 from each of the twenty autonomous republics, 5 from each of the eight autonomous regions, and 1 from each of the ten national areas, regardless of their respective populations); the number of electors in each constituency accordingly varied widely, as is the case in the U.S. Senate. In addition, 750 more seats were filled by *public organizations,* including the Communist Party and the trade unions with 100 seats each (see figure 2.1). The Congress, after it had met, would in turn elect a smaller Supreme Soviet that would conduct the daily business of legislation.

These were new, elaborate, and largely unfamiliar procedures; and they were ones to which many citizens had strong objections. The representation given to social organizations, in particular, appeared to violate the principle of one person, one vote; and the holding of selection conferences to approve final lists of candidates was also unpopular. Who needed such "elections before elections?" asked several of *Izvestiya's* correspondents (22 November 1988, 2). And why were such

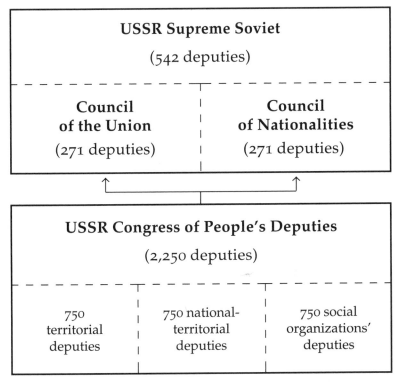

FIGURE 2.1
THE USSR CONGRESS OF PEOPLE'S DEPUTIES
AND SUPREME SOVIET, 1989–91

bodies as the stamp collectors given a seat—"what had this to do with the affairs of state?" asked a reader in *Moscow News* (no. 2, 1989, 8). Reflecting these concerns, selection conferences were avoided in Estonia, most of Lithuania, and some districts of Moscow so as to leave such choices—at least in principle—to the electorate (*Izvestiya*, 11 February 1989, 1; *Pravda*, 27 February 1989, 2). The main source of information for most voters was state television, followed by the local and national press. People were said to be looking for candidates who "knew the needs of their electors" and were honest and independent, for men rather than women, and for first-time candidates who were middle-aged and, other things being equal, party members (Levansky et al. 1989, 16–19; for more general accounts, see Komarovsky 1989; Kolosov et al. 1990; Brovkin 1990; Lentini 1991; and White 1991).

The most vigorously contested seat—for the city of Moscow—

showed both the changes that had taken place and the extent to which the reformed electoral system could still be manipulated from above. The two contestants were Boris Yeltsin, the sacked and disgraced Moscow party secretary who was now, in effect, the candidate of the "democratic opposition," and Yevgenii Brakov, director of the ZIL auto works, and the clear choice of the party authorities. Although he had been nominated by several branches, Yeltsin was not one of the candidates that the party leadership proposed for its 100 seats in the Congress, and according to Yeltsin himself, there was strong pressure to block his candidacy in any of the other constituencies. Yeltsin was eventually nominated for the Moscow national-territorial seat after a thirteen-hour selection conference; but he appeared only once on central television and every effort was made by party officials to hinder the production of his election material. In spite of everything, an increasingly charismatic Yeltsin drew enormous crowds for a series of public meetings at which he attacked party privileges, demanded improvements in food and housing, and called for the establishment of an all-union popular front as a means of countering the lack of debate within the CPSU and "apathy" within the wider society (see Yeltsin 1990).

The first and most significant result was the turnout. The election legislation and official commentaries had made it clear that the abuses of former years would not be tolerated. These had included fathers voting on behalf of their families, friends for their neighbors, and officials for anyone who stood in the way of an early and universal turnout. Voting took place over a slightly shorter period than had been customary in earlier years (from 7:00 A.M. until 8:00 P.M. rather than from 6:00 A.M. to 10:00 P.M.), and the date coincided with the introduction of summer time, which meant an earlier start. In some areas, notably Armenia, nationalists had conducted an active boycotting campaign (Moscow, they suggested, had sided with Azerbaijan in the Nagorno-Karabakh dispute), and the effects of the December 1988 earthquake were still in evidence. Voting in the Armenian town of Leninakan, for instance, had to take place in prefabricated huts or even tents.

The election provided voters with a real if still limited degree of choice (see table 2.1). A total of 9,505 candidates had been formally nominated; of these, 5,074 were officially registered as candidates, and 3,721 were placed on the ballot paper after selection conferences had considered all nominations (*Pervyi* 1989, 41). In spite of the intention of the law, in 399 constituencies there was just a single name on the ballot paper, but in more than two-thirds of constituencies there

TABLE 2.1

ELECTIONS TO THE USSR CONGRESS OF PEOPLE'S DEPUTIES,
MARCH 1989

_____ Nominations and Elections _____

| | Number of candidates | | | | Number | Filled on |
| | | On ballot | Per constituency: | | | of | first |
Type of seat	Registered	paper	1	2	3+	seats	round
Population-based	2,195	1,431	196	473	81	750	590
National-territorial	1,967	1,419	203	479	68	750	636
Public organizations	912	871	n.a.	n.a.	n.a.	750	732
Total	5,074	3,721	399	952	149	2,250	1,958

_____ Seats and Turnout _____

Republic	Population-based seats	National-territorial seats	Deputies[a]	Turnout (%)
Russia	403	243	1,099	87.0
Ukraine	143	32	262	93.4
Belarus	28	32	94	92.4
Uzbekistan	38	43	108	95.8
Kazakhstan	38	32	99	93.7
Georgia	14	59	91	97.0
Azerbaijan	14	48	72	98.5
Lithuania	10	32	58	82.5
Moldova	11	32	55	90.5
Latvia	8	32	52	86.9
Kyrgyzstan	8	32	53	97.0
Tajikistan	10	37	57	93.9
Armenia	8	32	53	71.9
Turkmenia	7	32	48	96.1
Estonia	5	32	48	87.1
USSR	750	750	2,249[a]	89.8

SOURCE: Based on the report of the Central Electoral Commission (*Izvestiya*, 5 April 1989, 1) and the report of the Mandates Commission to the First Congress of People's Deputies (*Pervyi* 1989, 41–44).

NOTE: Total electorate 192,575,165; valid vote 172,840,130; turnout 89.8 percent.

a. Including the 750 seats allocated to public organizations. In three districts (one population-based, two national-territorial) the results were declared invalid because turnout fell below 50 percent, making second elections necessary; 2,249 deputies had been properly elected by the time the Congress assembled.

was a choice and in one Moscow constituency as many as twelve candidates. In the event, in seventy-six constituencies where three or more candidates had been proposed, none secured more than half the votes, and a runoff between the two leading candidates was necessary. Unexpectedly, however, even "sensationally" for *Izvestiya,* in a further 195 constituencies with only one or two candidates there was no result because a majority of voters had crossed out the names with which they had been presented. This meant that in these constituencies the whole exercise would have to be repeated, beginning with the nomination of new and probably different candidates within a two-month period. In a further three constituencies there was a repeat ballot because fewer than half of the registered electorate had bothered to vote (*Izvestiya,* 5 April 1989, 1).

For Gorbachev, the results had been a "referendum in favor of perestroika" (*Pravda,* 27 April 1989, 1); for Yegor Ligachev, speaking for conservatives within the leadership, the whole process had been more like "political shock therapy" (1992, 75). A whole series of local leaders had been successfully returned, among them the first secretaries and prime ministers of Belarus, Estonia, Georgia, Kazakhstan, Moldova, the Ukraine, Turkmenia, and Uzbekistan, as well as the Russian prime minister, Vitalii Vorotnikov. There were, in fact, more party members among the successful deputies than ever before, 87 percent of the total, including those from the social organizations. And there were some striking victories for individual party leaders: the Astrakhan first secretary, for instance, won more than 90 percent of the vote, the Tambov first secretary won over 92 percent, and the first secretary in earthquake-stricken Spitak, in Armenia, obtained more than 93 percent of the vote in his constituency (*Pravda,* 1 April 1989, 1; *Izvestiya,* 1 April 1989, 1, and 30 March 1989, 1).

More unexpected was the number of defeats suffered by party and state officials; the weekly paper *Argumenty i fakty* reported that thirty-eight party first secretaries had been rejected by voters (no. 21, 1989, 8). The defeats suffered by local party and state leaders were especially remarkable. The prime minister of Latvia had been defeated, as had the prime minister and president of Lithuania. The runaway success of Yeltsin in Moscow—with 89.4 percent of the vote and a majority so large it went straight into the *Guinness Book of Records*—was a particular snub to the party authorities, given the attempts that had been made to frustrate his campaign. The most spectacular defeats of all were in Leningrad, where the list of casualties included the regional first secretary, Yuri Solovev, a candidate member of the Politburo who was standing as the single candidate in his constituency, as well as the second secretary, the chairman of the city soviet and his deputy, the chairman of the regional soviet, and the city party secretary.

A very high proportion of the successful candidates—88 percent—had been elected for the first time, including the first religious leaders and commercial farmers ever elected to a Soviet legislative body and a large number of writers and academics. Among them was a little-known law professor from Leningrad named Anatolii Sobchak. The local constituency had for fifty years been represented by a shipyard worker, but on this occasion the university's law faculty decided to put forward its own nominations, one of them its specialist on economic administration. Sobchak, whose platform emphasized legality and human rights, was in turn the single name put forward by the university to the local selection conference. Colleagues told him he was wasting his time; a party official he knew bet a bottle of brandy—"a truly precious commodity in perestroika-era Leningrad"—on the result.

But Sobchak, claiming inspiration by American civil rights activists, spoke at more than a hundred public meetings, turning the local subway station into a "political club" as well as participating in television debates between the candidates, the first of their kind that had ever taken place. Sobchak was accused of "wanting to castrate the working class" (another Leningrad professor had suggested that drug addicts and alcoholics be invited to seek voluntary sterilization); he was asked what he thought of the leading role of the Communist Party, if he was a Jew, and why there were no heroes of capitalist labor when there were heroes of socialist labor. In the end, he fell just short of victory on the first round but then took three-quarters of the vote in the runoff against a single opponent (Sobchak 1991, 13–26).

Elections in the Republics in 1990

The experience of the March 1989 elections led to a further consideration of the system. There was strong support for dispensing with some of the features of the new system that had given rise to the greatest number of objections, particularly selection conferences or constituency preelection meetings. The representation of social organizations was equally unpopular, and several candidates had promised, if elected, to campaign for the removal of this provision from the legislation (Komarovsky and Dugin 1989, 65). Georgii Barabashev and Viktor Vasilev, two Moscow University jurists who had helped to draft the new law, pointed out that there had in fact been few attempts to exclude contro-versial candidates and that the social organizations had provided a "compensation" mechanism by which women and young people, among others, had been able to improve their representation (1989, 11–13). It was argued, in reply, that members of social organizations enjoyed additional representation in a way that was inconsistent with the principle of an equal franchise (everyone could vote in his or her lo-cal constituency, but some could vote again as trade unionists, or as members of the CPSU, or in other ways). Arguments of this kind car-ried the greatest weight with the Soviet public (see, for instance, *Ob-shchestvennoe* 1989, 4–8), and they were influential when the law came to be revised later in the year.

Speaking to the newly elected Supreme Soviet in October 1989, Vice-Chairman Anatolii Lukyanov explained that any amendments to the electoral law involved both changes in general procedures and a greater tolerance of local variation in practices and institutions. Ukraine and the Russian Republic, for instance, both intended to convene Con-gresses of People's Deputies from which a smaller, working Supreme Soviet would be elected; the other republics had decided to elect a Su-preme Soviet by direct and popular ballot. There were also differences in the representation of social organizations and selection conferences, which were left to the republics to decide. The election law was modi-fied accordingly by the Second Congress of People's Deputies in De-cember 1989 (*Vedomosti,* no. 28, 1989, item 540). In the event, only the Russian Republic retained the complicated two-tier parliament that had been established by the USSR as a whole; only two republics (Ka-zakhstan and Belarus) decided to retain seats for public associations; and only four Central Asian republics retained selection conferences.

The republican and local elections that took place on the basis of this amended law were held over a period of months (see table 2.2), a departure from previous practices in which all the republics had voted on the same day (for a survey, see Commission 1990; Slider 1990; Taagepera 1990). Among the first to vote were the Baltic republics, in February and March 1990; nationalist candidates were overwhelmingly successful, and the three republics began to move toward indepen-dence under noncommunist administrations. In Lithuania, the Com-munist Party's leading role had been removed from the constitution the previous December; these were, in effect, the Soviet Union's first multiparty elections. The nationalist movement Sajudis won 90 of the 141 seats; a nationalist, Vytautas Landsbergis, was elected chairman of the new parliament; and on 11 March 1990 the republic announced that

TABLE 2.2

ELECTIONS AT REPUBLIC LEVEL, 1990

Republic	Date	Seats	Candidates	Index of com-petition[a]	Turnout (%)
Ukraine	4 Mar	450	3,901	8.7	84.7
Russia	4 Mar	1,068	6,705	6.3	77.0
Armenia	20 May	259	1,390	5.4	60.4
Moldova	25 Feb	380	1,892	5.0	83.4
Belarus	4 Mar	310	1,473	4.8	86.5
Tajikistan	25 Feb	230	1,035	4.5	91.2
Kazakhstan	25 Mar	270	1,031	3.8	83.9
Estonia	18 Mar	105	392	3.7	78.2
Lithuania	24 Feb	141	471	3.3	75.0
Turkmenia	7 Jan	175	526	3.0	93.6
Kyrgyzstan	25 Feb	350	878	2.5	92.0
Uzbekistan	18 Jan	500	1,094	2.2	93.5
Latvia	18 Mar	201	395	2.0	81.2
Azerbaijan	30 Sep	350	n.a.	n.a.	81.0
Georgia	28 Oct	250	n.a.	n.a.	69.9

SOURCE: Derived from central and republican press reports.

a. Calculated as the number of candidates divided by the number of seats.

it was reverting to the independent status it had enjoyed before its incorporation into the USSR in 1940. The neighboring republics of Estonia and Latvia adopted more cautiously worded declarations of independence on 30 March and 4 May respectively.

The Slavic republics voted on 4 March 1990. In the Russian Federation 6,705 candidates were competing for the 1,068 seats, with up to 28 candidates in a single constituency. The turnout was 77 percent, substantially lower than the corresponding figure a year earlier. As candidates had to secure an absolute majority of the votes that had been cast and elections were valid only if half the electorate voted, only 121 seats could be filled after the first round of voting. Among the successful candidates was Boris Yeltsin, who was chosen by over 80 percent of those voting in his home town of Sverdlovsk. Altogether 86 percent of the new Russian deputies were CPSU members, Yeltsin among them (*Izvestiya*, 5 March 1990, 2; *Pravda*, 17 May 1990, 1). In the Ukraine, 3,901 candidates were competing for the 450 seats available; turnout was high, at 84.7 percent, with nationalist and "green" candidates enjoying some success, particularly in the western regions of Lviv, Ivano-Frankivske, and Ternopil; the Democratic bloc, which grouped together most of the opposition, took 43 seats in the first round (Potichnyj 1992). In Belarus, which also conducted its elections in March, 1,473 candidates were standing for the 310 seats in the new parliament; turnout again was high, at 86.5 percent, and there was at least one "sensational" result when a journalist defeated a member of the Belarus Central Committee Secretariat (*Pravda*, 14 March 1990, 2).

The elections in Georgia were first postponed and then set for 28 October. In the event a nationalist coalition, Round Table/Free Georgia, took 54 percent of the vote, ahead of local communists with 30 percent (*Pravda*, 3 November 1990, 4). The republican parliament, under its new leadership, adopted a declaration of independence, which was confirmed by a referendum in March 1991, and the following October a veteran dissident and professor of Anglo-American literature, Zviad Gamsakhurdia, was elected the republic's first president with 86.5 percent of the vote.

The Armenian elections were complicated by the situation in Nagorno-Karabakh, a largely Armenian enclave in Azerbaijan that had been seeking to be reunited with the national territory since early 1988. After a period of direct rule from Moscow, the enclave had been returned to Azerbaijani sovereignty in November 1989; this precipitated widespread demonstrations, and nearly a hundred people were killed in January 1990 when a state of emergency had to be declared and imposed by force. There was a 95 percent turnout in the enclave itself, in spite of the presence of Azerbaijani troops (*Soviet Weekly*, 31 May 1990, 6); in Armenia as a whole, voters were less enthusiastic, and the turnout, already the lowest in 1989, was lower still—just over 60 percent.

There was least competition in Central Asia. In Uzbekistan a third of the seats in the February 1990 elections had only a single candidate, and 94.6 percent of the successful candidates—a much higher proportion than before—were CPSU members or candidate members of the party (*Pravda*, 16 February 1990, 1). This was typical of patterns across Central Asia, which were much closer to traditional Soviet forms of mobilization than to the exercises in limited choice that were beginning to take place in the towns and cities of the European USSR. The elections in Turkmenia produced one minor sensation when a collective farm milkmaid defeated the head of the ideology department of the republican Central Committee; voters, apparently, had been attracted by her "principled position" (*Pravda*, 10 January 1990, 1). Elections to the

Kyrgyz parliament took place in February 1990 (Huskey 1995a); so too did elections to the Tajik parliament, where over one-third of the successful candidates were party or state officials and only five were women (*Kommunist Tadzhikistana*, 2 March 1990, 1). The turnout, as elsewhere in Central Asia, was over 90 percent in both cases. In Azerbaijan, which voted in September, communist candidates won a decisive victory, but oppositionists secured twenty-six seats and a legitimate place in the political process.

In this second round of competitive elections voters had again been presented with a choice of candidates rather than of organized political alternatives. Yet there were still uncertainties about constituency boundaries, campaign spending, and electoral procedures more generally. What, for example, about the legal requirement that the single-member constituencies have equal numbers of electors? This was hardly the case in Latvia, where the number of electors varied from 2,800 to 127,300, as against a norm of 62,000. The smaller seats were generally in the countryside, giving rural areas more representation than urban ones although more than 70 percent of Latvia's population lived in towns, which, as it happened, were predominantly Russian (*Pervyi* 1989, 51). Nor was the problem confined to the Baltic. In Moscow, single-member constituencies varied from 139,236 to 379,906 electors as compared with a norm of 257,300. The distribution of seats by republic was also not strictly proportional. On the evidence of the preliminary results of the 1989 census, twenty-eight seats should have been transferred elsewhere, or fourteen if the 1979 census had been used as the basis of allocation (Berezkin et al. 1989).

Candidates, under an amendment to the 1988 election law, were supposed to compete under "equal conditions." Some, in fact, found their efforts hindered by official interventions of various kinds. In the Dnepropetrovsk region, a candidate found it very difficult to arrange places for his meetings and then found them occupied at the times that had been agreed on. Nor could he find a printer prepared to produce his election address. His opponent, who was supported by the local party first secretary, had no problems of this kind (*Pravda*, 22 March 1989, 3). Party officials were even prepared to intervene in the electoral campaigns of the clergy, a number of whom were candidates. At Elektrostal, just outside Moscow, the party secretary of a local plant went to churches two days before the ballot and demanded that a prayer service be held for one of the Orthodox priests who was standing, but not for the priest who was his competitor. In two other villages, leaflets in favor of this candidate were distributed together with church candles and holy objects (*Izvestiya*, 6 April 1990, 3).

There were particular difficulties about campaign expenditures. Candidates had equal access to radio and television, and their expenses were to be met from a "single fund created at the expense of the state as well as by voluntary contributions from enterprises, public organizations and citizens" (*Vedomosti*, no. 28, 1989, item 540). In practice, some candidates had the support of their workplaces, giving them access to printing resources and unpaid assistance of a kind that was not available to their competitors; and in Estonia and Lithuania individual or collective donations to particular candidates were permitted, although all such donations had to be monitored by the local electoral commission (*Narodnyi deputat*, no. 1, 1990, 65, 67). Other candidates went even further, offering inducements of a kind that would have been familiar in Hogarth's England: the director of a bread factory in Bashkiria arranged for his constituency to receive four years' supply of wheat, in Khabarovsk the director of a confectionery establishment distributed coupons for boxes of chocolates at the polling stations (he lost), and in Frunze an elderly bachelor was surprised to receive an invitation to the local gynecological clinic, whose director was a candidate in the constituency (*Izvestiya*, 11 February 1990, 1; *Moscow News*, no. 10, 1990, 5; *Izvestiya*, 8 February 1990, 2).

There was no shortage of more obvious violations of the electoral law. In a constituency in the Chechen-Ingush republic, for instance, 1,163 ballot papers were returned, although only 699 had been distributed (*Sovetskaya Rossiya*, 8 March 1990, 2); it was one of several constituencies in the republic where "significantly more voting papers were found than had been given out to voters or received officially for the election campaign" (Mikhaleva and Morozova 1990, 36). In another case, in the Moscow region, voters' choices marked in pencil had been erased and "new" votes cast in ink (*Trud*, 14 March 1990, 2). An electoral commission in the Bashkir republic had to be dissolved when 130 falsified ballots were discovered and the chairman of the commission, who was drunk when the investigating committee arrived, turned out to be related to one of the candidates whose electoral support had originally fallen short of what was needed by exactly the same number of votes (*Izvestiya*, 28 March 1990, 2). There were "numerous complaints of election law violations," observers concluded, including the "time-honored practice of one member of the family voting for the entire family," but there was no suggestion, at least in Russia, of "massive fraud" (Commission 1990, 106).

Electing a Russian President in 1991

Political life in prerevolutionary Russia had been dominated by an autocratic tsar. The Soviet leadership, by contrast, was nominally a collective one until March 1990, when an executive presidency was established (the idea had been considered briefly but rejected in the 1930s and again in the 1960s; see Lazarev 1990, 3–4). In the future, the revised constitution made clear, elections to the USSR presidency would be conducted by a direct and competitive popular vote. But in the turbulent and unpredictable circumstances then obtaining, it was agreed that in this first instance the president would be elected by the Congress of People's Deputies itself. Gorbachev, as expected, was successful, although only 71 percent voted in favor of his nomination—or 59 percent of the total membership of the Congress—in an uncontested ballot. For many observers it was a crucial mistake that at this point Gorbachev did not seek the endorsement of a popular ballot that he almost certainly would have won.

Following the March 1990 elections, Boris Yeltsin had been elected chair of the Russian parliament on 29 May 1990. Under Yeltsin's guidance the parliament became increasingly assertive: on 12 June it adopted a declaration of sovereignty in terms of which its own decisions had precedence over those of the USSR as a whole, and a series of legislative measures placed natural resources, foreign trade, and budgetary control under Russian rather than all-union jurisdiction. The Soviet president and he agreed on the direction of change, Yeltsin commented in October 1990, but not about its tempo; Gorbachev, for his part, saw their differences not in personal terms but as one between "two different political lines and programmatic aims" (*Pravda*, 18 October 1990, 5, and 28 February 1991, 2). During the following year, and particularly after he had secured a popular mandate as president of the largest of the republics in June 1991, Yeltsin's position became the dominant one.

The proposal to create a Russian presidency had not originally been controversial (see Eliseev 1992; Urban 1992; White, McAllister, and Kryshtanovskaya 1994a). At the first Russian Congress of People's Deputies, in May and June 1990, the proposal had the support of deputies from all the parliamentary factions. The "Communists of Russia" group, normally Yeltsin's most implacable opponents, were in favor of the change and themselves proposed to amend the constitution in this sense. Once Yeltsin had become parliamentary chairman and in July 1990 resigned from the CPSU, however, the issue of the presidency became more conflictual and the question of who might fill the position was soon a bitterly contested one.

The second Russian Congress of People's Deputies, in December 1990, agreed that the Supreme Soviet and its constitutional committee would consider appropriate amendments to the constitution. As a constitutional amendment would require a two-thirds majority in the Congress, Yeltsin's hard-line opponents were well placed to resist any change that would be to their disadvantage. The decision to call a referendum on the future of the USSR altered the position once again (on the referendum, see chapter 4). On 25 January 1991 the Russian Supreme Soviet was asked to "consider the appropriateness of asking additional questions in the referendum," in practice an invitation to approve an elected presidency; the proposal was approved on 7 February. On 17 March, the same time as the future of the USSR itself was being put to the vote, more than 76 million Russians voted and more than 53 million endorsed a presidential system.

An extraordinary third session of the Congress of People's Deputies had been called by deputies anxious to condemn Yeltsin's direct challenge to Soviet and communist authority. But the outcome of the referendum, and the open expression of public support on Moscow streets, influenced the Congress in a different direction, and on 5 April it agreed that a presidential election would be held on 12 June 1991. The Supreme Soviet was asked to prepare a law on the presidency as well as any amendments that might be necessary to the Russian constitution, and the changes were duly approved by the fourth Russian Congress of Deputies on 25 May.

Candidates for the Russian presidency would have to be citizens aged between thirty-five and sixty-five, and they could hold the office for no more than two five-year terms. Nominations could be made by political parties, trade unions, and public organizations, or other groupings that were able to collect 100,000 signatures in their support. The president could not be a deputy or a member of a political party; he enjoyed the right of legislative initiative, reported to the Congress once a year, and appointed the Russian prime minister with the consent of the Supreme Soviet.

From the outset, Boris Yeltsin was the front runner. In press interviews he claimed that the status of Russia as a republic within the USSR had been considerably enhanced since he had become parliamentary chairman: there was, for example, a separate Russian radio and television service, the first treaties had been concluded between Russia and foreign states, and the central leadership had "started to take Russia and the other republics into account." His own election program placed its main emphasis on "radical reform," above all in the economy, where the transition to the market would be pressed ahead more vigorously. Another priority was "civil peace and stability in society," perhaps through a roundtable agreement of the kind that had been concluded, in early April 1991, between Gorbachev and nine of the republican leaders (*Izvestiya*, 23 May 1991, 3).

Whose support was Yeltsin counting on? It was not an easy question to answer, for someone who had spent thirty years in the Communist Party. But the support he hoped for, he told *Izvestiya*, was the support "of the people who understand me and share my positions." The CPSU, Yeltsin thought, could itself have become a party of reform, and his vice-presidential candidate, Alexander Rutskoi, had just formed a grouping of members known as Communists for Democracy in support of the Russian chairman and the reforms he was conducting, but the party as a whole was heading for "further disintegration" (*Izvestiya*, 23 May 1991, 3). Speaking to an election meeting shortly before the poll, Yeltsin condemned the "totalitarian system" that had brought Russia to its crisis and promised to "fight the Lord God himself" to uphold the republic and its sovereignty (*Sobesednik*, no. 23, 1991, 7).

Yeltsin's main rival was the former Soviet prime minister Nikolai Ryzhkov, who favored a transition to the market but "not a market based on the deprivation and suffering of the workers" (*Izvestiya*, 7 June 1991, 3). Ryzhkov counted particularly on the support of the non-Russian areas of the Russian Federation, and on working people in factories, collectives, and state farms; he also expected the support of the Communist Party, although he was not its official candidate (*Izvestiya*, 23 May 1991, 3). The former interior minister, Vadim Bakatin, was understood to be Gorbachev's own choice for the Russian presidency. Bakatin had been a regional party first secretary and a member of the CPSU Central Committee from 1986 onward; his manifesto was based on "common sense," including a program of economic reform that would outlaw "illegal enrichment" and retain some price controls. It was, Bakatin suggested, a program of "radical centrism" (*Komsomolskaya pravda*, 31 May 1991, 1).

The three other presidential candidates attracted less initial attention. Vladimir Zhirinovsky, leader of the Liberal Democratic Party, was nominated by members of the fourth Congress of People's Deputies. Regarded by Yeltsin's supporters as a "clown who must be taken seriously" (Urban 1992, 198), Zhirinovsky based his appeal on a promise to restore Russia's national greatness and to cut the price of vodka. The "main slogan of his campaign," he told journalists, was "to defend Russians and the mass of ordinary people" (*Sovetskaya Rossiya*, 6 June 1991, 3). General Albert Makashov, chairman of the Olga-Urals military district, appealed to a rather different constituency, servicemen and workers in the military-industrial complex who were concerned by the far-reaching implications of Yeltsin's economic program. Speaking to the Russian parliament, Makashov called for the "sovietization" rather than privatization of property and went on to attack the "political prostitution" that was taking place around the country (*Izvestiya*, 23 May 1991, 2). The sixth and final candidate was Aman-Geldy Tuleev, chairman of the Kemerovo regional soviet and a miner; his campaign emphasized local autonomy, gradual economic reform, and "social defense" (Urban 1992, 199).

An eve-of-poll forecast had suggested the chances of success were "approximately equal" between Yeltsin and former prime minister Ryzhkov (*Izvestiya*, 4 June 1991, 6). Other surveys, based on more representative samples, predicted that the Russian parliamentary chairman might obtain about 44 percent, leaving Ryzhkov in second place at 31 percent (*Pravda*, 6 June 1991, 2). The final result, reported on 19 June, was a much more decisive win for Yeltsin, with almost three-fifths of the vote, than any of the opinion polls had indicated, leaving the candidate of the traditional communists, Nikolai Ryzhkov, with about a sixth, and the "serious clown," Zhirinovsky, in third place with less than a tenth. Gorbachev's favored candidate, Vadim Bakatin, won less than 4 percent (see table 2.3). The results from two constituencies were ruled invalid because of violations of the electoral law; there had been complaints, during the campaign, that bottles of vodka were being given out to those who promised to vote for Ryzhkov, and that "tourists" had been riding around Leningrad in buses, registering their votes in one constituency after another (*Pravda*, 6 June 1991, 2, and 14 June 1991, 1). And a constituency in Novosibirsk, in what was apparently an innocent mistake, had voted a day early.

For *Izvestiya* (14 June 1991, 1), the outcome was a "clear victory for the democratic forces," not simply because of Yeltsin's decisive success, but also because of the wins for reformers in the elections that took place on the same date for Moscow and Leningrad mayors, and the support given in Leningrad to the proposal to revert to the historic name of St. Petersburg. The Communist Party Secretariat less happily concluded that its leaders had "finally lost authority," leaving the party "without cadres and without power" (Center 1991e). Most voters, in fact, said they had favored the candidate that would "get Russia out of

TABLE 2.3

THE RUSSIAN PRESIDENTIAL ELECTION, 12 JUNE 1991

Candidate	Votes	Percentage of electorate	Percentage of valid vote
Yeltsin, Boris	45,552,041	42.8	59.7
Ryzhkov, Nikolai	13,395,335	12.6	17.6
Zhirinovsky, Vladimir	6,211,007	5.8	8.1
Tuleev, Aman-Geldy	5,417,464	5.1	7.1
Makashov, Albert	2,969,511	2.8	3.9
Bakatin, Vadim	2,719,757	2.6	3.6
Total valid votes	76,265,115	71.6	100.0
Invalid votes	3,242,167	3.1	
Nonvoters	26,977,236	25.3	
Electorate	106,484,518	100.0	

(Turnout 74.7 percent)

SOURCE: *Pravda*, 20 June 1991, 1.

its crisis," and very few thought they had been influenced by the organization that had made the nomination (*Pravda*, 2 July 1991, 3). The success that had been achieved by the Communist Party's most prominent opponents was nonetheless a heavy blow to its public standing.

Yeltsin's success also contributed to the breakup of the USSR itself. Initially, Yeltsin had favored a looser form of association, and on 20 August he was due to have signed a new treaty of union, with Gorbachev and other republic leaders, that would have brought it into existence. But the ceremony was forestalled by an attempted coup on 19 August, launched by a group of party hard-liners seeking to prevent the weakening of central authority that the new treaty would have involved. The coup collapsed after three days; its main result was to accelerate the dissolution of the state itself. On 1 December, in another referendum, voters in the Ukraine decided for independence; Yeltsin concluded there was no future in negotiating a new union, and on 8 December he agreed to establish a new Commonwealth of Independent States based initially on Russia, Ukraine, and Belarus. Gorbachev resigned as president of a state that no longer existed on 25 December, Yeltsin took over his office in the Kremlin, and the Russian parliament voted to withdraw from a treaty with the other republics that it had first approved in 1922.

Between 1985, when Mikhail Gorbachev became CPSU general

secretary, and December 1991, when he left office, Russia had moved from a republic of the Soviet Union without free or competitive elections to an independent state in which there were elections with a choice between candidates though not yet between parties. The principle that independently nominated candidates could stand for election had been established, as had the principle that candidates should be subject to common rules to ensure a fair chance for each. There was a genuinely secret ballot, and no more "passive voting." After a thousand years of autocracy and seventy years of communism, the principle that political authority must be based on the freely expressed consent of the electorate had been established, and voters had elected a president and parliament who would steer the new Russian Federation into the postcommunist era.

((@ 3 @))

What Can Influence
Russian Voters?

Russia came late to free elections, at a time when there were already thousands of studies of voting in dozens of different countries starting with the first social science survey of voters in the 1940 American presidential election (Lazarsfeld et al. 1944). The literature that is now available offers a wide range of generalizations about what can influence voting behavior, at least in liberal democracies. Conclusions differ from country to country and sometimes from election to election; the differences also reflect the contrasting interpretations of political scientists (see, for instance, Niemi and Weisberg 1984; Crewe 1994). Nonetheless, there is substantial agreement about three influences that shape voting in a normal election: political attitudes and party identification, economic conditions, and social structure.

A normal political science model of Russian voting would start by testing the influence of social structure: older and more educated voters, for instance, may differ from others, and there may be a "gender gap" between men and women. While these social differences are present in Russia as in other European societies, in established democracies they usually explain a limited proportion of the variation in votes. Economic influences, by contrast, are often considered the most important single factor in voting. If individuals feel prosperous or worse off financially, or believe one party but not another may improve their own economic circumstances, this can affect their vote. So too can judgments about the way in which the government is handling the national economy, particularly in Russia, where the transformation of a command into a market economy has produced extreme changes in the economic conditions of individuals and in the national economy as a whole.

In the abnormal conditions of Russia's first democratic elections, we also need to include some "abnormal" influences. In founding elections in new democracies voters are confronted with a choice between political regimes: there are proponents of the old authoritarianism, defenders of pluralistic institutions, and advocates of new forms of authoritarianism. The two 1993 referendums considered in chapters 4 and 5 were explicit efforts to mobilize popular support for the new system of government introduced under Boris Yeltsin. The parliamentary election of December 1993, which is the subject of chapters 6 and 7, was not so much a test of the appeal of individual candidates or parties as an occasion when leaders could present themselves as defenders of democracy or as advocates of an alternative view of Russia's future. The 1995 parliamentary election, examined in chapter 10, was not only about who should govern but also about the regime that determines how the country is governed.

A change of regimes gives rise to such distinctive issues as: How much freedom has been gained by the collapse of communism? And who is to blame—or held to be responsible—for Russia's new economic problems? Given that competing political parties were not allowed to organize in the Soviet period, there was no opportunity for party identifications to develop through a lifelong process of socialization into democratic party politics, as happens in an established democracy. Nor did the Soviet regime allow social organizations, especially political parties, to establish an identity independent of the party-state.

This chapter describes the variety of influences—political, economic, and social—that may be expected to shape the voting behavior of Russians in the novel circumstances of the postcommunist 1990s. Subsequent chapters test empirically which potential influences are actually most important in determining how Russians vote. The data analyzed in this and subsequent chapters come from the nationally representative New Russia Barometer (NRB) sample surveys, organized by the Centre for the Study of Public Policy, University of Strathclyde, as part of its ongoing program of monitoring mass response to transformation in the postcommunist societies of Central and Eastern Europe and the former Soviet Union. Each NRB survey covers political, economic, and social attitudes and behavior (see Rose and Tikhomirov 1995). The second NRB sample survey was undertaken in summer 1993, between the April referendum on the popularity of President Yeltsin and the December election of parliament (for a full set of questions and answers, see Rose, Boeva, and Shironin 1992). The third NRB survey was conducted in early spring 1994; it focused on the December 1993 election (for questions and answers, see Rose and Haerpfer 1994c). Both surveys interviewed large nationwide representative samples of the Russian population: 1,975 respondents in NRB II and 3,535 in NRB III. A fifth New Barometer survey followed the 1995 Duma election (Rose 1996b; for full details, see appendix A).

How Russians vote does not depend on what they are told on television or what journalists stationed inside the Moscow ring road see and hear; it depends on how they see the new institutions of Russia emerging, and how much they want to escape or return to the past. Hence, the emphasis in the New Russia Barometer surveys is not on whether people liked the personality of President Yeltsin or more or less "faceless" candidates for parliament, or whether they thought housing or health care the more important political issue. Instead, the New Russia Barometer focuses on whether people liked or disliked the communist political and economic regime—and how they have evaluated what has followed.

Political Attitudes in Postcommunist Russia

In the United States and Britain, voting studies emphasize party identification, formed by a process of intergenerational political socialization as children first learn to identify with the party of their parents (Butler and Stokes 1969). In the Russian Federation, the only party for the lifetime of most electors was the Communist Party of the Soviet Union. Every adult old enough to vote in a Soviet election had voted Communist at least once—often without conviction and sometimes in spite of his or her view of the party. But not every Russian became a member of the party. The incentives for membership were pragmatic as much as ideological, for possession of a party card was a condition of holding many jobs, and it could also be useful in obtaining material benefits such as consumer goods, subsidized holidays, or favorable treatment in the allocation of housing (McAllister and White 1995b).

When New Russia Barometer III asked people about membership in the Communist Party of the Soviet Union, there was no hesitancy in giving answers: only 2 percent did not respond. A total of 14 percent said they had been members, 24 percent said another member of their family had been a member, and 61 percent said that no one in their family had ever been a member. People who had been party members have shown marginal differences from nonparty members in some political attitudes, for example, attitudes toward capitalism and Marxism-

Leninism. The most striking feature of such comparisons is how small the differences are. For example, a majority of party members did not have a positive view of socialism (see White and McAllister 1996, table 5; Rose 1996b).

The distinctive feature of Russian voters today is that everyone has lived far longer under Communist rule than in a political system with competitive elections. By contrast, in established Anglo-American democracies the idea of being governed without elections is historically and psychologically inconceivable. In Germany, which has had a history of alternation between democratic and undemocratic regimes, the democratic institutions introduced by the 1949 Basic Law are now taken for granted. But no Russian can regard the current regime as established, and Russian politics today involves comparisons between the past and present regimes—and speculation about the possibility of another regime in the future.

In the Russian context, asking people to compare different regimes is not an abstract question of political philosophy, as it would be in an established democracy (cf. Kornberg and Clarke 1992). The collapse of the old regime implies that there was a significant level of dissatisfaction with what it represented. Events since that time imply a significant degree of dissatisfaction with the current regime as well. The New Russia Barometer accordingly measures attitudes toward regimes on a "heaven/hell" scale, in which +100 is the most positive rating that can be given to the regime and -100 the worst (cf. Rose 1992). The *regime scale* shows whether Russians are positive or negative toward a regime and how strongly or weakly they hold their views.

When Russians are asked to evaluate the former communist regime, just over half give it a positive rating and a third are negative, including 5 percent who are very negative, placing the communist regime at −100 (table 3.1). When Russians are asked to evaluate the current system, by contrast, more are negative than positive. Since a sixth give a neutral reply, the median Russian was neither positive nor negative about the regime. When asked to evaluate the political system as it is expected to be in five years' time, nearly half of the respondents are positive (sign of optimism) and the proportion that are neutral (often a mark of uncertainty) rises to a third. The aggregate profile of opinion emphasizes that even though the old regime did not rest on a broad base of support, the base of support for the new regime is even narrower.

All in all, Russians are very divided in their views of their systems of government past, present, and future. This is shown by the very

TABLE 3.1
EVALUATION OF POLITIAL REGIMES — PAST, PRESENT,
AND FUTURE

*Q: Here is a scale for evaluating how the political
system works. The highest mark is plus 100; the
lowest, minus 100.*
   *a. Where on the scale would you place the former
   communist regime?*
   *b. Where would you place our current system with
   free elections and a multiparty system?*
   *c. Where would you place our political system in
   five years?*

	Communist	*Current*	*Future*
Positive	51%	36%	49%
Neutral	13	16	34
Negative	36	48	17
Mean rating	4	−13	15
Standard deviation	58	51	48

SOURCE: Centre for the Study of Public Policy/Paul Lazarsfeld Society, New
Russia Barometer III (1994).

high standard deviation, a measure of the dispersion around the mean
rating. The standard deviation of 58 for the evaluation of the past communist regime means that a spread of opinion from plus 62 to minus 53
is required to cover two-thirds of respondents, and a sixth are even
more extreme on each end of the heaven/hell scale. Standard deviations are similarly large for ratings of the current and future regimes.

Many Russians are divided in their own minds about what to
make of political upheavals. This is shown by combining the assessments that people make about the old and the new regimes. The median group, 28 percent, are skeptics, giving both the old and new regimes negative ratings. The largest group, 36 percent, are positive
about the communist regime and negative about the current system,
compared to 21 percent who are positive about the new system and
negative about the communist regime. An additional 15 percent are
compliant, saying *da* (yes) to both systems (cf. Rose and Mishler 1994).

Given limited support for the current regime, New Russia Barometer III also asked people their views about alternative regimes (table
3.2; cf. Rose and Mishler 1996b). The first alternative offered was a re-

TABLE 3.2

POPULAR SUPPORT FOR ALTERNATIVE REGIMES

Q: Our current political system is not the only possible one. Some people say that another would be better for us. What do you think? Here are some statements; please tell me to what extent you agree with each of them.

	Strongly agree	Agree	Disagree	Strongly disagree	Don't know
Experts, not parliament and government, should make the most important economic decisions.	26%	28%	12%	6%	28%
We do not need parliament or elections, but instead a strong leader who can make decisions and put them into effect fast.	21	22	20	20	16
It would be better to restore the former communist system.	9	14	28	34	15
The army should rule.	3	7	23	55	12
The tsar should be restored.	4	5	18	52	21

SOURCE: Centre for the Study of Public Policy/Paul Lazarsfeld Society, New Russia Barometer III (1994).

turn to the communist regime, and 23 percent indicated this was their preferred option. In retrospect, Russians view the Soviet period as a time when prices were stable, employment was secure, living standards were more or less predictable, and the Soviet Union was a great world power. Nevertheless, fewer than half who give it a positive rating on the heaven/hell scale would like to return to the old regime. Most people giving a positive rating to the communist regime are not reactionaries but simply nostalgic for a more stable and equitable society. Altogether, more than three-fifths of Russians explicitly reject a return to a communist system, and those strongly opposed are almost four times as numerous as those strongly in favor of a restoration. This shows that the flaws of the communist system are seen as much greater than its benefits.

The prospect of bringing in the army is a familiar authoritarian alternative. The explosion of crime and inflation and unemployment that has followed market reforms might have been expected to encourage Russians to favor an institution that would be able to guarantee public order.

But the Soviet tradition of civil-military relationships has always emphasized political control of the military by party commissars and, in extreme circumstances, the execution of generals (Kolkowicz 1967); nor was the army seen as an independent social institution, as in some Middle Eastern or Latin American countries. Compulsory military service has given the great majority of Russian males firsthand experience of how the Soviet army works, from the bottom-up perspective of a lowly conscript. When Russians are asked whether they would prefer the army to rule, only 10 percent approve of the idea, and more than three-quarters reject it.

Another alternative to the present regime would be personal rule by a strong leader. The history of Central and Eastern Europe is full of examples of individuals who have sought to use their personal authority as a substitute for constitutional legitimacy. The Soviet Union, particularly in Stalin's time, had what was subsequently denounced as a "cult of personality"; this was also present in some other communist regimes, including China under Mao Zedong, North Korea under Kim Il-Sung, and Romania under Nicolae Ceausescu. Strong leadership may also be consistent with democracy, however; because parties and legislatures speak with so many competing voices, without strong leadership it may be difficult to give clear direction to government. For this reason, every American presidential election, features calls for strong and effective leadership (Rose and Mishler 1996a).

To test support for strong leadership, New Russia Barometer III first asked people whether they agreed or disagreed with the statement that a strong leader who could make decisions and put them quickly into effect was more important than parliament and elections. The replies once again showed that Russians were divided: two-fifths answered yes, two-fifths were against, and the median group were don't knows (table 3.2). By contrast, only 9 percent of Russians thought it a good idea to restore a tsar.

Since the transformation of Russia involves fundamental changes in the economy as well as in the polity, the New Russia Barometer posed a classic dilemma of political economy: should experts or elected officials make important economic decisions? The argument for allowing experts to decide about problems such as fighting inflation is that they should know what will be effective. But effective action imposes costs as well as benefits. The argument for elected officials to take decisions is that they know what the people want—even if they may not know how to achieve popular goals. The dilemma is particularly acute in Russia because in a command economy policymakers did not learn about tradeoffs between inflation and unemployment or consequences of budgetary deficits. New Russia Barometer III found that more than half of Russians wanted technocratic decision making, assuming that there were experts who would know what to do to put the economy right; more than a quarter were don't knows; and only 18 percent preferred such decisions to be made by parliament and elected government.

Because there is more than one alternative to government with competitive elections, the New Russia Barometer deliberately offered a wide range of alternatives to the current regime. The choices are not all compatible: few people, for instance, would want a return to the tsar and also a return to communist rule. Insofar as opponents of the current regime are divided, they are less threatening. Yet there are theoretical and empirical reasons to expect some Russians to be so dissatisfied with the present regime that they would prefer any of several authoritarian alternatives. When the five questions in table 3.2 were factor analyzed, the statistics showed that replies to questions about military rule, a strong leader, or a return to communist rule had formed a single dimension and can thus be used to create an authoritarianism scale (for details, see appendix B). Most Russians are *anti*authoritarian. A total of 28 percent explicitly reject all three authoritarian alternatives, and an additional 37 percent reject two. Only 3 percent endorse all three forms of authoritarianism, and an additional 15 percent endorse two of them. Those at the antiauthoritarian end of the scale outnumber the proauthoritarians by more than three to one.

A major difference between the old and the current regimes is in the competing meanings given to freedom. Marxist doctrines held that "true" freedom was impossible under capitalism because capitalism created a false consciousness among workers. Even if people said they felt free, this could not be the case because of objective forces that dictated those responses. The Soviet regime claimed that it enabled individuals to become free by taking collective decisions in the interests of everyone. There was thus no need for such "bourgeois" freedoms as a separation of powers or competing parties. The totalitarian apparatus of the state imposed severe restrictions on what individuals could choose to do or say, preventing people from expressing "antistate" opinions or acting in ways that the state—in practice, the party authorities—deemed inimical to the people's interests.

A classic philosophical rejection of communist totalitarianism is grounded in the liberal doctrine of freedom from the state. In Isaiah Berlin's words, this freedom is "the degree to which no man or body of men interferes with my activity"; it is "the area within which a man can act unobstructed by others" (1969, 122). This concept implies that freedom can differ from one area or domain of social life to another, and there can be differences in the extent to which individuals are free from obstruction by the state. In place of the communist idea of freedom achieved through state action, Berlin proposed what is effectively a consumer view of freedom—whether people actually find the state interferes with their lives or not.

To measure the extent to which Russians feel that the new regime offers *freedom from state controls,* the New Russia Barometer asked people whether they felt conditions were better, the same, or worse in eight different areas of social life (cf. Rose 1995d). The communist suppression of the institutions of civil society has produced a strong reaction (see figure 3.1). More than four-fifths of Russians feel freer today to decide about religious matters for themselves, and three-quarters feel freer to join any organization they like or say what they think. The key question about political activity does not make the mistake of assuming that political participation is a good in itself. In the old regime, exposure to political indoctrination was compulsory at school and the workplace and was unavoidable in the mass media. In a posttotalitarian society, freedom is the freedom to turn one's back on politics: more than half say they now feel freer to decide whether or not to take an interest in politics.

In four areas of social life, the median Russian did not consider that conditions had changed significantly: the freedom to travel or live anywhere one wants, fear of illegal arrest, or the expectation that government would treat everyone fairly. The fourth area, the respondent's sense that people like themselves could influence government, was included as part of the battery of freedom questions because it is central to conventional descriptions of a democratic civic culture (cf. Almond and Verba 1963; Putnam 1993). In fact, only 6 percent of Russians said they have more influence on government today than under Soviet rule, compared to 48 percent saying things have not changed, 20 percent saying their influence has lessened, and a quarter being uncertain. Yet even though Russians do not see themselves as better able to influence government, the freedoms gained are nonetheless real, for government is much less able to control what ordinary Russians can do.

A factor analysis of the eight freedom measures confirms a single

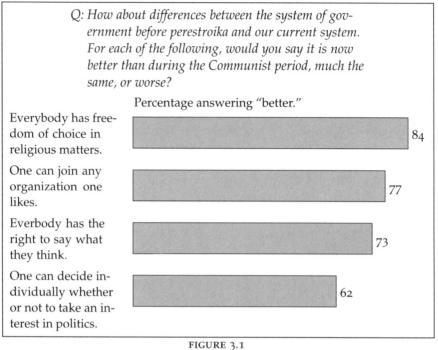

*Q: How about differences between the system of gov-
ernment before perestroika and our current system.
For each of the following, would you say it is now
better than during the Communist period, much the
same, or worse?*

Percentage answering "better."

Everybody has free-
dom of choice in
religious matters.   84

One can join any
organization one
likes.   77

Everbody has the
right to say what
they think.   73

One can decide in-
dividually whether
or not to take an in-
terest in politics.   62

FIGURE 3.1
INCREASE OF FREEDOM IN THE CURRENT REGIME

SOURCE: Centre for the Study of Public Policy/Paul Lazarsfeld Society, New
Russia Barometer III (1994).

distinctive dimension involving religious liberty, freedom to join or not
to join public organizations, saying what one thinks, and deciding
whether or not to take an interest in politics (see appendix B). The four
measures of freedom form a single underlying dimension constituting
the freedom scale used in subsequent chapters. A total of 35 percent of
Russians feel freer on all four counts, and an additional 50 percent feel
freer most of the time; 11 percent usually say they see no change in
freedom, with only 4 percent believing that their freedoms have usually lessened.

A representative democracy requires trust (Putnam 1993). People
must trust political parties to represent their interests, even if they do
not trust the government of the day. Moreover, people must also trust
institutions of civil society, such as churches, business enterprises, or
trade unions, which can mobilize support for parties. This is particularly the case with a fledgling party system in which the names and

characters of many parties will hardly be known because they are new and poorly organized. Through links with trusted social institutions, new parties can be identified as representing interests with which individual voters can identify (see Mishler and Rose, 1996b).

New Russia Barometer III asked people to indicate their level of trust or distrust in a range of sixteen different institutions, some explicitly governmental, such as parliament, others directly involved in the political process, such as parties, and still others significant in a normal civil society, such as the media. *Only one of sixteen institutions was positively trusted by half of Russians,* that is, rated between 5 and 7 on a seven-point scale (table 3.3). The church was trusted by 50 percent of respondents. The army ranked second, being positively trusted by 40 percent of Russians. The only other institutions trusted by as many as a fifth of Russians were peasants' organizations and the mass media (for a detailed discussion, see Rose 1994b).

Most institutions of Russian civil society are distrusted. Political parties rank highest on the distrust scale: 82 percent give parties a rating of 1, 2, or 3 on a seven-point scale, as against only 6 percent giving a rating of 5, 6, or 7. Such representative bodies as new and old trade unions, private enterprises, patriotic associations, parliament and civil service, the police, President Yeltsin, and the Russian government are distrusted by at least two-thirds of Russians. A substantial majority also distrust the courts, the mass media, and foreign advisers.

While there is a substantial degree of generalized distrust in institutions, there are differences between institutions in the degree of distrust. Factor analysis identifies four underlying dimensions (see appendix table B.2), and table 3.3 groups institutions accordingly. The resulting scales are best considered as measures of distrust, for an absolute majority of Russians show a distrust of *all* the institutions constituting the scales for state institutions, workers' organizations, and the market.

> *Distrust of state institutions (courts, police, civil servants).* A history of repression under the tsars as well as the commissars is often cited as evidence of the population's disposition to trust authority. In fact, this is not the case. The aggregate level of trust is low. Only 5 percent show trust in all three state institutions, an additional 7 percent show positive trust in two, and 13 percent in one. In sum, 75 percent of Russians do not trust the courts, the police, or civil servants.
>
> *Distrust of workers' organizations and patriotic groups.* In the Soviet Union trade unions were party-sponsored "transmission belts,"

TABLE 3.3
TRUST IN INSTITUTIONS OF RUSSIAN SOCIETY

Q: There are various public institutions in Russia, such as legislative and executive bodies, courts, and police. Please indicate your trust in them on a scale, where 7 denotes maximum trust and 1 denotes maximum distrust.

| | Great trust | | | | | | No trust | | Don't | Mean |
	7	6	5	4	3	2	1	know	score
State										
Courts	4%	4%	9%	16%	22%	17%	26%	2%	2.9
Police	5	2	8	13	21	19	31	1	2.7
Civil servants	3	2	7	15	24	20	27	2	2.7
Workers' organizations										
Old trade unions	6	4	8	11	18	16	34	3	2.7
Patriotic associations	4	4	7	14	18	16	33	4	2.7
New trade unions	2	2	4	10	20	18	40	4	2.3

Market								
Foreign organizations and experts advising government	3	3	7	12	15	16	41	3	2.5
Private enterprise	3	3	6	10	16	19	41	2	2.4
Traditional institutions								
Church	22	11	17	15	13	7	13	2	4.4
Army	14	9	17	20	16	9	14	1	4.0
Other institutions								
Peasants' organizations	10	5	11	18	19	12	21	4	3.4
Mass media	5	6	12	16	19	16	25	1	3.1
President Yeltsin	6	3	9	11	17	13	40	1	2.7
Parliament	2	3	7	16	24	17	29	2	2.7
Government	2	2	6	14	21	19	34	2	2.5
Parties	1	1	4	10	22	21	39	2	2.3

SOURCE: Centre for the Study of Public Policy/Paul Lazarsfeld Society, New Russia Barometer III (1994).

NOTE: The first four categories group institutions loading on that dimension in a factor analysis reported in appendix table B.2.

not free and independent representative bodies; hence, this factor is not a reflection of conventional social democratic values but more akin to what Lipset (1960) has labeled working-class authoritarianism. This point is underscored by the fact that trust in unions is associated with trust in patriotic groups. A total of 72 percent of Russians distrust all three institutions; only 2 percent show positive trust in all three, 7 percent in two, and 19 percent in one.

Distrust of the market (private enterprise and foreign groups aiding government). The introduction of the market in Russia is more popularly associated with the rise of the mafia than the rise of the Protestant work ethic. Those who have a positive view of both the market and the foreign advisers brought in from Western Europe and Washington to promote market institutions are a small minority, 6 percent of the total, with 13 percent trusting one of these groups. In other words, 81 percent do not trust market institutions at all.

Some trust in traditional institutions (church, army). In the Soviet Union, the regime controlled both the church and the army. But by the standards of that regime, they were regarded as separate from the main activities of the party and government. This distancing has left more scope for trust than is normal in Russia. The result is that Russians divide into three groups in their views of traditional institutions: 25 percent trust both church and army and an additional 40 percent trust one of them, as compared with 35 percent who trust neither.

Factor analysis also shows that six institutions listed at the bottom of table 3.3 are evaluated without regard to the generalized distrust of post-Soviet institutions. For example, even though parties, government, parliament, and President Yeltsin all have very negative ratings, distrust of each tends to be independent of other institutions.

Blame is the opposite of trust. The difficulties that have arisen in the political and economic transformation of Russian society make it evident that something has gone wrong or that something has been wrong for a very long time. A normal feature of democratic election campaigns is that the opposition parties blame incumbents for what has gone wrong, and incumbents blame their predecessors for the problems they have inherited. When both political and economic regimes are in turbulence, there are plenty of potential targets for blame. The New Russia Barometer thus offered a list of sixteen different institutions and asked people to say whether or not they thought each was to blame for the country's economic troubles.

Russians are ready to blame many different institutions for their difficulties (table 3.4). Many targets of blame are those who ought to be held accountable in terms of democratic theory. A total of 74 percent say the Russian government is definitely or somewhat to blame; 65 percent blame President Yeltsin, 60 percent the former prime minister, Yegor Gaidar, and 65 percent those who introduced reforms generally. There is some inclination to blame the old regime too: 66 percent say the *nomenklatura* is to blame, and 42 percent blame the communists. Russians are divided about how much of the blame should be put on their own shoulders. A striking feature of the answers is that there is no

TABLE 3.4

WHO IS TO BLAME FOR RUSSIA'S ECONOMIC PROBLEMS?

Q: Who is to blame for our economic problems and how much?

	Definitely	Somewhat	Not much	Not at all	Don't know
Government					
Russian government	43%	31%	10%	5%	11%
Russian president personally	40	25	14	10	11
Yegor Gaidar	39	21	14	10	16
Capitalists					
Foreign governments	10	12	12	37	29
Capitalists	10	11	10	39	30
Jews	5	3	5	62	25
Communists					
Former party *nomenklatura*	39	27	11	8	15
Communists	21	21	19	21	18
Other					
Disintegration of the USSR	47	22	9	9	13
Mafia	46	20	8	8	17
Those who introduced reforms	38	27	15	8	12
Local government	24	35	21	8	12
We Russians ourselves	22	27	16	23	12
Present Russian parliament	22	22	17	14	25
Businessmen	16	22	18	27	17
Workers	2	5	10	74	9

SOURCE: Centre for the Study of Public Policy/Paul Lazarsfeld Society, New Russia Barometer III (1994). Grouped by factor analysis reported in appendix table B.3.

tendency to blame foreigners: only 22 percent put some or a large amount of blame on foreign governments, and only 8 percent blame the very small Jewish population of Russia, a strikingly low figure in view of the history of Russian anti-Semitism (cf. Brym and Degtyarev 1993; Gibson 1994b; and subsequent discussion).

In apportioning blame, three distinct dimensions can be identified through factor analysis (appendix table B.3). The first factor directs blame at responsible state institutions and individuals: the president and prime minister personally, and the Russian government. An average of two-thirds of Russians definitely or somewhat blame each of these for the country's economic troubles. The second factor can be roughly labeled capitalist, including foreign governments and Jews as well as capitalists. But those blaming these three groups are not so numerous. By contrast, an average of 53 percent blame the two groups, communists in general and the *nomenklatura*, that constitute the third factor. A striking feature of the factor analysis is that public opinion does *not* link many institutions into a conspiratorial network of blame. For example, the mafia is blamed for many problems, but it is not statistically linked with blaming communists, capitalists, or government. The government factor that is blamed is personalized, emphasizing Yeltsin and Gaidar rather than local authorities or parliament.

Amid the turbulence of transformation, Russians can be fearful of foreigners as well as of their fellow citizens. Russian history is a reminder that while the country has emerged victorious from war, it has done so only after a bloody series of battles in which foreigners —Swedes, French, Japanese, or Germans—invaded Russian territory and sometimes reached the gates of Moscow itself. Threats to Russian security are also a recurring theme in the speeches of some military leaders and of nationalist politicians such as Vladimir Zhirinovsky. Hence, both the second and third New Russia Barometers asked whether any of a list of countries posed a threat to national security.

In fact, the majority of Russians do not feel threatened by foreign countries (table 3.5). None of the eight countries named, ranging from Japan to Belarus, was seen as a threat by a majority of Russians. Furthermore, the high percentage of don't knows indicates that a large number of Russians take little or no interest in what other countries are doing. The biggest perceived threats are seen as coming from other great powers; by contrast, neighboring countries such as Ukraine, Poland, and Belarus are seen as largely benign. Factor analysis identifies a single group of countries that tend to be linked as threats: China, Germany, the United States, and Iran (for the details, see appendix B).

TABLE 3.5

COUNTRIES THREATENING RUSSIA'S NATIONAL SECURITY

Q: Could any of the following states pose a threat to
our national security?

	Definitely	*Possible*	*Some*	*None*	*Don't know*
Japan	11%	32%	43%	33%	24%
U.S.	12	28	40	38	23
China	8	28	36	39	25
Iran	5	21	26	42	32
Germany	4	20	24	51	25
Ukraine	2	13	16	66	19
Poland	1	6	7	70	23
Belarus	1	3	4	79	17

SOURCE: Centre for the Study of Public Policy/Paul Lazarsfeld Society, New Russia Barometer III (1994).

Even though a variety of countries are seen as threatening Russia, the insecure are in a minority. For each country the median respondent sees no threat from the country or finds it difficult to say whether it poses a threat. Because most Russians normally do not feel threatened, the four-country scale measuring international threats is skewed heavily *against* anxiety. A total of 41 percent see no threat from any of the four countries named; 21 percent see a threat from one country, 21 percent from two countries, 10 percent from three, and only 8 percent from all four.

Russian intellectuals have traditionally been divided into two groups, a nationalist and chauvinistic group of Slavophiles praising what is unique in Russia's history, and a cosmopolitan group of Westernizers viewing foreign countries and particularly Western Europe as homelands of progressive ideas that Russia should emulate. The nationalist view was consistent with the Soviet doctrine that a Marxist-Leninist state had a unique role to play in leading the world to communism. The tradition of the Westernizers is consistent with post-Soviet efforts to introduce a market economy and a democratic political system.

In view of the strong vote for Zhirinovsky's nationalist Liberal Democratic Party at the December 1993 election, the third New Russia Barometer included a battery of questions to measure different aspects of Slav, chauvinist, and imperialist sentiments, such as valuing Slav traditions above Western traditions; a European identity; favoring tough action to defend Russians now living in other states of the former Soviet Union; and support for a high level of military force and nuclear weapons. Russians disagreed with each other in the answers they gave (see Rose and Haerpfer 1994c). The initial theory was that people would disagree in systematic ways, for example, dividing into Slavophiles and Westernizers, and/or along aggressive nationalist and pacifist lines. But factor analysis showed there was no consistent linkage between attitudes on one issue and another; the average correlation between six questions was only .06.

Because the New Russia Barometer uses an hour-long questionnaire, it collects responses to hundreds of different variables. Two criteria were used in selecting political variables for testing as potential influences on voting: theoretical significance and empirical impact. The attitudes discussed in the foregoing pages are meaningful not only theoretically but also empirically. Subsequent chapters will identify the circumstances and extent to which each may influence voting behavior. A number of additional influences, such as Slavophile, Westernizing, or nationalist sentiments, are not directly considered because initial analysis found they had no statistically significant effect when other influences, such as attitudes toward the communist regime or education, were taken into account.

Economic Influences in Postcommunist Russia

"It's the economy, stupid," is a familiar, conventional answer to the question, What influences voting behavior? Studies of voting behavior in Western nations often find economic conditions an important or the most important influence on party preferences (see Lewis-Beck 1988 for an overview). In a society making a double transformation from a command to a market economy as well as from an authoritarian regime to free elections, voters cannot ignore politically induced changes in the economy. Yet it would be misleading to draw conclusions about the state of the economy from official figures because Soviet statistics systematically exaggerated the performance of the old command economy and left out many activities in the "unofficial" shadow economies of importance to the economic well-being of ordinary Russians (cf. Grossman 1977; Rose 1993; Holzmann et al. 1995).

The proposition that economic conditions influence voting behavior is clear but also vague: it does not specify which particular economic conditions are significant. Is it the amount of money an individual has in her or his pocket or the state of the nation's finances? Is it the condition of the economy today, changes compared to what it was in the past, or future expectations of prosperity, a major benefit that opposition parties can promise amid the dislocations of transition?

At election time a person can vote egocentrically, reflecting the state of his or her household finances, or in sociotropic terms, assessing the economic well-being of the country as a whole (see Kinder and Kiewiet 1979, 1981; Kiewiet 1983). The two often go together because economic growth makes it possible for the majority of people to enjoy rising incomes, and inflation affects the cost of living of every household. But the impact of unemployment is uneven, affecting youths and uneducated people more than skilled workers, and having no direct effect on retired people. Moreover, individuals vary in their ability to see the potential connection between national changes and changes in their own household circumstances.

Time is the second important dimension because individuals can make economic assessments about current economic conditions, retrospective judgments about how well or badly the present compares with the past, and optimistic or pessimistic projections about what the future may bring (Fiorina 1981; MacKuen, Erickson, and Stimson 1992). Insofar as official economic statistics are credible, current Russian economic conditions are likely to be judged negatively. Inflation has driven up prices by more than 10,000 percent in the transition from a command to a market economy, and instead of growing, the official economy has contracted dramatically (see OECD 1995). Yet past economic conditions can also be judged negatively if Russians compare their conditions in the 1980s with the more prosperous East German communist state or with the very much more prosperous Federal Republic of Germany. The costs of transformation can also be viewed as a necessary investment in getting rid of old faults in order to create a booming economy in the future.

Microeconomic conditions. Today, as in communist times, there is no economic equality in Russia; some people are visibly better off and others badly off, whatever measure is used (cf. Rose and McAllister 1996). Because the economy is in the process of being transformed, money, the conventional measure of economic well-being in a market economy, is not a good measure of living standards. Inflation makes the relation between wages and prices fluctuate from month to month, from place to place, and even from product to product. Many staple goods are still sold at highly subsidized prices if they are bought, or produced without money changing hands—for example, food grown in a vegetable garden.

Given the difficulty of using money income as a measure of poverty, the New Russia Barometer asks people whether they have been doing without the basic necessities of food, clothing, heating, and electricity. Since economic transformation is bound to cause disruptions of everyday routines, the NRB also asks how frequently or infrequently people are doing without these necessities. We do not need to evaluate incomes in dollar terms to identify people in economic difficulty: Russians who frequently go without food, clothing they really need, and heating and electricity are on the verge of destitution (Rose 1995a).

Notwithstanding the trials of transformation, in NRB III fewer than 10 percent of Russians reported that they were continuously going without food, clothes, or heating. But only 43 percent of Russians said they had never gone without food during the preceding year, and only 22 percent said they had never gone without clothes of which they were in need. Heating and electricity have been the only goods in plentiful supply, regardless of nominal income; that is because the prices are artificially low as oil and gas are still not produced and sold at world market prices. The result is that the median Russian family sometimes went without one necessity or, less frequently, without two; a total of 19 percent report that their family never lacks any necessities (figure 3.2). Only 1 percent continuously lack one necessity and frequently do without others.

A prosperous modern economy is characterized by the widespread ownership of consumer goods by the mass of the population, not just a small elite. At the time the Soviet Union collapsed, Russia was not a land of consumer affluence; for example, a mechanically poor car required years of waiting (or bribes) to acquire, and telephones and color television sets were not found in every household. But neither was Russia a poor Third World country. New Russia Barometer III found that 24 percent of Russians had a car, 32 percent a dacha, 44 percent a telephone, and 75 percent a color television set. An index of consumer goods can be thus constructed, with the top mark a score of 4 for having all four of these goods and the bottom position 0 (zero) for households that have none. Russian households differ substantially in the possession of consumer goods: only 9 percent have a car, telephone, television, and a dacha, and 16 percent are without all these goods. There are 17 percent with three consumer goods, the median with 31 percent has two consumer goods, and 28 percent of households have only one.

The variation in ownership of consumer goods shows that there is scope for some Russians to feel economically aggrieved and others to

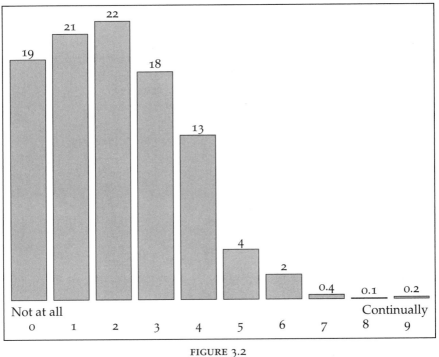

FIGURE 3.2
FREQUENCY OF PEOPLE DOING WITHOUT FOOD,
CLOTHES, AND HEATING (IN PERCENTAGES)

SOURCE: Center for the Study of Public Policy/Paul Lazarsfeld Society, New Russia Barometer III (1994).

NOTE: The scale was constructed by scoring how frequently respondents did without food, clothing, and heat or electricity in the past twelve months: 3 = constantly, 2 = often, 1 = sometimes, 0 = never. The scores for food, clothes, and energy were then combined.

feel relatively well off if they compare their conditions with other households. Furthermore, most Russians have good material reasons for wanting to improve their economic conditions in the future, whether relying on experts to make the economy work or on a return to communist controls or on their own official or unofficial economic initiatives.

When Russians are asked to evaluate their current household economic conditions, two-thirds report that they are unsatisfactory as against a third saying they are satisfied (table 3.6). The great majority of those who are dissatisfied report that their standard of living has fallen

TABLE 3.6
EVALUATION OF HOUSEHOLD ECONOMIC CONDITIONS
(VALUES IN PERCENTAGES)

Q: (Past) How does the current economic situation of
your family compare with five years ago?
(Current) How do you rate the economic situation
of your family today?
(Future) What do you think your family's economic
situation will be in five years' time?

Past		Current		Future	
Much better before	34	Very satisfied	3	Much better in future	6
A bit better before	31	Fairly satisfied	27	A bit better in future	21
The same	11			The same	13
A bit worse before	11	Not very satisfied	50	A bit worse in future	7
Much worse before	8	Very unsatisfied	17	A lot worse in future	6
Don't know	5	Don't know	3	Don't know	47

SOURCE: Centre for the Study of Public Policy/Paul Lazarsfeld Society, New Russia Barometer III (1994).

by comparison with what it was in the days of the Soviet command economy. In addition to widespread dissatisfaction with current economic conditions, there is a significant minority who have gained from transformation. In the New Russia Barometer III one in five not only were satisfied but also reported that their standard of living had been rising since the move to the market. When asked about the economic future of their family, nearly half show uncertainty, saying they do not know what their economic conditions are likely to be in five years' time. Among Russians who do have an opinion, those who expect their conditions to improve outnumber those who expect conditions to worsen by a margin of two to one.

Evaluating macroeconomic change. In established market economies, change usually occurs at the margin: good news or bad news in the rate of economic growth, unemployment, or inflation is measured in a few percentage points, and a small minority of the electorate is without work at any given time. Economic change in Russia is fundamental rather than marginal: the transformation of the economic regime is meant to be as complete as the transformation of the polity. Prices are to be set by supply and demand rather than by planners; investments are to be for profit rather than in response to demands from the military-industrial complex; shops can stock imported goods as well as what the planners plan; workers are free to seek higher wages or new jobs, and employers to make unwanted labor unemployed.

The great majority of Russians were socialized in an environment in which abstractions such as socialism and capitalism were frequently invoked as symbols. But they had little meaning to the ordinary person. As the Soviet joke ran: What is the difference between capitalism and socialism? Answer: Under capitalism, man exploits man; under socialism, it is the other way round. Therefore, it is not meaningful to ask Russians what they think about the market economy or capitalism, symbols that lack a widely accepted clear meaning.

Because every Russian has experienced a command economy with controlled prices, controlled wages, no unemployment, and chronic shortages of consumer goods, the New Russia Barometer asks people to evaluate the old regime with which they are familiar, the current economic system, and the economic system as they expect it to be in future (table 3.7). Three-fifths of Russians have a positive view of the old socialist economy. By contrast, only one in seven had a positive view of the state of the economy as it was in the third year of reform. The proportion with positive expectations of the future is higher, but is still less

TABLE 3.7

ECONOMIC REGIMES EVALUATED — PAST, PRESENT, AND FUTURE

Q: Here is a scale for evaluating how the economy works. The highest mark is plus 100; the lowest, minus 100.

a. Where on the scale would you place the socialist economy in 1989?

b. Where would you place our current economic system?

c. Our economic system in five years' time?

	Socialist	*Current*	*Future*
Positive	61%	14%	44%
Neutral	12	10	25
Negative	27	76	31
Mean rating	16	−46	1
Standard deviation	53	46	54

SOURCE: Centre for the Study of Public Policy/Paul Lazarsfeld Society, New Russia Barometer III (1994).

than half. Thus the majority of Russians do not expect their economic regime by the end of the century to be as satisfactory as it was in 1989, toward the end of Soviet rule. The large standard deviations show that there are big differences among Russians in their evaluations of economic regimes, as there are in their evaluations of forms of government.

Social Structure

The classic Lipset-Rokkan (1967) model of the origins of political parties emphasizes the historic importance in Western democracies of two dimensions of social structure: cultural cleavages along lines of religion or ethnicity, and economic cleavages between urban and rural populations and between industrial workers and the possessors of capital. But the relevance of this model in postcommunist Russia is problematic (cf. Mair 1996). One reason is that the great mass of the population is sometimes uniform, rather than divided: for example, virtually the entire population is Russian speaking. Second, Stalinism destroyed the capacity of social institutions to organize for political action independently of the Communist Party.

The limitations of the Lipset-Rokkan analysis are clearest in the field of cultural divisions. Formally, the population of the Russian Federation is multiethnic. The state itself recognizes this: dozens of different nationalities are officially recognized and inscribed on the internal passport that each citizen is obliged to carry. More than four-fifths of the population is Russian, however, thus requiring any minority to attend to the views of Russians if it wishes to be successful in electoral politics. Furthermore, the remaining fifth is divided into more than a hundred different ethnic groups. Since the population of Russia is almost 150 million, even if an ethnic group claims more than a million members, a party representing an ethnic minority would be swamped in a Russian election.

Regional differences are a fact of life in every society, and especially in Russia. The distance between Moscow and Vladivostok is vast, whether measured in miles or in time zones. The social differences between regions are not necessarily so great, however, for much of Siberia and Russia east of the Urals has been settled relatively recently by the movement of Russians eastward. In that respect, parts of Russia resemble the American West, drawing together people whose family roots and traditions are from other parts of the country. In testing influences on voting, Russians are here divided geographically between those living east of the Urals in Asiatic Russia and the population living west of the Urals. Because of the distinctive cultural positions of Moscow and St. Petersburg, residents of these two cities are classified separately when testing for the effect of urban residence on voting. The majority of Russians live in cities a long way from the dollar economy that visiting foreigners see in the capital.

While the Russian Orthodox church has traditionally been a national church, for generations the Communist Party kept a tight grip on it, limiting its resources and personnel and ensuring its support of the regime (Anderson 1994). The party authorities, moreover, waged an aggressive campaign to convert the Russian people from Orthodox Christianity to scientific Marxist-Leninist doctrines, including atheism. The results were mixed. New Russia Barometer II found that 41 percent described themselves as Orthodox, 24 percent as agnostics, and 25 percent as atheists, with the remaining tenth scattered among many smaller groups. When asked about church attendance, only 9 percent said they attended as often as once a month. When New Russia Barometer III asked whether people considered themselves religious, there was a similar three-way division, with 26 percent saying yes, 33 percent indicating indifference, and 29 percent replying no, with the remainder don't knows. The communist offensive has failed to root out all religious beliefs, but at the same time relatively few Russians are regular church attenders. In parallel with secularization in Western Europe, Russians have increasingly become indifferent to religion rather than dividing between believers and anticlerical secular groups (White, McAllister, and Kryshtanovskaya 1994b).

Communist ideology stressed class conflict outside the communist bloc but claimed that the socialist measures of Lenin and Stalin had abolished class conflict in their own societies. Whereas urban/rural conflicts were part of the classic mobilization of parties in Western societies and agrarian parties have persisted in Scandinavia, in the Soviet Union the collectivization of farming turned agricultural workers into employees rather than independent peasants or farmers. It remains possible to distinguish between urban and rural residents; and we can do so on the basis of the quarter of the New Russia Barometer respondents who live in the countryside.

Conventional Western categories of class are doubly dubious in Russia today. In the Soviet Union, the Weberian categories of class, status, and power did not have their conventional meaning, for class (that is, money or other material resources controlling life chances) was often less important than power (that is, Communist Party membership), and high status was awarded to workers rather than to the nobility. The collapse of that system has created new bases for inequality, ranging from knowledge of English or German to membership in a mafia-type organization with the power to extort money from businessmen.

In this study we use education, important in the determination of socioeconomic status and economic success in market economies, as the equivalent of a measure of class. The Soviet Union promoted mass education, especially in the postwar era. Hence, elementary education tends to be confined to the oldest generation. Secondary education is here differentiated from technical education, imparting a higher level of skill, and from higher education equal to a college degree or professional postgraduate qualification. Because of the desire to promote technical and engineering qualifications without regard to general education, a second indicator of education was introduced in New Russia Barometer III: whether or not a person had at least a hundred books in his or her home. A total of 49 percent of Russians lived in such "bookish" households.

In many theories of political behavior age is regarded as significant, and this is also true in the Soviet case (cf. Inglehart 1977; Rose and Carnaghan 1995). Old people are less likely than others to depart from the political values and beliefs into which they were socialized up to fifty years previously. The searing experience of the invasion of Soviet Russia by Nazi Germany in 1941 affected the older generation directly. Old people also have distinctive interests: for example, government policy on pensions affects their monthly income. By contrast, young Russians belong to a generation with a very different experience from that of their elders: the youngest Russian voter was only a child when Mikhail Gorbachev took office. Furthermore, younger voters have not had the time to form stable political orientations or party identifications.

As part of Soviet egalitarianism, women were mobilized into the labor force along with men, so at the end of the USSR there was virtually no difference in the participation of men and women in the working population. The leadership of the Communist Party, by contrast, was overwhelmingly male; so were a disproportionate number of those in leadership positions in Soviet society. The collapse of the Soviet Union has now made it possible to articulate women's interests independently of party orthodoxies. Hence, the chapters that follow test the influence of gender too.

While Russian voters share many characteristics of voters in established democracies, the society in which they live does not. It is making an unprecedented double transition: from a command economy to private enterprise, and from communist rule to a form of democracy. It is a society with high levels of education and urbanization, and its members have needed a great deal of political sophistication to deal with the realities behind the party-approved view of life in the Soviet Union in which they lived. But they have learned to keep their distance from government and to be suspicious of party politics, and they have had little of the Western experience of a choice of candidates and parties at genuinely competitive elections. Russian voting behavior, in these circumstances, reflects many of the characteristics of voting in the liberal democracies; it also has a number of distinctive features of its own.

◖◖ 4 ◗◗

Referendum
or Opinion Poll?

In most countries, government is based on periodic elections in which the people choose their representatives in parliament. But parliamentary elections are not the only way in which the electorate can pass judgment on matters of public policy. A *referendum* is another means available to citizens in a modern democracy as a form of popular vote (cf. Suksi 1993; Butler and Ranney 1994; Gallagher and Uleri 1996). A referendum can be defined as (1) a vote on a constitutional issue (2) that is held according to established legal procedures prescribed by act of parliament or in the constitution itself and (3) that produces a decision binding on government.

The purpose of holding a referendum is to give the people as a whole an opportunity to decide about a major issue of public controversy. Referendums are often held on matters of conscience: for instance, in Ireland in 1995, on whether divorce should be permitted. They may also be used to resolve a constitutional issue: whether a new constitution should be adopted or an existing constitution amended. And in the United States they can be used to pass judgment on tax increases. Inasmuch as the electorate is supposed to be the ultimate source of sovereignty in a democracy, once a referendum outcome is known, there is no higher court of appeal. In this way, for instance, the United Kingdom agreed to remain within the European Community in 1975, but the Norwegians decided to remain outside it in a referendum held in 1994.

Sometimes a referendum degenerates into a plebiscite, a vote called in circumstances manufactured to authorize a government to do what it is determined to do anyway. Hitler was notorious for using the plebiscite to give the appearance of popular endorsement to his actions. The principal features of a "manufactured" plebiscite are a question designed to give the answer the government wants, excessive governmental influence on the campaign and the count, and a ballot that is often without constitutional authority.

An *opinion poll* is a sample of the electorate rather than a tabulation of the views of the entire population. From a statistical point of view this is hardly a limitation because a properly representative sample can reflect a large electorate with a high degree of accuracy. An advantage of a public opinion poll is that dozens of questions can be asked of the same individuals, measuring many nuances of attitudes. The answers can be subjected to sophisticated analysis to find out what kinds of people voted on opposite sides of an issue and what was on their minds when they made their decisions. A secret ballot on a simple referendum question, by contrast, makes it impossible to capture the range of opinions that voters may entertain. From a political point of view, however, a small sample of the electorate lacks the authority of the electorate as a whole. Politicians interested in legitimating what they do require a ballot in which everyone has the opportunity to vote.

The referendum was a well-established institution in Eastern Europe, although not in Russia, before the onset of communist rule. There were six countrywide referendums during the interwar years in the Baltic republics, and one each in Bulgaria and Romania (Butler and Ranney 1994, 176–78). There was no Soviet referendum at all during the same period, although there was provision for an exercise of this kind in the "Stalin" constitution approved in 1936 and in the "Brezhnev" constitution of 1977. It was not until March 1991 that the first—and as it turned out, last—Soviet referendum was held, on the future of the state itself. The outcome was a clear vote in favor of retaining the USSR as a "reformed federation," which was hardly decisive; but a referendum on the Russian Federation at the same time established an elective presidency, and the practice of consulting the people directly has continued into the postcommunist 1990s on the basis of further legislation (*O referendume* 1995).

The Referendum in Soviet Political Thought

The notion of a referendum had a long history in Soviet political thought. Lenin and Stalin had both spoken positively of a popular vote as a means of exercising the right of national self-determination, and it was approved in the same sense by the Petrograd Soviet and then by the Bolshevik government (Towster 1948, 53). The 1936 constitution went further, indicating in Article 49 that the Presidium of the USSR Supreme Soviet could conduct a "national poll (referendum)" on its own initiative or on the demand of one of the union republics. But no such exercise was ever held, and the constitution itself was adopted by a Congress of Soviets rather than by nationwide ballot.

The referendum was mentioned in the 1961 CPSU program, which insisted that "discussion by the people of draft laws and other decisions of national as well as local significance must become the rule" and "the most important draft laws must be submitted to a nationwide vote (referendum)." It was conceived in the Khrushchev era as part of a broad process of democratization by which power was to be transferred from the state apparatus to elected institutions and the state itself gradually superseded by "communist self-administration" (Hill 1980, 100–103). The principle of a popular vote of this kind was in line with the notions of direct democracy that were current in the Khrushchev years, and with an increasing recognition that there could be a diversity of interests under communist rule that needed to be expressed and reconciled.

A detailed examination of what a referendum might mean in Soviet practice was published by Viktor Kotok (1964). Kotok defined a referendum as "the confirmation of one or another state decision by way of popular voting, according it a definitive and obligatory character." He went on to identify "voting by the people" as the "concluding stage in the process of popular lawmaking, which is preceded by other stages of the people's participation in the creation of a law or another legal act." He proposed the adoption of a special "law on the all-union referendum," which would state what laws would be placed before the people for a vote, who would have the initiative in putting the question to a popular vote, who would conduct the voting, and how it would be organized. Kotok envisaged comparable laws at the republican level and a special law for local referendums. They were also appropriate for major constitutional changes, and for questions on which the two chambers of the Supreme Soviet were in disagreement—they were, in fact, always unanimous (Kotok 1964, 126, 128).

A number of other scholars commented favorably on the idea of a referendum as part of a range of mechanisms for taking account of public opinion (for instance, Safarov 1963; Baitin 1965). In the mid-1970s the dissident historian and commentator Roy Medvedev thought the referendum a "particularly effective form of direct democracy," of value in extending knowledge and civic responsibility as well as in resolving constitutional disputes. It was a way in which the willingness of republics to remain part of the USSR could regularly be tested, perhaps through a "compulsory referendum in each republic at least once every ten years" (Medvedev 1975, 147, 280). The referendum, moreover, had become an established part of the constitutional practice of several East European states by this time, among them Bulgaria and the German Democratic Republic, although the practice was still heavily stagemanaged (Mishin 1987).

Under Brezhnev, there was little attempt to extend these or other forms of direct democracy, although somewhat greater use was made of "national discussions" as a means of allowing a broadly regulated discussion in the official media. The referendum was not abandoned in principle, but there were no official proposals to make use of it, and the 1977 constitution, like its predecessor, was adopted by a majority vote in the Soviet parliament after a further "national discussion" in which four-fifths of the adult population were reported to have participated, in practice by attending meetings organized by the authorities (Brezhnev 1978, 518).

The constitution made formal provision for national discussions on the "most important questions of state life," and made clear that they might be "put to an all-national vote (referendum)" (Article 5). There was similar provision for a referendum on draft legislation and on matters on which the two houses of parliament were unable to reach agreement (Articles 114 and 115). And yet, like much else in these constitutions, the reference to a referendum was essentially symbolic because there was no legislation to define the terms on which questions should be put to the people in this way. Nor was there any means of determining whether the results should be binding or merely consultative—although in 1977 the Presidium of the Supreme Soviet had committed itself to the preparation of the necessary legislation (Ponomarev 1982, 34).

It was only after Gorbachev's adoption of the principle of democratization in early 1987 that the referendum became more than a constitutional abstraction. A first step forward was taken in the summer of 1987 when a new law on the "national discussion of important questions of state life" was adopted (*Vedomosti*, no. 26, 1987, item 387). In April 1990 a law on local government provided in general terms for "local referendums and other forms of direct democracy" (*Vedomosti*, no. 16, 1990, item 267). Then in December 1990 a law "On Voting by the Whole People (Referendum of the USSR)" was approved by the Congress of People's Deputies, coming into immediate effect. This identified a referendum as "a means, through voting by the whole people, for the adoption of laws of the USSR and other decisions on the most important questions of the life of the state" (Article 1). Under Article 4, a referendum could be conducted (1) to adopt a new law of the USSR; (2) to amend or rescind a law of the USSR, or part of such a law; (3) to adopt decisions "predetermining the basic content of laws of the USSR or other acts"; or simply (4) to "determine public opinion on other important questions within the jurisdiction of the USSR" (*Vedomosti*, no. 1, 1991, item 10).

A Russian law, similar in its basic principles to the Soviet law, had been approved in October 1990, and it was this law that governed the referendums that took place in 1991 and 1993 (text in *Rossiiskaya gazeta*, 2 December 1990, 1, 7; as amended in *Sbornik* 1993). A referendum was defined as a "national vote on the most important questions of state and public life," and its decisions had "supreme legal force." Referendums were called by the Congress of People's Deputies or Supreme Soviet on their own initiative or on the demand of at least a million voters or a third of the members of the Congress. At least half the electorate had to vote if the referendum was to be valid; a proposition was carried if at least half of those voting were in favor, and it could be modified only by another referendum. More than fifty years after the constitution had first referred to it, the legislation setting out the circumstances in which a referendum might be held had finally reached the statute book.

The Soviet and Russian Referendums of March 1991

For President Gorbachev, the referendum was an opportunity to assert his own authority over the republics; many leaders of the republics, including Russia, saw it as an opportunity to assert their own authority against centralized rule from Moscow. Faced by challenges to the integrity of the state as a whole, Gorbachev saw an all-union referendum as a means of appealing directly to the people on a new treaty of union that would replace the agreement originally concluded in 1922. On 17 December 1990, speaking to the Fourth Congress of People's Deputies, he suggested that a referendum be held "so that every citizen could declare 'for' or 'against' a Union of Sovereign States on a federal basis," with the result to be a "final verdict." He also proposed a referendum on the private ownership of land (*Chervertyi* 1991, vol. 1, 83, 87–88).

The Congress declared itself in favor of both proposals on 24 December, and also in favor of maintaining the USSR as a "renewed federation of equal sovereign republics" in which the rights and freedoms of people of all nationalities would be "fully guaranteed." On 16 January 1991 the Supreme Soviet agreed to the wording of the question and set a date. "Nobody but the people themselves," it declared, "can take upon itself the historic responsibility for the fate of the USSR" (*Pravda*, 18 January 1991, 2).

The holding of the first referendum in Soviet history, on 17 March 1991, was itself an "enormous achievement of perestroika," Gorbachev declared in a television address to the nation (*Sud'bu* 1991, 10). The wording of the question nonetheless left many issues open and made the exercise much closer to a plebiscite called to endorse government policy. What, for instance, was meant by a "renewed" federation? Did it have to be socialist? By what mechanisms would the "renewal" take place? What guarantees of the rights of each nation could be offered, and by what mechanisms would they be upheld? Most critically, what was the meaning of "sovereignty" in this context: would the "renewed federation" itself constitute a sovereign state, and if so, what would its rights be in relation to the "sovereign" republics it comprised? How many republics would be members of the federation? What would happen if a republic voted no?

Some republics found the wording of the question so unsatisfactory that they modified its application to their territory. In Kazakhstan, where the question was changed entirely, the reference was to a "union of equal sovereign states"; in Ukraine, voters were asked whether their republic should be part of a union of sovereign states on the basis of the declaration on the state sovereignty of the Ukraine of 16 July 1990. Similar modifications were made to the wording in Azerbaijan, Uzbekistan, and Kyrgyzstan. The authorities in six republics (the three Baltics, Armenia, Georgia, and Moldova) refused to hold the referendum in any form and instead organized their own ballots on other dates, seeking endorsement of their policies of national independence. Other republics, provinces, and cities appended questions of specific local interest, ranging from the issue of landownership in the Mari autonomous republic to the construction of an atomic power station in two regions and the recall of an elected deputy in a district of the city of Sverdlovsk. The most important addition was in Russia, where it was agreed in February to put the question of a directly elected presidency to voters in the republic (*Pravda*, 20 February 1991, 2; for a full list, see Radio Liberty 1991).

The referendum soon became a contest between Soviet President

Mikhail Gorbachev and the chairman of the Russian parliament, Boris Yeltsin. In this contest, Gorbachev stood for the Communist Party leadership and central rule; Yeltsin represented reformist forces determined to oppose the party *nomenklatura* and prepared, if necessary, to see the USSR dissolve into a group of independent states. The traditional instruments of communist power, including the official media, came out strongly in favor of a resounding "yes." The new publications of the democratic opposition—newspapers such as *Nezavisimaya gazeta* and *Kuranty*, both published in Moscow under the auspices of the city soviet, which was under the control of reformers and radicals—urged electors to vote against a reformed USSR but in favor of a Russian presidency and a directly elected mayorate in the capital itself.

Gorbachev had clearly intended the referendum to be a device by which he could outflank his separatist opponents. And party officials did their best to deliver the result he wanted, organizing meetings in workplaces in support of the referendum and maintenance of the USSR with extensive coverage on television and a steady buildup of propaganda in the media more generally. The campaign was to climax with addresses by Prime Minister Pavlov on 14 March, by Parliamentary Chairman Lukyanov on 15 March, and by Gorbachev himself on the eve of the poll. The party authorities also gathered information on attitudes to the union in an opinion survey in seventeen different regions (Center 1991a). Yeltsin, for his part, used the referendum to create a Russian presidency that would permit him to mount a more effective challenge to Gorbachev and what radicals had begun to call "the Center."

The referendum set records for the number of votes cast—just under 150 million, or slightly more than 80 percent of the eligible electorate; and it took place in an orderly manner. The Ministry of Internal Affairs reported that nationalists had organized some "hooligan actions" in Moldova, but elsewhere there were just isolated incidents such as the careless use of firearms that wounded the chairman of an electoral commission near Odessa (Center 1991d). The results, however, were far from decisive, and all sides felt able to claim victory (table 4.1).

Of those who cast valid votes, 77.8 percent favored a renewed federation; as a proportion of the electorate, the figure was a much lower 61.1 percent. And more than one voter in five voted against. The "renewed federation" was supported strongly in most republics, particularly in Central Asia; in Turkmenia, with a reported 97.9 percent in favor, the result exceeded the turnouts recorded in democratic coun-

TABLE 4.1
USSR AND RUSSIAN REFERENDUMS,
17 MARCH 1991

_____ A. The USSR referendum _____

Q: *Do you consider it necessary to preserve the Union of Soviet Socialist Republics as a renewed federation of equal sovereign republics in which the rights and freedoms of people of all nationalities will be fully guaranteed?*

	Number	Electorate (%)	Voters (%)
In favor	113,519,812	61.1	76.4
Against	32,303,977	17.4	21.7
Invalid votes	2,757,817	1.5	1.9
Total votes	148,581,606	80.0	100.0
Total electorate	185,647,355	100.0	

SOURCE: Derived from *Izvestiya*, 28 March 1991, 1, 3.

_____ B. The Russian referendum _____

Q: *Do you consider it necessary to introduce the post of RSFSR president, who would be elected by a republicwide popular vote?*

	Number	Electorate (%)	Voters (%)
In favor	53,385,175	52.5	69.9
Against	21,406,152	21.0	28.0
Invalid votes	1,633,683	1.6	2.1
Total votes	76,425,110	75.1	100.0
Total electorate	101,776,550	100.0	

SOURCE: Derived from *Izvestiya*, 26 March 1991, 2.

tries with compulsory voting and could "hardly be considered reliable" (Davydov 1991). In Russia and the Ukraine, support for the union was less than the overall average, 71.3 percent and 70.2 percent respectively. Moscow and what was still Leningrad voted for the "renewed federation" by tiny majorities; in Gorbachev's own district in the capital, 375 voted against the proposition and 376 in favor, the only uncertainty being whether the general secretary or his spouse had cast the decisive ballot (*Nezavisimaya gazeta*, 21 March 1991, 1).

For his part, Boris Yeltsin won the support of 53 percent of electors and nearly 70 percent of voters in the Russian Federation for a directly elected presidency. While this was not quite as convincing a margin of victory as Gorbachev could claim in the all-union referendum, it was a big win, particularly in view of the organized opposition of the Communist Party. Moreover, the Russian presidential election that followed in June 1991 gave Yeltsin a popular mandate that Gorbachev had not sought on becoming the first-ever Soviet president.

Gorbachev declared the vote a mandate for the "renewal and strengthening of the union state" and pressed ahead with the negotiation of a new Union Treaty, to be signed in April or May. In the event, it was not ready for signature until 20 August, the day after the attempted coup had been launched, and so it never came into effect. Gorbachev continued to pursue his goal of devising a replacement for the Soviet Union that retained a form of all-union statehood or at least of citizenship, and as late as December 1991 he was suggesting a "plebiscite" on the establishment of the Commonwealth of Independent States that succeeded the USSR (*Izvestiya*, 11 December 1991, 2). But there was, in the end, no further vote on an all-union basis.

The Russian Referendum
of April 1993

Political developments in the postcommunist Russian Federation centered initially on the relation between President Yeltsin, who could claim the mandate of popular election in June 1991, and the Congress of People's Deputies elected in March 1990. The Congress, led by its increasingly influential Speaker, Ruslan Khasbulatov, included a substantial representation of Communists and showed little sympathy for the market-oriented reforms then being promoted by Yeltsin and his government. At the first Congress of Deputies since the demise of the USSR, held in April 1992, an attempt to debate a motion of no confidence in the government was narrowly defeated and a resolution was adopted that called for "basic changes" in the reform program, including substantial increases in public spending (*Vedomosti*, no. 17, 1992, item 899). The government promptly resigned, warning that the adoption of a resolution of this kind would prejudice economic reform and the assistance promised by the West. Its resignation, however, was not accepted, and the Congress adopted a more moderately worded resolution that supported the principle of a "fundamental transformation" of the Russian economy (*Vedomosti*, no. 17, 1992, item 900). In a separate action, the Congress required Yeltsin to give up the position of acting prime minister that he had held, together with the presidency, since November 1991.

On 15 June 1992 Yegor Gaidar, the grandson of a famous children's writer, was appointed acting prime minister; the title "acting" signified that he had yet to acquire the formal endorsement of the Congress of Deputies. Gaidar was young (at this time, just thirty-six) and a graduate of the economics faculty of Moscow University. He had worked as an academic and then in journalism, first in the Central Committee's theoretical fortnightly *Kommunist* and then for three years in the economics department of *Pravda*. After a further period in academic life, in November 1991 he had been appointed deputy chairman of the Russian Federation government and its minister of finance. By this time, Gaidar had become a convinced marketeer, and, he was the main architect of a program of privatization launched by presidential decree in December 1991 and of the liberalization of prices that followed in January 1992. He was associated, controversially for most Russians, with the doctrine of "shock therapy," a rapid transition to a market economy, and his well-fed appearance was something of a political handicap at a time of sudden and widespread scarcity.

The tensions between president and parliament deepened at the seventh session of the Congress of Deputies in December 1992. Yeltsin on 1 December, accepted that there had been some mistakes in tactics but insisted that the strategy of reform was not responsible. Khasbulatov, in a speech that was warmly applauded, replied that the reforms had led to a collapse of production and called instead for the "socially oriented market" that had operated successfully in Europe, Canada, Israel, and China (*Rossiiskaya gazeta*, 2 December 1992, 3–5). The Congress went on to insist that Yeltsin present a number of candidates for the position of prime minister, which was formally still vacant. In the voting Gaidar finished a poor third and stood down. His place was taken by Viktor Chernomyrdin, a former deputy prime minister and member of the CPSU Central Committee with a background in the gas industry. Chernomyrdin told the Congress he was in favor of reforms, but "without deepening the impoverishment of the people" (*Izvestiya*, 16 December 1992, 1–2); his appointment was taken to represent the end of "shock therapy" in its original form.

Yeltsin responded to these reverses by an appeal to citizens, complaining of a "creeping coup" by those who had failed in August 1991; the only way forward, he argued, was to hold a referendum in January 1993 to ask Russians if they trusted president or parliament to extricate the country from its "economic and political crisis" (*Izvestiya*, 10 December 1992, 1). The Congress countered with a proposal that there should be early elections to both institutions. After discussions brokered by the chairman of the Constitutional Court, it was agreed in the end that there would be a referendum on 11 April 1993 and that it would place the basic principles of a new constitution before the Russian people (*Izvestiya*, 14 December 1992, 3).

Yeltsin proposed four more specific questions when the Congress met for its eighth session on 7 March 1993, including one that asked if Russia should be a presidential republic and another that asked about the private ownership of land. The Congress, in reply, stripped Yeltsin of the emergency powers he had been granted in November 1991 and ordered him to act in accordance with the Russian constitution, in terms of which Congress was the "supreme body of state power" and the president merely its "chief official" (*Rossiiskaya gazeta*, 13 March 1993, 1). The Congress also reversed the earlier decision to hold a referendum on 11 April, ordering that the funds that had been saved should be spent on accommodating soldiers returning from Eastern Europe (*Federatsiya*, no. 31, 1993, 1). At the conclusion of the Congress, Yeltsin's staff announced that they would nonetheless be holding a popular vote—which would not have the full force of law—on the date originally announced (*Rossiiskaya gazeta*, 16 March 1993, 1).

Yeltsin's personal response to this challenge emerged in a television address to the Russian people on Saturday, 20 March, when he called for the introduction of a "special form of administration." Under these provisions the ordinary rights of citizens would be unaffected, but parliament would be unable to overrule whatever decrees the president or his government chose to adopt. In the meantime, Yeltsin promised, there would be a "national vote" on 25 April at which the president and vice-president would ask for an expression of confidence, and which would also provide an opportunity to approve the basic provisions of a new constitution and electoral law (*Delovoi mir*, 23 March 1993, 1).

The address was supported by his government but condemned by the chairman of the Constitutional Court as an "attempted coup" and denounced by Vice-President Rutskoi, the prosecutor-general, and parliamentary representatives. When the text of Yeltsin's decree was eventually published, on 24 March, it did not in fact make reference to a "special form of administration" and called for no more than a vote of confidence in the president and an expression of opinion on the draft constitution and electoral law (*Rossiiskaya gazeta*, 25 March 1993, 1). The Congress of Deputies was hurriedly convened to consider this new challenge to its authority.

When it met on 26 March, an attempt to impeach the president was carried but fell short of the two-thirds majority that was required. The outcome was a further compromise: a formal referendum would be held on 25 April, which required parliamentary approval, but it would consider somewhat different questions from those the president had originally suggested (*Rossiiskaya gazeta*, 1 April 1993, 3).

For many Western commentators, the deadlock was one between a "communist-era parliament" and a "democratically elected president." In fact, Yeltsin had himself been elected under Soviet legislation with a communist running mate, and the Congress had its own popular mandate from the competitive elections that had taken place in 1990. What had become a deepening constitutional crisis reflected the existence of dual and conflicting mandates. At a time of rapid economic reform, which was leading to high inflation and factory closures, the deputies had political incentives to call for a slowdown in the implementation of policies that appeared to be threatening the living standards of their constituents. While they had elected Yeltsin as their chairman in May 1990 and supported his resistance to the attempted coup in August 1991 (when Khasbulatov himself stood beside Yeltsin outside the parliament building), thereafter the Congress had become increasingly opposed to Yeltsin's growing tendency to rule by decree, bypassing elected representatives.

The task of governing Russia was becoming virtually impossible because of conflicting authorities granted by the Russian Federation constitution to both parliament and the president. Originally approved in 1978 and amended repeatedly since, the constitution had become a self-contradictory document. As long as both parliament and the president derived their powers from the constitution, parliament could annul the president's decrees until the end of its term in the spring of 1995; the president had no power to dismiss the parliament or even suspend its operation and was therefore at its mercy as far as his economic and other policies were concerned. The parliament became increasingly determined to achieve Yeltsin's removal from office and so had an interest in impeaching him, or at least forcing a presidential election before the end of Yeltsin's five-year term in the early summer of 1996. Yeltsin, for his part, resorted increasingly to emergency measures because of what he saw as parliamentary obstruction of his reforms.

The referendum on 25 April presented the electors with four questions reflecting these conflicting perspectives: confidence in Boris Yeltsin as president, support for his social and economic policies, the calling of early presidential elections, and the calling of early elections to the Congress of People's Deputies. Yeltsin's supporters campaigned for "yes, yes, no, yes." Why, they asked, should they have to "reelect a President the people trust"? (Anfinogenov et al. 1993). His opponents, by contrast, called for "no, no, yes, yes"—against the president and his policies, but in favor of early presidential and parliamentary elections (see, for instance, *Pravda*, 8 April 1993, 1). In the campaign, most of the mass media were firm supporters of Yeltsin, and the president himself offered direct inducements to a variety of constituencies: his promises included increased grants for students, improved retirement benefits, and better salaries for significant segments of the workforce. As before, a variety of other questions of more local concern were put to the electorate on the same date in the Far East and in Moscow (*Izvestiya*, 21 April 1993, 1, and 22 April 1993, 2; for a more general account, see Mendras 1993).

Voting in the April Referendum

The results of the referendum were mixed, both from Yeltsin's point of view and from that of his opponents (see table 4.2). A first concern was turnout, partly that the legal requirement of the law on referendums could be satisfied (at least 50 percent of the electorate had to take part for the exercise to be valid), and partly that the result should have the political force that each side had hoped to achieve. The turnout was a disappointing 64 percent, 16 percent lower than the USSR referendum two years earlier but enough to ensure that the outcome was legally binding. There was no voting at all in the Chechen republic, and in Tatarstan the turnout was just 22.6 percent.

Among those who did vote, Yeltsin won almost 60 percent for his presidency and 54 percent for his economic reform program—a result that contradicted the polls, which had predicted a majority for the pres-

TABLE 4.2
VOTING IN THE RUSSIAN REFERENDUM, 25 APRIL 1993

	Yes			No			Invalid		Total	
	Number of votes	Percent-age of votes	Percent-age of electorate	Number of votes	Percent-age of votes	Percent-age of electorate	Number of votes	Percent-age of votes	Number of votes	Percent-age of electorate
Q1: Do you have confidence in the president of the Russian Federation, B.N. Yeltsin?										
	40,405,811	58.7	37.7	26,995,268	39.2	25.2	1,468,868	2.1	68,869,947	64.2
Q2: Do you support the economic and social policy that has been conducted since 1992 by the president and the government of the Russian Federation?										
	36,476,202	53.0	34.0	30,640,781	44.6	28.6	1,642,883	2.4	68,759,866	64.1
Q3: Should there be early elections for the president of the Russian Federation?										
	34,027,310	49.5	31.7	32,418,972	47.1	30.2	2,316,247	3.4	68,762,529	64.1
Q4: Should there be early elections for the people's deputies of the Russian Federation?										
	46,232,197	67.2	43.1	20,712,605	30.1	19.3	1,887,258	2.7	68,832,060	64.2

SOURCE: Based on *Rossiiskaya gazeta*, 6 May 1993, 1.

NOTE: The electorate was 107,310,374.

ident but a defeat for his policies (*Izvestiya*, 10 April 1993, 2). This was balanced by a failure to secure the support of half the registered electorate for early parliamentary elections—a difficult task on the turnout recorded because the Constitutional Court had ruled that, for early presidential as well as parliamentary elections, a majority of voters would not be sufficient.

Support varied across the country, and in many areas the electorate refused to endorse the president and his policies (the full results appeared in *Rossiiskaya gazeta*, 19 May 1993, 2–3). In Russia as a whole, 58.7 percent of voters had expressed their confidence in Yeltsin personally, but in twenty-six of the eighty-seven republics and regions that voted there was less than majority support for the Russian president, and in eighteen there was a majority against. And in thirty areas there was a majority against his socioeconomic policies. Broadly speaking, the Urals (which were Yeltsin's home base), the Far East, and most of Siberia, Moscow, and St. Petersburg, and the northwest (Archangel and Murmansk) were strongly pro-Yeltsin; the North Caucasus, the Volga republics, the black-earth zone of central Russia, including the Belgorod, Kursk, Penza, Smolensk, and Tambov regions, and the Amur and

TABLE 4.3
REASONS FOR ABSTENTION IN THE REFERENDUM

	Percentage of nonvoters		
	Primary reason	*Secondary reason*	*Not mentioned*
Alienated, apathetic			
Would not make any difference	79	17	4
Didn't understand what it was about	56	26	18
Thought referendum a bad idea	33	52	15
Better if experts decide how country is governed	33	51	16
Physical, legal impediments			
Too ill to vote	25	10	65
Away from home; name not on electoral register	25	7	68
Authorities did not organize a vote locally	7	20	73

SOURCE: Centre for the Study of Public Policy, New Russia Barometer II (1993).
NOTE: Nonvoters only (*N* = 478).

Chita regions east of Lake Baikal were most firmly opposed. Compared with the 1991 presidential election, Yeltsin's position had strengthened in twenty-one regions, mostly those with a strong export orientation; but in fifty his position was weaker (*Segodnya*, 8 June 1993, 3).

New Russia Barometer II asked nonvoting respondents to give two major reasons for their abstention. The results (see table 4.3) suggest that the major reasons were alienation and apathy rather than practical difficulties associated with getting to the polls. Almost four-fifths of nonvoters said they did not believe the vote would make any difference to the outcome, and more than half said they did not understand what the referendum was about. Only a quarter of nonvoters mentioned being away from home, not being listed on the electoral register, or being too ill to vote as primary reasons for their abstention.

The combined answers to questions in New Russia Barometer II suggest that most Russians were broadly in favor of gridlock at this time: that is, a political order in which neither president nor parliament had supreme authority. Overall, 30 percent supported a strong president; another 30 percent supported a strong Congress; 21 percent favored a mutual veto; and a further 20 percent rejected all these options. Still more clearly, there was strong support for a "government of experts rather than politicians" (78 percent were in favor and only 21 percent against); and the Supreme Court was seen as a body that should have the right to intervene in the event of a dispute between president and parliament (83 percent agreed, with only 16 percent against).

The referendum was a plebiscite, in that President Yeltsin sought to manufacture popular endorsement by asking voters to approve a set of vaguely specified policies. Forcing a yes/no vote about his popularity made the ballot a crude measure of preferences. The New Russia Barometer tested the strength or weakness of support or opposition to President Yeltsin at this time. Table 4.4 shows that only a small minority of those who reported voting in the referendum were wholeheartedly in support of the Russian president. Only 4 percent said they trusted Yeltsin "a lot," and only 7 percent of voters said they entirely approved of the policies that Yeltsin and his government had been pursuing. The proportion of Russians who expressed absolutely no confidence in Yeltsin and his policies was four to six times larger, but still a minority. The majority gave qualified support or expressed qualified disapproval. These reservations were hidden by the stark yes/no choice offered by the referendum ballot; the shallowness of Yeltsin's support helps help to explain the subsequent decline in his public standing (see chapter 8).

TABLE 4.4

POPULAR ATTITUDES AND REFERENDUM QUESTIONS

	Electorate	Voters only
a. Do you trust the president of the Russian Federation?		
Yes, a lot	4%	4%
Yes, somewhat	30	33
Not much	40	39
Not at all	27	24
b. Do you support the policy that the president and		
government have pursued since 1992?		
Yes, a lot	6	7
Yes, somewhat	18	21
Not much	44	43
Not at all	33	30

SOURCE: Centre for the Study of Public Policy, New Russia Barometer II (1993).

Standard multivariate regression statistics can be used to relate the range of potential influences reviewed in chapter 3 to support or opposition to Yeltsin and his policies in the referendum (figure 4.1). Political attitudes had the greatest influence on referendum voting: those in favor of the new regime and disliking its communist predecessor were most likely to support Yeltsin's policies. So were those who believed that they had gained more freedoms than before. Economic attitudes were also important predictors of the referendum vote. Yeltsin supporters were not particularly inclined to endorse the transitional economic system as of April 1993. But they were much readier to make negative judgments about the socialist system and to take an optimistic view of the future of the economic system. Four social factors were each of secondary influence: those who lived in urban areas, ethnic Russians, and religious believers were more likely to be positive about the Russian president's social and economic policies; but net of other influences, women were less likely than men to endorse them.

Yeltsin claimed he had been given the authority he wanted. But he ignored a fact unprecedented in Soviet elections but common in established democracies: the electorate divided more or less evenly, and the minorities were sufficiently large to have hopes of becoming the majority in the next vote. The New Russia Barometer shows that the support of yes voters was not unconditional. The April 1993 referendum was

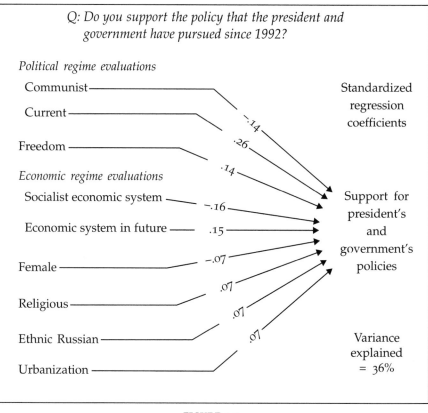

FIGURE 4.1
WHO SUPPORTED THE YELTSIN GOVERNMENT'S POLICY
IN THE REFERENDUM?

SOURCE: Centre for the Study of Public Policy, New Russia Barometer II (1993).

NOTE: Voters only ($N = 1,487$).

less a vote in favor of the Russian president and his policies than it was a vote against the communist past. For Yeltsin and his supporters, it was a verdict that justified pressing ahead with a constitution establishing presidential superiority to the legislature and judiciary. For his opponents, it was a result that owed a great deal to media manipulation and exposed the limits of Yeltsin's support, particularly outside the large cities and in non-Russian areas (see, for instance, Khasbulatov's response as reported in *Rossiiskaya gazeta*, 30 April 1993, 3–4). Gridlock, clearly, would continue.

⟪⚭ 5 ⚭⟫

A Weak Yes
for a Constitution

What is a constitution? A familiar answer is: the rules of the game that determine who does what in government, and how disputes are resolved between different branches of government (Finer et al. 1995). A constitution is a political document, as it sets out the rules under which political groups compete for power; it has been described as a "power map" (Duchacek 1973). It also specifies the rules for reconciling conflicts that are the lifeblood of the political process. It allocates functions and powers among various institutions of government and seeks to regulate their relationship. The constitution also defines the status of citizens and their rights in relation to government.

How is a constitution normally adopted? By negotiation between representatives of competing parties and groups, that is, by elites who are then expected to abide by the rules adopted. A constitution is not negotiated above politics: "problems of the country tend to take a back seat to the problems of the people at the negotiating table" (Weaver and Rockman 1993, 465). Making a new constitution effective is also a political problem, as neither governors nor governed have experience of novel rules and institutions. No hard-and-fast rules can be laid down about what is and is not necessary to create a democratic constitution. As Linz and Stepan emphasize, the artful "crafting" of an agreement is the essence of bargaining (quoted in Di Palma 1990, 8). The need for bargaining between prodemocratic and antidemocratic groups often makes it difficult to draw a line between reform and revolution, for there are significant continuities with some institutions from the past (cf. O'Donnell and Schmitter 1986).

Because the problems of governing are endless, the adoption of a democratic constitution is not the end of politics. A constitution cannot ensure economic growth, full employment, or the absence of crime. It is about procedures; it licenses public disagreements about what government ought to do. As Huntington (1991, 258) emphasizes, elite commitment is tested by "the way in which political leaders respond to their inability to solve the problems confronting their country."

The countries of Central and Eastern Europe adopted their post-communist constitutions in a variety of ways (Howard 1993; for the texts, see Raina 1995; International Institute 1995). Usually, it was the outcome of a bargain among elites in conditions of high uncertainty, sometimes while Soviet troops were still in the country, for example, in Bulgaria and Hungary, or after they had left, as in the Czech Republic and Slovakia. Normally a referendum was not felt necessary, even when, as in Czechoslovakia, the division of the state itself was involved; the elites agreed and have kept to their bargain subsequently. The Baltic countries presented a special case in that they had been annexed by the Soviet Union under the terms of the Nazi-Soviet Pact of 1939. When independence was resumed, the constitutions that came into effect were those of the late 1930s, before Soviet control. In 1992 Estonia and Lithuania went on to adopt new texts based on their predecessors; Latvia remains under its restored constitution of 1922.

Toward a New Russian Constitution

The Russian case was different in that there was no precommunist constitution to fall back on and no elite consensus about the document that should take its place. There was widespread agreement that the constitution inherited from Soviet rule, itself repeatedly amended, needed to be replaced and "desovietized"; there had been at least 300 changes since its original adoption in 1978 (*Moscow News*, 19 March 1993, 1). The USSR Congress of People's Deputies, when it met in 1989, had agreed to begin drafting a new Soviet constitution; the newly elected Russian Congress, in June 1990, established a constitutional commission, chaired by Boris Yeltsin, for the same purpose. By August a draft had been agreed on, and it was published in November 1990 (see Sakwa 1993b, 79–83; Tolz 1993; Moore 1995; the successive texts are available in *Konstitutsionnyi vestnik* 1990–93, and in *Konstitutsii* 1993). A second draft, which reflected the continuing discussion, appeared in October 1991, and at the fifth Russian Congress of People's Deputies in November 1991 Yeltsin urged that it be adopted without delay, as the old constitution had "outlived itself" (*Konstitutsionnyi vestnik*, no. 9,

1991, 56). The Congress agreed only to "take note" of the new draft, and the much-amended constitution of 1978 continued in effect.

A third draft of a new constitution was published in March 1992 and discussed at the sixth Congress of People's Deputies the following month. The Congress approved the basic principles of the new draft on 18 April but called for further discussion and revision. The Speaker, Ruslan Khasbulatov, explained that the aim was a document that would incorporate an "effective parliament and an effective president." Parliament, under the draft, would have to give its approval to presidential nominations to high office and could not be dissolved by presidential decree; the president, for his part, could not be removed from office by a parliamentary vote, nor could the government that he nominated (*Proekt* 1992, 3–6; the draft, as approved, is on 19–81). The Congress, at the same time, revised the existing constitution extensively, adding a new section on human rights and the separation of powers. It also agreed to incorporate a Federal Treaty, signed on 31 March 1992, that was intended to regulate future relations between Russia and its larger republics. A further version of the new draft appeared in November 1992 as part of this continuing process of discussion and revision (for the text, see *Konstitutsionnyi vestnik,* no. 13, 1992).

By the spring of 1993, when Yeltsin's opinion poll referendum was held, the differences had crystallized into two alternative drafts: a parliamentary version, drawn up by its constitutional commission, and a presidential draft drawn up within the executive branch and published shortly after the referendum had taken place (the texts appear in *Konstitutsionnyi vestnik,* no. 16, 1993; the presidential version was published in *Izvestiya,* 30 April 1993, 3–5; Yeltsin outlined its basic principles in *Izvestiya,* 24 April 1993, 1). The two drafts had a good deal in common. They agreed that the new Russia should be a presidential republic based on a separation of powers and with human rights defined in terms of the "generally recognized principles and norms of international law." In both cases the president was to be chosen by popular election for a maximum of two five-year terms; he was to take a leading role in foreign affairs and would head the armed forces and make appointments to key positions. In both drafts the prime minister was to be nominated by the president but confirmed by parliament; the president could submit draft legislation, but the Russian government, that is, the premier and departmental ministers, were to be the main originators of policy.

The presidential draft, however, gave much greater powers to the chief executive; Vice-President Rutskoi even called it "monarchical" (*Ne-*

zavisimaya gazeta, 8 May 1993, 2). The parliamentarians proposed that
there be a vice-president; in the presidential draft, the president would
rule alone. The parliamentary draft reserved to parliament the right to
call a referendum; in the presidential version it would be called by the
president himself. Most important, while both drafts gave the president
the power to call elections, only the presidential draft allowed the chief
executive to dissolve parliament on his own authority if the parliament
rejected his nomination as prime minister for a third time; this was a
"formidable, even overwhelming weapon in the event of a conflict between the legislature and the executive" (Moore 1995, 48).

Responding to success in the April referendum, Yeltsin announced
that he was calling a constitutional conference with a view to producing a single, approved version that could be adopted as a new Basic
Law, resolving the constitutional crisis that he considered the "main
obstacle to the implementation of reform" (the text of his decree appeared in *Izvestiya,* 22 May 1993, 1). Yeltsin made it clear that the conference version would be based on his own presidential draft but that
there would also be scope for amendment and for the consideration of
alternative proposals (*Izvestiya,* 2 June 1993, 2). There was some opposition within the parliament to these arrangements, Speaker Ruslan
Khasbulatov describing the conference as "one way of unconstitutionally adopting a constitution"; his own suggestion was a referendum on
three different drafts: the presidential, the parliamentary, and one put
forward by a group of communist deputies (*Izvestiya,* 1 June 1993, 1).
Other parliamentary spokesmen, however, including the Deputy
Speaker, expressed their willingness to take part, and in the end the
parliament agreed to the conference, provided its own draft was used
as the basis of discussion (for these developments, see Tolz 1993; Moore
1995, 49–50).

The conference began on 5 June 1993, with three main tasks: the
writing of a draft constitution, the establishment of a method for its
adoption, and a preliminary decision on the process of electing a new
parliament (*Rossiiskie vesti,* 8 June 1993, 3). There were 762 representatives of a wide diversity of opinion; Khasbulatov and some of his followers stormed out after describing the new draft as "tsarist." But by
26 June the conference had agreed on a very much revised version of
the presidential draft, and it was formally approved on 12 July (*Rossiiskie vesti,* 29 June 1993, 1; *Izvestiya,* 13 July 1993, 1). Only three articles of
the presidential draft were left untouched, and an entire chapter on the
"principles of the constitutional system" was added, drawn from the
parliamentary draft. The principles it contained—federalism, the sepa-

ration of powers, the priority of human rights—had been incorporated at various points in the version proposed by the president. Yeltsin described the new text as "neither presidential nor parliamentary" (*Izvestiya*, 13 July 1993, 1; the text itself was published in *Izvestiya*, 7 July 1993).

The Supreme Soviet, influenced by Khasbulatov, refused to endorse this version and instead produced another parliamentary draft on 14 July. Further negotiations opened in August, leading to the formation of a constitutional working group on 8 September. Headed by Nikolai Ryabov, the Deputy Speaker of parliament, it was charged with reconciling the conference draft with the new parliamentary draft and presenting proposals for a single approved text to President Yeltsin by 15 September. The revisions, Ryabov explained, would focus on the "system of state power" section of the conference draft with a view to finding a "compromise between a purely presidential and a purely parliamentary form of government" (*Segodnya*, 16 September 1993, 1). The Supreme Soviet, meanwhile, appointed a delegation of its own to "hold consultations with the president" in order to work out a compromise (*Nezavisimaya gazeta*, 11 September 1993, 1).

The revised parliamentary draft, in fact, was close to the version that the constitutional conference had approved. But it was important, at least for Khasbulatov, to insist on the authority of the Congress of People's Deputies, over which he presided, as an expression of the will of the electorate. Part of the tension arose from the personal rivalry that had developed between Yeltsin and the parliamentary chairman. Khasbulatov, an economics professor in his early fifties, had become Acting Speaker in July 1991 with Yeltsin's support and had stood beside the Russian president outside the White House at the time of the attempted coup. But he had used his office to establish an independent political position and to articulate what was in effect a doctrine of the sovereignty of parliament. Government, he insisted, should be accountable to parliament rather than to the "collective Rasputin" that surrounded the president (*Izvestiya*, 9 February 1993, 1, and 10 April 1993, 1). A broadly representative parliament was needed to review public expenditure and legislation as it did in other countries and to balance what would otherwise be an overstrong executive (*Narodnyi deputat*, no. 12, 1992, 7–8, 13–14, and no. 13, 1992, 7–8). And the proper way to adopt a new constitution, Khasbulatov argued, was by a decision of the Congress of People's Deputies or by a referendum that the Congress itself had called (*Rossiiskaya gazeta*, 10 June 1993, 3).

Yeltsin placed more emphasis on the strengthening of central authority, in the circumstances of early postcommunist Russia. To reduce the presidency to a figurehead, he warned the Congress, would lead to chaos and regional separatism; only a strong executive could preserve the integrity of Russia and with it the continuity of reform (*Rossiiskaya gazeta*, 8 April 1992, 1). The Congress, he complained, tended "just to reject, just to destroy"; too many of its deputies were engaged in "cheap populism and open demagoguery ... and in the final analysis, the restoration of a totalitarian Soviet-Communist system" (*Izvestiya*, 10 December 1992, 1). He had received his authority directly from the Russian people, Yeltsin made clear in early 1993, and he did not necessarily consider he was bound by a constitution that had been repeatedly amended since he had sworn to abide by its provisions as Russian president (*Rossiiskie vesti*, 4 March 1993, 1). In the end, he resolved the dispute with parliament by stepping outside it.

The October Crisis and a Draft Constitution

The constitutional crisis deepened when Yeltsin, in a television address on 21 September 1993, promulgated a decree on "gradual constitutional reform" that suspended the parliament and called new elections for 11–12 December. The elections would be to a State Duma, which was to be the lower house of a new parliament. Yeltsin claimed that the Supreme Soviet had blocked the process of economic and constitutional reform and that the security of Russia and its people was a "higher priority than formal conformity to contradictory norms created by the legislative branch of government." An entirely new constitution would be presented by the time of the elections, and in the meantime government would be conducted directly by the president and his ministers (*Rossiiskie vesti*, 22 September 1993, 1). In further decrees Yegor Gaidar was brought back as minister of economics and first deputy prime minister; parliamentary property was transferred to the presidency; and the parliamentary newspaper, *Rossiiskaya gazeta*, was suspended and its editor replaced.

Yeltsin, his supporters acknowledged, was in technical violation of the constitution; but they argued that the constitution was a document of the Soviet period and that there was no other way of resolving a deepening constitutional deadlock. Western governments were supportive, impressed by Yeltsin's promise of early parliamentary elections and by an undertaking that he would call an early presidential election in June 1994. For Yeltsin's opponents, by contrast, the decree was a step toward dictatorship. The Constitutional Court met the same evening

and declared it a violation of ten different articles of the Russian constitution and grounds for impeachment. When the Congress of People's
Deputies was assembled for an emergency tenth session on 23 September, it condemned Yeltsin's action as a "state coup" and voted for his
dismissal. Alexander Rutskoi was sworn in as acting president, and the
first appointments were made to an alternative administration.

The new administration had its base in the White House, where
the parliament held its meetings and where Yeltsin himself had led the
resistance to the August 1991 coup. Its telephone links with the outside
world were cut off, the electricity supply was severed and the water
supply was reduced; toilets on upper floors became unusable, and
meetings had to be held by candlelight. But increasing numbers of supporters began to assemble outside the building, many with red flags
and in a defiant mood, and they began to put up makeshift barricades
in order to defend the White House against a possible attack. Tensions
increased when the government on 28 September ordered the White
House to be sealed off by troops, and a warning was given that there
would be "serious consequences" for anyone who remained in the
building after 4 October (*Rossiiskaya gazeta*, 1 October 1993, 1).

Time was running out, but attempts were still being made to negotiate a compromise. Most important was a "zero option" suggested by
Valerii Zorkin, chairman of the Constitutional Court, under which
Yeltsin's original decree would be withdrawn; so would the vote to impeach him, and there would be simultaneous parliamentary and presidential elections. Yeltsin's supporters responded that it would be dangerous, in a state with nuclear weapons, to hold elections on this basis
and risk a "power vacuum." But several centrist politicians supported
Zorkin's initiative, among them Mikhail Gorbachev, former prime minister Nikolai Ryzhkov, and the reform economist Grigorii Yavlinsky, and
there was further support among regional leaders throughout the country. Direct negotiations began on 1 October under the auspices of the
Orthodox church in a desperate attempt to reach a last-minute accord.

The crisis came to a head on the weekend of 3–4 October when a
demonstration of about 10,000 parliamentary supporters marched to
the White House, raised the blockade, and encouraged Rutskoi and
Khasbulatov—and many Western journalists—to believe that a popular insurrection had taken place in their support. The demonstrators
took control of the Moscow mayor's office, immediately opposite the
White House. Rutskoi and Khasbulatov at this point urged the crowd
to "take Ostankino" (the main television center, which went off the air
for some time) and to "take over the Kremlin."

After a day in which the regime itself had appeared fragile and in which Yeltsin had shown little clarity of purpose, armed forces were deployed on the morning of Monday, 4 October, and the White House was subjected to an artillery bombardment. It soon became the "Black House" as flames engulfed its upper stories. By the early evening Rutskoi, Khasbulatov, and their supporters had been forced to surrender; Yeltsin, in a television broadcast later the same evening, accused the parliamentarians of an "armed rebellion" that had sought to establish a "bloody communo-fascist dictatorship." Khasbulatov and Rutskoi were eventually charged with "inciting public disorder" and imprisoned, but they were released in February 1994 when the Duma voted an amnesty for them and for the conspirators of August 1991. According to the official report, 145 people lost their lives and more than 800 were wounded in the bloodiest street fighting in Moscow since 1917 (*Izvestiya*, 25 December 1993, 1).

Yeltsin moved to consolidate his advantage by proposing a further draft of the constitution involving a considerable extension of his own powers. Most changes in the draft that was published on 10 November were minor, but several were significant, particularly those that related to the relationship between the central government and the republics and regions. The existing draft had incorporated the Federation Treaty, concluded in the spring of 1992; the November draft left it out, undermining the position of what were now to be known as "subjects of the Federation." The republics and regions, in a related change, were no longer to be considered "sovereign," with their own citizenship. And the position of the government in relation to the president was further weakened; under a new article it would be required to resign on the election of a new president, the president would have the right to preside over its meetings, and he could dismiss it without reference to parliament (Moore 1995, 55–56; the revised draft appeared in *Izvestiya*, 10 November 1993, 3–5).

The draft constitution was strongly presidentialist. It was the president who defined the "basic directions of domestic and foreign policy" and represented the state internationally. The president would be directly elected for a period of four years and for not more than two consecutive terms The president had to be at least thirty-five years old; there was no upper age limit as in earlier drafts, presumably because Yeltsin would be just over sixty-five when he was due for reelection. The president had to be a Russian citizen of any nationality and must have been resident in the country for at least the previous ten years. The president would have the right to appoint the prime minister, subject to the approval of parliament, and, on the prime minister's recommendation, to appoint and dismiss deputy premiers and other members of the government.

Under the new draft the president appointed a whole range of other top officials. He nominated the chairman of the State Bank and judges to higher courts (including the Constitutional Court, which was supposed to determine the legality of his own decisions). He headed the Security Council and appointed his "plenipotentiary representatives" throughout the federation. The president was the commander-in-chief and approved the "military doctrine of the Russian Federation" (a constitutional novelty); he appointed and dismissed the high command, as well as senior members of the diplomatic service. Additionally, the president could call elections or referendums (a new power); he could declare martial law or a state of emergency; he could issue his own decrees, which had the force of law, and have his own staff. He could dismiss parliament, in appropriate circumstances, and initiate legislation; and he would give an annual "state of the union" address to the Federal Assembly, the new two-chamber parliament. He could still be impeached, but only for serious antistate crimes and after a complicated procedure had been followed.

The prime minister and government, under the new constitution, exercised "executive power" but in a clearly subordinate capacity. The chairman of the government, or prime minister, was appointed by the president "with the consent of the State Duma"; the Duma could reject the president's nomination, but if it did so three times it would be dissolved and new elections would be called. The prime minister proposed the members of his own government, subject to the approval of the president. The prime minister was responsible for determining the "activity" of the government as a whole and for "organizing its work": this included preparing a state budget and regulating financial and monetary policy, as well as managing education, science, health, and social security and taking charge of public order, defense, and foreign affairs. The government could issue its own directives, but within the framework established by presidential decrees as well as by the laws and constitution.

The Duma had some influence over the composition of the government, although government was hardly "responsible" in the sense understood in parliamentary democracies. In particular, the Duma could pass a vote of no confidence in the government; the president could either dismiss the government or ignore the vote, but if a further vote of no confidence was passed within three months, the president had to announce either the resignation of the government or the dissolution of the Duma itself. These "big bang" powers were unlikely ever to be used. The president, meanwhile, had begun to build up a staff of his own that in numbers and effective authority tended to marginalize the government still further. The constitution referred only to the "Executive Office (Administration) of the President of the Russian Federation"; the president, in fact, was able to use his administration as well as the newly established Security Council and representatives in the Russian regions to bypass the prime minister and his ministerial colleagues whenever he wished to do so.

The new constitution was one in which the rights of the citizen were more fully recognized than in previous Russian constitutions or in the earlier drafts. There was to be "ideological" and "political diversity," together with a "multiparty system." There could be no state or official ideology. The Russian state was to be a secular one, based on the separation of church and state, with religious organizations independent of political control and equal before the law. There were guarantees of free movement within or across the frontiers of the federation. Citizens must be allowed to have access to any information about them that was held by public bodies, and censorship was specifically prohibited. There was to be freedom of thought and speech, and of assembly and association. In the courts, similarly, all would have the right to a qualified defense lawyer and were to be presumed innocent until proved guilty.

The new Russian state would also be a "social" one, with policies that aimed to ensure "adequate living standards and the free development of every individual." Many of its provisions were strongly reminiscent of documents adopted in the Soviet period about social rights and welfare. For instance, everyone would have the right to free medical care and to a free education from preschool to university level. Everyone had the right to life, though there would still be a death penalty for "particularly grave crimes." There could be no torture or "cruel or degrading treatment or punishment." Everyone would have the right to work in safe and hygienic conditions and at a rate of pay that was not below the minimum wage. Everyone would have a right to rest and leisure and to state support in the event of old age or disability. And there would be a right to housing, "free or at a reasonable charge" to whose who needed it. All these rights were spelled out in a separate chapter of the constitution, one that was "entrenched" and could not be modified by the legislature.

There was barely a month in which to discuss the new constitution and the changes involved, both to the existing constitution and to the drafts that had already been published. Lawyers and political scientists were generally positive, though there were many reservations. Leonid Mamut, for instance, was particularly pleased that the basic principles of a legal and democratic state had been specified in the new constitution; from now on, at least legally, there could be no "single and obligatory ideology" or the "monopolization of power by a single political party." Sergei Sitorkin was particularly pleased by the way that human rights, with a whole chapter of their own, had been defined by reference to international legal norms, and by the provision that the new Duma appoint the first-ever commissioner on human rights (*Literaturnaya gazeta*, no. 46, 1993, 1). Viktor Sheinis, a lawyer who had helped to shape the new draft, thought the right balance had been struck between president and parliament: the Federal Assembly could dismiss the government, but the president could dismiss the Assembly. And Evgenii Kozhokin was pleased by the way in which the federal relationship had been defined. But there were other views. Evgenii Ambartsumov, chairman of the parliament's foreign affairs committee and another academic, was concerned that this was a "presidential constitution," more so than in America or France, and with a "consultative, almost decorative parliament." Russia, he agreed, needed a presidency, but a "rational, not an absolute one." Yeltsin, personally, was no dictator. But what if someone like Zhirinovsky took his place? (ibid.) Indeed, if any of Yeltsin's successors took on the "ready-made dictatorial mantle" that the constitution provided, argued political scientist Georgii Shakhnazarov, the whole country could be "returned to the Gulag era" (*Rabochaya tribuna*, 9 December 1993, 1–3). Andranik Migranyan, another parliamentarian with an academic background, pointed to the danger that the president might nominate a prime minister who was opposed by a majority in the Duma: in this way, he thought, "we once again risk having a political crisis" (*Literaturnaya gazeta*, no. 46, 1993, 2).

Other commentaries were still more critical, particularly of the range of powers concentrated in the hands of the new presidency. A group of party leaders and deputies, mostly from the organized left, charged in an open letter that the president had accumulated "dictatorial" powers, and called for a constituent assembly that could more adequately discuss a new document (*Pravda*, 19 January 1994, 1). Many republics were wary of the centralizing thrust of the new draft—Bashkortostan, for instance, insisted it was still "sovereign" under its own constitution. And the Russian Association of Gays and Lesbians called for a boycott because the new constitution "did not reflect the interests of sexual minorities" (*Kommersant,* 16 November 1993, 4).

Political parties took views that reflected their attitude to Yeltsin and the reform movement generally. Gaidar's "Russia's Choice" called for the constitution to be adopted, although they saw "dangerous gaps" in the sections that defined the relationship between president, parliament, and the courts. The Party of Russian Unity and Concord took a similar view, though they intended to propose a number of amendments once the new constitution had been adopted. Yavlinsky's "Yabloko" group, by contrast, called for a vote against the new constitution, believing matters of this kind should be decided by parliament rather than by popular vote. Vladimir Zhirinovsky of the Liberal Democrats was more positive, explaining that a "state can't live without a constitution any more than a person without a passport"; a draft constitution that his own party had produced was in fact remarkably similar to the version that Yeltsin was putting to the electorate (*Nezavisimaya gazeta,* 8 December 1993, 5). Zyuganov's communists, however, had urged their supporters to oppose an "antipopular constitution" even before the final draft had been published (these and other responses were reported in *Moskovskie novosti,* no. 49, 1993, 10A); and Anatolii Lukyanov, the former parliamentary chairman, told *Pravda* that the new constitution gave Yeltsin powers that could only be compared with those of the Emperor Napoleon III in nineteenth-century France (10 December 1993, 3).

Voting and Voters in the December Referendum

Yeltsin had called for a "single agreed draft" of the constitution in his decree of 21 September, and in another decree on 15 October 1993 he set out the basis of a "national vote (*golosovanie*)" on a draft that had not yet been published. The ballot paper would contain a single question: "Do you approve of the Constitution of the Russian Federation?"; the answer would be yes or no, with voters crossing out the alternative they rejected. The draft constitution would be adopted if a majority of voters decided in favor, provided that at least half the electorate had taken part. This was not a referendum in terms of the Russian law on referendums of 1990, which would have required at least half the electorate to offer their support; and its legal basis remained in some doubt even after it had taken place.

The official outcome of the referendum, as it was called in practice,

TABLE 5.1

THE RUSSIAN REFERENDUM, 12 DECEMBER 1993

Q: Do you approve of the constitution of the Russian Federation?

	Number	Percentage of electorate	Percentage of valid vote
In favor	32,937,630	31.0	58.4
Against	23,431,333	22.1	41.6
Invalid votes	1,818,792	1.7	—
Total votes	58,187,755	54.8	100.0
Total electorate	106,182,030	100.0	

SOURCE: Derived from *Rossiiskie vesti,* 25 December 1993, 1.

was a weak majority in favor of the new constitution (see table 5.1). The reported turnout was 54.8 percent, or just over 53 percent after subtracting spoiled and invalid papers, barely enough to satisfy the requirement that half the electorate take part. Of those who cast a valid vote, 58.4 percent declared in favor of the draft constitution. There was no voting in the Chechen republic and low participation levels in several other republics or regions: in Tatarstan just 13.9 percent of the electorate went to the polls. There were majorities against the draft constitution in 8 of the 21 republics and 10 of the other 68 regions; the largest negative majority was in Dagestan, where 79.1 percent rejected the new draft (the official results were published in *Byulleten,* no. 1 (12), 1994, 34–38).

Yeltsin declared himself satisfied that this was sufficient support to make the draft document the new constitution of Russia, and when he commented on the results, he laid most emphasis on the adoption of this new Basic Law. It meant, he told journalists, that a "final line" had been drawn under the Soviet communist system, and it was an "important step into the future" (*Izvestiya,* 23 December 1993, 1; the text of the new constitution, as approved, appeared in *Izvestiya,* 28 December 1993, 4–6). The new constitution came into force when the results of the vote were announced, on 25 December 1993.

The status of the new constitution was questioned on at least three grounds. The first challenge was legal. The much-amended 1978 constitution specified that a referendum had to be called by the Congress of People's Deputies, not the president; and the referendum law of October 1990 made clear that at least half the registered electorate had to give their approval for a proposition to be adopted. This requirement had not been met, as less than a third of the registered electorate had voted in favor. Yeltsin had called for a "plebiscite" (*golosovanie*), in which a majority of voters was sufficient; but the law made clear that a referendum, not a simple expression of opinion, was the appropriate mechanism for decisions on the "most important questions of public life." The existing constitution also made clear that any changes required the support of two-thirds of the Congress of People's Deputies, and, if they related to federal matters, of Russia's republics and regions. There had been several forms of consultation, including the constitutional conference, but no attempt had been made to secure the endorsement of the Congress or the regions. And there were other improprieties, such as the chairman of the central electoral commission calling for a vote in favor of the new draft in spite of his supposedly independent position (*Rossiiskaya gazeta*, 11 December 1993, 1).

Second, there were doubts about the authenticity of the voting figures and allegations of misreporting in order to produce the "official" (that is, government-desired) result. There was little dispute that the draft constitution had been supported by a majority of those who had voted. But under the rules for a "national vote," as Yeltsin had set them out, the result would be invalid if fewer than half the electorate took part. Observers at the polls estimated that between 38 and 43 percent had voted, well short of this figure (*Konstitutsionnyi vestnik*, no. 17, 1994, 32). And the size of the electorate itself appeared to have been manipulated to make it easier to declare that a majority had exercised their rights. As journalist Alexander Minkin reported, the authorities had begun to celebrate the adoption of the new constitution at midnight on election day. But very different figures were reported of the number of voters who were supposed to have supported it, from 29.3 to 32.9 million. And the electorate, which had been 107.3 million in April, was reported at 105.2 million in December, and when the final results were published in mid-February, at 106.2 million. Where, asked Minkin, had all the voters gone? (*Moskovskii komsomolets*, 11 January 1994, 1).

Third, the inability or unwillingness of the Central Election Commission to publish a detailed breakdown of the results even two months after the vote implied substantial inconsistencies in counting or reporting the results. Under the regulations that Yeltsin approved on 15 October (*Rossiiskie vesti*, 19 October 1993, 1, and 21 October 1993, 3), each district electoral commission was to report the number of electors on its list, the number of unused ballot papers, the number of papers distributed on the day of the election, the number found in the ballot boxes after voting had been completed, and the number that were invalid (such as "unofficial" ballot papers, or those in which both answers had been crossed out). They were also required to calculate the number of valid votes cast *for* the draft constitution and the number *against.* The various totals were then to be added together at constituency level and passed on to the Central Election Commission in Moscow. The official return eventually reported these totals, but for each of the eighty-nine units of the federation rather than for the districts or individual constituencies. This made it harder to verify the result and encouraged speculation, although it was likely that incompetence and inexperience were more often involved than systematic falsification.

As far as the electorate was concerned, the referendum was not so much about legal clauses that had been debated between the president's staff and parliament; as it was about apportioning blame for how the country had been governed in the past and how it was to be governed in the future (see figure 5.1). Those who blamed the government and capitalists for the country's economic problems or were Communist Party members were likely to vote against the constitution, and those who blamed the communists for economic problems were likely to vote for it. Moreover, those who rejected the old communist regime and welcomed new freedoms were likely to support the new constitution.

National economic conditions had no influence on voting on the constitution. The only economic influence of any significance was destitution: those who were hardest hit by changes were more likely to vote against the constitution. Similarly, the links between the social structure and voting in the constitution were modest: opponents of the new draft were disproportionately younger and more likely to live in European than in Asiatic Russia, a result that may at least in part have been attributable to Yeltsin's own Siberian origins.

What did Russians expect the new constitution to do? The third New Russia Barometer survey asked people whether they thought the new constitution would help to establish a lawful and democratic Russian state. Only 14 percent agreed, as against 30 percent who took the opposite view. The largest group, well over half, thought it "difficult to say" whether the new constitution would lead to a democratic state governed by the rule of law. And would the constitution, in the face of challenges from the republics for autonomy or even independence, guarantee the unity and territorial integrity of Russia? Only 13 percent thought it would do so; 27 percent thought it would not; and again the

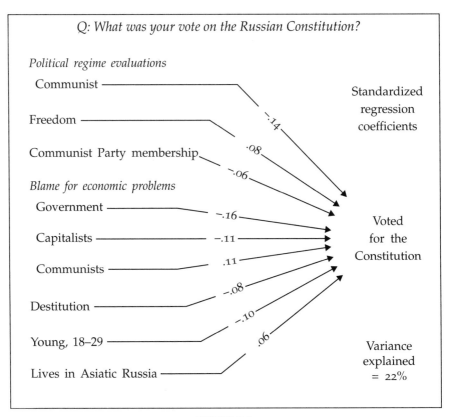

FIGURE 5.1
WHO SUPPORTED THE CONSTITUTION?

SOURCE: Centre for the Study of Public Policy/Paul Lazarsfeld Society, New Russia Barometer III (1994).

NOTE: Standardized regression coefficients predicting who voted in favor of adopting the Constitution. Estimates exclude nonvoters (N = 1,913); the sample has been weighted to the referendum results.

largest group, 60 percent, had no clear opinion. There was indecision about what the new constitution might achieve, and insofar as people had opinions, they were skeptical about its effects.

Voters can be divided into four groups according to their views about the impact of the constitution and how they voted (figure 5.2). The largest group were "pessimistic supporters," 36 percent of the total: they favored the new draft but were doubtful of its ability to ensure a lawful, democratic state. The second largest group were "pessimistic

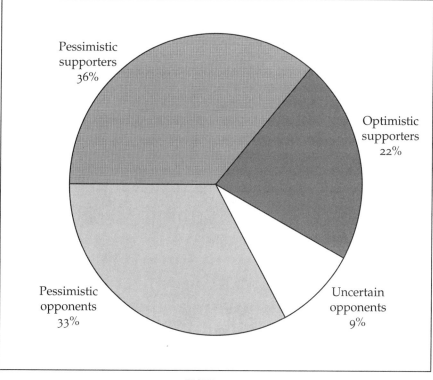

FIGURE 5.2

PESSIMISTIC SUPPORTERS CARRIED THE CONSTITUTION

SOURCE: Centre for the Study of Public Policy/Paul Lazarsfeld Society, New Russia Barometer III (1994).

NOTE: Using the survey question on the approval of the constitution (see table 5.2) and the question on the new constitution ensuring a lawful and democratic state (see table 5.3), the four groups are defined as follows:

Optimistic supporters approved the constitution and said that the constitution would ensure a lawful and democratic state.

Pessimistic supporters approved the constitution but answered no or don't know to the second question.

Uncertain opponents disapproved of the constitution and answered don't know to the second question.

Pessimistic opponents answered no to both questions.

Percentages exclude nonvoters ($N = 1,913$) ; the sample has been weighted to the referendum result.

opponents," opposed to the new constitution and believing it would not guarantee a lawful and democratic state. Together, these two groups encompassed more than two-thirds of voters. "Optimistic supporters" were 22 percent of all voters, and "uncertain opponents" were just 9 percent. Within the voting public, pessimism about the constitution was predominant.

Whereas the new constitution was definitely presidentialist, the electorate was not (figure 5.3). Only a quarter said they believed the president should be more important than parliament, and a similar

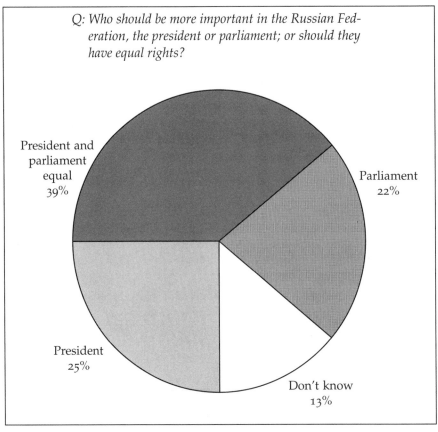

Q: Who should be more important in the Russian Federation, the president or parliament; or should they have equal rights?

President and parliament equal 39%

Parliament 22%

President 25%

Don't know 13%

FIGURE 5.3
WHERE SHOULD POWER BE?

SOURCE: Centre for the Study of Public Policy/Paul Lazarsfeld Society, New Russia Barometer III (1994).

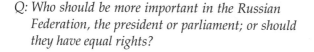

Q: Who should be more important in the Russian Federation, the president or parliament; or should they have equal rights?

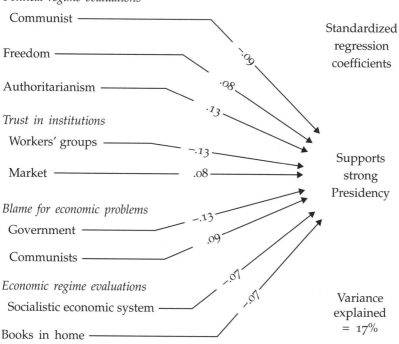

FIGURE 5.4
SUPPORTERS OF A STRONG PRESIDENCY

SOURCE: Centre for the Study of Public Policy/Paul Lazarsfeld Society, New Russia Barometer III (1994). Sample weighted to referendum results.

proportion favored parliament being more important. The largest group thought the two should have equal powers—the position in Washington but not the case in Moscow after the shelling of the White House. The fact that gridlock could result from giving equal rights to president and parliament was of concern to politicians wanting more power—but not to Russians inclined by experience to distrust a "too powerful" state (cf. Rose 1994b). Even among those who voted in favor of the constitution only 36 percent said they wanted the president to be more important; a larger percentage favored the president and parliament being equal in authority.

Supporters of a stronger presidency in 1993 tended to be in favor of reform, reflecting Yeltsin's perceived position at that time (figure 5.4). They were likely to evaluate the communist regime and the communist economic system negatively, to view gains in freedom positively, and to lay blame for the country's economic problems on the communists rather than the government. Supporters of a strong president also tended to be higher on the authoritarianism scale, a reminder that the "strong leader" tradition in Russia is not a tradition of constitutional leadership as that term is understood in a rule-of-law state. More "bookish" people were also more suspicious of granting the president stronger powers.

The outcome of the referendum gave Russia a new constitution after three years of reform. But it was not clear whether the constitution had achieved its primary aim of establishing a new set of rules of the political game. Russia had a new constitution, but it had been achieved in ways that prejudiced its long-term future.

⟪⟨ 6 ⟩⟫

Electing a Parliament

The drafts of the new constitution revealed different understandings of the role of an elected parliament. Both the presidential and parliamentary drafts provided for a popularly elected two-chamber assembly. For Yeltsin and his associates, the parliament was to be called a Federal Assembly and would consist of a Council of the Federation and a State Duma of 300 deputies. The parliament wanted a Supreme Soviet with two chambers: a Federal Assembly and a State Duma with 450 deputies. Yeltsin rejected any use of the term *soviet* on the grounds that it indicated an institution of "communist totalitarianism" (*Trud*, 2 July 1993, 1). In both cases the upper house would consist of two representatives of each of Russia's republics and regions, and the lower house would be elected every four years from single-member constituencies on a first-past-the-post basis (the 1993 Duma had been elected for two years because its purpose was transitional). The parliamentary draft, however, placed the parliament before the president, describing him as the "highest official" of the Russian state; the presidential version put the presidency first and described him as the "head of state," with parliament a more limited and "representative" institution.

When President Yeltsin dissolved parliament on 21 September 1993 and called for elections, the Duma as he conceived it would consist of 400 deputies, 130 from national party lists chosen by proportional representation and 270 from single-member districts (*Izvestiya*, 22 September 1993, 1, and 24 September 1993, 3). An amendment on 1 October changed the number of deputies to 450, to be elected in equal numbers on a party-list and single-member-district basis, and set out more detailed arrangements (*Polozhenie* 1993). On 11 October, another presidential decree announced that the Federation Council was to be elected on the same date, with two members being chosen by each republic or region on the basis of a simple majority (*Rossiiskaya gazeta*, 12 October 1993, 1, 4; see figure 6.1). A decree of 9 October announced

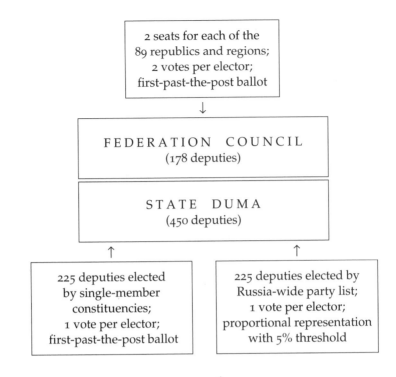

FIGURE 6.1

ELECTIONS TO THE RUSSIAN FEDERAL ASSEMBLY,

DECEMBER 1993

elections for new, smaller bodies of local government, and many such elections took place on 12 December. Yeltsin also announced that a presidential election would be held in June 1994, two years ahead of schedule. This helped secure the support of Western governments for what was an acknowledged breach of the constitution; in the event, no such election was held.

Voters had at least four decisions to make when they went to the polls on 12 December in the first Russian general election since the end of Soviet rule: one about the constitution, the second, third, and fourth about voting for the two chambers of the new Russian parliament. In the election of the Council of the Federation, voters in each of the eighty-nine republics and regions of the federation could select two candidates. There were two ballots for the Duma. One was a choice between lists of candidates for 225 seats elected by proportional representation (PR), a complete innovation in Soviet terms. A nationwide PR ballot, in the view of presidential advisers, would advantage prominent reformers and encourage the formation of political parties. "No proportional representation, no parties," as Viktor Sheinis, a deputy who was one of its authors, told journalists (*Rossiya*, no. 35, 1993, 3). The other Duma ballot offered a choice of individuals seeking to represent one of the 225 single-member districts.

The old election law had required a turnout of 50 percent for the results to be valid; the regulations reduced this to 25 percent. In elections to the party-list section of the Duma, parties or (in the language of the decree) "electoral associations" were required to secure at least 5 percent of the votes across the whole country to secure representation. For the single-member districts and for the Council of the Federation the candidate with the largest number of votes would win provided the turnout requirement of 25 percent was met, and provided, initially, that the vote "against all" did not exceed the number of votes cast in favor of the candidate with the largest individual vote—a requirement that was dropped at a later stage.

The Contenders

The suspension and bombardment of parliament created an inhospitable environment for the conduct of Russia's first postcommunist elections. There was a brief period of censorship: fifteen newspapers were banned on the grounds that they had contributed to the "mass disorder in Moscow," and three others were suspended. *Pravda* and *Sovetskaya Rossiya*, two of the papers that were suspended, were also instructed to change their names and replace their editors (in the end, both retained their distinctive titles but did not appear for an extended period). A state of emergency in Moscow, incorporating a ban on rallies and demonstrations and a curfew, lasted until 18 October. The Constitutional Court was suspended and its chairman forced to resign; the prosecutor general was dismissed and replaced with a Yeltsin loyalist. A wide range of opposition groups were suspended, for a time, on the grounds that they had been involved in the "events" of 3–4 October. Several were eventually legalized, including the Communist Party of the Russian Federation and the People's Party of Free Russia led by Vice-President Rutskoi, who was under indictment for his role in the October events. A number, including the National Salvation Front and the Russian Communist Workers' Party, remained suspended and were unable to take part in the elections.

All the national parties or movements registered with the Ministry of Justice were eligible to nominate candidates for the Duma seats allocated by proportional representation, provided that they could secure at least 100,000 signatures of electors, with no more than 15 percent from any of the republics or regions. Several found it impossible to do so by the deadline, midnight on 6 November. A total of 130 parties were eligible to nominate candidates; 35 attempted to gather the necessary signatures, and 21 submitted formal nominations (*Izvestiya*, 9 November 1993, 2). Eight of these were disallowed, on the grounds that there were irregularities in their documentation; the other thirteen parties or movements were registered by the Central Electoral Commission for the party-list section of the Duma (*Izvestiya*, 11 November 1993, 1). The thirteen registered party lists contained the names of 1,717 candidates (Ryabov 1993).

In the single-member constituencies of the State Duma 1,567 candidates were registered by the Central Electoral Commission to contest 224 seats; no vote was held in the Chechen republic because of unsettled political conditions in the area. This was an average of seven candidates per single-member district. There were 490 nominations for 176 seats in the Council of the Federation, with no ballot in the Chechen republic, an average of 2.8 candidates per seat (*Izvestiya*, 21 November 1993, 1).

The parties or electoral blocs that contested the election were all very new (see table 6.1). Half had been founded earlier the same year; many were ad hoc alliances formed for the purpose of contesting the elections, and only three dated from 1990, when political parties had been formally legalized. The December elections did not provide a clear and coherent choice between parties. For a start, most electoral alliances were groupings, not individual parties. And many party-sponsored candidates did not belong to the parties that had nominated them. Among the Liberal Democrats, for instance, 42 percent of the deputies did not belong to the party and two belonged to other parties. Nationally about 30 percent of the party-list candidates were not members of the party or alliance for which they stood (Lentini 1994b, 3). Of the candidates in single-member constituencies, "almost 60 percent" did not have a formal party affiliation (*Izvestiya*, 8 December 1993, 4).

The main group supporting the introduction of a market economy was Russia's Choice, which began to form soon after the April referendum and held its founding congress in mid-October 1993. Its list was headed by Yegor Gaidar, the economist who had been acting prime minister in 1992 and had been reappointed as a first deputy prime min-

TABLE 6.1

PARTIES AND BLOCS IN THE DECEMBER 1993 ELECTIONS

Party	Leader(s)	Founded
Liberal Democratic Party	Vladimir Zhirinovsky	1990
Democratic Party of Russia	Nikolai Travkin	1990
Communist Party of the Russian Federation	Gennadii Zyuganov	1990
Democratic Reform Movement	Gavriil Popov	1992
Agrarian Party of Russia	Mikhail Lapshin	February 1993
Constructive Ecological Movement (Cedar)	Anatolii Panfilov	March 1993
Russia's Choice	Yegor Gaidar	Summer 1993
Party of Russian Unity and Concord (PRES)	Sergei Shakhrai	October 1993
Yavlinsky-Boldyrev-Lukin bloc (Yabloko)	Grigorii Yavlinsky	October 1993
Civic Union for Stability, Justice, and Progress	Arkadii Volsky	October 1993
Women of Russia	Alevtina Fedulova Ekaterina Lakhova Natalya Gundareva	October 1993
Dignity and Charity	Konstantin Frolov	October 1993
Russia's Future–New Names	Vyacheslav Lashchevsky	October 1993

ister in September 1993. It included other government leaders such as Foreign Minister Andrei Kozyrev, Privatization Minister Anatolii Chubais, and Finance Minister Boris Fedorov, as well as Ella Pamfilova, minister of social security and the only woman in a leading position on a party list outside Women of Russia. It also included the head of the presidential administration, Sergei Filatov, and it was the most clearly pro-Yeltsin grouping, although the president did not support it openly. Russia's Choice took "Freedom, Property, and Legality" as its slogan; it stood for a continuation and extension of Russia's transition to a market economy based on private property through budgetary reform, the elimination of import subsidies, and a steady reduction of taxation ("Not the salvation of the weak but assistance to the strong"). It also favored a reduction in the military-industrial complex, support for shareholders and entrepreneurs, and the privatization of land (for this and other party platforms, see "Izbiratelnye," 1993, 2, and *Izvestiya,* 28 October 1993, 4). Russia's Choice nominated the most candidates on its list, 212; it had the support of the largest number of banks and commercial enterprises; and it was clearly the "favorite of the pre-election campaign" (*Izvestiya*, 30 October 1993, 4).

Other ministers, including Deputy Premiers Sergei Shakhrai and Alexander Shokhin, headed the list put forward by the Party of Russian Unity and Concord (PRES), whose founding congress took place on 17 October 1993. It described itself as the "party of Russian statehood" and gave particular prominence to the interests of Russians distant from the center; its founding congress was deliberately placed in Novgorod rather than Moscow. PRES favored a more gradual program of economic reform, including "sensible protectionism" and an "active industrial and scientific-technical policy" as well as the development of competition and private initiative. It was thought to enjoy the covert support of Prime Minister Viktor Chernomyrdin. The Yabloko (Apple) bloc was named after its three leaders, headed by economist Grigorii Yavlinsky, along with Yuri Boldyrev, a Leningrad deputy who had become head of the national audit office, and Vladimir Lukin, who had stepped down in September as Russian ambassador to the United States. It placed a greater degree of emphasis on the assertion of Russia's national interests in world affairs than did Russia's Choice, and while supporting the move to the market, saw itself as a "constructive opposition" to the policies of the Yeltsin-Gaidar government. It also placed more emphasis on demonopolization than on privatization.

A substantial number of parties distanced themselves from the market without endorsing the old command economy or appealed for support on other grounds. For example, Women of Russia was formed in October 1993 on the basis of the Union of Russian Women, originally a CPSU front but one that had become increasingly assertive on behalf of its members in the late Soviet period. It aimed to increase women's representation to influence social policy and argued that the market was "not an end in itself, but a means of improving living standards." The Civic Union for Stability, Justice, and Progress, headed by Arkadii Volsky of the Russian Union of Industrialists and Entrepreneurs, represented the interests of factory managers rather than new private entrepreneurs.

Nikolai Travkin's Democratic Party of Russia stood for a mixed economy and a more limited presidency. Other groupings included The Future of Russia—New Names (based on the Russian Union of Youth and representing younger age groups); Dignity and Charity, which sought to represent veterans, invalids, and Chernobyl victims; and Cedar (*Kedr*), an environmentalist group. The Democratic Reform Movement, headed by a former Moscow mayor, Gavriil Popov, placed particular emphasis on human rights and democratization; its list of candidates included St. Petersburg Mayor Anatolii Sobchak and Alexander Yakovlev, formerly the "architect of perestroika" but now a Yeltsin adviser.

The Communist Party of the Russian Federation, headed by its chairman, Gennadii Zyuganov, was the only CPSU successor party able to compete for seats in the new Duma. In the view of the Communists, the elections were illegal, but the party was prepared to participate so as to "prevent the dictatorship from being legalized" (*Megapolis-Ekspress*, no. 45, 1993, 17). The Communist Party of the Russian Federation stood for the establishment of a "strong and determined opposition"; more particularly, it wanted the restoration of political and economic stability, a more powerful parliament, and an end to the "unrestrained rise in prices and mass impoverishment of the people." While not opposed to a market economy as such, the Communists were hostile to a further extension of private and particularly foreign ownership, and they favored a high degree of state control of economic activity. The party was critical of some aspects of the communist past, such as authoritarianism and hostility to organized religion, and it was much more emphatically nationalist than its predecessors, seeing the collapse of the USSR as a betrayal of Russian interests. Its list of candidates included Anatolii Lukyanov, the former Supreme Soviet chairman who had been arrested following the August 1991 coup, and many former deputies and party officials.

In their opposition to the Yeltsin-Gaidar administration, the Communists were supported by Mikhail Lapshin's Agrarian Party, founded in February 1993, which reflected the interests of state and cooperative rather than private agriculture. "The renewal of Russia," declared the Agrarians, "must begin with its foundation—the countryside." The party favored a policy that gave the land to those who were prepared to work it themselves, but not its general sale; and in the national economy they argued for a "socially oriented market" involving a gradual transition to market relations under the control of the state, together with a range of guaranteed social rights including the right to work and state support for the less prosperous. Lapshin himself had formerly directed a state farm; the Agrarians' list of candidates also included Vasilii Starodubtsev, a collective farm leader who had taken part in the attempted coup of 1991, the writer Valentin Rasputin, and Ivan Rybkin, a former CPSU district secretary who later became the Duma's first chairman. The Agrarians were the most successful of all the parties in collecting signatures in support of their nominations —half a million, more than twice as many as any other; Lapshin told journalists he could easily have collected another million (Rodin 1993).

The Liberal Democratic Party of Vladimir Zhirinovsky challenged many conventions with an extreme nationalist line. The economy, argued the LDP, could be revived very quickly by ending foreign aid, stepping up arms sales, and cracking down on organized crime. The LDP stood for a strong state sector with limited privatization, no shift to private ownership of land, and no overt unemployment. There should also be a strong and unitary system of government, including the restoration of a Russian state "within the boundaries of the former USSR," and a strong executive presidency; and the LDP favored a strongly pro-Slavic and anti-Western foreign policy, particularly in the former Yugoslavia. The LDP had a well-educated membership and more than half its candidates were university or college teachers, but in practice it was a vehicle through which Zhirinovsky could articulate his own extreme positions, particularly on foreign policy. He suggested, for instance, that there could be "new Hiroshimas and Nagasakis on Japan," and "another Chernobyl" on Germany; and his autobiography, *Last Push to the South,* argued that the secret of world peace was Russian control of Pakistan, Afghanistan, and Turkey, and "Russian soldiers washing their boots in the Indian Ocean" (Zhirinovsky 1993).

In a manner that was in some ways reminiscent of Yeltsin's antiestablishment campaign of 1991, Zhirinovsky sought to be all things to all men. To the military-industrial complex he promised an end of the conversion of the defense sector. Pensioners were offered improved social security; crime would be solved "in a few months" by shooting gang leaders; and unemployment would simply be forbidden. Foreigners and Jews were offered as scapegoats for Russia's problems, including (inaccurately) "the Jew Gaidar," although Zhirinovsky's own father was Jewish and he had been called Edelstein until the age of eighteen (*Izvestiya,* 5 April 1994, 2). Although Zhirinovsky was never a CPSU member, repeated reports stated that the Politburo had ordered the KGB to establish his party as a manageable rival when its own monopoly became unsustainable (see, for instance, *Izvestiya,* 14 April 1994, 2). Zhirinovsky was also the politician who complained most about the fact that many Russians were being forced to leave former Soviet republics because they were Russians. An aspect of Zhirinovsky's character less commented upon was that many found him funny in a crude and sinister way—a combination of Hitler and Charlie Chaplin. In a broadcast, for instance, he compared the Soviet period to a variety of sexual acts: the revolution was rape, the Stalin period homosexual, Khrushchev was masturbation, the Brezhnev and Gorbachev years political impotence, and his own victory would be orgasm (cf. Frazer and Lancelle 1994).

The existence of multiple parties and ballots for the two chambers of the new parliament—and sometimes local councils as well—offered Russian electors more choices than ever before (the Central Electoral Commission called it a "superalternative choice"—*Izvestiya*, 11 November 1993, 1). In Moscow, for instance, electors could choose two from among the five candidates nominated for the city's seat in the Council of the Federation: an urban economist, two members of the presidential administration, a local government official, and a writer. For the party-list section of the Duma, Muscovites made the same choice as elsewhere in the country from the thirteen electoral alliances on the PR ballot. For the other half of the Duma, the city was divided into fifteen single-member constituencies offering a variety of more particular choices. For instance, in the city's southwestern constituency, No. 204, there were nine candidates: a manager, the head of a commercial bank, two other members of the presidential administration, two senior researchers, a local government official, a teacher, and a member of the full-time staff of the Liberal Democratic Party. All were men, mostly in their forties or fifties. Initially, voters were to be given the choice of writing "against all" on their ballots, but this was withdrawn by presidential decree on 6 November although it still appeared on the ballot paper (*Rossiiskaya gazeta*, 11 November 1993, 4).

The mixture of electoral systems made the value of a vote variable. Proportional representation meant that individuals casting ballots for a party list could secure representation in the State Duma as long as the party that they voted for won at least 5 percent of the vote, the minimum needed to share in the distribution of proportional representation seats. The first-past-the-post rule for gaining a single-member seat, by contrast, produced a large number of wasted votes. Differences between constituencies in the number of electors introduced another form of distortion.

The single-member constituencies were supposed to satisfy three requirements: each of the eighty-nine units of the federation was to have at least one; each of the constituencies was to consist of a unified territorial area; and there was to be no more than 15 percent variation in the number of voters between constituencies within each of the Russian regions and republics (*Polozhenie* 1993). This third condition was not always met. The normal number of voters in each constituency was set at 470,000; but in the Astrakhan region, for instance, there were 737,800, while in the Evenk autonomous area in northern Siberia the total electorate was only 13,800. The ten sparsely populated autonomous areas—such as the Koryaks, with 24,600 electors, and the Nenets, with 32,500 electors—did best out of the allocation of seats. Constituencies in large cities and in central Russia, by contrast, were usually of average or slightly above-average size (Treivish 1993; the constituencies were listed, with the size of their electorates, in *Izvestiya*, 13 October 1993, 4, and 14 October 1993, 4). In the Federation Council there were necessarily big variations because the council represented administrative units, not individuals of voting age. Hence there were an equal number of seats for the Evenks and Koryaks with their tens of thousands of electors, and for Moscow and St. Petersburg, with their millions.

The Campaign

At all stages there was an atmosphere of improvisation as officials, parties, and candidates sought to cope with an unrealistically tight schedule amid the uncertainties of a turbulent political situation. The election campaign was low key, given the short time available and most parties' and electoral alliances' lack of experience or organization. The unusually cold weather and the limited circulation of the national press meant that the candidates largely fought through television—available, by 1993, to 98.7 percent of Russian households; radio reached 95.9 percent, and the commercial networks 18.2 percent (Goskomstat 1993, 570; more general accounts of the December 1993 elections include Hough 1994; Hughes 1994; Lentini 1994a, 1994b, and 1995; Sakwa 1995; and Wyman et al. 1994, 1995).

In the aftermath of the "October events" there were worries in Russia and abroad that the elections might not be free and fair. Yeltsin's most obvious opponents, Parliamentary Chairman Khasbulatov and Vice-President Rutskoi, were under arrest. The opposition press was heavily handicapped when the Russian Ministry for the Press and Information banned a number of its publications, a decision for which it had no legal authority; *Pravda* reached a compromise with the ministry, but it reappeared only on 10 December, two days before the election; its nationalist-communist counterpart *Sovetskaya Rossiya* won a ruling that the ministry had acted unlawfully, but it was unable to resume publication until after the election. The parliament's own paper, *Rossiiskaya gazeta*, was taken over entirely by the Russian government.

There were big differences in resources between the various parties. Reflecting the support received from banks and private business, campaign expenditure by Russia's Choice was twice that of the next wealthiest party, the Liberal Democrats, and ten times that of the Communist Party (*Segodnya*, 28 December 1993, 11). President Yeltsin sought to allay some criticism by a decree of 29 October, "On informational guarantees for participants in the election campaign of 1993," which ordered Russian television and radio companies to provide an hour's free time to all the electoral associations during the three weeks before polling day and established a tribunal to resolve disputes (*Izvestiya*, 30 October 1993, 4). But it did not cover paid advertising or regional broadcasts, where there were wide divergences in spending. Russia's Choice, for instance, bought 180 minutes on the first television channel, twice as much as any other group (*Izvestiya*, 10 December 1993, 4). The Liberal Democrats bought more radio advertising than any other party, but the disproportionate share of editorial time in favor of Russia's Choice gave it the largest overall share (Lange 1994, 119).

The electoral regulations prescribed that each candidate for the single-member districts in the Duma would have the right to a single appearance on television and to a radio broadcast; the parties and electoral alliances were guaranteed at least an hour of free time on state television and radio during the three weeks before the election (*Polozhenie* 1993, Art. 28). Candidates and electoral alliances were granted an allocation of state funds and could in addition use their own funds and individual donations provided these did not exceed twenty times the minimum monthly wage in the single-member or thirty times in the party-list sections of the Duma. No donations were permitted from foreign states, organizations, or individuals, and an account had to be rendered not later than sixty days after the election (*Polozhenie* 1993, Art. 32). In the end, there was no simple relationship between spending and votes. Russia's Choice got the lowest electoral return on its investment (television appearances by the corpulent Gaidar were not always helpful), and the Agrarians, Communists, and Women of Russia all did well without spending any of their limited resources on commercials (*Segodnya*, 28 December 1993, 11; Pestrukhina 1994; slightly different figures appear in Lange 1994, 117).

During the campaign and on election day there were several independent attempts to monitor the fairness of the elections. The European Union, in the largest of these exercises, sent observers to seven different parts of the country to observe the campaign and the vote. While acknowledging that opposition parties had been given television time during the campaign, the observers noted plenty of bias. They deplored a program attacking Zhirinovsky, "the Hawk," broadcast by the premier television channel on the eve of the poll (and which may have backfired, boosting his appeal), and concluded that "pressure, particularly with regard to the draft constitution, was directly and indirectly applied by the government on all media." They concluded that the media's editorial coverage was "deeply flawed," not simply in terms of partisan bias but also in the "fundamental lack of analysis" and a "conspicuous unwillingness to challenge and question the assertions and policies of the candidates," particularly in the electronic media (Lange 1994, 39). Other studies agreed there had been "blatant bias" toward Russia's Choice on state television (Hughes 1994, 133–34).

In the campaign there were irregularities of many other kinds. Each party, for instance, had to gather 100,000 signatures from different parts of the country to secure a place on the party-list ballot. Some, such as the "August" bloc promoted by Konstantin Borovoi and his wealthy Party of Economic Freedom, found it impossible to do so in the time available; the strongly anti-Yeltsin Russian All-People's Union claimed that the police had raided its offices and stolen documents with 20,000 signatures in order to prevent it from participating (*Komsomolskaya pravda*, 9 November 1993, 1). Another would-be contender, the Christian Democrats, reported that their telephones had been cut off three days before the deadline for qualifying (*Izvestiya*, 9 November 1993, 2). Party organizers could sometimes buy signatures from passers-by; the price rose sharply as the deadline approached (*Izvestiya*, 6 November 1993, 2). Although the parties were meant to report their spending and keep within prescribed limits, some admitted that their real outlays were three or four times greater than the costs reported to the Central Electoral Commission, and "almost all" made use of sponsors paying advertising and other bills directly. The source of the funds on which the Liberal Democratic Party had drawn remained a mystery even after its accounts had been submitted (Pestrukhina 1994).

What kind of candidate were voters actually looking for? According to a survey in Moscow, St. Petersburg, and Yaroslavl, the ideal candidate was a man (64 percent) aged between 43 and 55 (53 percent) and with a higher education (70 percent). Occupation was less important, with 28 percent preferring a representative drawn from the business world and 23 percent a lawyer (*Argumenty i fakty*, no. 49, 1993, 2). Journalists found even more outspoken preferences. A pensioner told interviewers, "I really like Sobchak. He's always well dressed and clean shaven." A young kiosk saleswoman thought "Gaidar, Zyuganov, and Zhirinovsky [were] the sexiest"; a student, by contrast, thought Zhirinovsky would "talk too much" in bed and preferred Vladimir Shumeiko: "What shoulders—an athlete!" Another interviewee, a photographic model, preferred to go out with "normal people," but a young woman librarian was willing to accompany Yavlinsky or Shakhrai to the theater, Travkin to a football match, or Borovoi or Zatulin to a restaurant ("they have lots of money"). The candidate she described as the "most passionate," Ruslan Khasbulatov, was unfortunately sitting in Lefortovo jail.

The media published a variety of polls of public opinion during the campaign; publication, however, was banned during the last ten days of the campaign. A comparison between the figures published by the media and the election results makes clear that many were based on amateurish samples and methods that were unintentionally or knowingly biased or were circulated with more concern to influence the morale of campaigners and the result than to advance the cause of science. Moreover, the volatility of an "amateurish" electorate meant that there was great scope for voters to make choices at the last minute or to change their minds. At the outset of the campaign *Novaya ezhednevnaya gazeta* (5 November 1993, 3) led with an extravagant claim that Russia's Choice would take up to 50 percent of the vote. Other surveys claimed Russia's Choice would obtain at least 41 percent, with a further 33 percent supporting other reformist parties (*Argumenty i fakty*, no. 44, 1993, 2). In late November a poll showed Russia's Choice still had 29 percent of the electorate behind it, with just 3 percent supporting the Liberal Democrats (*Segodnya*, 25 November 1993, 1). In the last polls it was able to make public, the most authoritative of the survey organizations, the All-Russian Public Opinion Research Center, put Russia's Choice in the lead, with over 25 percent of the vote; the Liberal Democrats, by contrast, were in the "zone of defeat" with less than 3 percent (*Segodnya*, 30 November 1993, 1).

As late as 9 December, in an illegal eve-of-poll survey, *Ekspress-khronika* (10 December 1993, 1) reported that Russia's Choice "would win." The fragmentation of voters between parties and a high level of don't knows and nonvoters, however, meant that victory was forecast on the basis of the 15 percent that expressed a preference for Russia's Choice, with the Liberal Democrats second at 10 percent and the Communists third at 7 percent. The trend in the preelection polls prior to the imposition of the publication ban showed that the Liberal Democrats were gaining ground and Russia's Choice receding. A Western survey, conducted during the period of the ban, found a continuing trend toward the Liberal Democrats as polling day approached (Miller et al. 1996). The outcome was nonetheless a serious embarrassment for Russian pollsters. As two leading analysts wrote after the election, "we must honestly acknowledge that all the polling organizations were wrong, without exception" (Dmitriev and Toshchenko 1994, 46); the veteran pollster Boris Grushin called the whole exercise a "fiasco" (1994, 9; see also Shlapentokh 1994; Rose 1995b).

The Results

The elections saw a continuation of the trend of declining rates of participation in Russian elections. According to the official figures, just 54.8 percent of the registered electorate went to the polls, a far cry from the impossibly high 99.99 percent voting in the early 1980s, the 74.7 percent in the Russian presidential election of June 1991, or even the 64.6 percent in April 1993. Reduced turnout reflected a fall in the level of interest in politics of ordinary Russians and may also have reflected some uncertainty about how and whether to vote when confronted with completely new parties, institutions, and choices. All the party-list seats in the Duma were filled, but only 219 of the 225 single-member seats: there were no elections in the Chechen republic, no election could take place in the Naberezhnye Chelny constituency in Tatarstan because just a single candidate had been registered, and in four other constituencies in the republic the level of turnout was too low to validate a winner. In the elections to the Federation Council there was no voting, once again, in the Chechen republic; the Chelyabinsk region and Tatarstan failed to return any members, and the Yamal-Nenets autonomous area returned only one, because of insufficient turnout. Hence, only 171 of the 178 seats of the Council of the Federation were filled on 12 December.

Nonvoters, according to survey evidence, were twice as likely to live in cities of over a million as in rural areas and were twice as likely to be under thirty as over fifty-five; they were also more likely to be unemployed and to be women, and less likely to attend church (Wyman et al. 1994, 259). Turnout was also lower among those who owned their own businesses and among those who lived in the pro-Yeltsin Urals. By contrast, more than 70 percent of all pensioners voted, and those who were employed in the state sector were more likely to have voted than their counterparts in private industry (Sedov 1994, 29). These figures imply that parties differed in their capacity to mobilize their natural supporters. Students and the younger generation, normally more re-formist in sympathies, were less likely to vote than older electors, who have tended to be more in favor of the old regime (cf. Rose and Carnaghan 1995).

Nearly half the successful candidates in the single-member districts received less than 30 percent of the vote, and only a fifth secured an absolute majority. More generally, there were large votes "against all the candidates" (in some constituencies up to 17 percent) or spoiled papers (up to 7 percent of the total in some single-member constituencies) (*Segodnya*, 21 December 1993, 2). This made it easier to understand why President Yeltsin, in an amendment to the original regulations, had removed the requirements to report the vote "against all" and to pronounce the election valid only if the candidates had collectively secured a larger vote than the vote "against all" and not simply a 25 percent turnout (for the amendment, see *Rossiiskaya gazeta*, 11 November 1993, 4; the vote "against all" was nonetheless reported).

As the early results started coming in on election night it became clear that the Liberal Democratic Party had made a sensational breakthrough in the party-list section of the Duma, a breakthrough confirmed by the final results, which put Zhirinovsky's party first, Russia's Choice second, and the Communist Party third. Television programs that were to have covered the expected victory of the reformers had to be cut short as the outcome became increasingly embarrassing to the studio guests; "technical difficulties" were blamed as transmission ceased at 3:30 A.M., and distinguished guests at official receptions such as Al Gore, the vice-president of the United States, found they were attending a wake rather than a victory celebration. Gaidar's immediate reaction was that the reformers had suffered a "bitter defeat" (*Izvestiya*, 15 December 1993, 2). The next day a Moscow paper put it even more dramatically, warning that Russians had "woken up in a new state" after the "Communo-Fascists' success" (*Vechernyaya Moskva*, 13 December 1993, 1).

The success of Zhirinovsky came as a surprise to the great majority of political commentators, who traditionally concentrated on interpreting the politics of government and normally paid little attention to its opponents and the wider society. At the start of the election campaign, polls consistently indicated that the LDP would be lucky to get over the 5 percent threshold necessary to qualify for a share of the proportional representation seats, and Zhirinovsky's own standing was "close to zero" a month before the election. This implied that the campaign had given a big boost to the impudent nationalist (Klyamkin 1993, 40; similarly, Shokarev and Levinson 1994, 31; Wyman et al. 1995, 598; Miller et al. 1996). According to the survey evidence, Zhirinovsky's voters were the least committed of the major blocs: only a third had made up their minds to support the Liberal Democrats at the outset of the campaign and more than a third made their decision in the last week (*Segodnya*, 25 December 1993, 2). By contrast, more than twice as many Communist voters had made their choice before the start of the campaign (Shokarev and Levinson 1994, 33). The LDP vote, in fact, was boosted by exceptional circumstances. In particular, the authorities had excluded a number of groups connected with the "parliamentary insurrection" of September and October; and others, such as the Christian Democratic Movement and Sergei Baburin's Russian All-People's Union, had failed to collect enough signatures to secure a place on the PR ballot. The result of such exclusions was to concentrate the attention of those wanting to make a nationalist or antiregime choice on Zhirinovsky or, to a lesser extent, the Communists and Agrarians.

A close examination of the full returns shows a very different picture: no single party could be said to have won the election, as each of the ballots produced a very different outcome. Zhirinovsky's party came first among the electoral alliances, but it finished fifth in the single-member constituencies of the State Duma, where unaffiliated candidates won more than three times as many seats as the LDP.

By definition, the party-list system forces voters to choose a party, however weak their commitment. Yet in the December 1993 election, 7.5 percent of Russians spoiled their ballots or wrote that they opposed all 13 parties on the list. The "antiparty" share of the list vote thus ranked seventh among all the groups in table 6.2. Five parties or groupings failed to obtain any seats because they did not take 5 percent of the vote, the minimum required to participate in the sharing out of seats by proportional representation. Collectively, just under 9 percent of those voting for a party list were unrepresented in the State Duma. Stated positively, 91 percent of Russians voting for a party list saw some of their representatives returned to the Duma, a higher degree of proportionality than achieved in Spain and equal to that of Norway or Belgium. The distribution of the 225 party-list seats among the nine parties qualifying for a share was conducted without difficulty and in accord with strict rules of proportionality.

The election of representatives from single-member districts is a much stronger test of the capacity of parties to organize support nationwide. To secure a place on the party list, Russian parties needed

TABLE 6.2

ELECTIONS TO THE STATE DUMA, DECEMBER 1993

Party/bloc	PR party list			Single-member constituencies		Total seats	
	% votes	seats	% seats	seats	% seats	N	%
Russia's Choice	15.51	40	17.8	30	13.3	70	15.6
Liberal Democratic Party of Russia	22.92	59	26.2	5	2.2	64	14.2
Communist Party of the Russian Federation	12.40	32	14.2	16	7.1	48	10.7
Agrarian Party	7.99	21	9.3	12	5.3	33	7.3
Yabloko	7.86	20	8.9	3	1.3	23	5.1
Women of Russia	8.13	21	9.3	2	0.9	23	5.1
Party of Russian Unity and Concord	6.76	18	8.0	1	0.4	19	4.0
Democratic Party of Russia	5.52	14	6.2	1	0.4	15	3.3
Civic Union	1.93	—		1	0.4	1	0.2
Democratic Reform Movement	4.08	—		4	1.7	4	0.9
Dignity and Charity	0.70	—		2	0.9	2	0.4
Russia's Future–New Names	1.25	—		1	0.4	1	0.2
Cedar	0.76	—		—		—	—
Against all	4.36	—		—		—	—
Spoiled ballots	3.10	—		—		—	—
Independents	—	—		141	62.7	141	31.3
Postponed	—	—		6		6	
Total		225		225		450	

SOURCES: Based on *Rossiiskaya gazeta*, 28 December 1993, 1; *Byulleten' Tsentral'noi izbiratel'noi komissii Rossiiskoi Federatsii*, no. 12 (1994), 67.

to secure 100,000 valid signatures nationally. While nominations in the single-member districts required the signatures of 1 percent of voters in a constituency, about 4,000 to 5,000, to contest all 225 seats would have required nearly a million signatures. Even then, the candidate nominated would not appear on the ballot paper as a party standard-bearer, as the law on elections specified that such candidates were to be described by name, date of birth, occupation, and place of residence, but not by party affiliation (*Polozhenie* 1993). Furthermore, the ballot procedure meant that Moscow-based parties had to convince politicians of some standing locally that it was in their interest to promote a national party label rather than run a personal or local campaign. There was no shortage of candidates ready to stand in single-member seats; the average district had at least seven candidates. The deficiencies were on the side of the parties, for the most part Moscow-centered and often elitist. It was easier for parties to recruit individuals centrally to stand on a national list, which might mean campaigning from a Moscow television studio or party headquarters, than to recruit people who would campaign in the mud of the countryside or the snows of Siberia.

Well-organized parties can and do nominate candidates in hundreds of single-member constituencies. The Federal Republic of Germany is a particularly striking example, and the Russian electoral system, awarding half the seats by party list and half by single-member seats, is very similar in principle to its German counterpart. The difference is in the parties: the Christian Democrats, the Social Democrats, and smaller parties in Germany have no difficulty fielding hundreds of candidates nationwide, as they are well-established parties with tens of thousands of party workers. In the vastness of the United States, the Republican and Democratic parties virtually monopolize representation in the U.S. Congress. The American example is relevant to Russia inasmuch as it too emphasizes that politicians elected from single-member districts are not beholden to national party organizations, as is the case when the position assigned an individual on the party list is critical for victory or defeat.

In the single-member contests, it was candidates independent of all parties who won the biggest share of the vote (table 6.2). Russia's Choice showed some capacity to generate support nationwide; it came in second in the number of single-member seats won, doing almost as well there as in the party-list ballot. The Communists came in third in single-member seats won, but took only half as many as in the PR ballot. Helped by their rural focus, Agrarian candidates were able to win a dozen seats. The most revealing failure in the single-member districts was the showing of the Liberal Democrats; Zhirinovsky could only claim that five of his candidates were able to come in first in districts where their own names and reputations rather than the television appearances of the party leader were most important.

Overall, a "nonparty," the independents, were the big winner of the State Duma election, taking almost a third of the seats, more than twice the number of seats won by Russia's Choice, which finished second. The Liberal Democratic Party did well enough in the party-list vote to finish third in aggregate, although its 14 percent share of the seats was far less impressive than the "sensational gains" headlined by the media on the basis of its unexpected lead in the party-list ballot. The organized support of the Communist Party across the country enabled it to finish fourth in total seats.

The ballot in the Federation Council again produced a very different result. The election of council members appeared similar in form to the election of Duma members from single-member constituencies—in both cases, candidates were not allowed to identify their party on the ballot, and seats were allocated on a first-past-the-post basis to the two highest-ranking candidates. The strategy of nomination was very different in the two elections. For positions in the Duma, an average of more than half a dozen candidates contested each seat, whereas for the Federation Council there were usually only two or three candidates for the two seats. Voters, in practice, were not asked whom they wanted to represent the republic or region, but which of three candidates should not become a representative or whether, in ways reminiscent of earlier elections, they simply wanted to protest against candidates who would anyway be elected. The vote for the Federation Council was in effect a "no party" contest, in which candidates stood on local or regional or personal grounds.

Elections to the eighty-nine constituencies in the Federation Council produced different clusters of parties and groups. Councillors describing themselves as independents, as in the Duma, were the largest group. Their numbers were augmented by almost a third of councillors who labeled themselves according to broad or vague tendencies, such as "centrist opposition" or "moderate reformers," thus preserving their flexibility of bargaining with parties of all sorts in Moscow. Russia's Choice was exceptional in doing better in the Federation Council than in the Duma elections, perhaps a reflection of the belief of local leaders that it would have most influence in the new government. Equally, local leaders were more likely to have been nominated by President Yeltsin and were therefore more likely than candidates for the Duma to support the parties that favored his policies. The Liberal Democrats, by contrast, were unable to elect a single representative.

Were the results authentic? Election officials could also point to the presence of observers from more than fifty foreign states and financial help from abroad, including $10 million from the U.S. government to improve electoral administration (*Izvestiya*, 26 October 1993, 1). Foreign observers gave only qualified endorsement to the work of the Central Electoral Commission, particularly noting its inability to report results at the local and polling station levels. The Central Electoral Commission claimed that its inability to release comprehensive results, as is done in Western nations, was due to "logistical and practical" considerations (Barnes 1994, 6). The commission also complained that it was given less than half the staff it needed to deal adequately with its novel and massive organizational tasks. The fact that a presidential decree on 20 December 1993 made the commission a permanent body was cited by opponents as evidence that it might be likely to favor the Yeltsin administration and the parties that supported it.

Given the critical importance of securing a 50 percent turnout for the adoption of the constitution, its opponents raised questions about whether the actual turnout had cleared that barrier, as the reported turnout did (see chapter 5). The way the count was organized was almost bound to lead to mistakes, concluded Western analysts, because for the first time in Russian history district electoral committees did not exist, leaving each of the higher-level election authorities to deal with the returns from up to 3,500 different polling stations. The Central Electoral Commission received more than 95,000 sets of results, and many of these were incomplete or incorrect. Press reports indicated serious irregularities in a number of areas. For instance, in the Archangel region, the 434 electors on the Solovetsky Islands had managed to cast a total of 1,604 votes (Anokhin 1994); in another case, in Moscow, large numbers of deceased "voters" were recorded as living in a building once inhabited by Nikolai Gogol, author of the classic *Dead Souls* (Kagarlitsky 1995, 4). The supervisor of a polling station in Moscow committed suicide, leaving behind a letter in which he confessed he had "grossly deceived the people" (Tolz and Wishnevsky 1994, 2).

By law, the results for the State Duma and Federation Council were meant to be published within a month of the ballot. In fact, results were not published until more than two months after the event; and when they appeared in a communication to the new parliament and then in the bulletin of the Central Electoral Commission, they were incomplete. There was no reference to the number of ballots cast "against all" even though a national total was provided. In single-member districts, the only figure given was the number of votes cast for the candidate declared the winner; no figures were given for any of the other candidates. Kronid Lyubarsky, a journalist with the weekly paper *Novoe vremya* and himself a candidate, was one of the first to make a fuss. In his own constituency, No. 110 in the Moscow region, the only figure reported was the total vote for the winner, General Stolyarov, who obtained 12 percent of the recorded turnout; Lyubarsky was unable to find out how well he had done himself (1994b). Results for the party-list ballot were officially reported at the national level and for the country's eighty-nine administrative units, aggregates with an average of more than a million electors each. They were not reported by lower-level units of analysis, such as the polling station, ward, city, or subregion, thus making it impossible to check allegations of manipulating vote totals where they had first been counted; and the papers themselves were destroyed some months afterward. Our own analysis is based on a preliminary set of data produced on 21 December 1993 for the presidential administration (*Predvaritelnye* 1993) and the official but less complete returns published in the bulletin of the Central Electoral Commission (*Byulleten*, no. 1 [12], 1994, 34–80).

Undoubtedly, there were many minor errors in the hastily organized conduct of an election by amateurs unaccustomed to organizing a competitive ballot. Reports of Western observers could not be conclusive evidence, however, for no one individual or team could cover more than a handful of polling stations on election day. Moreover, it was the count that was decisive, not the conduct of the voting, and no observers were allowed into the headquarters of the Central Electoral Commission as the final count was being tallied (*The Times*, 18 December 1993, 15). Past history would support allegations that errors were not random, as officials sought once again to show their commitment by "improving" the results by increasing support for officially approved candidates. But it was not always clear which party or candidate carried the official imprimatur, and particularly in single-member seats and the Federation Council, local interests could differ from interests in Moscow. Insofar as false reporting occurred, the official results are likely to have overestimated support for the governing parties and understated opposition.

In an attempt to deal with allegations of fraud, a commission was set up under the auspices of the presidential administration headed by Alexander Sobyanin, a physicist associated with Russia's Choice. Since there were more than 100 million electors and almost 100,000 polling stations, it was impossible for the committee to investigate all allegations in detail. Instead, Sobyanin developed a mathematical model to impute turnout in each administrative unit, given its socioeconomic characteristics. In addition, he produced a statistical model that predicted what the vote for each party ought to have been on the basis of assumptions that he made about the relationship between socioeconomic characteristics and voting behavior. Sobyanin then proceeded to treat the results of his statistical model as if they were the actual expression of mass behavior.

The results reported by the Electoral Commission were then compared with the "true" vote as imputed by Sobyanin. Sobyanin assumed that deviations were evidence of electoral malpractice. On this basis, it was concluded that only 46 percent of the registered electorate had voted, almost 9 percent less than the official turnout. Assuming that statistical estimates were totally accurate also gave Russia's Choice about 2 million more votes than were reported on the party list ballot. Even more striking, the report argued that Zhirinovsky's Liberal Democrats had secured up to 6 million "extra" votes thanks to electoral malpractices (*Vek,* no. 18, 1994, 3; *Segodnya,* 10 March 1994, 10). The gaps between statistical estimates and the official results were attributed to three types of fraud: an increase in the total number of votes cast in order to push turnout over the 50 percent mark necessary to validate the constitutional ballot; adding votes to parties favored by election officials; and subtracting votes from parties they opposed (Vyzhutovich 1994).

The allegations of Sobyanin were challenged on many sides (see, for instance, *Moskovskie novosti,* no. 29, 1994, 6). Methodologically, the procedure was faulty because no statistical model can ever be 100 percent accurate; there is always a degree of random fluctuation in the patterns observed. Moreover, Sobyanin relied on a classic, quasi-Marxist materialist determinism in assuming that socioeconomic influences determined the party choices. As chapter 7 will demonstrate, they were of secondary importance by comparison with political opinions and values. Politically, the calculations were implausible because they appeared to show that public officials had worked against the parties of government, especially Russia's Choice, and also the party which many had formerly belonged to, the Communist Party. There was alleged to be a massive conspiracy among government officials to help the most antigovernment party, the Liberal Democrats, by padding its electoral support in every polling station.

The Central Electoral Commission insisted there were "no grounds for doubting the voting results," and pointed out that relatively few disputes taken to court had confirmed irregularities. They also rejected some of Sobyanin's original and more specific charges. Sobyanin's involvement in party politics led opposition parties to dismiss the conclusions of his committee as the self-serving charges of an interested party (Kostyukov 1994). Even if irregularities existed at the lowest level, they could only influence hundreds of votes, and insofar as they were due to amateurism or incompetence, errors would tend to cancel out. The systematic organization of a nationwide conspiracy on behalf of one or more parties, especially antigovernment parties, was inherently improbable, given that the election had been monitored by more than 50,000 representatives of all parties and thousands of candidates.

The official certification of the outcome, confirming the new constitution as in place and naming individuals who could claim seats in parliament, preceded the publication of the final results. There was no incentive for the winners to launch an investigation of deficiencies in the process that had given them what they wanted. If the constitution had not been adopted in a valid manner, the deputies themselves would have been deprived of their mandate and their decisions would have lost all legal force, and former Vice-President Rutskoi, Ruslan Khasbulatov, and the other leaders of the "October events," who had been amnestied by parliament in February 1994, would return to prison. Equally, the presidential administration could hardly wish to be deprived of a constitution it had devised in order to establish a strong executive. And in any case, the new Duma was a transitional one—it would hold office for just two years. For all the contenders it was increasingly the new Duma, which would be elected in December 1995 for a normal four-year term, that became the main electoral preoccupation.

✽ 7 ✽

Mobilizing Demobilized Russians

In a civic culture voters not only have a choice between parties but also believe that the party with which they identify can be trusted to represent their views in government (Almond and Verba 1963, 123ff.). In Lipset and Rokkan's (1967) classic formulation of the emergence of a modern party system, leaders of major social institutions—churches, business associations, trade unions, anticlerical groups, and so forth —could draw on the trust of their members to organize support for political parties. The outcome was the mobilization of large numbers of citizens in support of democratic norms.

But what happens if voters distrust parties? In France a tradition of *incivisme* reflected circumstances in which many electors had an antiparty mentality (see Converse and Dupeux 1966). In such circumstances an election may be democratic in the sense of offering voters a choice between competing elites. When the choice is between distrusted parties, however, an election is only a choice between greater and lesser evils. Individuals can vote to turn out one group of rascals but the only result is that another group of rascals gains power. Free elections remain valid even if there is a "missing middle" of trusted parties, but the outcome is not representative government as this term is understood in established democracies.

For seventy years, party politics in the Soviet Union was the politics of the Communist Party. Socialization by the party occurred in school and in party-sponsored youth organizations. Having a party card was often necessary to secure a good job, enter a profession, or gain promotion. It also brought material benefits. The party articulated the "objective" truth of Marxism-Leninism. And while Marxist-Leninist doctrines were subject to frequent reinterpretation, they were never subject to a popular referendum or a free election. Critical decisions about government were made by the *nomenklatura*, based on a practice of "democratic centralism" that was far more centralist than democratic.

The Communist Party used its organizational network to control the major institutions of government and prevent the creation of the independent institutions of civil society. In Stalin's days, a high priority was given to the ruthless elimination of organizations that might challenge party authority. Trade unions were turned into communist satellites; the press, book publishers, and broadcasters became mouthpieces for the party line; churches were subject to subtle and not so subtle controls. Its domination of institutions was consistent with the party's totalitarian ideology. As the inquisitor proclaimed in Arthur Koestler's *Darkness at Noon*, "There is no salvation outside the party." Ironically, one of the clearest results of communist rule was to discredit the idea of party itself. When Russians are asked to state their level of trust for different institutions in society, political parties are almost invariably at the bottom. In the 1993 New Russia Barometer, only 6 percent of Russians indicated positive trust in parties, and the average level of distrust was the highest among all sixteen institutions surveyed (see table 3.3).

The unvarying insistence on supporting the party-state in the Soviet Union had the similarly perverse effect of demobilizing voters. Ritual conformity and apathy were widespread. Attending church or listening to rock music were minor forms of dissent, involving identification with institutions and values that the party scorned. Intellectuals could become internal émigrés, concentrating on abstruse questions of no concern to party commissars such as pure mathematics or the musicology of the Italian Renaissance. Dissident groups could discuss ideas contrary to party doctrines—provided that the group was small enough to prevent infiltration by the KGB. Private expressions of dissent could be tolerated by the authorities as long as they did not take the form of public challenges (Shlapentokh 1989).

Many Russians reacted to such pressures by becoming "negatively integrated" in the political system, and this legacy remains in postcommunist Russia. As chapter 3 made clear, the great majority of Russians see major gains in freedom from the communist effort to mobilize and control their everyday lives. It is particularly significant that one of the major gains in freedom is the right to decide for oneself whether or not to take an interest in politics. Whereas voting for a single slate of party-approved candidates was compulsory in a totalitarian election, in a civil society freedom can take the form of not having to vote at all (see Fish 1995; Rose 1995e).

Negative integration also means that the state is not subject to influence by ordinary citizens. When the New Russia Barometer asked whether the influence of ordinary people on government is greater today than under the old regime, only 8 percent said it was and 27 percent thought they had less influence than in a regime that denied free elections and most civil liberties. The largest group, almost two-thirds of the total, thought their influence on government was no more and no less than it had been under communist rule.

Russian distrust of new institutions of government is much greater than in other postcommunist countries (see figure 7.1). In every political system, including established Western democracies, there is always a significant number of citizens who believe they cannot do much to influence government (Dalton 1996; Hayes and Bean 1993). In a country as vast as the United States, an individual's lack of a sense of political efficacy may simply reflect the problems facing a single individual in an ocean of 250 million Americans. In postcommunist countries, the important point is comparison between the old and new regimes. In Central and Eastern Europe, twice to four times as many people feel better able to influence government today than in Russia, and few feel their political influence has diminished. The contrast with Russia is stark.

Given that the starting point of the Russian electorate is distrust of the party-state, we would predict that most Russians would not identify with political parties, that the minority who identified would have a weak attachment to a party, and that most Russians would use the multiballot electoral system to split their tickets between candidates for different parties or independents. These predictions are tested in the first section. A lack of party identification does not mean a lack of political values or a passive consensus about values. Given multiple parties, the motives of voting for parties are likely to be heterogeneous. The predicted influences are likely to include differences in how voters evaluate the performance of the old regime and that of the current regime, economic well-being, and social structure location. The second section examines the influences that lead Russians to support different parties. The concluding section shows the extent to which parties draw voters who agree in their evaluation of the old communist regime and the new competitive party system.

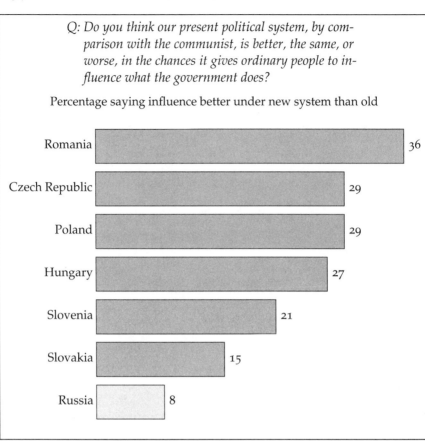

Q: Do you think our present political system, by comparison with the communist, is better, the same, or worse, in the chances it gives ordinary people to influence what the government does?

Percentage saying influence better under new system than old

FIGURE 7.1
OPPORTUNITY FOR ORDINARY PEOPLE
TO INFLUENCE GOVERNMENT

SOURCES: Paul Lazarsfeld Society, New Democracies Barometer III (1994); Centre for the Study of Public Policy/Paul Lazarsfeld Society, New Russia Barometer III (1994). See Rose 1995d, 464 ff.; and Rose and Haerpfer 1994b.

The Absence of Party Identification

Classic American studies of voting have argued that an individual's party identification is critical for voting. The formation of party identification in turn reflects a lengthy process of political socialization begun in childhood. Second, party identification remains stable over a long period of time. Third, party identification is separate from the act of voting, for even if a person does not vote in an election, he or she can still identify with a party. Party identification is a filter through which individuals view the political world; "in the competition of voices reaching the individual the political party is an opinion-forming agency of great importance" (Campbell et al. 1960, 128).

In an established democracy, a majority of voters have sufficient trust in a party to identify with it. Stable partisans are a ballast in the electoral system, preventing extreme swings between parties and the entry of "flash" parties promoting popular but impossible goals or achievable but undemocratic actions. Without the anchor of partisanship, we would expect volatility in popular support and instability in the names, leaders, and platforms of the competing parties.

In the United States and Britain, seven-eighths or more of the electorate identify to some extent with a political party (see table 7.1). By contrast, in Russia more than three-quarters of the electorate lack any party identification. Even though party loyalties are being challenged by new parties and independent movements in Western nations, four times as many Britons and Americans identify with a political party as do Russians. The percentage of Americans who strongly identify with the Republican or Democratic parties is greater than the number of Russians who have even a weak party identification, and in Britain a similar pattern is found.

The low aggregate level of identification can be explained by the fact that every party except the Communist Party is a new party; most

TABLE 7.1

PARTY IDENTIFICATION IN RUSSIA, THE UNITED STATES,
AND BRITAIN

	Russia	United States	Britain
Identifies with party			
Very close	4%	28%	19%
Somewhat close	9	33	44
Not very close	9	27	29
Total identifiers	22	87	92
Does not identify with party	78	13	8

SOURCES: Russia: Centre for the Study of Public Policy/Paul Lazarsfeld Society, New Russia Barometer III (1994). United States: Stanley and Niemi 1994, 158, table 5.1. Britain: British Election Study (1992).

were founded in an election year and some only to fight the election (cf. table 6.1). Furthermore, they were not linked with organizations that had their roots in civil society, as there had been no opportunity for a civil society to develop during the period of Soviet rule. The parties were led by politicians whose names and faces had been appearing on television for months, not decades. In such circumstances, what distinguishes the fifth of Russians who do identify with a political party?

In the United States and Western Europe, party identification is assumed to correlate with attitudes favoring democracy itself. In Russia, the opposite is the case. Figure 7.2 shows that the significant influences on party identification include authoritarianism, Communist Party

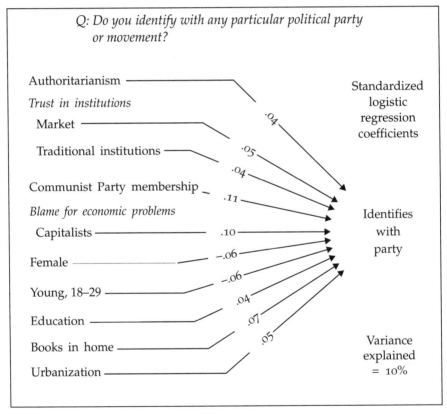

FIGURE 7.2
WHO IDENTIFIES WITH PARTIES?

SOURCE: Centre for the Study of Public Policy/Paul Lazarsfeld Society, New Russia Barometer III (1994).

membership, blaming capitalists, and trust in traditional institutions. Social structure has a secondary influence. More educated people and those who read books are more likely to have a party identification, which is consistent with findings in established democracies. Party identifiers are also likely to be older, as the development of partisanship is cumulative through a lifetime.

Party identification varies substantially between parties. The Communist Party, the only legal party in the Soviet Union up to 1990, has the highest proportion of committed identifiers. NRB III found that 59 percent who voted Communist in 1993 also identified with the party. This level of identification is more than double the 25 percent of Yabloko voters who identified with their newly formed party. Among the parties claiming to represent an established social group, 36 percent of Agrarian voters also identified with it, significantly more than the 25 percent that identified with Women of Russia as well as voting for it. The relatively clear ideology of Russia's Choice, emphasizing promarket reforms, did not produce a sense of identification: only 32 percent expressed any persisting attachment. Similarly, only 35 percent of those voting for Zhirinovsky's Liberal Democrats had any degree of identification with that party.

The demobilization of the Russian electorate means that most people are not partisans in the Western sense and the majority are to a significant degree "antiparty" (see figure 7.3). The largest group in the electorate are *uncommitted, untrusting voters,* individuals who name a party they will vote for, but do not identify with it and do not trust parties in general. This group constitutes two-fifths of the Russian electorate. An additional third are *antiparty nonvoters;* they distrust parties and do not name a party for which they would vote. Because they abstain, the influence of the antiparty electors is felt only indirectly at the ballot box. But insofar as democracy requires a positive commitment from the great mass of the citizenry, the absence of commitment to a party by almost three-quarters of the electorate is a serious limitation on the capacity of the Russian government to mobilize popular support for its actions or to claim to represent the mass of citizens.

The result is that Russian elections do not register popular commitment to the parties that are elected. The civic-minded voter who identifies with a party and trusts parties is in a small minority. Only 2 percent of the electorate are *strongly committed partisans,* trusting parties in general and identifying with the party for which they vote. An additional 20 percent are *committed partisans,* who identify with the party for which they vote but do not trust parties in general.

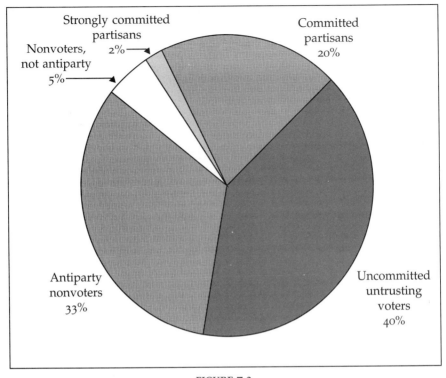

FIGURE 7.3

DEMOBILIZED VOTERS PREDOMINATE IN THE ELECTORATE

SOURCE: Centre for the Study of Public Policy/Paul Lazarsfeld Society, New Russia Barometer III (1994).

NOTE: *Strongly committed partisans* have party identification, name party vote, and trust parties.

Committed partisans have party identification, name party vote, and do not trust parties.

Uncommitted untrusting voters have no party identification, name party vote, and do not trust parties.

Antiparty nonvoters have no party identification, will not vote, and do not trust parties.

Nonvoters, not antiparty, have party identification, will not vote, and trust parties.

Split-ticket voting is another indication of weak party attachment. In the United States, where voters are asked to make choices for a multiplicity of offices at federal elections, between 13 and 30 percent of voters have split their ticket between Republican and Democratic candidates for the presidency, the House of Representatives, and the Senate in elections since 1952. Since 1976, an average of exactly one-quarter of the electorate have split their tickets at national elections (Stanley and Niemi 1994, table 4.7; McAllister and Darcy 1992), and a similar proportion have split their tickets in votes for the House of Representatives and the Senate. In Britain, by contrast, ticket-splitting is impossible because voters cast a single vote for a candidate seeking to be the sole representative of a parliamentary constituency.

In the December 1993 election, each Russian voter was offered both party-list and single-member ballots for seats in the State Duma and a ballot for representatives in the Federation Council as well. Differences in ballot forms and nomination practices encouraged split-ticket voting. Whereas a party vote was mandatory in the proportional representation list ballot, in the single-member districts of the Duma and in the Federation Council the ballot did not identify candidates with any party, and in a confused political situation many candidates preferred to run as independents making a personal or local appeal, rather than identify themselves with a Moscow-based party elite.

Ticket-splitting was the norm in the election. A survey by the Public Opinion Research Center (VTsIOM) shortly before election day found that among those who said they knew how they would vote, 70 percent were planning to vote for different parties—or for a party and an independent candidate—in the two ballots for the State Duma, and an additional 11 percent said they would vote for different parties at the Duma and Federation Council level (see figure 7.4). Only 19 percent indicated they would vote a straight party ticket, virtually the same proportion as those who identify with a party. The level of split-ticket voting in Russia in 1993 is thus about three times higher than that normally found in an American presidential election. Paradoxically, the greatest degree of political consistency is shown by individuals who do not vote, as they have no opportunity to scatter preferences among parties and independents. When the partisan inclinations of the electorate as a whole are examined, the proportion of Russians ready to vote, and to vote for only one party on election day, drops to 11 percent.

The preeminence of demobilized voters goes a long way to explain why Russian opinion polls cannot produce a good guide to election outcomes a few months or even weeks before an election is held (Rose

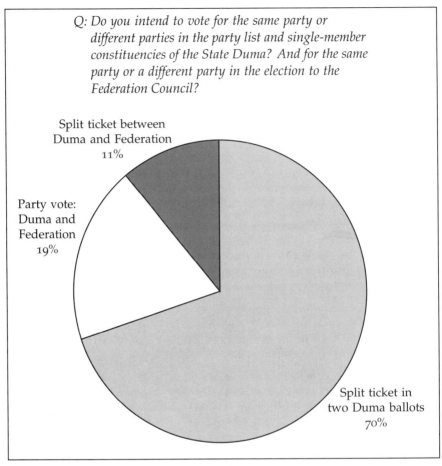

Q: *Do you intend to vote for the same party or different parties in the party list and single-member constituencies of the State Duma? And for the same party or a different party in the election to the Federation Council?*

Split ticket between Duma and Federation 11%

Party vote: Duma and Federation 19%

Split ticket in two Duma ballots 70%

FIGURE 7.4
SPLIT-TICKET VOTING PERVASIVE

SOURCE: VTsIOM, December 1993.

NOTE: N = 1,303. Estimates are for voters only and were derived by cross-classifying responses to two questions listed above.

1995b; cf. Gibson 1994a; Shlapentokh 1994; White 1995). When a large majority of Russian voters do not identify with a party, the standard question, "For which party would you vote if an election were held this Sunday?" has little meaning. Since most Russians who volunteer an answer name a party with which they do not identify, the critical element is not the name of the preferred party but the proximity of an election. Since most Sundays are not election days, the typical poll produces an ephemeral response to a nonevent.

The fragmentation of parties further limits the value of opinion polls as forecasting instruments. In almost every Russian survey asking questions about party preference, including the New Russia Barometers, the largest single bloc of electors is the don't knows. Typically, the don't knows run at 40 percent of the electorate, more than twice the percentage likely to vote for the leading party. The remaining three-fifths of the electorate is divided among more than a dozen different parties, giving the average party 5 percent of the support of the electorate. The don't knows are thus about eight times as numerous as the average party.

If don't knows were stable—which is not the case—their views could be ignored and excluded from reports of opinion poll results. But the transient nature of don't knows means that some will vote, if only to oppose a particular party or candidate. Even more likely to destabilize projections is the fact that the majority of those who state a preference do not identify with a party. The horse-race character of media coverage of an election campaign compounds problems by making a party that is the weak and temporary preference of a tenth of the electorate appear to be the "winner."

Who Supports Which Party?

In a one-party system, political lines are clearly drawn. Because elections are irrelevant, everyone in party politics must work within the one party that controls the state. Dissidents also recognize the supremacy of the ruling party; breaking its monopoly of power is their primary goal, and opposition gives dissidents a degree of unity. The conflict between the Communist Party and dissidents in Central and Eastern Europe was often framed in "a language of philosophic and moral absolutes, of right against wrong, love against hate, truth against falsehood" (Garton Ash 1990, 51f). In Russia, the conflict was within the Communist Party and then between president and parliament. In each case, raw power decided the outcome.

The openness of choice after generations of monolithic party rule places both politicians and voters in a quandary. Voters can respond by not voting, but politicians who respond by leaving politics pass to their successors the problem of deciding what parties offer the electorate. The register of political associations in Russia in the 1990s is overwhelmingly a list of failures. Hundreds of groups have gained legal recognition, but only thirteen parties secured a place on the party-list ballot in December 1993 and only eight were successful in winning seats; the other parties failed to win sufficient votes to qualify for seats in the Duma and split, merged, or simply dwindled away.

Some of the classic Lipset-Rokkan dimensions of party competition are completely absent in postcommunist Russia. Unlike Britain, where Scots, Welsh, and a variety of Northern Ireland nationalists compete and sometimes win seats in parliament, no ethnic minority party was visible in the 1993 Russian election. The breakup of the Soviet Union saw to that. The Liberal Democrats were the nearest equivalent to a nationalist party, as Vladimir Zhirinovsky used Russian nationalist rhetoric. Nor did any party make an explicit religious or antireligious appeal, and only Zhirinovsky made anti-Semitic remarks in public. New Russia Barometer III shows this is consistent with public opinion, as Jews rank next to last among sixteen groups that are sometimes blamed for the country's economic problems (see table 3.4). In debates about the economy, Russia's Choice was the party most clearly committed to the introduction of the market in Russia. In view of the costs associated with economic transformation, many political parties pressed for state action to protect people against the disadvantages of the market while promising to keep its benefits. The Agrarian Party was distinctive in making an appeal to a clearly defined economic and geographical constituency, and Women of Russia appealed to a distinctive gender group.

In theory, a charismatic leader could mobilize a large popular following to support a new regime, democratic or otherwise, and such leaders have emerged in Latin America, fascist Europe, and some of the other communist states. At the inception of the new Russian Federation, President Yeltsin could lay some claim to this status, as he had challenged the power of the Communist Party of the Soviet Union at the ballot box in June 1991 and led the resistance to the attempted coup two months later. At the December 1993 election, however, there was no Yeltsin party. Unlike General de Gaulle in the Fifth French Republic, Yeltsin preferred to play off factions and interests against each other rather than create his own following. Only two parties were organized around the personalities of their leaders: Yabloko, led by Grigorii Ya-vlinsky, and the very different Liberal Democratic Party of Vladimir Zhirinovsky.

A unique feature of the communist legacy is competition between parties about which can restore the most popular features of the old regime or protect the people against the most disliked features of the new. The Communist Party of the Russian Federation has a unique claim to defend the old regime, as it is the lineal heir of the former Communist Party of the Soviet Union. Unlike Italy, where the breakup of the Communist Party has led to some competition between parties to claim the legacy of the "achievements" of communism, in Russia only one party has emerged as a substantial force identified with that cause. This is its weakness too, for such an identification means that it cannot gain votes from those who believe that there was nothing good about the past. Russia's Choice and Yabloko have promoted themselves as parties that are critical of authoritarian communist practices and strongly in favor of individual rights and a civil society. In the case of Russia's Choice, the protection of individual political rights is combined with an emphasis on individuals promoting their own interests in the marketplace. Yabloko has been less clear-cut about economic policies. Many other parties have viewed both the authoritarian past and present-day reforms in an ambivalent manner.

In postcommunist societies, the identification of party cleavages is both experimental and empirical. It is experimental as politicians leading new political groups can formulate an image from a very wide array of alternatives, for example, whether to project a clear image that would attract some voters and repel others or a "catchall" image that seeks to appeal to everyone, if not very clearly or strongly (see Kitschelt 1995). Party leaders decide which audiences they are targeting, what they say, and how to run their campaigns.

Parties differ in their success in mobilizing votes from groups defined by social characteristics, by economic conditions, or by political attitudes. Here, we test the influence on votes for six parties that came highest in the party-list ballot for the State Duma. Together, the Liberal Democrats, Russia's Choice, Communists, Agrarian Party, Yabloko, and Women of Russia took three-quarters of that vote and more than five-sixths of the party-list seats. A total of thirty-one different influences —political, economic, and social—are introduced into multivariate equations concerning party preferences. Figure 7.5 shows the extent to which a party's voters differed from the national average on characteristics that are statistically significant influences. Appendix table B.1

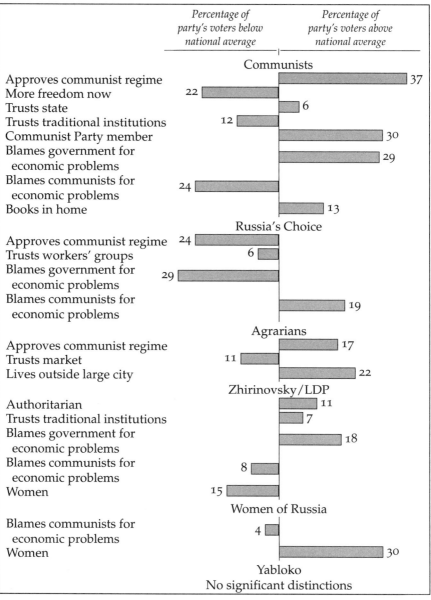

FIGURE 7.5
DISTINCTIVENESS OF VOTERS FOR EACH PARTY

SOURCE: Centre for the Study of Public Policy/Paul Lazarsfeld Society, New Russia Barometer III (1994).

NOTE: The figures give all the statistically significant variables on the party's vote in a logit regression; cf. appendix table C.1.

gives the average value for each potential influence among the electorate as a whole; appendix table C.1 lists in detail all the statistically significant and insignificant influences on voting for the six largest parties.

Voters for the *Communist Party* were much more influenced by political values than by organizational membership. While Communist voters were disproportionately likely to have been members of the Communist Party of the Soviet Union, many who belonged to the old party did not vote for its successor in the Russian Federation. It tended to receive the votes of individuals who not only belonged to the party but also believed in much that the party stood for. In their household economic circumstances, Communist voters were not significantly different from a cross-section of the population. But whatever their level of formal education, the party's voters tended to be more bookish than the average.

Support for *Russia's Choice* was based solely on political values, not economic circumstances or social structure. Its voters disproportionately rejected the communist regime and blamed it for the country's problems. The partisanship of Russia's Choice voters was apparent in their readiness to say that the new government, with which party leader Gaidar was identified, was not to blame for the country's economic problems. Consistent with support for the market, Russia's Choice voters were also inclined to distrust workers' groups.

The supporters of Vladimir Zhirinovsky's *Liberal Democratic Party* were distinctive in their preference for authoritarian alternatives rather than a government based on free elections. They were more likely to blame the current government than the Communists for economic problems and to trust traditional institutions. LDP voters were also disproportionately male. In view of the extreme character of Zhirinovsky's appeals, it is also important to emphasize what his voters did *not* endorse. An initial statistical analysis included a host of measures of aggressive and nationalist attitudes, such as spending more on the armed forces, retaining nuclear weapons, believing that Russia was threatened from abroad and that Russian nationals in the other former Soviet republics should be protected, readiness to use force in the near abroad, and commitment to Slav traditions. Some of these nationalist attitudes were expected to influence support for Zhirinovsky. In fact, none was significant. This suggests that the Liberal Democratic vote was a nonideological protest vote. Those with nationalist views were not a bloc, nor did they support any one party.

As its name suggests, the *Agrarian Party* drew support disproportionately from rural areas and small towns, rather than big cities. Politically, its voters were likely to favor the former communist regime and to distrust the market. They were defending the interests of collective farms and those who depend on collective farms and opposed to individuals farming on their own account.

Although feminist pressure groups exist in most established democracies, a party claiming to represent the interests of women, such as *Women of Russia,* is exceptional on the European scene. Its name reflects its electoral appeal: more than four-fifths of its voters were women. Its supporters lacked virtually any other distinctive characteristic, however, as they were not different in their economic views and were only marginally different in not blaming Communists for the country's economic difficulties. Since more than half the Russian electorate is female and Women of Russia secured only 8 percent of the party list vote, the party could not claim to represent Russian women; five-sixths of Russian women endorsed other parties.

Up to a point, *Yabloko* succeeded in appealing to voters for all kinds of reasons, as none of the social, economic, and political variables we measured had any significant influence on its vote. Grigorii Yavlinsky was relatively popular, or at least less unpopular than the leaders of other parties. One reason for its diffuse but limited support may have been that Yabloko was not identified with either the old communist regime or the more recent reforms led by Russia's Choice.

Representative government assumes that political parties reflect the interests and values of an identifiable segment of the electorate. Insofar as each party's voters are cohesive, sharing a number of attitudes and interests, a party can claim to speak for a particular section of the society. The large number of parties in Russia makes it easier for a party to represent a distinctive bloc: the smaller the party, the easier it is for its supporters to be alike in their political values, economic conditions, and social structural characteristics.

Russian parties differ greatly in the extent to which they represent a well-defined bloc of voters (see figure 7.6). The party with the longest history and inherited organizational strength, the Communists, had the most cohesive bloc of supporters: 36 percent of the variance in the Communist vote can be explained statistically by a range of social, economic, and political influences. A new party representing reform political values and the market, Yegor Gaidar's Russia's Choice, was also relatively cohesive: 23 percent of its vote can be explained in the same way. It thus contrasts with Yabloko, which placed considerable emphasis on the personal appeal of its leader, economist Grigorii Yavlinsky, as well as on its support for market reform. Voters for Zhirinovsky's Lib-

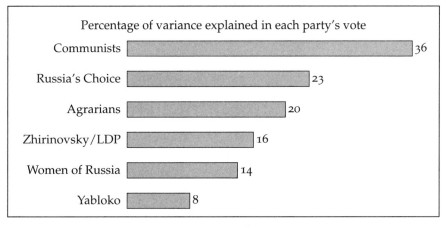

FIGURE 7.6
VARIABLE COHESIVENESS OF PARTIES

SOURCE: Centre for the Study of Public Policy/Paul Lazarsfeld Society, New Russia Barometer III (1994).

NOTE: Figures are pseudo R-squared values based on logistic regression models. See appendix C for details of estimation and appendix table C.1 for full details.

eral Democrats were less cohesive in their political and economic values and in their social characteristics; the Agrarian Party was much more united, with a clear focus on the economic interests of voters in rural Russia. Women of Russia also targeted a clearly defined group, but its intervention had the effect of splitting the female vote into a feminist minority and a much larger group of women who did not vote on the basis of gender.

Patterns of Party Competition

In seeking votes, Russian party leaders were not so much competing against each other as experimenting with mobilizing support in very different ways. We cannot apply the Lipset and Rokkan model of social cleavages because it implies *pairs* of opponents, for example, a clerical and an anticlerical party. In Russia, this situation did not develop, as parties did not generally call forth opposition from their logical alternatives. Women of Russia, for instance, was not balanced by Men of Russia, and the presence of an Agrarian Party did not lead to the formation of an Urban Party.

Only two parties appeared to compete at complementary and opposing ends of the same political dimension. Both Russia's Choice and the Communists appealed for support on the grounds of *political values*, while differing greatly in the values that each emphasized. Communist voters were endorsing what might be called "Red conservatism," a defense of the accomplishments of the old regime and rejection of the new. By contrast, supporters of Russia's Choice were characterized by a commitment to reform and rejection of the past.

Women of Russia and the Agrarian Party pursued a *social-interest* strategy, mobilizing votes from groups that shared common social structural characteristics. Women of Russia emerged as a pure social-interest party, as its voters disagreed about whether the old days were good or bad and about whether reform was good or bad. The Agrarian Party had a narrower appeal than its name suggested because it endorsed collective farms, repelling a significant number of the entrepreneurially minded. The Agrarian Party could not claim to speak for the countryside as a whole because it won less than a third of the vote in rural constituencies. Each interest group party failed to mobilize the majority of those for whom it claimed to speak.

Yabloko's strategy avoided close identification with a clear-cut position in terms of political values, economic policies, or social interests. As an economic reformer in the Gorbachev era, Yavlinsky could talk the language of reform, but having broken with Yegor Gaidar and never having served in the Yeltsin government, he was also free to blame the reform government and claim he could do better. The result was a "fuzzy" image. Yabloko's low vote and the even lower vote for other parties with a "fuzzy focus" leader is a caution against assuming that Russian politics has become as leader oriented as personalistic American election campaigns.

Zhirinovsky's Liberal Democrats followed a hybrid strategy. The high vote for the party on the list ballot and the absence of support in single-member districts emphasizes the importance of the party leader's television appearances in attracting votes. Zhirinovsky's appeals to authoritarianism and traditional institutions make clear that a part of his support could be identified with reactionary political values. But the blame that it placed on the government for the country's economic problems also shows that the LDP vote contained an element of pure protest. Given the variety of motives leading people to vote LDP, the limited identification with the party and its lack of ideological cohesion, there is no basis for describing the 23 percent who cast a party-list vote for the LDP as committed to its leader's neonationalist creed. The party's vote drew support from those who for disparate reasons wanted to vote for the party that most clearly reflected a rejection of both reform and Red conservatism.

The parliamentary election offered voters a chance to express their views about the constitution too. No major party campaigned on a platform favoring the abandonment of free elections, although Zhirinovsky hinted that he had little use for constitutional restraints. Of the six major parties reviewed here, the Communists and Yabloko campaigned for a "no" vote on the constitution, Russia's Choice and the LDP—for different reasons—for a "yes." The NRB survey indicates that the Communists had considerable success in mobilizing their supporters to vote against the constitution and that Russia's Choice had comparable success in mobilizing support in favor of its adoption. The supporters of other parties tended to divide in the referendum.

We can characterize the position of each party toward the Soviet system and the new regime by the views its voters expressed about each of them. Figure 7.7 plots the position of each party's voters on a continuum of support for the old and new regimes. The closeness of each party to the least-squares regression line shows that this is a meaningful dimension for comparing all six major parties.

At the opposite ends of the continuum are Russia's Choice and the Communists. Yabloko voters also tended to be relatively close to the reform end of the continuum. But this does not mean that the 1993 parliamentary election was a contest for or against the change of regime: Russia's Choice and the Communists won only 28 percent of the party-list vote between them, and even the addition of Yabloko leaves a large majority of voters somewhere in the middle.

A total of 40 percent of the list vote was cast for three big parties whose supporters tended to be divided in their views about the regimes, with the Agrarians and Women of Russia more inclined to see some favorable points in both and Zhirinovsky's voters more negative. The remaining third of the voters scattered their choices among a majority of smaller and (in most cases) unrepresented parties in the State Duma.

The fragmentation of votes, the lack of identification or active distrust of parties, and the transient nature of preferences have led some to argue that Russians dislike open disagreement between competing parties and criticism of those in power (see, for instance, Sakwa 1993b). In Soviet times the fact that people were not allowed to express divergent preferences for parties was even cited as tautological "proof" that Russians disliked free elections and democracy.

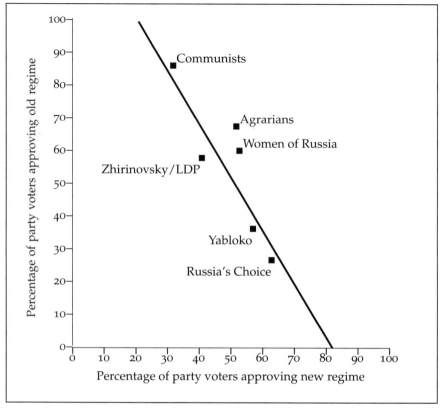

FIGURE 7.7

WHERE PARTY VOTERS STAND ON OLD AND NEW REGIMES

SOURCE: Centre for the Study of Public Policy/Paul Lazarsfeld Society, New Russia Barometer III (1994).

NOTE: The equation for the regression line is $y = 136 - 1.65x$. R-squared = 0.74.

In postcommunist Russia it is possible to ask people how they feel about elections and competing parties, and the New Russia Barometer did just that. Six months after the violent breakdown of relations between parliament and president, the third New Russia Barometer asked Russians whether or not they thought it possible that parliament might be suspended and party competition limited. Respondents divided into three groups: 38 percent said they thought it possible, 37 percent thought it difficult to say, and only 25 percent were confident that the suspension of parliamentary elections was very unlikely.

When Russians were asked whether they would actually like to see parties abolished and parliament dissolved, a different division emerged. Only 21 percent said they would approve the abolition of representative institutions, as against 39 percent saying they would disapprove. Again, there was a large bloc of 39 percent unsure about whether they would approve or disapprove.

The large number of Russians undecided about maintaining parliament means that the 1993 elections were neither a firm endorsement nor a rejection of representative institutions. Altogether, Russians divided into five groups of unequal size. Hopeful authoritarians, approving the suspension of parliament and believing it possible, constituted only 14 percent of the population. Frustrated authoritarians, who would have welcomed the suspension of parliament but did not think it likely to happen, were 8 percent. Both groups were outnumbered by the 25 percent of confident democrats, disapproving the suspension of parliament and not thinking it likely to happen. Their ranks were augmented by 14 percent of anxious democrats, disapproving an end to representative institutions but fearing that it could happen there. While democrats outnumbered authoritarians, the critical bloc for the future consisted of the 39 percent who were uncertain whether parliamentary government in Russia is desirable or not, and often uncertain about whether it will survive.

ᐧᐧᐧ 8 ᐧᐧᐧ

Boris Yeltsin and the
Russian Presidency

Strong personalized political leadership had been the Russian tradition from tsarist times. It was institutionalized in the Soviet period by the dominance of Josef Stalin as general secretary of the Communist Party. Yet after Stalin there were countervailing forces, including the development of a substantial element of collective constraint on the leader. At the same time, effective authority began to shift from party to state, with an increase in the number and powers of the committees within the USSR Supreme Soviet and in the authority of the Soviet government itself. The general secretaryship of the party had been separated from the position of prime minister after the fall of Khrushchev in 1964 to avoid excessive concentration of power in the hands of a single person. And yet when Mikhail Gorbachev became general secretary in 1985, he could claim he was more powerful than any of his counterparts on the world stage: the virtually unassailable leader of a party that could not itself be challenged through the ballot box, the media, or the courts of law (*Izvestiya*, 6 April 1991, 1).

Russia came late to a presidency, as it had come late to free elections. The Soviet Union was a republic, with the chair of the Presidium of the Supreme Soviet the titular head of state. Carrying out ceremonial duties, he had no real political power. Only in 1988, with the resignation of Andrei Gromyko, did Gorbachev become head of the Presidium as well as party leader. Gorbachev assumed an additional and newly established post in 1989 when he became chair of the whole of the Supreme Soviet. The presidency was not formally constituted as an office until March 1990, when Gorbachev became the first—and as it turned out, last—president of the USSR. There was no Russian presidency until June 1991, when Boris Yeltsin, already chair of the Russian parliament, was elected to that post (see chapter 2). In both their cases, the presidency was a position of executive authority. Neither Gorbachev nor Yeltsin, as former prime minister Nikolai Ryzhkov remarked, liked the idea of "reigning like the Queen of England" (Nenashev 1993, 26).

The introduction of the Soviet presidency, and subsequently a presidency of the Russian Federation, was part of a trend toward presidencies throughout the Soviet successor states. Tajikistan established a presidency in November 1990; and by 1994, when Belarus adopted a new constitution, each of the member states of the CIS had an executive head of state (Sakharov 1994). In the Central Asian republics, the post was occupied by an authoritarian ruler of a distinctive, "sultanistic" type (cf. Roeder 1994). In Kazakhstan, for instance, Nursultan Nazarbaev was elected unopposed with 98.8 percent of the vote in 1991, and after four years his tenure was extended to the year 2000. In Uzbekistan, Islam Karimov won a similar extension of his term with 99.6 percent support. And in Turkmenia, 99.99 percent of voters in a 1994 referendum gave President Niyazov the traditional title of *turkmenbashi* (leader of the Turkmen) and extended his term to 2002. In Central and Eastern Europe new constitutions differed in the extent to which the office of president was a ceremonial post, as in the Czech Republic, where it was first held by the dissident playwright Vaclav Havel, or a post claiming political authority, as in Poland, where the dissident leader Lech Wałesa was elected to the office in December 1990 (cf. Taras 1993; Baylis 1996).

The introduction of a strong executive president as part of a process of democratization has been questioned by many students of comparative politics, who have argued that a separately elected president is less likely to encourage democratic consensus than government by a prime minister accountable to parliament. This is because political disagreements between a separately elected president and legislature can lead to constitutional crises—as they clearly did in postcommunist Russia (cf. Lijphart 1992; Shugart and Carey 1992; Sartori 1994; Linz and Valenzuela 1994). Guillermo O'Donnell (1993, 1367), drawing on the experience of Latin America, has argued that many new democracies with popularly elected presidents become "delegative democracies" in which whoever is elected to the presidency can do whatever he thinks appropriate without regard to constitutional constraints, accountability to a popularly elected parliament, or public opinion.

The Emergence of a Russian Presidency

The idea of a Soviet presidency had first been considered at the time of the adoption of the 1936 constitution. Stalin, however, opposed it, and the idea made no further progress. It was also considered in 1964 during preparatory work for the constitution eventually adopted in 1977. A presidency was proposed to Gorbachev by his advisers as early as 1985 (Kuznetsov 1996, 95); and in 1988, during preparations for the 19th Party Conference, the idea was once again examined before a decision was made to establish the rather different position of chair of the Supreme Soviet, normally to be held by the party general secretary and similar to a parliamentary speakership (Lazarev 1990, 3–4; Shakhnazarov 1993, 73). Gorbachev was still committed to a renewal of the system of elected soviets, rejecting the idea of a presidency on the grounds that it would lead to an undue concentration of power in the hands of a single person (*XIX Vsesoyuznaya* 1988, vol. 2, 129). The idea of presidential government surfaced once more in 1989, when it was formally proposed to the Second Congress of People's Deputies by veteran dissident Andrei Sakharov and urged on Gorbachev by his closest advisers (Shakhnazarov 1993, 137f.; Zlobin 1994; Kuznetsov 1996, 96–97).

Gorbachev then made an about-face, proposing the creation of an executive presidency among the radical changes presented to the Central Committee plenum of February 1990, which agreed that the constitutionally guaranteed "leading role" of the party should be relinquished. A presidency, he argued, would ensure swift action could be taken in circumstances that required it, particularly where the economy, ethnic relations, or public order were concerned (*Materialy* 1990, 19). Parliamentary chairman Anatolii Lukyanov, who presented the proposals to an extraordinary Congress of People's Deputies in March 1990, told them that an institution of this kind would encourage a broader political dialogue and help to establish a popular consensus. The president, he explained, would be able to act decisively in the event of emergencies, and he could help to resolve the impasse that had developed between the Soviet government and the Congress of Deputies. Nor, claimed Lukyanov, was there any reason to fear that the presidency would lead to a new form of authoritarian rule; there was an "entire system of safeguards" against this, including limits on age and tenure and the ability of the Congress—if enough deputies voted accordingly—to recall the president and overrule his decisions (*Vneocherednoi* 1990, vol. 1, 17–18). Leaders in the republics were particularly concerned about the possible exercise of presidential power to suspend the operation of their own parliaments, and there was a majority in favor of a formal separation of the presidency and the party leadership, although not the two-thirds majority that would have been necessary to pass the proposal into law (Gorbachev, as a result, retained both positions). Others were more inclined to accept the proposals as a means of ending a damaging "vacuum of power," and in the end the establishment of the presidency was approved by a vote of 1,817 to 133, with 61 abstentions (*Vneocherednoi* 1990, vol. 1, 58–61, 395–96, 193).

Although the president was normally to be elected by popular ballot for a maximum of two five-year terms, the Congress of Deputies agreed that at a time of political tension and instability Gorbachev could be elected by the Congress of Deputies itself. The oldest member of the Congress, literary scholar Dmitrii Likhachev, issued an impassioned warning that if they did not elect a president without further delay—and he was old enough to remember the revolution of 1917 —there was a real danger of civil war (*Vneocherednoi* 1990, vol. 2, 385–86). Gorbachev was duly elected on 15 March, although he received only 71 percent of the vote of Congress members in an uncontested ballot. He conceived of the presidency as a means of guaranteeing the "irreversibility" of perestroika, Gorbachev explained in his acceptance speech, and as a means of strengthening the institutions of socialist self-government; and he promised to act not as the representative of a particular political group but as the "agent of the people as a whole" (*Vneocherednoi* 1990, vol. 3, 55, 56, 62).

The new Soviet president was required to brief the Supreme Soviet on the "most important questions of the USSR's domestic and foreign policy" and had the right to propose candidates for the premiership and other leading state positions. He could suspend legislation, and in particularly grave circumstances introduce direct presidential rule. The president headed a Council of the Federation, consisting of the heads of state of the fifteen union republics, and a Presidential Council; after December 1990 he also headed a newly formed Security Council with overall responsibility for defense and public order. Gorbachev nominated Gennadii Yanaev, a former trade union and party official, to the new vice-presidency at the same time, explaining to the Congress of Deputies that he needed a "person he could trust." It was an unfortunate choice, as Yanaev became head of the attempted coup in August 1991.

In September 1990 Gorbachev's powers were extended further when he was given the right to institute emergency measures to "stabilize the country's sociopolitical life." This extension of an already impressive range of powers deepened the concerns of liberals and of his political opponents. The new presidency, Boris Yeltsin warned, had more powers than Stalin or Brezhnev; the office was an attempt to constitutionalize an "absolutist and authoritarian regime that could ultimately be used to provide a legal pretext for any high-handed act" (*Pravda*, 16 December 1990, 2). Gorbachev himself drew attention to a cartoon in which he had been shown trying on a tsar's crown for size (*Pravda*, 1 December 1990, 4). But as Gorbachev reminded a gathering of miners in April 1991, he had voluntarily surrendered the extraordinary powers that he possessed as general secretary of the CPSU. Would he have done so if he had been seeking unlimited personal authority? (*Izvestiya*, 6 April 1991, 1).

Although the powers of the president were extensive, the new laws also imposed limitations. He could be impeached by a two-thirds vote of the Congress of Deputies. His ministerial nominations required the approval of the Supreme Soviet, which could force the resignation of the government as a whole if it voted accordingly. Indeed, the Fourth Congress of People's Deputies in December 1990 saw an attempt to force the resignation of the newly elected president when a Communist deputy accused Gorbachev of responsibility for "destruction, collapse, hunger, cold, blood, tears [and] the death of innocent people." Gorbachev survived comfortably, but 423 of the 1,898 deputies who voted supported the call to place a vote of confidence on the Congress agenda (*Chervertyi* 1991, vol. 1, 12, 34).

In confrontations of this kind Gorbachev lacked the ultimate mandate of a democratic reformer: popular election. The votes that he won were elite votes, conducted within the framework of the Communist Party of the Soviet Union and the Soviet state. As elections were held in the republics and as they installed leaders who were more obviously "the people's choice," a group of alternative leaders began to develop who could claim a popular mandate to challenge the Soviet president and the Soviet state itself. The challenge to central authority was greatest in Russia, after Boris Yeltsin won a popular election against five opponents in June 1991 (see pp. 35–40); he used this popular mandate to dominate the negotiating process as the USSR came to an end.

Once Russia became an independent state, it required a constitution of its own. The document approved in the December 1993 referendum created what *Izvestiya* described as a "superpresidential republic" (12 October 1994, 4; see also Okunkov 1996). Even though a presidential election was meant to be held every four years, Yeltsin was allowed to serve the full five-year term to which he had been elected in June 1991. Whereas the Soviet constitution and the Russian system each authorized an elected vice-president, the 1993 Russian constitution made no mention of a position of this kind, a consequence of the conflict that had arisen between President Yeltsin and his vice-president, Alexander Rutskoi. In the event of the president's incapacity, the prime minister becomes acting president, and an election to fill the vacancy should be held within three months. The president can be impeached, but only for serious antistate crimes and after the Duma votes an indictment of treason or a charge of equivalent gravity, the Supreme Court agrees there is a case to answer, and the Constitutional Court confirms that the proper procedures have been followed. Both chambers of the parliament must then vote in favor of impeachment by a two-thirds majority of their respective memberships before the president can be removed from office.

The Russian presidency was influenced by practice elsewhere, particularly France, which has historically shifted between a democratic system and an undemocratic regime ruled by a Bonapartist "man of destiny" (cf. Hayward 1993; Hazareesingh 1994). In the Fifth French Republic, established in 1958, the president has constitutional powers to impose his will on government for limited periods and for stated purposes, such as resolving a deadlock about the budget. In both countries the method of electing the president emphasizes personal appeal as against party endorsement. A large number of candidates run in the first ballot; assuming no candidate secures as much as half of the total, a second ballot is held between the two with the greatest support to make sure that the president is the choice of a majority of voters, either as a positive good or as the "lesser evil." In France, the president is elected for seven years as against the Russian norm of four.

The Russian presidency differs fundamentally from the American presidency, for, reacting against the monarchy of George III, the U.S. Constitution was designed to prevent the emergence of a strong executive. The Madisonian system accordingly gave great powers to Congress to initiate legislation and to check the president. The growth of the modern American presidency has created an executive that can propose a different policy from that of Congress, but the two must resolve their differences by bargaining, if government is not to be stalemated (see, e.g., Neustadt 1960; Rose 1991). By contrast, the Russian practice, even more than in France, gives the presidency broad decree powers.

The Yeltsin Presidency

Boris Yeltsin was born in the village of Butko in the Sverdlovsk region of western Siberia in 1931, the son of peasant parents. According to his autobiography, he was lucky to be alive at all: the priest nearly drowned him when he was being baptized, remarking calmly, "Well, if he can survive such an ordeal it means he's a good tough lad." Both his father and his uncle were persecuted in 1934 when they fell foul of the campaign against "kulaks," who were rich or simply more efficient farmers. They were accused of conducting anti-Soviet agitation and though protesting their innocence were given three months' hard labor; Yeltsin himself, though only three, remembered the "horror and fear" years later (*Izvestiya*, 28 September 1993, 7; Yeltsin 1994, 121–25). Yeltsin's childhood was a time of the Stalin-induced famine that followed agricultural collectivization; there were always shortages of food, and the family might not have survived the war without the milk and, sometimes, the warmth of their nanny goat. Yeltsin lost two fingers in an accident, he broke his nose and contracted typhoid fever, and his father beat him regularly. But he did well at school and graduated as an engineer at the Urals Polytechnical Institute, where he perfected his volleyball techniques and met his future wife (Yeltsin 1990; for biographies see Morrison 1991; Colton 1995).

After completing his studies, Yeltsin worked as a construction engineer, managing a large state enterprise that specialized in prefabricated housing. In 1961 he joined the CPSU, becoming a full-time local party functionary in 1968 and in 1976 first secretary of the Sverdlovsk regional party organization. In this capacity he ordered the destruction of the Ipatyev house in which the tsar's family had been shot in 1918 and which had become a shrine to the old order. Yeltsin's managerial qualities—he had, on his own account, become "steeped in command-administrative methods"—caught the attention of the central leadership, and in early 1985 he was invited to Moscow to take up a position in the party apparatus as head of its construction department. In December 1985, after Mikhail Gorbachev took office, Yeltsin transferred to the position of first secretary of the Moscow city party organization in succession to a disgraced Brezhnevite, Viktor Grishin.

When Yeltsin arrived in Moscow, he was a little-known outsider from the provinces who had never worked in the national capital. His outspoken comments soon attracted attention. His speech at the 27th Party Congress in early 1986 sharply criticized corruption and official privilege. In October 1987—according to those who were present, almost by accident (Vorotnikov 1995, 167)—he was called to speak to the Central Committee meeting that was considering Gorbachev's address on the seventieth anniversary of the revolution. Why, asked Yeltsin, in all that time had they failed to feed and clothe the people they claimed to represent? And why had a cult of personality developed around the Soviet leader and his wife? (*Le monde*, 2 February 1988, 6; an edited version appeared in *Izvestiya TsK KPSS* no. 2, 1989, 239–41).

While glasnost licensed the expression of more than one opinion, it was not a charter for freedom of speech, especially for party officials, and Yeltsin was removed from the Moscow party secretaryship shortly afterward. In the latterday equivalent of a show trial of the 1930s, he was denounced by a succession of speakers, accused of arrogance, incompetence, and even Bonapartism (*Pravda*, 13 November 1987, 1–3). He was moved to a junior ministerial position at the State Construction Committee and dropped from the party Politburo in February 1988; his political career appeared to be at an end. Even his membership of the CPSU was in doubt as the Central Committee, in a decision without postwar precedent, voted to investigate his increasingly outspoken statements to determine if they were compatible with party membership (*Pravda*, 17 March 1989, 1).

His own outspokenness and the attacks on him by the party establishment gave Yeltsin a substantial public following, for he articulated many popular grievances. In the relatively open elections of March 1989 he won 89 percent of the vote in the Moscow national-territorial constituency running against an officially supported candidate (see chapter 2) and became a member of the newly elected Supreme Soviet after one of the deputies originally chosen stepped down in his favor. Yeltsin became joint chairman of the radical Inter-Regional Group of Deputies, a kind of parliamentary opposition, and an increasingly vocal critic of official privilege and the party's political monopoly. In the Russian elections of March 1990 he was elected by another huge majority in his native Sverdlovsk and began using his position to advance the claims of the republics—and especially of Russia—against the apparatus of the central state and the Communist Party of the Soviet Union.

Yeltsin's speeches avoided the ideological symbols common in Marxist-Leninist disputes. Instead, he called for the private ownership of land, independence for the republics, financial autonomy for factories and farms, freedom of political association, and freedom of conscience (*Materialy* 1990, 68–69). Asked if he was still a socialist, Yeltsin replied with another question: What did this mean? The USSR had experienced the "developed socialism" of the Brezhnev years; there was Pol Pot socialism; in Hitler's Germany there was national socialism, and there were many different kinds of capitalism. What was the point of arguing about definitions? (*Argumenty i fakty*, no. 22, 1990, 3). Yeltsin's statements during his 1991 campaign for the Russian presidency did little to clarify what specifically he favored. Once a month, Yeltsin told interviewers, he attended a religious service. He was in favor of "radical reform," a transition to the market, and the preservation of peace and stability—but so was Gorbachev. Their major difference was Yeltsin's insistence that Russian laws must prevail over those of the USSR (see *Izvestiya*, 23 May 1991, 3). In general, he explained, he was happy to rely upon his intuition (*Izvestiya*, 11 June 1992, 3). A close analysis of his speeches found the Russian president "predictable in only one respect—his unpredictability" (*Pravda*, 10 June 1991, 2).

Exercising the powers of a president is a very different task from criticizing government from the outside. The presidential administration has both formal and informal sides. Formally most important is the executive office of the president, divided into fifteen departments and comparable in many ways to the central party apparatus of the late Soviet years. The president also has a staff of senior counselors, and more than ninety analysts (*Prezident*, no. 1, 1995, 5; Okunkov 1996, 109–40). Another section consists of presidential support services, including Yeltsin's personal security office headed until June 1996 by former KGB general and regular tennis partner Alexander Korzhakov, whose hard-line and often controversial views were attacked as a reactionary influence on the Russian president. In addition, there are presidential representatives on government committees and a Security Council, similar to the Defence Council of the late Soviet years. The presidential administration is at least as large as the CPSU bureaucracy it was intended to replace: some estimates estimate it as having 40,000 employees (*Rossiya*, no. 41, 1994, 4).

As an outsider, Yeltsin found himself in the position of an American governor who ends up in the White House with little knowledge of how the presidency works. A political leader in this position tends to trust those who have won his personal favor rather than those who are expert in managing the government bureaucracy. This creates a system of "court politics," involving struggles for advantage between official advisers, cronies, and intimates. As an overburdened president, Yeltsin was in danger of having staff take decisions in his name in the belief that by arrogating this power to themselves they were "protecting" the president from distractions and difficulties. One of Yeltsin's ex-advisers, Vyacheslav Kostikov, told journalists that a common expression among Yeltsin's staff was "It is no business of the tsar," that is, aides rather than the president himself would make the decision (quoted in Beeston 1996). This meant that it could often be "very difficult to sort out the intricacies of the relationships among the internal Kremlin structures responsible for drafting presidential decisions" (*Kommersant-daily*, 8 June 1995, 4; for insiders' accounts, see Filatov 1995; and Kostikov 1996).

The outsider president faced a government dominated by insiders, who were very often holdovers from the Soviet regime. Huskey (1995b) has described Yeltsin as resolving problems by governing "through the presidency"—that is, going around the government rather than working through the ministries that were formally responsible for the functions of state. He could not use the purge, the classic Soviet method of disposing of those loyal to the old leaders. Nor would removing a few key individuals reform the ministries, as they were supported by an intricate web of ties that integrated departments of state with other key interests and institutions, such as the military-industrial complex. Even if large numbers of ministry officials had been pushed into early retirement, Yeltsin lacked loyal and competent officials to replace them. And as efforts at economic reform made clear, the presence of a small number of Western advisers, many non-Russian speaking, was not adequate to ensure that his wishes prevailed over those of the government bureaucracy—and often over those of the wider society (cf. Aslund 1995).

The buildup of the president's office inevitably created friction between the presidency and the government of the Russian Federation, headed by the prime minister. It was the prime minister's "government" that reported to parliament. The president's own entourage was a kind of supergovernment, often decisive in making big decisions. When policies went wrong, as they often did in the economy and, latterly, in Chechnya, Yeltsin blamed the prime minister and individual ministers as scapegoats, while he claimed to be "above" day-to-day activities, especially mistakes. It is a tactic that is not unknown in democratic politics. As John F. Kennedy once remarked apropos a risky diplomatic initiative: if it works, it will be another White House success, and if it doesn't, it will be another State Department failure.

The relationship between the president and the Russian government headed by the prime minister was difficult, whether the prime minister was reformer Yegor Gaidar or, after December 1992, former Central Committee member and industrial manager Viktor Chernomyrdin. The prime minister depended on the continued favor of the president, and there was repeated speculation about his future whenever the president appeared dissatisfied with policy failures—or jealous of his success. The prime minister could also find his position usurped by members of the presidential entourage, such as security chief Alexander Korzhakov, who told television viewers a week before the 1995 Duma election that he would not be voting for the prime minister's party (Bershidsky 1995, 1). Yeltsin could also play deputy prime ministers off against the prime minister, as when first deputy premier Oleg Soskovets, rather than Chernomyrdin, accompanied the president on his 1994 visit to the United States.

The president and the prime minister were both targets of attack by the Duma, and the election of the president and Duma at different times made for friction between institutions elected in different political climates and responsible to different political constituencies. Furthermore, the president's nomination of a prime minister required Duma approval. This was not easily secured, making a designated prime minister spend months in an acting capacity, as Yegor Gaidar did from June until December 1992 when the Duma failed to confirm his candidacy and he resigned. The need for confirmation by the Duma has also made it difficult to fill the politically important and electorally unpopular post of chair of the State Bank. After Viktor Gerashchenko's resignation in October 1994, Tatyana Paramonova was appointed acting bank head, but identification with presidential policies led to her repeated rejection, and it was not until November 1995 that the Duma could be persuaded to accept Sergei Dubinin.

The continuing friction between president, prime minister, and parliament led to calls for reform. For example, it was argued that the president and parliament should be chosen on the same date so as to maximize the chance that they would have a common program of government. There were also calls for a conventional parliamentary system as in Britain or Scandinavia, with government led by a prime minister accountable to a popularly elected assembly rather than a president (*Izvestiya*, 15 March 1994, 1, 4). The Communist Party was very critical of the presidency, and party leader Gennadii Zyuganov called for it to be abolished altogether as "one of the first actions of a new president, if one is elected from the opposition" (1994, 188–89). In October 1995 he charged that the existing Russian presidency was poorly adapted to Russia's multinational population or to the country's federal system of government, and called for it to be placed under the control of an elected body (*Pravda*, 24 October 1995, 1).

While President Yeltsin could, if he chose, blame ministers for failures, the many layers of government between his own position and that of officials on the ground meant that he had to be continuously vigilant to prevent officials usurping his authority to "go into business" for themselves, whether in the literal sense of exchanging political favors in return for cash payments or in the political sense of pursuing a particular line of foreign or domestic policy that he had not specifically authorized.

The demands of office impose great physical and mental burdens on the incumbent, and Boris Yeltsin is no exception (cf. Post and Robins 1993; L'Etang 1995). Yeltsin was confined to a hospital in 1993 suffering from a nerve disease, radiculitis, which caused pain that could require strong sedation (*Le monde*, 11 September 1993, 11). In April 1995 a spring holiday was extended by a week because of the president's high blood pressure, and in July 1995 he was rushed to a hospital complaining of acute chest pains; appointments were canceled, and a scheduled visit to Norway had to be postponed. In October 1995 there was a recurrence of the same cardiac difficulties; Yeltsin was in the hospital for more than a month and did not return to his Kremlin desk until the end of December. A series of carefully staged media events showed the president being briefed by the prime minister and making a number of appointments. But while the president was ill, the Russian government carried on, allowing his entourage to engage in "palace intrigues with far-reaching consequences" (*Izvestiya*, 1 November 1995, 2).

Bouts of depression and drinking also affected the president's behavior. Yeltsin admitted that he sometimes allowed himself a glass "or maybe two" of brandy on a Sunday evening with his family, or some beer after visiting the bathhouse (*Argumenty i fakty*, no. 16, 1993, 3). His parliamentary critics were more outspoken. "It's time to stop the public drunkenness of our president," a Communist deputy demanded after an unsteady performance during Yeltsin's first visit to the United States. "When he's shown on television he can't stand up without support" (*Nezavisimaya gazeta*, 16 May 1992, 2). There was further criticism in early 1993 when the president, defending himself against impeachment, spoke uncertainly before the Russian parliament and had to be assisted from the hall. The following year, Russian troops withdrawing from Germany were treated to a "stirring rendition of 'Kalinka' under the impromptu conductorship of the president" (*Guardian*, 29 March 1993, 18, and 9 September 1994, 12). A number of advisers who expressed their concern about this event were left behind during Yeltsin's next trip to America, which included a canceled appointment with the Irish prime minister when his return flight touched down at Shannon airport (*Argumenty i fakty*, no. 39, 1994, 2). The president's bodyguard explained that he had overslept; others were more inclined to blame in-flight refreshment. Former Vice-President Rutskoi later accused Yeltsin of being in a "permanent state of visiting Ireland" (*Lipetskaya gazeta*, 2 March 1995, 2).

Russians and the Yeltsin Presidency

In every political system, leadership is a function of popular support for the president as an individual as well a function of the constitutional powers of the office, and this is particularly so when the office is new and the individual is a fresh political personality. When Russians are asked to select the characteristics of an ideal president, a majority select three traits as important: education, decisiveness, and Russian nationality. Boris Yeltsin meets all three qualifications, for he is a graduate in engineering, showed decisiveness in challenging the Communist establishment, and is a Russian by nationality and—with all his faults—by character (see table 8.1). At least two-fifths also think a president should have no connections with the old *nomenklatura* and should be above reproach in his personal life. As a full-time official of the Communist Party for a quarter-century before becoming a critic of the party and as a heavy drinker, Yeltsin fails to meet these standards. Yet a substantial proportion are prepared to accept a president who had some experience of management in the Soviet period, and 45 percent to allow the "usual human weaknesses." Nor does former membership of the

TABLE 8.1

CHARACTERISTICS OF AN IDEAL PRESIDENT AND OF BORIS YELTSIN

Ideal President	Ideal %	President Yeltsin
Highly educated	75	Degree in construction engineering
Decisive	59	Often shown
Russian nationality	59	Yes
Not connected to *nomenklatura*	49	Party official 20+ years
Beyond reproach in personal life, without bad habits	43	Stable marriage but many drinking bouts
Male	42	Yes
Never in Communist Party	29	Member 30+ years
Believes in God	25	Baptized; occasional churchgoer

SOURCE: Ideal attributes: survey reported in *Moskovskie novosti*, no. 33, 1993, 11A.

Communist Party appear to matter very much to ordinary Russians (*Moskovskie novosti*, no. 33, 1993, 11A).

The ups and downs of support for an individual leader are not so much a reflection of an individual's personality, which is relatively unchanging through the years, as the result of the performance of the government for which a leader is responsible and, in the case of Russia in the 1990s, the performance of a fledgling regime.

Politically, Yeltsin's career was launched as a critic of the establishment. He could not claim to have been the first to challenge Communist orthodoxy, as Gorbachev himself had initiated perestroika, but Yeltsin was much more radical in his criticisms, not only attacking old-guard Communist practice but also Gorbachev himself for not going far enough in radically changing the institutions that affected the lives of the great majority of Soviet citizens. In doing so, he was backing the people, and especially the Russian people, against the party and its leader.

The longer President Mikhail Gorbachev's policy of perestroika lasted, the less popular it was. Even four years after the collapse of the Soviet Union, only 14 percent of Russians said they thought it was the right step to have taken. The majority, 53 percent, described perestroika as necessary but implemented so incompetently that it had done more harm than good, and a quarter were against it in principle (Levada 1995, 4). As a radical critic, Yeltsin could endorse what was necessary and desirable about perestroika, while blaming President Gorbachev for what was unpopular and unsuccessful. This tactic made Yeltsin, as president of the Russian Federation, more popular than Gorbachev, as president of the Soviet Union; indeed Yeltsin had become more popular by the summer of 1990 shortly before he was elected speaker of the Russian parliament (see figure 8.1). When the Russian Public Opinion Research Centre (VTsIOM) asked Soviet citizens to rate Gorbachev on a scale of 1 to 10 in July 1990, his score was 5; but by March 1991 his rating had dropped to 3.4, and it was lower still when the Soviet Union collapsed at the end of the year. By contrast, Yeltsin stood at 8 in the summer of 1990—the highest rating he ever achieved—and his public standing was half again as high as that of the Soviet president at the end of the following year.

The emergence of the Russian Federation as an independent state not only made Boris Yeltsin the unchallenged leader of Russia but also placed him in the hot seat, with responsibility for all that happened—including all that went wrong. The ambiguous benefits of incumbency are common to leadership in every political system, and in

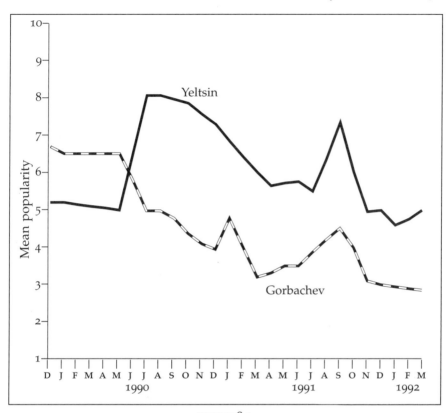

FIGURE 8.1
GORBACHEV AND YELTSIN, 1989–92

SOURCE: VTsIOM.

NOTE: Nationwide stratified random samples with about 2,000 interviews each. Rating scale: 1–10.

established democracies presidents and prime ministers expect to see their popular support move both up and down during their period of office (Rose 1991, chap. 13; Edwards and Gallup 1990; Rose 1995c). The important point for a leader is that, however unpopular a person may be at midterm, popularity should be on an upswing at election time.

VTsIOM has regularly tracked Yeltsin's popular support by asking nationwide samples to rate his standing on a scale from 1 (bottom) to 10 (top). Since every political figure will make enemies as well as have supporters, no leader can expect to average a mark close to 10. But a leader with a broad base of support should normally have a rating above the midpoint in the scale, as Yeltsin did after he publicly resisted the attempted coup of August 1991. Throughout his period as president of an independent Russia, however, Yeltsin's rating has consistently been below the midpoint of a 1-to-10 scale.

Unlike most leaders in established democracies, Yeltsin's popularity has not fluctuated up as well as down. Instead, there has been a steady downward trend. In January 1992, when the federation was brand-new, his average rating was 4.5 out of 10; by January 1996, it was 3.1. The underlying downward trend in Yeltsin's rating is charted by the least squares regression line in figure 8.2. Instead of the ups and downs of political fortune canceling out during the first four years of his presidency, Boris Yeltsin more often lost support than gained it. The steadiness of the downward trend is demonstrated by the strong correlation between the regular VTsIOM ratings of the president and the underlying trend. In a complementary fashion, the ratings substantially above or below trend identify times when the president was doing better or worse than the underlying trend.

The peak of Yeltsin's popularity as Russian president (with a rating of 4.9) was reached in March 1992, a few months after the inauguration of the new federation and less than a year after his successful campaign for election as Russian president. But this was a "honeymoon" effect, and reform soon became unpopular as inflation accelerated and uncertainties about the economy increased. By the end of 1992, Yeltsin's rating had fallen to 3.9, and he called a referendum in April 1993 in an attempt to mobilize popular support in his struggle with the parliamentary opposition. The referendum was successful in giving a qualified endorsement to Yeltsin and his policies (see chapter 4), and his popularity rating rose to 4.4 in May 1993. But the boost in public opinion did not last long; by June 1993, Yeltsin's rating was again back on trend, and by August 1993 it had fallen to 3.5. The confrontation with parliament mobilized support for the president once again, and in October 1993 Yeltsin's rating rose to 4.5, the same as it had been in the first month of the new federation. But the support gained in the shootout with parliament was temporary. By the time of the December parliamentary election, the president's popularity rating had again fallen to 3.6.

In the December 1993 parliamentary election the president sought to be "above" the conflict between parties, not running a slate of candidates of his own and not explicitly endorsing any one party. In this

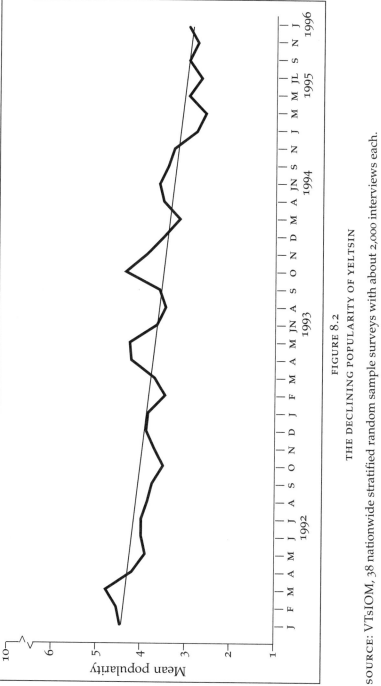

FIGURE 8.2

THE DECLINING POPULARITY OF YELTSIN

SOURCE: VTsIOM, 38 nationwide stratified random sample surveys with about 2,000 interviews each.

NOTE: Regression line values: *R*-squared = .63; slope = .042. Rating scale: 1–10.

way, he hoped to retain room for maneuver with whatever coalition of interests dominated the new Duma. But without a party of his own in parliament, Yeltsin and his government were vulnerable to pressures from deputies who did not owe anything to his endorsement. The contrast with the Fifth French Republic is striking. Even though General de Gaulle shared Yeltsin's distaste of party politics, he did launch a Gaullist party that could provide a core of support in the French parliament.

The new Duma that met at the beginning of 1994 had more democratic legitimacy than its predecessor, but it was no more ready to cooperate with the president. The third New Russia Barometer, in the spring of that year, found that a majority of voters in all parties in the Duma expressed distrust of Yeltsin; they differed only in their degree of distrust. Among Communist voters, 92 percent were inclined to distrust him, and among voters for Russia's Choice 81 percent distrusted him. The least distrustful party was Yabloko; even there, 65 percent distrusted the president. Yeltsin sought to maintain his position by playing critics off against one another, a classic stratagem of "within the beltway" politics (or, in the case of Moscow, within the ring road). These tactics, however, did not gain popular support. In March 1994 Yeltsin's popularity hit a new low of 3.2, and after a slight recovery, it headed down again later in the year (see figure 8.2).

Military action against the breakaway Russian republic of Chechnya in December 1994 had a very strong political dimension, for there were forces within the Moscow elite lobbying strongly for measures to be taken to "punish" rebels against the authority of the Russian state, and these views were represented within the president's own entourage. Some of Yeltsin's staff apparently believed that a "small victorious war" in the Caucasus would restore his reputation as a man of action and would attract the support of all who favored the maintenance of a strong Russian state, whatever the politics of its leadership might be (*Izvestiya*, 14 December 1994, 3). Military action would also avoid the damaging criticism that the president was "soft" on Russia's enemies or prepared to countenance the breakup of the Russian state.

In the event, neither the war in Chechnya nor the opinion polls turned out as the president would have wished. Predictions that Chechen resistance would swiftly be overcome had to be abandoned; by the beginning of 1996, at least 30,000 lives had been lost and there was no end in sight. Chechen guerrillas were meanwhile extending hostilities to other parts of Russia, including the seizure of hostages outside their own borders in June 1995 and January 1996. The president blamed his advisers and the military for all that went wrong. But the Russian people blamed the president; his rating fell to 2.9 in January 1995 and as low as 2.7 in March, before recovering slightly. Whereas Yeltsin's popularity had averaged 4.1 out of 10 in 1992, in 1995 the average rating was 2.9. By the end of 1995, only 2 percent "completely supported" the Russian president, 28 percent were "in disagreement with some of his actions," and the largest group, 52 percent, thought he "should resign." By this time, Yeltsin had become even more unpopular than parliament and the prime minister (*Ekonomicheskie i sotsialnye peremeny*, no. 6, 1995, 56–57).

The link between support for Yeltsin and evaluation of political and economic regimes is confirmed by a more detailed examination of the New Russia Barometer surveys. In summer 1993, when NRB II asked people if they trusted Boris Yeltsin, trust was not high. The single most important influence on trust was an individual's rating of the current regime (beta: .37); in other words, those favorable to the new regime were more likely to trust the Russian president. In a complementary fashion, those more favorable to the old Communist regime were the most likely to distrust him. Yeltsin's status at that time as a reformer is shown by the fact that the more people felt a sense of increased freedom, the more they were likely to trust him. The economic situation of an individual's family did not influence views about the president. Judgments about the economic regime paralleled political regime evaluations, except that those more dissatisfied with the current economic system were also more likely to trust the Russian president. Age and ethnicity were of minor significance (see figure 8.3). The link between trust in Yeltsin as president and approval of his policies is confirmed by a second regression analysis of support for Yeltsin's policies, which produced very similar results.

The fall in the president's popularity in the spring 1994 New Russia Barometer can be explained by the same influences as in 1993; those more positive about the new regime were more likely to be pro-Yeltsin, and those more positive about the Communist regime were the most anti-Yeltsin. The president's problem was that more people had begun to rate the old regime positively than the year before. Moreover, the lower variance that was explained in 1994 (20 percent as against 29 percent in 1993) indicates that dissatisfaction with the president was becoming more diffuse as he was no longer seen as a clear-cut reformer, now that Gaidar had been replaced as prime minister by an *apparatchik* from the old regime, Viktor Chernomyrdin.

The decline in support for Boris Yeltsin was marked by a shift in

FIGURE 8.3
TRUST IN YELTSIN, 1993

SOURCE: Centre for the Study of Public Policy, New Russia Barometer II (July 1993).

popular views about how disputes between president and parliament should be resolved. Disputes between the two institutions are inherent in any system in which each is separately elected and each can claim constitutional authority for its decisions. In the United States, disputes between the White House and Congress reflect the preference of the authors of the Constitution for a political system of checks and balances. In France, the independent authority of a popularly elected president and of the popularly elected National Assembly, with a prime minister accountable to both, creates tensions when the institutions are controlled by different parties.

In the second New Russia Barometer survey in summer 1993, just before the violent confrontation between the president and the Supreme Soviet, just over half those with an opinion said that the president should have the power to suspend the Supreme Soviet and rule by decree. In the third NRB survey, six months after the violent confrontation between the president and parliament, the largest group favored president and parliament having equal rights. In the fourth NRB survey (figure 8.4), the proportion that approved a president's acting unilaterally to resolve a deadlock with parliament had fallen by four percentage points and support for the parliament acting as a check on the president had increased (Rose 1995f). In NRB II, exactly half the respondents thought the Supreme Soviet should have the power to stop the president from taking actions to which it objected. By NRB IV, two years later, almost two-thirds—64 percent—endorsed the idea that parliament should be able to stop a presidential action to which it objected, a significant swing away from the centralist doctrines that President Yeltsin had been promoting.

Although the 1993 Russian constitution is "presidentialist" in its distribution of authority, Russian public opinion has become "antipresidentialist." When individual views about rule by decree and parliamentary veto are combined, in the 1995 New Russia Barometer the largest single group, 35 percent of the total, favored the Duma having a veto over presidential actions and opposed presidential rule by decree. By contrast, fewer than one in five Russians approved the president's ruling by decree and denying Parliament the right to veto presidential actions. In the middle are two groups that appear closer to the eighteenth-century American Founding Fathers, more skeptical of all claims to unchecked authority than of President Yeltsin and his entourage. The median bloc of Russians favor some form of gridlock, with 18 percent not wanting to vest power in either institution and 29 percent wanting both president and Duma to have the power to check the other. Russian opinion thus tends to favor resolving constitutional disputes about government action by compromise or bargaining rather than by the traditional hammer of power.

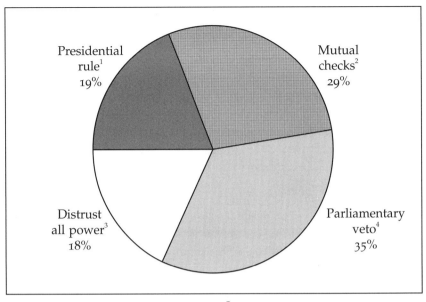

FIGURE 8.4

PREFERENCE FOR GRIDLOCK IN RUSSIAN GOVERNMENT

SOURCE: New Russia Barometer IV (spring 1995) as reported in Rose and Tikhomirov 1995, 25.

NOTES:

    1. Approves rule by decree; rejects parliamentary veto.

    2. Approves parliamentary veto *and* rule by decree.

    3. Disapproves both veto and rule by decree.

    4. Approves parliamentary veto; rejects rule by decree.

9

Taking Positions for the 1995 Duma Election

After December 1993, Russia had a parliament, a president, and a constitution freely endorsed by the electorate—but it was far from clear whether the country had a workable system of government. To begin with, the procedure for electing the Duma divided deputies between the representatives of single-member districts and those of party lists. Duma members in their turn were inclined to attribute their victory to the attacks they had made on President Yeltsin and government policies, not to the alternatives they had themselves proposed. There was no consensus among critics about what government ought to do; there was no political incentive to present an alternative program; and even if the 450 disparate members of the Duma were to speak in a clear, collective voice, there was no assurance that their views would be heeded by the Russian government, still less by the president and his entourage.

The choice of the party-list method of electing members of the Duma compelled politicians accustomed to operating in cliques and cabals to operate in unfamiliar ways. This was also true of "outsiders," such as Boris Yeltsin, who was a breakaway leader from the Communist Party, and of technocratic reformers such as Yegor Gaidar, who was an academic and a journalist rather than a grassroots party organizer. It was thus necessary to "create democracy from scratch" (Fish 1995, 214). Paradoxically, the end of Soviet rule made it harder, not easier, to organize parties, as there was no longer an overriding need for unity in the fight to create a new form of Russian government. The Duma elected in

December 1993 became an arena in which there were many disagreements, but they often reflected personal and local, rather than philosophical, differences.

The adoption of a presidentialist constitution secured Boris Yeltsin the authority to govern—but it also made him responsible when things went wrong. Yeltsin's rise to the presidency had been achieved by declaring all-out opposition to the party and state authorities. He was not interested in the ideology of the market economy, just as he was not interested in Marxist-Leninist doctrines. Now that power was in the hands of his own government, there was no indication that he had any clear ideas about what that government ought to do—and much evidence to the contrary. Although not a dissident in the classic East European sense, his position was analogous to that of Polish President Lech Wałesa. Wałesa secured his place in Polish history as the leader of the Solidarity movement in the early 1980s, but as the first elected president of postcommunist Poland he displayed limited capacity to govern and was rejected by the voters in his bid for reelection in 1995.

Russia had no shortage of problems at the beginning of the new Duma. The official economy was shrinking, while inflation was still driving up prices. Many workers were caught in a world between unemployment and employment; they still held jobs, but they might not be paid for months on end, and even the largest enterprises were close to insolvency. Relations with the other newly independent states of the former Soviet Union were unresolved; and there were challenges to the authority of Moscow from within the Russian Federation, above all from the Chechens, who had formally declared independence in November 1991. The new constitution laid down procedures within which the government was supposed to operate, but it gave little guidance about what should be done in the face of such unprecedented challenges.

Politics was pervasive in the shaping of public policy. Popularly elected representatives wanted to proclaim opinions they thought would be popular or give vent to their own feelings and preoccupations. Ministers had a personal stake in avoiding blame or, if possible, claiming success. Yeltsin and his entourage had an even greater interest in spotlighting government actions for which the president could claim credit and avoiding association when failure loomed and others could be blamed. Around each ministry and each major decision there was a network of competing lobbies, all seeking to influence the outcome and often pursuing their private or corporate interests as well as—or instead of—anything that might resemble the public interest.

Collectively, elected politicians and policymakers constituted a minute portion of the Russian electorate, and neither the Duma nor the president could be sure of what the next election result would be, or even whether another election would be held on schedule for the Duma and the presidency. In conditions of great uncertainty, politicians had to respond simultaneously to problems that were too big to be ignored, such as the plight of the economy, and to problems that were too personal to be neglected. For example: What party should I join (or organize) to fight the next election? Who is the best candidate to back in the presidential election? And since institutions were not firmly established, what electoral law is most in my interest? This unstable balance of interests, institutions, procedures, and competitive politics shaped Russian politics between the first and second elections to the Duma.

Policies and Politics

The economy had been a chronic source of difficulty to Soviet policymakers. In the early 1920s, in reaction to the shortcomings of "war communism," Lenin recommended a New Economic Policy that allowed small-scale private trade and ownership. Successive Five Year Plans, launched initially in 1928 under Stalin, changed this accommodation between private ownership and political control into a command economy with centralized administration of prices, wages, and investment, in which ideological politics, personal favoritism, and bureaucratic interests competed. The Soviet economy could succeed, albeit with much inefficiency, in advancing military prowess or exploring outer space, but it was less successful in providing an adequate range of consumer goods or even an assured food supply. Brezhnev sought to ameliorate conditions through a policy characterized as "welfare state authoritarianism," offering workers more consumer goods in exchange for political quiescence (Breslauer 1978; Cook 1993). But the economy resumed its downward trajectory, and by the mid-1980s, when Gorbachev began to develop perestroika, it was in danger of becoming an "example to the rest of the world how not to conduct its economic life" (Nikolai Shmelev in *Znamya*, no. 7, 1988, 179; more generally Kornai 1992).

The Soviet economy began to contract before the collapse of the state. Even allowing for the shortcomings of Soviet and post-Soviet official statistics, the picture that emerges from official data is consistent with other evidence (see, e.g., European Bank 1995; Holzmann et al.

1995). Instead of growing or simply stagnating, in the last two years of Soviet rule the official economy contracted by a sixth. The slide downward continued or even accelerated thereafter. In the first year of the new Russian Federation, the official economy contracted by 19 percent. In the election year of 1993, it contracted an additional 12 percent, and it continued to contract in each of the next two years (see table 9.1).

TABLE 9.1
CUMULATIVE DETERIORATION OF THE RUSSIAN ECONOMY

	1989	1990	1991	1992	1993	1994	1995
Gross domestic product	100	96	84	68	60	51	49
Consumer prices	—	100	144	3,338	28,071	56,985	82,629

SOURCE: Calculated from European Bank 1995, 185f.

Quoting annual rates of economic change substantially underestimates the cumulative effect of contraction of the economy and inflation, for each year's change adds its impact to what happened before. Thus the 13 percent contraction in the official economy in 1994 was sufficient to reduce it to barely half of what it had been in 1989, because the economy had already shrunk by two-fifths between 1989 and 1993. The 4 percent contraction in the national product in 1995 might be described as good news inasmuch as it marked a substantial reduction in the annual rate of deterioration. But it pushed the official economy below half its 1989 level, and real wages were down over the same period by more than two-thirds. Russian researchers calculated that the contraction of the official economy was greater than anything the USSR had experienced during World War II, and greater than the depression in the United States at the end of the 1920s (*Pravda*, 21 June 1995, 4).

Of course, the official economy is only part of the story, as the breakdown of the command economy allowed the unofficial economy to boom and fortunes to be made in dealings that were never entered in national accounts. Western institutions monitoring Russian trade estimated that in some years in the 1990s, when the Russian government claimed it was impoverished and in need of an International Monetary Fund loan, Russian businessmen were actually *exporting* billions of dollars gained from unofficial trading to bank accounts abroad (see, for instance, *Rossiiskaya gazeta*, 20 April 1993, 5). At the household level, Russians found goods for immediate purchase in shops without the queues or waits of many months that had been experienced in former times: in

1992, on the evidence of NRB I, 30 percent of Russian shoppers had to spend two hours or more getting what they wanted, but by 1995 only 28 percent were doing so. Some Russians, by this time, were already participating in an unofficial consumer boom, and luxury automobiles were selling faster than almost anywhere in the outside world.

But social differences were widening rapidly: in 1995, the richest 10 percent of the population was earning up to twenty-five times as much as the least-well-off 10 percent. But for the mass of the population, economic transformation resulted in an immediate lowering of living standards and a heightened sense of economic insecurity by comparison with the old system. Officially, up to a third of Russians had incomes below the poverty line; 7.8 percent were officially out of work in 1995 and a further 20 percent were not receiving their wages on a regular basis (*Rossiiskaya gazeta*, 29 February 1996, 3). Low income did not necessarily mean destitution, for every Russian household was involved in several economies in addition to a regular job. Some were involved in social economies in which no money was needed because people grew some of their own food or exchanged help with one another, and some made money in the cash-in-hand shadow economy. This enabled many Russians with incomes below the official poverty line to get by (Rose and McAllister 1996). Moreover, the cumulative legacy from Soviet times of stress, disregard for occupational health, and environmental pollution had led to an increase in death rates, especially for males, and a fall in life expectancy that was "unparalleled in the civilized world" (*Argumenty i fakty*, no. 30, 1995, 13; *Segodnya*, 27 January 1995, 6; cf. Feshbach and Friendly 1992).

The collapse of the communist system destroyed what was left of the command economy but left open what was to be put in its place. In economic terms, perestroika implied that the economy should become more responsive to market forces, including international trade, which meant importing Western goods and selling Russia's raw materials abroad. When Boris Yeltsin placed Gaidar and his colleagues in charge of economic policy in late 1991, it signaled a commitment to market reform. Gaidar and his team sought to speed up the reform process, but quickly ran into obstacles thrown up by the entrenched bureaucracy; they also faced popular resistance, as policies began to bite, and the obstacle of ignorance as the jump from a nonmarket to a market economy had never been attempted before (see Aslund 1995; Leitzel 1995; Nelson and Kuzes 1995). By December 1992, when Gaidar was replaced as premier by Viktor Chernomyrdin, an old-style politician from the energy monopoly, it signaled a tilt against the market. But it was too late to undo what had been done or to stop the momentum already in train.

The economy was not the only problem facing Russia's governors: the breakup of the Soviet Union left a further legacy of unresolved nationality issues. Russians accounted for 83 percent of the population of the Russian Federation, and one-sixth of the Russians of the former Soviet Union lived outside its new territory. This meant that after 1991, 25 million Russians were residents of the other successor states. Numerically, the largest concentrations were in Ukraine (11.4 million) and Kazakhstan (6.2 million). Measured in a way that is politically more meaningful, as a proportion of the local population Russians were a substantial presence in Kazakhstan (38 percent of all residents, or nearly as many as the Kazakhs themselves), Latvia and Estonia (34 and 30 percent respectively), Ukraine (22 percent), and Kyrgyzstan (almost 22 percent). In urban areas, especially the capitals of successor states, Russians and the Russian language were often preponderant (*Rossiiskii* 1994, 37; cf. Shlapentokh et al. 1994; Chinn and Kaiser 1996).

The most pressing challenges came from ethnic minorities within the boundaries of the Russian Federation. Although minority nationalities were linguistically diverse and widely dispersed territorially, through geographical concentration even half a million people could become an organized force for political change. Moreover, the Soviet practice of recognizing dozens of different nationalities in issuing internal passports to its citizens gave official recognition to groups using their new freedoms to articulate demands for distinctive treatment that officials did not want to grant (cf. Bremmer and Taras 1996). The breakup of the Soviet Union encouraged minorities such as the Chechens—nearly a million strong—to assert claims for their own independence. In other republics that were constitutionally a part of the Russian Federation, such as Tatarstan and Bashkortostan, diamonds, other minerals, and oil gave local politicians the incentive to extort as much profit as they could from these resources by whatever means available. For example, the Tatars held a referendum on local autonomy in the spring of 1992 after the Moscow government and the constitutional court had ruled it illegal.

Violence also gained prominence with an increase in crime, especially organized "Mafia-style" crime. Homicides, for instance, doubled in three years, and contract killings doubled in the single year of 1994 (*Nezavisimaya gazeta*, 11 April 1995, 1; *Kommersant-daily*, 23 February 1995, 14). A professional killing could be arranged "as easily as, say, a restaurant dinner" (*Izvestiya*, 5 November 1993, 3), and hitmen could be hired to conduct "conversations" with reluctant debtors (*Argumenty i fakty*, no. 22, 1992, 8). Three members of the Duma were victims of the crime wave, shot dead by assassins. Businessmen were another target. The president of Rosbiznesbank, Ivan Kivelidi, poisoned in August 1995, was one of forty-six bank directors and staff killed since January 1992 (*Izvestiya*, 5 August 1995, 1). Journalists were also at risk. The *Moskovskii komsomolets* reporter Dmitrii Kholodov was blown up in his office in October 1994 after he began uncovering massive corruption in the Soviet armed forces stationed in East Germany. And the television journalist Vladimir Listev was shot dead in March 1995 in a murder that appeared to be connected to the sale of commercial advertising. In 1994 twenty-four journalists were killed in the former USSR in the course of their duties, and another twelve lost their lives in the first four months of 1995 (*Izvestiya*, 4 May 1995, 1). Ordinary people were vulnerable, too, particularly if they were elderly and lived alone.

Whatever the issue, the government of the day wants to generate a "feel good" factor. It may try to do so by engineering an economic boom or by scoring a military or diplomatic success to generate national pride. In complementary fashion, the opposition parties have a vested interest in creating a "feel bad" factor, spotlighting problems and blaming them on the government of the day. The Russian parliament elected in December 1993 had lots of members with reasons of this kind for trying to make the government look bad.

In early postcommunist Russia, "feel bad" arguments had the larger following, especially when the new regime was compared with the pre-perestroika Soviet Union. This is shown by changes in the "heaven/hell" scales used in the New Russia Barometer to measure approval of new and old political and economic regimes (figure 9.1). At the commencement of the Russian Federation, half the Russians who were asked gave a positive rating to the communist regime; the new regime was endorsed by only one in seven. By summer 1993, 36 percent expressed a positive view of the new political system, and a similar proportion held this view in 1994. By spring 1995, however, the proportion approving the new regime was little more than a quarter, and this remained the position in the fifth New Russia Barometer survey conducted at the start of 1996. Those holding a positive view of the former communist regime were not thereby endorsing a return to the stagnation of Brezhnev or the terror of Stalin, yet their views did offer hope to antireform parties, above all the restyled Communist Party of the Russian Federation. Given the link between attitudes toward the regime and toward President Yeltsin, they were also evidence of his diminishing popular appeal.

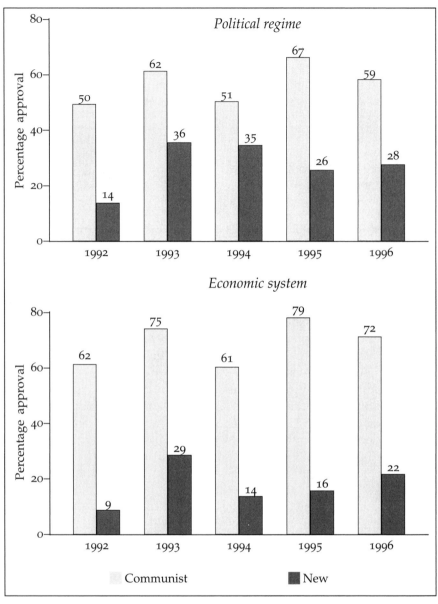

FIGURE 9.1
GROWING DISSATISFACTION WITH NEW SYSTEMS,
NOSTALGIA FOR OLD

SOURCE: First four annual New Russia Barometer surveys as reported in Rose and Tikhomirov 1995, 17, 49. January 1996 results from Rose 1996b, 22–23, 47–48.

In each annual New Russia Barometer survey, the percentage approving the transitional economic system has been lower than that approving the new political regime. In contrast, the percentage endorsing the old command economy has always been higher than the proportion endorsing the old communist political regime. The "high" point in endorsement of the transitional economy to date has been low, 29 percent giving it a favorable rating in 1993. In the same survey 75 percent gave a positive rating to the command economy. Since then, the minority viewing the new economic system positively has fluctuated, from one-seventh in 1994 to just above a fifth in January 1996 (Rose 1996b).

Forming, Reforming, and Abandoning Parties

The old Soviet regime could easily produce assemblies that were representative in a sociological sense because the party decided who would be elected. It could gather a substantial quota of manual workers, women, and other social groups because the party itself controlled all stages of the nomination and election process. The outcome was a Supreme Soviet that had a large proportion of workers and collective farmers, young people, and non-Russians. But the Supreme Soviet was not representative in the democratic sense, for the members had been selected by the party rather than freely chosen by the electorate to represent their own interests.

Unlike its predecessors, the new Duma was freely elected, but its membership was no longer directly representative of the society that had chosen it. As in Western parliaments, the deputies were nearly all university graduates. All but two had some higher education, and many were academics or highly qualified specialists. Public officials and enterprise managers were also well represented. Only 13 percent of the new deputies were women, much less than in the Scandinavian countries, but more than in Britain or France (cf. Rose 1996c, 183). The political parties were also less prominent than had been expected. Fewer than 70 percent of deputies elected on the party lists were actually members of the party that had nominated them; most of the rest were not members of any party. And only 43 percent of the deputies elected from single-member districts were party members (*Rossiiskaya federatsiya*, no. 2, 1994, 14; full biographies of the new deputies were published in Rybkin 1994).

The strength of parties in the Duma that assembled in January 1994 differed significantly from that produced by the results of the December election. Initially, Duma rules recognized as parties only the eight organizations that had won 5 percent of the vote in the party-list ballot. This left more than 150 independents and representatives of smaller parties elected in single-member districts without an institutional status (cf. table 9.2). After the new Duma had assembled, some of these "orphans" sought a home in a party that had party-list members. The Agrarian Party gained more than twenty seats this way, and Sergei Shakhrai's Party of Russian Unity and Concord gained more than ten recruits in the same manner (Halligan and Mozdoukhov 1995).

TABLE 9.2
PARTY AFFILIATION OF DUMA MEMBERS, 1993–95

| | Dec. 1993 election | 1994 | | 1995 | | Change |
		Jan.	Dec.	Mar.	Oct.	
Party list groups						
Russia's Choice	70	76	71	55	49	−21
Liberal Democratic Party	64	64	60	55	55	−9
Communist Party	48	45	46	46	47	−1
Agrarian Party	33	55	54	52	51	+18
Yabloko	23	27	27	27	27	+4
Women of Russia	23	23	22	22	20	−3
Party of Russian Unity and Concord	19	30	31	22	13	−6
Democratic Party of Russia	15	15	15	8	11	−4
New deputy groups formed in Duma						
New Regional Policy	–	67	64	39	37	−30
Stability/Our Home Is Russia	–	–	–	35	37	+37
Russia/Rybkin's Bloc	–	–	–	35	36	+36
Independents	141	47	57	51	57	−84

SOURCE: December 1993: table 6.2, p. 128. 1994–95: Halligan and Mozdoukhov 1995.

Because of the practical advantages of being part of an organized group in a chamber of 450 members, Duma members immediately voted to allow all the deputies elected on the basis of a party list to form their own parliamentary "fraction." It was also agreed to allow deputies to form "groups" provided they had at least thirty-five members. By 1994, this led to a deputy group called New Regional Policy becoming the second largest in the new Duma, with over sixty members (Rybkin 1994, 10). New Regional Policy claimed to represent regional and industrial interests, for which its leader, Vladimir Medvedev, an oil bureaucrat, was particularly well qualified (table 9.2). Party factions as well as registered groups were represented on the Council of the Duma, which allowed them to share in agenda-setting and the detailed negotiation that took place within the council; they also enjoyed a number of organizational privileges within the Duma itself.

The new Duma considered a proposal that deputies elected on the party list should have an imperative mandate, requiring them to remain with the party or resign. The proposal was rejected, however, allowing deputies owing their seats to a party list to change their allegiance, and permitting independents and representatives of single-member districts to migrate from one party to another. During the two-year life of the Duma, deputies moved repeatedly, some on their own initiative and others as a result of political shocks, the founding of new parties, or "infant mortality" among the parties created to contest the 1993 election. When the Duma began its work, there were eight organized fractions as well as New Regional Policy; by the summer of 1995, they had been joined by the "Stability" group, which spoke for the prime minister and government, and "Russia," formed by a group of single-member district representatives who had left the New Regional Policy group. Several very prominent politicians left the grouping that had initially sponsored their entry to the Duma: Ella Pamfilova, Gennadii Burbulis, and Mikhail Poltoranin left Russia's Choice; Nikolai Travkin left the Democratic Party he had founded; and Alexander Shokhin left the Party of Russian Unity and Concord. The balance of support for the government remained broadly constant, but this concealed an increasing tendency of collectivist parties to vote in its favor, while former allies among reformers such as Yabloko moved against the government, in many cases because of the Chechen war.

Notwithstanding the fissiparous nature of parties in the Duma, there was one issue that simplified divisions: whether or not to support the government. Criticisms came to a head on 21 June 1995, when the seizure of hostages in the town of Budennovsk by Chechen guerrillas led to a vote of no confidence in the Russian government for its handling of the campaign; it was approved by 241 to 72 (*Izvestiya*, 21 June 1995, 1). If a similar motion passed within three months, it would have required the president either to dissolve the legislature or to appoint a new government. Yeltsin therefore threatened a dissolution if there was a second vote of no confidence; a second vote on 1 July passed by 193 to 117, but it fell short of the majority of all deputies necessary for adoption. A move on 12 July to impeach President Yeltsin, initiated by the Communist Party, attracted only 168 votes in its favor instead of the

226 that would have been necessary to approve it (*Izvestiya*, 13 July 1995, 1).

In the no-confidence vote of 1 July most parties showed a high degree of cohesiveness in voting for or against the government (figure 9.2). Three large parties—the Liberal Democrats, the Communists, and the centrist Democratic Party of Russia—were virtually united in their condemnation of the government. Other parties, for example, New Regional Policy and Women of Russia, showed a high degree of cohesion in refusing to bite the hands they hoped would feed them. Faced with unattractive alternatives, Yegor Gaidar's Russia's Choice swung almost solidly behind the president and government at this point. Only two of the eleven fractions in the Duma divided, the Agrarians and Yabloko. The position of some Agrarian deputies was influenced by a prevote government announcement that agricultural subsidies were to be increased. Yabloko's split reflected its loose structure and three-person

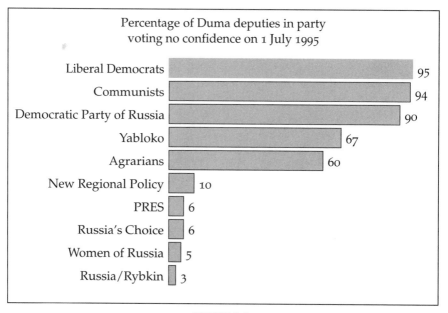

FIGURE 9.2
COHESIVENESS OF PARTIES IN VOTE OF NO CONFIDENCE
IN GOVERNMENT

SOURCE: Halligan and Mozdoukhov 1995.

leadership, as well as tensions among its deputies because of the Chechen war.

Within the Moscow ring road, the twists and turns of politicians and parties in the Duma were of immediate significance, but what did the voters make of the institution meant to represent them? The answer is: not a lot. When a 1995 survey by the International Foundation for Electoral Studies asked a representative sample of Russians if their deputy had been back to meet the voters since being elected, only 19 percent said yes. Twice as many said that their deputy had not been back, and the largest group, 41 percent, simply had no idea whether or not their deputy had sought to keep in touch with his or her district. Nor did voters expect deputies to be interested in their concerns (figure 9.3). Only 5 percent thought deputies were primarily concerned to help their constituents; just over a quarter thought they wanted to help their constituents as well as themselves; but three-fifths thought elected representatives were only interested in looking after their own interests.

The Duma's reputation was not improved by the somewhat disorderly way in which it conducted its affairs. A sitting on 9 September 1995, which had been meant to discuss the NATO bombings in Bosnia, was particularly remarkable (Gessen 1995). The deputy who set things in motion was Nikolai Lysenko, leader of the far-right National Republican Party. Desperate to attract press attention, he chose this moment to attack a long-time foe, Orthodox priest Gleb Yakunin of the Democratic Party. As Yakunin was returning to his seat, Lysenko seized his cross; another deputy from the Stability group rushed forward to separate them but became involved in the melee. Two women deputies tried to restore order—"women have always interfered in fights," one of them told journalists—but at this point Vladimir Zhirinovsky joined in. He elbowed one of the women out of the way (she suffered a concussion) and then turned on the other, seizing her in an armlock and removing her spectacles. "We are voting," the Speaker, Ivan Rybkin, reminded them. "I wish you could push buttons the way you do that." A bloodied Yakunin later announced he would be taking legal action against Lysenko for the theft of his cross, for banditry, and for offending the sensibilities of believers. The press gave rather more attention to Zhirinovsky's assault on a woman deputy, describing it as "the Duma's solution to women's issues."

An ambitious attempt to bring order to this political and legislative turmoil was launched in spring 1995. After discussions with President Yeltsin, Prime Minister Chernomyrdin announced that he would launch a new, centrist political party to compete in the December

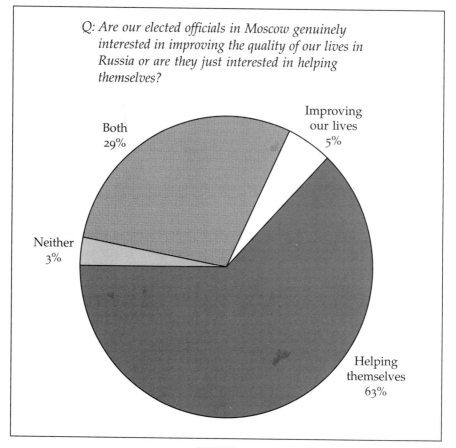

Q: Are our elected officials in Moscow genuinely interested in improving the quality of our lives in Russia or are they just interested in helping themselves?

Both
29%

Improving
our lives
5%

Neither
3%

Helping
themselves
63%

FIGURE 9.3
WHOM ARE DUMA MEMBERS INTERESTED IN HELPING?

SOURCE: A nationwide sample survey of 4,070 Russians conducted in July 1995 by the Institute for Comparative Research (CESSI), in collaboration with American Viewpoint and the Response Center, and sponsored by the International Foundation for Electoral Systems (IFES), Washington, D.C.

Duma election, Our Home Is Russia. Russia, he explained, had had "enough shocks and revolutions"; he called instead for "agreement and stability" (*Izvestiya*, 26 April 1995, 1). The new party's founding congress took place on 12 May, and Chernomyrdin was unanimously elected its first chairman. "Our Home," announced Chernomyrdin, would work in parallel with "Accord," another new movement of a more left-wing character set up under the chairmanship of Duma

Speaker Ivan Rybkin. President Yeltsin welcomed the formation of the two blocs in a speech, declaring them the embryo of a Russian two-party system (*Rossiiskaya gazeta*, 26 May 1995, 1–2); it was a development he had inspired, with a view to providing a natural party of government that would sustain the reform process and Yeltsin himself through the parliamentary and then presidential elections.

The image of Our Home was not helped by its close connection with Gazprom, the huge energy concern that Chernomyrdin had headed before joining the government; there were persistent and damaging rumors that he had become one of the richest men in Russia when the company was privatized. Our Home quickly became known as the party of power, whose purpose was to sustain the government within which its members held leading positions; it was also known as the party of the fuel and power complex (*Kommersant-daily*, 16 August 1995, 3). Rybkin's bloc, for its part, failed to gather the support of a single major party, including his own Agrarians (*Izvestiya*, 23 August 1995, 2). Later in the year it lost the backing of General Boris Gromov, who had commanded Soviet troops in Afghanistan and who established another group, called My Fatherland (*Izvestiya*, 21 September 1995, 2). The process of party formation was a continuing one, as the attempt to maximize the number of "responsible" deputies in the State Duma as a means of sustaining the president and his reforms had not yet succeeded (*Segodnya*, 19 May 1995, 3). The factions, however, had begun to give some coherence to the legislative process more generally, and for some they were already the "nuclei of future parliamentary parties" (Remington and Smith, 1995, 483).

Negotiating the Election Law

From the disinterested perspective of an armchair philosopher, election laws can be evaluated by their contribution to the representation of electors and the creation of a democracy. But the politicians who draft and vote on electoral laws are anything but disinterested; they know (or think they know) what laws best suit themselves. Public choice theories postulate that election laws are intended to represent not so much the interests of voters as the interests of the politicians who enact the laws. On this assumption, the rational thing for politicians to do is to vote for the measures that are most likely to secure their reelection. As most people have little interest in or knowledge about electoral law, public opinion normally allows politicians substantial leeway in drafting these laws.

While the debate on a new electoral law was in full swing within the Moscow beltway, an International Foundation for Electoral Systems survey found that 73 percent of those interviewed said they had no idea whether or not the election laws of Russia worked well or needed reform. When asked a follow-up question about which type of electoral system they preferred, 41 percent again had no opinion or refused to say; 30 percent thought there should be no change; a preponderance of party-list seats was favored by 22 percent, and more single-member seats by 7 percent. Even the existing law was poorly understood: a majority (51 percent) thought prisoners could vote, and more than a third (34 percent) thought a family member could vote on their behalf, a legacy of communist times when abstention was riskier than personation. At the same time, 53 percent of Russians believed that elections could "change something in the life of our country," which in turn suggested some commitment to the classic function of elections, the ability to "throw the rascals out" (IFES 1995).

Electoral reform had been placed on the agenda in February 1994, when President Yeltsin referred to it in an address to the Federal Council and cautioned against a repeat of the experience of December 1993. The first priority of the president and reformers was to strengthen the position of the Russian government in the Duma through gaining seats for Our Home, the party of the prime minister. A strong showing for this party and its associates would make it easier for Yeltsin to exercise his presidential authority and run a successful campaign for the presidency in 1996. Second, the president and his entourage wanted at all costs to avoid the shock of December 1993, when Zhirinovsky's Liberal Democrats had emerged the surprise winners in the party-list section of the Duma elections, and the Communists had also done well. The presidential goals were therefore to reduce the number of party-list seats, disadvantaging Zhirinovsky and the Communists, and to increase the number of single-member districts, where local officials who depended on presidential patronage would have a better chance of influencing the outcome.

There were other arguments in favor of an emphasis on single-member districts, some of which were similar to points that had been put in constitutional debates in other countries. Party lists were said to give too much power to national party offices in Moscow, which filled their lists with other politicians from the capital and neglected the claims of outlying areas. They lacked the direct link with voters that was provided by a constituency election (*Nezavisimaya gazeta*, 12 April 1995, 2). The progovernment paper *Rossiiskie vesti* argued that if the new Duma included a large number of competing parties, it would become as ineffective as the Italian parliament had been until the recent changes in that country's electoral system (1 April 1995, 2). Parties, in any case, were, as the chairman of the Central Electoral Commission put it, "in an embryonic state" (*Trud*, 8 April 1995, 1), and could hardly be expected to supply the coherent program of government that parties provided in other countries.

Duma members had a rather different agenda. Collectively they had an interest in boosting the power of their own institution, and individually they had an interest in winning reelection. The latter goal meant that they were inclined to favor a low minimum turnout requirement—no more than 25 percent—to make the election valid. The president's preferred minimum turnout of 50 percent made it possible for the elections to be declared invalid, allowing him to govern without a Duma. The Duma was also more inclined to favor the representation of political parties, strongly influenced by deputies such as Yabloko's Viktor Sheinis, who had helped shape the original law. As Sheinis acknowledged, no electoral system was perfect. But he denounced the "dreadful unfairness" of the single-member seats, which deprived electors who voted for unsuccessful candidates of any representation at all. With a single round and a result determined by a simple plurality, well over half the electorate would be without any representation in single-member seats (*Moskovskie novosti*, no. 19, 1995, 8; similarly, *Segodnya*, 18 May 1995, 5).

The party-list ballot was expected to make the Duma more cohesive because the need to rank candidates would encourage party discipline (*Novoe vremya*, no. 18, 1995, 8–9). Stronger parties in their turn would strengthen democratic government by making it harder for the president and his entourage to dominate the policy process. Stronger parties could also help party leaders, as well as the president, to set the political agenda (*Segodnya*, 2 June 1995, 2). It would be destabilizing, in any event, to change the electoral system before every election in order to extract a temporary advantage. The national element in the party-list system also meant that the Duma could represent the interests of Russia as a whole. Single-member districts represented particular regions and republics. If the Duma became an aggregation of local interests, who would formulate policy for the nation as a whole and help maintain its territorial integrity? (*Nezavisimaya gazeta*, 12 April 1995, 2). Given these conflicts of principle and self-interest, it was not surprising that the new electoral law had a long and difficult passage (see McFaul and Petrov 1995; Razmustov 1995).

An additional option, canvassed with varying degrees of enthusi-
asm almost up to polling day, was that the election should be canceled
altogether, or at least postponed. The most prominent exponent of this
view was Vladimir Shumeiko, speaker of the Federation Council and
normally a Yeltsin loyalist. The new parliament, Shumeiko argued,
should hold office for two further years, and so too should Boris Yeltsin. Most of the deputies, he told the upper house in June 1994, were
"just beginning to understand what [was] required of them." If there
was an election soon, many would begin to "spend more time thinking
about their preelection campaign than working to make laws"
(*Izvestiya*, 23 June 1994, 2). A former presidential aide, Gennadii
Burbulis, argued similarly for "two more years" so that state institutions and presidential contenders would have a chance to establish
themselves (*Argumenty i fakty*, no. 27, 1994, 3). To suspend elections
would have involved a constitutional amendment, which in turn
would have required a referendum, or else the suspension would have
to be imposed by presidential fiat, a step toward dictatorship. In the
event, there was no open support for the proposal from any of the major parties or from the president.

A draft electoral law reflecting the president's views was submitted to the Duma on 1 November 1994, based on preparatory work
undertaken over the summer by the Central Electoral Commission.
The bill proposed increasing the number of single-member districts to
300, with the remaining 150 allocated to party lists on a Russia-wide
basis. Another change was that candidates included in a national list
could not at the same time run for election in an individual constituency. The national lists would themselves have to be nominated by at
least 250,000 voters, not 100,000, and no more than 7 percent could be
drawn from any republic or region, instead of the 15 percent that the
law had previously allowed. The presidential draft also proposed that
parties or alliances that had reached the 5 percent barrier in the December 1993 party-list vote should not be required again to collect the signatures needed for nomination.

The bill was approved on first reading by the Duma in late November. The Duma's committee on legislation had introduced more
than a thousand amendments, including a reversion to the 50:50 balance between single-member districts and party lists (*Moskovskie
novosti*, no. 15, 1995, 8). The amended bill was approved on a second
reading on 15 March 1995, and after lengthy discussion on a third reading on 24 March 1995 it was approved by a vote of 257 to 36 with only
one abstention. To become law, however, the bill also required the ap-

proval of the Federation Council, which rejected it with equal decisiveness on 12 April. The "traditional hostility of regional leaders for party
leaders" had played a part, commented *Rossiiskie vesti* (14 April 1995,
1). In addition, the regional leaders represented in the upper house had
a direct interest in a Duma electoral system that would give them the
greatest possible influence over the outcome. Federation Council members thus tended to favor single-member districts. Undeterred, the
Duma confirmed its own version of the new law in three readings on
21 April, retaining an equal balance between single-member districts
and party lists; but it was rejected once again by the Federation Council
on 4 May by a margin of 114 to 11 (*Kommersant-daily*, 5 May 1995, 1).

Under the Russian constitution, the Duma has the power to override the upper house if two-thirds of its members decide accordingly.
On 11 May the election law was approved again by 302 to 73 and sent
directly to the president for his signature. Yeltsin complained that the
equal division between local constituencies and national lists was "un-
just," however, and that a Duma elected on this basis would "not represent the people" (*Segodnya*, 16 May 1995, 2). On 23 May, "taking into
account the opinion of the Federation Council," he vetoed the new
draft. The Duma once more voted in its favor, but not by the two-thirds
majority that would have been necessary to override the presidential
veto. Yeltsin refused to withdraw, and a conciliation committee had to
be appointed to find a way forward.

In the end, the conciliation committee found a formula that "could,
by a considerable stretch of the imagination, be called a compromise"
(*Kommersant-daily*, 10 June 1995, 3). The revised bill was approved by
the Duma on 9 June by a substantial 264 to 45 majority. It was approved by the Federation Council on 14 June, but by less than the half
of the total membership that the constitution required. The Duma,
Shumeiko had warned, would overturn any veto they might impose,
and the president would then go ahead and approve the law; it was
also important to "hold the elections on time to show the world that we
respect our constitution and that Russia is building a civil society"
(*Segodnya*, 16 June 1995, 1). After all-night consultations, the Federation
Council approved the revised bill by a large enough majority on 15
June. On 21 June the legislative marathon finally came to an end when
the revised draft was signed by President Yeltsin, concluding what
Nezavisimaya gazeta described as "more than two years of intense political struggle" (29 November 1995, 5; for the text, see *Rossiiskaya gazeta*,
28 June 1995, 3–7, and *O vyborakh deputatov* 1995).

The net effect of the mobilization of conflicting presidential and

Duma interests was an election law with relatively few changes compared to the law that had regulated the elections of December 1993. In particular, the 50:50 balance between single-member constituencies and national party lists remained intact. The national lists, however, would consist of a Moscow section of no more than twelve candidates, together with a much longer regional list; members of the central list could not stand elsewhere, while members of the regional list could also put themselves forward in single-member districts. The Duma moved toward the president in accepting that government employees and journalists could run for office without resigning, provided they did not make improper use of their positions. The president had favored a 50 percent minimum turnout requirement or else a second round between the two leading candidates in the single-member districts. The law retained the Duma's view that a 25 percent turnout requirement was sufficient and a single round of voting more appropriate.

In addition to a new law about electing deputies, in October 1994 the Duma had approved a set of basic guarantees of electoral rights. Citizens abroad were given the same right to vote as those in Russia, and the franchise was extended to all Russian citizens except prisoners and those pronounced incompetent to exercise those rights by a court (*Ob osnovnykh* 1995). Legislation on the election of a Russian president was approved in April 1995; there were few changes apart from a significant increase in the number of signatures required to submit a valid nomination. To disadvantage smaller and more recently formed parties, President Yeltsin proposed a threshold of 2 million, twenty times more than the number required in 1991. The Duma lowered the number of signatures to 1.5 million in the draft adopted on 24 March and reduced it to 1 million in the final version adopted on 21 April, but left unchanged the requirement that no more than 7 percent of signatures could come from any one republic or region. This was approved by the Federation Council, and the law was signed by President Yeltsin on 17 May 1995 (*Rossiiskaya gazeta*, 23 May 1995, 4–8, and *O vyborakh Prezidenta* 1995). New legislation on the "general principles" of local government elections followed in August 1995 (*Ob obshchikh printsipakh* 1995).

There was controversy, too, about the manner in which the Federation Council should be formed, and a possibility that this dispute could lead to postponement of the forthcoming Duma ballot because of the absence of agreement about the upper house. The constitution laid down that it should be "formed," but did not explicitly require it to be elected, as had happened in December 1993; it simply indicated that the manner of its formation would be established by future legislation. A bill providing for the election of the Federation Council was approved by both houses in June 1995 but was rejected by the president on 12 August on the grounds that it was unconstitutional. The same day, the Duma failed to overturn the presidential veto. Yeltsin favored a greater emphasis on ex officio membership in the Federation Council in order to assure "stability"; it should include regional heads of government, most of whom he had appointed, and it would be less likely to consist of active legislators who might resist presidential initiatives. For their part, having originally been elected, council members were more inclined toward the representative principle. After two further attempts, a bill was passed in late November establishing a new selection procedure for the Federation Council. It was rejected by the council itself, but the Duma overrode its veto on 5 December and President Yeltsin signed the new law the following day (*Sobranie zakonodatelstva Rossiiskoi Federatsii*, no. 50, 1995, item 4869).

According to the new Federation Council law, the governors of every republic and region and the heads of each of their legislatures would ex officio become members of the Federation Council when its current term expired. About a third of the governors had already secured their local positions as a result of competitive elections, and those who had not been elected in this way would have to submit themselves to local elections before December 1996.

Yeltsin's supporters favored the law because their views were well represented among regional governors, many of whom were Yeltsin appointees. The president's opponents knew that if there was no agreement on the formation of the Federation Council, the Duma elections would have to be postponed. There was an attempt by opponents to challenge the law in the Constitutional Court, but the Court refused to consider the matter. This ended what *Segodnya* described as the "longest-running soap opera of the new Russian parliamentarianism" (8 December 1995, 1).

The new law on electoral districts, adopted in the late summer, altered virtually all of them to some degree (see *Sobranie zakonodatelstva Rossiiskoi Federatsii,* no. 34, 1995, item 3425). There was criticism that the Central Electoral Commission had sought to merge parts of opposition strongholds in the countryside with larger and more reform-minded urban areas (*Izvestiya*, 11 July 1995, 1). There was also some concern that more than 2 million electors had somehow "disappeared" from the electoral register since the April 1993 referendum, even though the population itself had fallen by just 300,000 (*Argumenty i fakty*, no. 29, 1995, 2). There were additional worries about an attempt to computerize the voting process. A new state automated system was introduced for the 1995 and 1996 elections, giving rise to fears of the "adjustment" of results. Domestic computer producers were particularly annoyed that the order had been placed abroad (*Kommersant-daily*, 2 June 1995, 3). Officials, in reply, made clear that there were safeguards, and that computer-generated election figures would be used for "consultative purposes" only (*Segodnya*, 7 April 1995, 2; the presidential decree that established the system appeared in *Rossiiskaya gazeta*, 11 March 1995, 4).

Holding the election was nonetheless in doubt up to the last minute, when a group of deputies and activists sought to suspend it by challenging its constitutionality. A Duma elected under the new law, they argued, would directly represent only a small minority of voters because of wasted votes for parties and candidates that failed to secure election. How could this satisfy the constitutional requirement that the Russian parliament represent all citizens? (*Moskovskie novosti*, no. 75, 1995, 4). But the Constitutional Court refused to consider the case, and on 17 September the Central Electoral Commission began collecting nominations for party lists and candidates. Like it or not, Russian politicians had to switch their attention from life within the Moscow beltway to the choices of 100 million voters spread across the eight time zones of the Russian Federation.

ᢙ 10 ᢘ

The 1995 Duma Campaign

The minimum definition of democracy is that free competitive elections offer voters a chance to endorse the government of the day or turn it out in favor of opposition parties (Schumpeter 1952). A separately elected president and representative assembly complicate this principle but do not contradict it. In France, the president of the republic appoints as prime minister the party leader most likely to command the support of a majority in parliament. Thus, when the French electorate gave a majority to the right, a Socialist president had to "cohabit" with a prime minister of a different party; a president of the right must in turn respect a parliamentary majority of the left (see, e.g., Hall et al. 1994; Keeler and Schain 1996). In the United States, midterm congressional elections do not change control of the White House, but a government divided between Republicans and Democrats is a frequent occurrence (see, e.g., Cox and Kernell 1991; Thurber 1991; Jones 1994). Moreover, a big swing in votes in midterm congressional elections can produce a big change in the political climate, as the Republicans under Newt Gingrich demonstrated in 1994.

The new Russian Federation, rooted in a violent confrontation between president and parliament, has not yet established conventions to regulate relations between president, prime minister, and Duma. Yeltsin supporters could claim that the Duma election was no concern of the president, since his name was not on the ballot and he was not a member of a political party. Hence, when Duma votes were counted, it could not be said that the president had won or lost the election. Yeltsin's uncertain health—after his heart attack in October 1995 he spent most of the campaign convalescing—made him appear outside the battle, although he did warn voters against the Communists in an eve-of-poll broadcast (*Rossiiskaya gazeta*, 16 December 1995, 1, 3). Implicit in the president's role was the assumption that whatever happened in the

Duma vote on 17 December, Russia would still be governed by the Yeltsin administration.

The president's distancing himself from the parliamentary election could be considered a denial of democratic accountability or as "delegative" democracy in the Latin American style, in which a president claims to know what is best for the country without reference to other representative institutions (cf. O'Donnell 1994). The prime minister, Viktor Chernomyrdin, could not take this view, as his office is vulnerable to a no-confidence vote by the Duma. But the constitution hedges the impact of no-confidence votes in such a way that the process is too cumbersome to operate as a continuing check. In an effort to build support for himself, his ministers, and his presidential patron, Chernomyrdin organized "Our Home Is Russia" to contest the Duma election. The prospect of a presidential election six months after the Duma ballot encouraged Yeltsin's potential challengers to make the best possible showing in December 1995 in order to establish a position as front-runner, and some of the parties—such as the Congress of Russian Communities, grouped around General Lebed and the former Security Council secretary, Yuri Skokov—were best interpreted as vehicles giving their leaders a head start in the presidential race.

In effect, the Duma election was a halfway house on the road to democratic accountability: it did offer the Russian electorate a chance to vote for or against the government of the day, but there was no way in which voters could choose a new government. In addition to constitutional and presidential barriers to change, the division of the opposition into dozens of parties meant there was no party or coalition of parties readily identified as an alternative government, as happens in multiparty systems such as Germany as well as in the British two-party system. The majority of Russians felt dissatisfied and used the opportunity to vote against the government. The result left Boris Yeltsin in office, but it did not leave Russian politics the same as before.

Parties as Irrational Actors

Empirical theories of political science tend to model elections as a rational process in which politicians seek votes and office. Parties do not stand for anything in the old-fashioned ideological sense, and they are representative only in the instrumental sense of saying what voters want in order to win election. The theory is most developed in studies of American elections, but attempts have also been made to apply it to the analysis of postcommunist elections (see, e.g., Kitschelt 1995). Like economic theory, these public choice models of vote seeking are based on a priori assumptions about how politicians are expected to behave; they are not based on evidence drawn from everyday political life.

The 1995 Duma election offers a good test of the applicability of rational actor models to Russian politics, for unlike the elections of December 1993, politicians had plenty of time to make calculations and form strategic alliances in pursuit of their own interests. Furthermore, politicians were no longer flying blind concerning the preferences of voters. Zhirinovsky's success in 1993 indicated substantial support for a nationalist appeal, and there was also substantial support for Communists. The low vote for Gaidar's Russia's Choice indicated limited electoral support for reformers and the disadvantages in being the party of government when government was unpopular.

Since winning votes is but a means to the end of winning seats in the Duma, the way in which the electoral system converts votes into seats is a very important part of any rational calculation. Although 225 Duma members were to be elected by proportional representation, the law required parties to cross a 5 percent threshold to qualify for the award of seats. This high threshold was intended to prevent an undue proliferation of parties, as is the case in Germany. Where a low threshold exists, as in the Netherlands, a dozen parties can easily win seats in parliament. Countries with a lower threshold tend to have more parties in parliament, and they are more likely to have coalition governments (cf. Taagepera and Shugart 1989).

The simplest goal of a rational politician in the Russian setting would be to form a party that will win at least 5 percent of the vote (more than 3 million votes in total), thus securing more than twenty seats in the Duma. In 1993, although only three parties won more than 10 percent of the party-list vote, eight cleared the 5 percent barrier (see table 6.2). But the more parties contesting an election, the fewer the number that can be confident of being above the threshold. Furthermore, to clear the 5 percent barrier, new parties would have to take votes from parties that did not have a lot of votes to spare. Presidentialist parties had another rationale for putting forward lists of party candidates: to increase the media exposure of their leaders. But the election also threatened to expose the weakness of would-be presidential candidates if their parties failed to clear the threshold. A nationally known personality standing as a candidate in a single-member district could hope that even if the party did not win any list seats it might boost the leader's campaign for a single-member seat.

If only two parties contest seats, in a free and fair election both would be certain to clear the 5 percent barrier. If no more than six national parties contested the election, most would be expected to clear the barrier, as the average vote per party would be 16.7 percent. But parties take an unequal share of the vote: some get more than the average and others less. In a six-way division of the vote a party could still clear the 5 percent threshold with less than a third of the average vote. But if twelve parties compete, with the leader winning 20 percent of the vote and the second 15 percent, the remaining ten parties have only 65 percent of the vote to share out among them. In such circumstances, the probability of some parties failing to win any seats rises substantially. With more than two dozen parties it was possible, as Sergei Shakhrai of the Party of Russian Unity and Concord pointed out, that only one would reach the 5 percent threshold and thus take all 225 party-list seats (*Izvestiya*, 23 September 1995, 2). It would be theoretically possible for no party to win any seats, for if two dozen or more parties each won the same share of the vote, all would fall below the 5 percent threshold.

The rational way to maximize representation in the Duma is simply stated: form alliances that add electoral support, even if doing so blurs ideological lines or requires sharing the fruits of victory. In the early months of 1995, however, the press was full of reports of the formation of new political parties, rather than coalitions. In January, a Federal-Democratic Movement of Russia was formed (*Izvestiya*, 17 January 1995, 1); in February, Boris Fedorov's Forward, Russia! (Fedorov 1995); in March, the Party of Popular Conscience and the Party of Workers' Self-Management (*Segodnya*, 23 March 1995, 3; *Pravda*, 10 March 1995, 5). Our Home Is Russia and Ivan Rybkin's bloc were both formed in the spring; and in May, Yavlinsky made clear that Yabloko would be unable to form an electoral pact with Gaidar's Russia's Choice (*Izvestiya*, 18 May 1995, 2). Duma members who had formed a new faction in parliament and who wanted to run again had to find a national list that would accept them or else form a list of their own: two further groupings, "Duma-96" and "Stable Russia," were formed on this basis.

To be eligible to nominate candidates, an electoral association had to be registered with the Ministry of Justice not less than six months before the election; hence, there was a flurry of activity throughout the early months of 1995 for politicians to register their parties. At one point it appeared that any group of politicians with a backer who had enough money to rent a room for a press conference could announce the formation of a new party. In a fluid situation, the mere announcement of a party might be used as a bargaining counter for a politician wanting to secure a top slot on the list of an established party or to bargain with other would-be party leaders about the terms of combining to their mutual advantage. According to the Central Electoral Commission, more than 270 parties or other organizations were initially registered and recognized as having the right to take part in elections at the national level; in 1993 there had been just 147 (*Rossiiskaya gazeta,* 19 September 1995, 2). While many so-called parties existed only on paper, there were indications that Russia might "take the world record for the number of electoral associations per head of population" (*Segodnya,* 18 August 1995, 2).

Public and privately commissioned opinion polls gave ample warning of the risk that politicians faced of their parties failing to clear the 5 percent barrier. After allowing for nonvoters and don't knows, the polls showed that those with voting intentions were relatively evenly divided among the parties and implied that the majority would have difficulty in clearing the threshold and qualifying for Duma seats. For example, the spring 1995 New Russia Barometer found that the clear winners were "don't know," with 31 percent, and "won't vote," with 27 percent; at that time no party or alliance could claim the support of more than 7 percent of the electorate. Even after excluding those not intending to vote and assuming that the behavior of don't knows did not alter the relative strength of parties, only four parties were endorsed by as many as a tenth of intending voters (Rose 1995f, 55–56).

The nomination procedure gave parties an incentive to combine. To be eligible for a place on the party-list ballot, an electoral association had to collect at least 200,000 signatures from eligible voters, with no more than 7 percent coming from any one of Russia's regions or republics. All these signatures had to be presented to the Central Electoral Commission by 22 October (*Kalendarnyi* 1995). The law made financial inducements or any form of pressure illegal, and each elector was allowed to endorse no more than a single list of nominees (Article 39). Press reports, however, made clear that many of the parties ignored these laws in obtaining their signatures. A week before nominations closed, prospective signatories in the Belgorod region were being offered 2 kilograms of flour, and in Krasnodar a bottle of beer; the average price of a signature had reached 2,000 rubles, about 50 cents at the prevailing rate of exchange (*Izvestiya,* 14 October 1995, 4). A few days later the average charge for a professionally collected signature had reached $4 to $5; indeed there were "centers for political consultation" that were prepared to organize the entire campaign for their clients, from the collection of signatures to public speeches and, "for the laziest," even an electoral program (*Izvestiya*, 18 October 1995, 2).

The electoral law made no direct reference to political parties. Lists of candidates could be put forward by electoral associations, which were bodies formed for the purpose of contesting elections, or by electoral blocs, which were combinations of two or more electoral associations (*O vyborakh* 1995, Articles 32, 33). The construction of party lists gave further opportunities for coalition building. Each party was allowed to nominate twelve names on a national list; these candidates were guaranteed a seat in the Duma if a party cleared the 5 percent barrier. This gave leaders of electoral associations the opportunity to determine who would be certain of winning a place in the Duma—if their association or bloc could clear the 5 percent threshold. Additional candidates had to be nominated on regional lists; since residence in the region was not a requirement for being nominated, such candidates could be Muscovites. The allocation of seats to individuals on regional lists followed a complex procedure taking into account the votes a party won in each region, and the number of seats remaining after candidates on the national list had been accommodated (Articles 37, 61, 62, 70).

Too many parties would make a "mockery" of democracy, the chair of the Central Electoral Commission declared. At the outset of the campaign he thought only seven to nine parties or blocs would be able to win seats in the new Duma (*Segodnya*, 21 September 1995, 2). As many as sixty-nine different groupings began to collect the signatures required; many, however, were unable to achieve the target, and some did no more than announce the launch of a campaign that did not even produce a valid list of candidates (*Izvestiya*, 24 October 1995, 2). Nomination papers and lists of candidates were filed with the Central Electoral Commission, whose chair had promised that all would be "X-rayed" for authenticity (*Izvestiya*, 28 September 1995, 2). The commission found irregularities in the documentation of two of the major parties, Derzhava and Yabloko, and initially refused to register them (*Rossiiskaya gazeta*, 2 November 1995, 5, 6). Its refusal was overturned shortly afterward by the Supreme Court (*Nezavisimaya gazeta*, 5 November 1995, 1).

In the end, forty-three electoral associations or blocs were registered, with 5,675 candidates included in their lists (*Kommersant-daily*, 29 November 1995, 3). Such a degree of party competition demonstrated the irrationality of Russian politicians, at least as that term is understood in Western political science. Instead of combining into parties with a reasonable chance of clearing the 5 percent barrier, the proliferation of parties turned the barrier from a hurdle that most parties could clear into a mountain that few could surmount. The maximum number of parties capable of clearing the threshold was twenty, if each got exactly 5 percent of the vote and the remaining twenty-three parties won no votes at all. Thus, even before a single vote was cast, a substantial majority of parties were condemned to winning nothing. On average, a party could expect only 2.3 percent of the vote; thus, even if a party won twice the average vote, it would still not win any party-list seats. The greater the pool of "wasted" votes, that is, ballots cast for parties that were not awarded any list seats in the Duma, the bigger the jackpot of seats shared by the small number of parties able to clear the 5 percent threshold. Positions on the ballot paper were allocated by lot; Women of Russia drew first place; the Union of Housing and Municipal Workers of Russia was placed last on the ballot.

In single-member seats a very different logic applied, for the candidate who came first in the popular vote won the seat, however large or small the candidate's share of the vote. With only two candidates in a race, one was sure to get more than half the vote, but as the number of candidates contesting a district rose, the minimum required to win tended to decline. The single-member electoral system thus encouraged candidates who could be sure of mobilizing a significant bloc of votes in a district, for example, a factory manager or the head of a large collective farm, to enter the election even if their core support was well under half the local electorate. To win in a district, such a candidate could either broaden his or her core vote or encourage a large number of other candidates to come forward, thus splitting the total vote and lowering the number of votes needed for victory. In a single-member district, a candidate who could mobilize anything from an eighth to a quarter of the vote had a chance of victory.

In the event, about 2,700 candidates were nominated in the single-member districts, an average of 12 for each of the 225 seats available. More than 1,000 candidates were nominated by independent groups of electors, and the remainder by 60 different parties or alliances (*Kommersant-daily*, 29 November 1995, 3; for the number of parties, see *Nezavisimaya gazeta*, 14 December 1995, 1). The Liberal Democrats made valid nominations in 83 percent of the single-member districts, the Communists in 80 percent; in addition, the Congress of Russian Communities, Our Home Is Russia, the Agrarians, Russia's Democratic Choice, and Yabloko made nominations in more than half of them (*Nezavisimaya gazeta*, 14 December 1995, 1).

In social composition, Women of Russia was most distinctive, for all its candidates were women. The Liberal Democrats nominated the smallest proportion of women, 6 percent. Communists and Agrarians tended to field the oldest candidates. The candidates of the party of government, Our Home Is Russia, and of Women of Russia were the most likely to work in government itself (see Haas et al. 1995, 13).

Parties and Candidates

The forty-three parties and movements that took part in the election could be divided into five broad "camps" (cf. *Financial Times*, 11 December 1995, 2; Pribylovsky 1995; see also *Pravda*, 16 November 1995, 1; McFaul and Petrov 1995; Markov 1995; Schneider 1996). Of course, any classification involves oversimplification and tends to exaggerate the coherence and distinct identity of what were rarely "parties" in a Western sense and more often tactical alliances or the followings of individual leaders (for interviews with leaders and discussions of programs, see *Transition* 1995).

1. *Liberal reform* parties were committed to democracy and market reform, and critical of the Chernomyrdin government for backsliding on both counts. The most important was "Russia's Democratic Choice (RDC)—United Democrats," led by former prime minister Yegor Gaidar. The bloc included Gaidar's Russia's Choice party, founded in June 1994, together with the Peasant Party of Russia, led by Yuri Chernichenko, and the Social Democratic Party, formed in 1995 and led by the "father of perestroika," Alexander Yakovlev. Gaidar's party had emerged as the largest of the parliamentary factions after the 1993 Duma election, but Gaidar himself had resigned from office and Russia's Choice had lost ground as some of its deputies gravitated toward the Chernomyrdin government, while others took up a more sharply critical position. So too did Gaidar after the outbreak of the Chechen war, leading to an open rift with President Yeltsin and Gaidar's announcement in February 1995 that the party would not support Yeltsin for a second term. The RDC list was headed by Gaidar, together with the former parliamentary ombudsman who had become internationally known for his condemnation of the Chechen war, Sergei Kovalev, and actress Lidia Fedoseeva-Shukshina.

There were several other strongly liberal and promarket blocs including "Common Cause," led by businesswoman Irina Khakamada, which championed the "unheard majority," including women at home, pensioners, the disabled, teachers, and youth (Khakamada 1995). There was also a Christian Democratic Union, led by deputy Vitaly Savitsky, which gave particular emphasis to social problems including human rights and the death penalty; and a Federal Democratic Movement, based on the ideas of Andrei Sakharov and led by the former chair of Moscow's Antimonopoly Board, Oleg Novikov, with the well-known former KGB general Oleg Kalugin and poetess Rimma Kazakova as the other names at the top of its national list. The Party of Economic Freedom, led by the wealthy founder of the Russian Goods and Raw Materials Exchange, Konstantin Borovoi, was close to Gaidar and other monetarists.

Yabloko (Apple), led by economist Grigorii Yavlinsky, favored a "socially oriented" market concerned with the less privileged. It was critical of Yeltsin for his attempt to convert the presidency into a "monarchy with unlimited powers," but was equally critical of the "bolshevik methods" that had been followed by Gaidar and other "radical democrats" in the recent past. Yabloko's list was headed by Yavlinsky, former Russian ambassador to the United States Vladimir Lukin, and economist Tatyana Yarygina. Yuri Boldyrev, one of the original leaders, had resigned as deputy chairman in opposition to what he considered to be Yavlinsky's authoritarian management, but he retained his party membership. Yabloko's aim, according to Yavlinsky, was to show that there was a "democratic alternative to the current regime." It criticized the shelling of the White House in October 1993 and the increasingly oligarchical and (in its view) criminal character of the ruling elite, and promised to strengthen the place of parliament within the Russian constitution (*Izvestiya*, 13 July 1995, 2; *Deklaratsiya* 1995).

Among other proreform movements, "Forward, Russia!" was headed by former Finance Minister Boris Fedorov; founded in 1994, it was particularly conspicuous for its firm defense of Russian unity, including Chechnya. What would the United States government have done, Fedorov asked, if Texas had tried to leave the Union? At the same time, Forward, Russia! took a sharply hostile position toward the Chernomyrdin government and called for faster, more extensive privatization and other measures to curb the state bureaucracy (*Liberalnyi* 1995). The name of the grouping itself was borrowed from Silvio Berlusconi's successful right-wing movement in Italy, "Forza Italia!" Fedorov saw his party as the political equivalent of the U.S. Republican Party, with Yabloko the Democrats. Because of his outspoken defense of Russian unity and populist rhetoric, opponents made less flattering comparisons of Fedorov with Vladimir Zhirinovsky.

Another reform party, the "Pamfilova-Gurov-Vladimir Lysenko" bloc, was less stridently monetarist and nationalist. Formally an association of the Republican Party, headed by Lysenko and based originally on the liberal Democratic Platform within the old Communist Party of the Soviet Union, and the Committee of Soldiers' Mothers, it was in practice a grouping of the supporters of its three well-known leaders. Ella Pamfilova, the most prominent, had been minister for social welfare in the Chernomyrdin government but had resigned in 1994; before that, she had headed the commission on privileges in the USSR Supreme Soviet, earning a reputation as an advocate of social justice. Alexander Gurov had been head of the department on organized crime of the Interior Ministry, lending the group some "anti-Mafia" credentials. The other elements in its program were tax and military reform and attention to the needs of the less advantaged (*Platforma* 1995).

2. The main *progovernment* party was Our Home Is Russia, founded in spring 1995 as a political movement to sustain the Chernomyrdin government in the Duma elections and intended to offer the base for a presidential campaign by Boris Yeltsin in June 1996. Our Home was the "party of power": a coalition of the postcommunist political and economic *nomenklatura*, differing in views but sharing a common interest in the maintenance of their official position. Above all, it represented the energy complex, with which Premier Chernomyrdin had a close association, and the military-industrial complex, with which First Vice-Premier Oleg Soskovets was connected. Chernomyrdin's reputed wealth as a result of the privatization of the gas industry, of which he had been chairman, attracted unfavorable publicity, and some dubbed the group "Nash dom, Gazprom" (Our Home Is the Gas Industry). It was the wealthiest of the parties and nominated the largest number of candidates, 396.

Our Home's list of candidates was headed by Chernomyrdin, followed by film director Nikita Mikhalkov (whose *Burnt by the Sun* had won an Oscar in 1994) and General Lev Rokhlin, who had led the assault on Grozny but refused to accept a state prize for his achievement. It also included Nikolai Travkin, who had founded and led the Democratic Party of Russia. Our Home stood for the construction of a "democratic civil society" with the support of all who wanted "progress without revolutionary upheavals" and were "tired of disorder" (*Programma* 1995a); stability, in the view of commentators, was in fact its "basic and almost its only slogan" (Markov 1995, 72). In addition to being able to use the state machinery, Our Home received heavy support from finance and big business. It was able to spend liberally on campaign publicity, and to attract celebrities, such as the German supermodel Claudia Schiffer, to its public events. But it was not clear that show business glitz would compensate for the gray and middle-aged image of the prime minister, who had never before run for public office. Our Home's campaign slogan—"On a firm foundation of responsibility and experience"—emphasized its bureaucratic orientation.

Sergei Shakhrai's Party of Russian Unity and Concord (PRES) was also progovernment and had performed relatively well in the 1993 elections. Essentially a collection of Shakhrai's supporters, it had originally formed part of Our Home Is Russia but withdrew to campaign separately when it failed to secure enough high-ranking places in Our Home's national list of candidates; Shakhrai himself was offered the seventh or eighth place, but there were no places for his colleagues. In 1993 PRES had won votes in peripheral and non-Russian areas, but Shakhrai's earlier supporters were dismayed by his firmly progovernment position in the Chechen conflict. Its list was headed by Shakhrai, Valerii Bykov (a biochemist responsible for the preservation of Lenin's corpse), and the Siberian politician Vladimir Ivankov; its program emphasized a new relationship between the federal government and the regions. "Cedar" represented environmentalists, but was close to the agencies that enforced government policy; its list was headed by party chair Anatolii Panfilov and included Sergei Zalygin, respected editor of the literary journal *Novy mir*. The Muslim movement "Nur" was also close to government thinking and was influenced by Islamic church leaders.

"Women of Russia" had a more ambiguous position. Based originally on the Soviet-era Committee of Soviet Women, it had come to reflect the views of the president and of the party's leader, Ekaterina Lakhova, a doctor from the same part of Russia as Boris Yeltsin, who had chaired a commission on women, the family, and demography for the government. In a sense, it sought to be the female half of the "party of power"; yet it had also supported a move by the Communists and Agrarians to halt the process of privatization. In the Duma, Women of Russia was "one of the most pragmatic" parties in that it "more often than others voted for diametrically opposite proposals" (*Izvestiya*, 5 November 1995, 4). When it came to voting on the "most bitterly contested questions of principle, the party usually abstained or voted in a way that suited the government" (*Sovetskaya Rossiya*, 11 November 1995, 4). In addition to Lakhova, the party's leaders were Alevtina Fedulova, chair of the Russian Union of Women and a former member of the CPSU Central Committee, and Galina Klimantova, chair of the Duma Committee on Women, Family, and Youth Affairs. Women of Russia emphasized social welfare and military noninvolvement in its program; its slogan pointed out that "without women, there is no democracy!" (*Programma* 1995b). But its special claims for support were weaker than in 1993, inasmuch as many women were prominently placed on other party lists or indeed led lists of their own, as did Pamfilova and Khakamada.

3. *Social-welfare parties* generally supported the government but also emphasized the need to protect the less fortunate from the full rigors of market reform. The Ivan Rybkin bloc, headed by the Duma Speaker, was created in early 1995 as a putative left-center counterpart to Our Home Is Russia, but it failed to gather support, and Rybkin was expelled from the leadership of his own Agrarian Party in September 1995 for being too propresidential. The Federation of Independent Trade Unions and the Industrial Party also deserted Rybkin, and even after the bloc had been registered, several of its leaders left because of Rybkin's weak direction, among them General Boris Gromov (who had been second on the original party list), economist Stanislav Shatalin (who had been third), and singer Iosif Kobzon. Rybkin's bloc called for a greater degree of attention to social welfare within the context of market reforms, but its program remained diffuse (see *Predvybornaya platforma* 1995). In addition to Rybkin, its list included Yuri Petrov, who had formerly headed Yeltsin's administration.

The social-welfare category also included Trade Unions and Industrialists of Russia—the Union of Labor, founded in September 1995 and headed by trade union leader Mikhail Shmakov, former vice-premier Vladimir Shcherbakov, and former co-chair of the Civic Union Arkadii Volsky. It called for policies favoring industry and domestic producers (*Osnovnye polozheniya* 1995). "My Fatherland," closely connected with Stanislav Shatalin's "Reform" foundation, drew on the support of former Komsomol first secretary Viktor Mishin and General Gromov. The "Transformation of the Fatherland" bloc was a grouping of regional elites, headed by the Sverdlovsk regional governor Eduard Rossel. The Social Democrats combined such different groups as the Russian Social-Democratic Union headed by Vasilii Lipitsky and the Democratic Reform Movement headed by economist and former Moscow mayor Gavriil Popov. Lipitsky and Popov headed its list, together with economist Oleg Bogomolov. The pro-welfare group also included the Party of Workers' Self-Management, headed by prominent eye surgeon Svyatoslav Fedorov; its list included former Prosecutor General Aleksei Kazannik (for its program, see *Za blagopoluchie* 1995).

4. A more conventional range of parties represented *communist* alternatives, led by the Communist Party of the Russian Federation (CPRF) (Lysenko 1995; Ishiyama 1996). The CPRF was the only party with a mass membership, claiming half a million, more than all the others put together; it was one of the few that had a network of activists throughout the country; and it was virtually the only party that was more than the fan club of its leader. Unlike almost all other groupings, the rating of party chair Gennadii Zyuganov lagged behind that of the party itself. The CPRF had three main elements: a national communist or reformist section represented by Zyuganov; a social-democratic section represented by the former Russian party leader Valentin Kuptsov; and an orthodox Marxist-Leninist section headed by the former editor of its journal *Kommunist,* Richard Kosolapov. Without rejecting private property in principle, the CPRF said it needed to reflect "social justice." Its symbol was a book as well as a hammer and sickle, representing the "union of workers of town, country, science and culture," and it emphasized religion, morality, and traditional values too (*Tretii III S"ezd* 1995, 96–118). Its program was described as an exercise in "selective nostalgia" (Belin 1995, 25) and as showing "iron-fisted populism" (Sakwa 1996, 17).

The CPRF national list was headed by Zyuganov, together with a Vladivostok procurator and former deputy chair of the Russian Congress of People's Deputies, Svetlana Goryacheva, and Kemerovo regional council chair and former presidential candidate Aman Tuleev. Its regional lists included former Supreme Soviet chair Anatolii Lukyanov, who had been indicted for his support of the attempted coup in 1991, and many others who had been prominent in the Soviet period. The party's electoral manifesto called for the formation of a "national patriotic majority" in the new Duma, which would restore the right to employment and to free education and health care. The party also promised to hold down prices, return "strategic" industries to public ownership, develop a more independent foreign policy, defend the rights of Russians abroad, and bring back a "single union state" on a voluntary basis. Although the party was opposed to presidential rule in principle and would retain it only for a limited, transitional period, the manifesto looked forward to the "victory of our presidential candidate" in the June election (*Za nashu* 1995; also *Dialog,* no. 10, 1995, 3–9).

The Communists were allied in rural areas to the Agrarian Party, representing state and collective farms. Their leader was Mikhail Lapshin, director of the "Behests of Lenin" farm in the Moscow region; other leading figures included Alexander Zaveryukha, who was vice-premier in the Chernomyrdin government, Alexander Nazarchuk, who was minister of agriculture, and Vasilii Starodubtsev, one of the conspirators in August 1991 and chair of a thriving collective farm in the Tula region. The Agrarians' slogan was "Fatherland, People's Power, Justice, Welfare." In practice, they stood for state government support of agriculture and opposed land privatization, arguing that it would lead to a fall in production and to ownership by speculators rather than farmers themselves (see *Programma* 1995c; also *Dialog,* no. 11–12, 1995, 13–18).

Other left-wing electoral associations included "Power to the People!" led by former prime minister Nikolai Ryzhkov and Duma deputy Sergei Baburin, which was less uncompromising on economic questions than Zyuganov's party and more nationalist (its platform appeared in *Pravda,* 12 September 1995, 2). "Communists—Working Russia—for the Soviet Union" was a hard-line coalition of the Russian Communist Workers' Party and the Russian Party of Communists headed by Viktor Anpilov, a skillful street orator imprisoned after the October events of 1993 who favored the restoration of the Soviet system by whatever means were necessary (see *Predvybornaya pozitsiya* 1995).

5. There were a variety of *national and imperial patriotic* groupings, including Vladimir Zhirinovsky's Liberal Democrats and the Derzhava (Great Power) movement headed by former vice-president Alexander Rutskoi. The Liberal Democrats had done best in the 1993 party-list vote, but their parliamentary faction had been unstable and Zhirinovsky had shown some willingness to cooperate with the Chernomyrdin government by supporting the 1994 and 1995 budgets. The party's earlier appeals had also been undermined by the emergence of other nationalist groupings, such as Sergei Baburin's Russian All-National Union, which had formed a common electoral front with Power to the People. The Liberal Democrats were strongly nationalist and anti-Western in their foreign policy, in favor of the restoration of federal control in Chechnya, and both promarket and protectionist in domestic economic policy (Zhirinovsky 1995). They were well financed, had a national network of activists, and enjoyed good relations with the armed forces. But the Liberal Democrats owed most to their leader, a campaigner who identified the problems of ordinary Russians and sug-

gested simple remedies, such as reviving arms exports or shooting the leaders of organized crime.

The Congress of Russian Communities (KRO) was distinctive in embracing both Russian nationalism and socialist-style economics. Its most prominent leader was former General Alexander Lebed, who had led the 14th army in the Dnestr region of Moldova until a cease-fire was concluded. He was dismissed in spring 1995 when his outspoken views began to embarrass the Ministry of Defense. Lebed was a charismatic figure who had opposed the Chechen war and a contender for the presidency. Newspapers credited him with the "brain of Albert Einstein and the physique of Arnold Schwarzenegger" (*Financial Times*, 3 June 1995, 8). KRO's other leaders were former chair of the Security Council Yuri Skokov, who had close ties with the military-industrial complex, and the chair of the Democratic Party of Russia, Sergei Glazev, who was minister of foreign trade and the only member of the administration to resign when the Russian parliament was dissolved by presidential decree in September 1993. KRO also drew on the support of Lyudmila Vartazarova, leader of the Socialist Workers' Party, former justice minister Yuri Kalmykov, and industrialist Konstantin Zatulin.

KRO had been founded in 1993 to represent Russians living outside the federation. It included supporters of the fullest possible restoration of the Soviet empire (Zatulin) as well as convinced federalists (Kalmykov) and former separatists. It embraced moderate Russian nationalists, but also such socialists as Vartazarova. There were opponents of "Zionism" as well as radical democrats; there were Communists and Orthodox monarchists. The central elements in KRO's program were the gradual reconstitution of the USSR by peaceful means, defense of Russians abroad, a crackdown on crime, support for traditional Russian institutions such as the church and family, and a greater degree of social protection and state support in economic matters (*Budte s nami* 1995; see also *Dialog*, no. 11-12, 1995, 32–39). KRO was very critical of the government's economic program and blamed Yeltsin personally for the collapse of the USSR, the "October events" of 1993, and the excesses of privatization. But it had its own difficulties, partly because of the inconsistencies in its program but also because of the unresolved ambitions of its leaders: Skokov, for instance, told journalists that Lebed lacked "education" and would not even be able to be minister of defense, let alone president (*Obshchaya gazeta*, 29 June 1995, 8).

Many parties were more difficult to classify: to give just two examples, Eduard Limonov's National Bolshevik Party and the Beer Lovers' Party. Limonov, a controversial novelist, "advocated everything from banning imported food to invading Russia's neighbours" (*The Times*, 9 December 1995, 16). The Beer Lovers had begun as a joke, but registered as a party in April 1995 with a program favoring cheap beer, cheap vodka, low taxes, "a man for every woman and a woman for every man." One initiative was to hold a party near the Ukrainian border town of Lugansk intended to "wash away the borders with beer." The Beer Lovers were informally associated with the "Subtropical Russia" Movement, whose declared aim was the introduction of a temperature of 20 degrees Celsius throughout the country, summer and winter; the party did not specify how its program was to be realized.

The Media Campaign

Unlike 1993, the rules set out for media coverage of the 1995 Duma election by the Central Electoral Commission on 20 September 1995 were fully considered and detailed. They covered access to time on radio and television as well as election material in the press; however, only state-funded or assisted media were affected (*Vestnik*, no. 6, 1995, 78–90). Under the regulations, these media were to refrain from bias in their news coverage, and specific rules were laid down for the conduct of debates and roundtable discussions. Between 15 November and 15 December, the national television and radio channels had to distribute one hour of free time daily among the forty-three parties and associations on the ballot. Arrangements for individual candidates in single-member districts were made separately by regional electoral commissions, allowing each candidate about ten to twenty minutes of radio or television time during the campaign and free advertising in the local press. Parties and candidates could buy additional commercial broadcasting or press advertising.

The Central Electoral Commission gave each party 80 million rubles ($18,000) for its campaign, and regional electoral commissions contributed to the campaigns of individual candidates. The central commission instructed that all funds were to flow through special temporary accounts in the national savings bank. Political associations were allowed to spend up to 10.9 billion rubles ($2.4 million) on their campaigns, and individual candidates up to 437 million rubles (about $95,000). Individuals could donate no more than 874,000 rubles ($188) to an individual candidate or 1.3 million rubles ($282) to a party, and companies or other bodies could donate no more than 8.74 million rubles ($1,880) to an individual candidate and 87.4 million rubles ($18,800) to a party. There could be no contributions from foreigners, state enterprises, military units, or charitable or religious organizations, and parties and candidates were not allowed to buy more time on state radio and television than was provided free of charge. But there were no formal restrictions on the payments for collecting signatures in order to secure a nomination, which was the longest and most expensive part of the electoral campaign. Enforcement was a big problem, and the parties and candidates were as much aware of this as was the Central Electoral Commission. The regulations were thus a "declaration of good intentions" (*Izvestiya,* 1 August 1995, 2; for the regulations themselves, see *Izvestiya,* 29 July 1995, 1).

The European Institute for the Media, which monitored campaign coverage on behalf of the European Union, concluded that free time had been allocated "fairly and in accordance with the regulations," in spite of a "few minor complaints" (1996a, 19). Political advertising, for instance, had been clearly distinguished from editorial opinion in the federal broadcast media. Unacknowledged advertising in the newspapers and on some regional channels, however, was "commonplace," and the volume of advertising on national radio and television was much greater than the total that all the parties had been allowed to spend on their campaigns. Several parties exceeded the legal limits by a considerable margin. Our Home Is Russia bought nearly a quarter of all political advertising, worth about $4 million at the published rate, well in excess of its permitted $2.4 million maximum (see table 10.1). Most parties used brief spot advertisements; Our Home Is Russia's were consistently the longest. At the other extreme, the Communist Party bought no commercials, relying on its local network of activists; so did its ally, the Agrarian Party (European Institute for the Media, 1996a, 19–20, 32–33).

Editorial coverage in the broadcast media was unevenly distributed too, with a "slant toward Our Home Is Russia and (to a lesser extent) Russia's Democratic Choice" and an "editorial bias against some opposition parties." Our Home Is Russia again took nearly a quarter of all editorial coverage on the five central television channels, followed by Russia's Democratic Choice (table 10.1). In the opinion of the European Institute for the Media, both were "overexposed"; the same was true of radio coverage, which "devoted a few minutes to the most important parties, yet gave generously to OHR and RDC." The Institute found a "clear absence of journalistic political analysis, debating programs, and in-depth interviews with the main candidates."

TABLE 10.1

ADVERTISING AND EDITORIAL COVERAGE ON TELEVISION,
1995 DUMA CAMPAIGN

Party	Paid time		Editorial time	
	Minutes	Percent	Minutes	Percent
Agrarians	3	0.1	20	0.7
Communist Party	10	0.5	160	5.9
Congress of Russian Communities	215	11.6	109	4.0
Forward, Russia!	32	1.7	137	5.0
Ivan Rybkin's bloc	151	8.5	199	7.3
Liberal Democrats	176	9.5	200	7.3
My Fatherland	137	7.4	34	1.2
Our Home Is Russia	431	23.5	670	24.7
Pamfilova bloc	24	1.3	11	0.4
Power to the People	3	0.1	18	0.6
Party of Workers' Self-Government	22	1.3	60	2.2
Russia's Democratic Choice	103	5.5	346	12.8
Trade Unions/Industrialists	35	1.9	131	4.8
Women of Russia	36	2.0	63	2.4
Yabloko	43	2.3	88	3.2
Other twenty-eight parties	419	228	476	175
Totals	1,840	100.0	2,722	100.0

SOURCE: Derived from European Institute for the Media (1996b, 32, 34); based on paid and editorial times on central television (ORT, RTR, NTV, MTK, and TV-6) from 19 November to 16 December 1995.

The central press had a disproportionate influence on elite opinion and the political agenda; although it was "quite pluralistic," there was little or simply negative coverage of Zhirinovsky's Liberal Democrats and a "tendency to support the centrist and reform-oriented parties" (European Institute for the Media 1996b, 34, 35, 40). But local and regional press had an important role to play too, for half the candidates were elected in single-member districts. Altogether, 42 percent of Russians at the start of 1996 read local and regional newspapers, far more than the collective readership of such major national newspapers as *Izvestiya*, *Pravda*, and *Trud*. Even if each local paper showed a substantial bias, many local biases could offset each other nationally. Thirty-two percent of the electorate were insulated from press bias entirely because they did not read any newspaper regularly (Rose 1996b, 41).

To appeal to readers, newspapers paid attention to human interest aspects of the election. For instance, what were the party leaders like in their daily lives? From whom did they take advice? And what did they drink? Yegor Gaidar, it emerged, took Andrei Sakharov as his role model; he took advice from his wife; he had a maid; and he drank whiskey and soda. But he refused to say if he was religious or how he had proposed marriage. Vladimir Zhirinovsky drank Zhirinovsky vodka; he greatly respected the prerevolutionary Russian premier Stolypin and Charles de Gaulle; and his favorite music was late Beethoven. If he had a fault, it was the same as his main virtue: impulsiveness. The KRO leader Alexander Lebed, by contrast, had no role model, no car, no housemaid, and didn't drink at all, but he could make an omelet, which was his favorite food. He liked Russian traditional music, and if he had a different career it would have been as a carpenter (*Argumenty i fakty*, no. 50, 1995, 6). Boris Fedorov of Forward, Russia! took Theodore Roosevelt and Margaret Thatcher as his models; Irina Khakamada of Common Cause chose Margaret Thatcher and drank "a little gin and lots of tonic."

Parties also tried to get their message across by posters and leaflets, which generally featured the party leader in a statesmanlike pose. A poster for Russia's Democratic Choice showed Yegor Gaidar gazing thoughtfully into the middle distance above the slogan: "Everyone talks. He acts." Another warned voters against "Bolshevik revenge" and urged them to "make a sensible choice." The most numerous and expensive posters were produced for Our Home Is Russia, many featuring the prime minister. Playing on the party's name, some showed the premier with his hands steepled like a roof; others called for the support of those "to whom their home is dear." Others showed the premier admiring a well-nourished rooster, whose early morning call was meant to remind voters of the party's slogan: "Don't sleep through the future of Russia!"

The Congress of Russian Communities featured its own leaders, Alexander Lebed and Yuri Skokov, in a warm handshake above the slogan "Join us"; the two men parted ways soon after the election. The Pamfilova-Gurov-Lysenko bloc made as much as it could of the photogenic and widely recognized Pamfilova; she reminded voters that it was "better to have kindergartens today than young offender institutions tomorrow." Eye surgeon Svyatoslav Fedorov was pictured in front of his hospital; his television commercials made the point "You have eyes." Where appeals were expressed in terms of policy, they were often vague or unrealistic. Rutskoi's Derzhava, for instance, promised to introduce public order "once and for all," to secure a "society of social justice" with everyone guaranteed an income at least twice the level of subsistence, and to restore Russia as a military power on the basis of its own traditions, not an "alien way of life" imported from the West. Ivan Rybkin's bloc made a series of more specific but even less realistic promises, including the payment of salaries without delay, "sensible prices" for goods and services, free medical treatment, and guaranteed employment and pensions.

Zhirinovsky's Liberal Democrats pitched their appeal almost exclusively in terms of the leader, who was typically pictured with the Russian parliament as a backdrop. Sometimes the slogan was bland, such as "Vote for the LDPR," but often it made a more direct appeal, such as "I'll get Russia up off its knees!" The party's printed leaflets attacked the "corrupt 'democratic' nomenklatura," promised to defend ordinary people against wealthy "new Russians," and told Muscovites that public transport would run on time, that the streets would be clean, and that new housing would go to city residents rather than "southern Mafiosi."

The organized Left gave more attention to socioeconomic issues. Viktor Anpilov's "Communists—Working Russia—for the Soviet Union" called on voters to support the "restoration of Soviet power; a reversion to socialism; and the rebirth of the USSR." Nikolai Ryzhkov's "Power to the People" called more cautiously for central regulation of the economy, support for domestic producers, and an end to war and poverty. The Communist Party itself made relatively little use of posters and leaflets, placing more emphasis on grassroots campaigning by its activists; it was, however, one of the parties that attempted to use a campaign jingle, which began "Khochesh zhit ty zanovo, Vybirai Zyuganova" (If you want to live once again, vote for Zyuganov).

December discouraged outdoor meetings, and geography and the size of the electorate made face-to-face contact between national leaders and the great majority of voters impossible. The mass media, and especially television, offered the only means for party leaders to project themselves, their policies, and their personalities to a large audience. Russia's Democratic Choice commercials showed a finger seeking out the party's number on the ballot paper, and then making a "sensible choice." Our Home Is Russia used the slogan "Choose the future, vote for NDR." But many of its efforts had only the vaguest connection with the party. The Congress of Russian Communities, by contrast, made a much clearer impression with the warning "Comrade bureaucrat, don't take bribes," followed by Lebed in full military uniform telling them, "I don't advise it."

Among the undecided voters, television and radio were the most frequently cited sources of information, and voters were particularly interested in seeing what Vladimir Zhirinovsky was up to (Levada 1996). The Liberal Democratic flaunted political commercials that were dubbed "porno-politics." One commercial featured a scantily clad singer in a smoky nightclub undoing her bodice while singing the praises of the party leader. In another, Zhirinovsky appeared on stage with an exotic stripper who told him, "Spank me, I want a man who will spank me" (*The Times*, 16 December 1995, 14). Yabloko, a party bearing the Russian name for Apple, featured in one of its commercials an apple falling off a tree and landing on the head of a figure resembling Isaac Newton. In another, a country lass tells her young man, who is eating an apple with gusto, "You love the apple more than me!" He replies, "I vote for Apple, but it's you I love." Other commercials were more straightforward but also focused on the party leader: Boris Gromov—"a man you know"— fronted the commercial that was put out by "My Fatherland"; Ivan Rybkin's bloc showed photographs of its leader's early life, urging viewers to "Vote for Ivan!"; and Boris Fedorov presented viewers with his entire family.

There were several set-piece television debates, although the multiplicity of parties and leaders made it impossible to hold a simple confrontation between alternative prime ministers, as in the British House of Commons or an American television debate between two presidential candidates. In one debate Vladimir Zhirinovsky caused a minor sensation by throwing a glass of water at his opponent, Viktor Anpilov (*Argumenty i fakty*, no. 7, 1996, 3). In another, Yegor Gaidar faced a Communist deputy, Yuri Ivanov, who attacked him for his subservience to Western interests. All campaigning was meant to end on election eve, Saturday, 16 December 1995. But there were "media events" that circumvented this rule: Chernomyrdin was featured on central television attending an ice hockey match, Zyuganov was briefly covered on independent television attending a concert, and independent television put out a preelection program of its animated puppet cartoon "Kukly" (Dolls), which made fun of all the party leaders.

Politicians hoped the publicity attracted by campaigning would increase their vote. But exposure can turn voters off rather than turn them on. In the opinion of political journalist Yekaterina Yegorova (1995, 2):

The debates can be called debates in name only. The talk was sluggish,

boring and all about past sins. Russian politicians in general have problems communicating their ideas. They are deaf to the arguments and
positions of their opponents. This is expressed in the way they carry
themselves. During debates the politicians often avoid making any eye
contact with one another and keep their hands folded tightly, signalling
that they are entirely closed psychologically.

Now it was for voters spread across eleven time zones to make their
choice.

⟪ 11 ⟫

Russians Vote Against

The 1995 Duma election was Russia's first normal election. By contrast with the one-party elections of the Soviet period, voters were offered a rich variety of choices. Whereas the 1993 Duma ballot had been held at the same time as a vote on the constitution, the new constitution was in place before the second Duma election was called. In spite of persistent speculation that the election would be postponed by those in power, the vote took place when specified by law, and international observers pronounced the contest free and the counting of votes fair. With forty-three parties on the ballot, there was no shortage of choice and the result represented a diversity of political opinions.

Nevertheless, Russian elections have not yet become normal in the classic democratic sense, for the Russian government is not accountable to the Duma, as in a normal parliamentary system. Although the contest featured great, even excessive, party competition, the vote could not change control of government. The fragmentation of competing parties and the large number of independents and "one-person" parties winning seats in single-member districts meant that no one party could win a majority of the 450 seats in the Duma. Moreover, even if one party or bloc controlled the Duma, the constitution makes it difficult for Duma members to vote no confidence in the prime minister without risking that the president will force a dissolution, putting their own seats at risk. Moreover, there are precedents for the president ignoring votes in the Duma and ruling by decree or *force majeure*.

The Duma election was not normal in the Russian sense either, for it offered the population a chance to vote against the government of the day. In Soviet days this was unthinkable; everyone was expected to turn out and vote for the Communist Party of the Soviet Union (see table 1.3, p. 11). The Communist legacy has encouraged the Russian government to use the state apparatus to campaign for support for the powers that be. But in a free election, voters are not compelled to cast their votes as the government wants. As in Schumpeter's classic model of democracy, Russians can cast protest votes about how the country is being governed. In the event, the Duma vote showed a negative consensus, rejecting parties identified with government. But there was no agreement about who should govern or how the country ought to be governed.

Public opinion was also not normal, insofar as the word implies that most people regard their system of government as stable. In Russia, political and economic transformation results in the opposite being the case. Mass dissatisfaction with the system goes far beyond voting against the government of the day while accepting that the regime remains unchanged. In the statistical sense of a norm being majority or median opinion, the "normal" state of the Russian electorate is dissatisfaction tinged with anxiety and even fear.

When Russians are asked to evaluate the political situation, more than half describe it as tense, and a third describe it as critical or explosive (table 11.1). Such anxieties were not induced by the election; they are the normal, day in and day out views of the Russian people. Consistently, less than 5 percent view the political situation as normal in the sense of being calm or favorable. Russians usually see the political situation as tense; this is the opinion of an absolute majority in every monthly VTsIOM monitoring survey since the question was introduced in March 1993. The lowest proportion fearful of a political explosion was 18 percent in July 1994. After the outbreak of the war in Chechnya, as many as 43 percent saw the situation as explosive in January 1995. In the fifth New Russian Barometer survey immediately after the 1995 Duma election, 35 percent were fearful of a crisis or explosion, the average figure for the preceding two years. Month in, month out, year in and year out, five-sixths or more of Russians see the political situation as tense, critical, or explosive.

In an established democracy an election is usually a time when the government engineers a "feel good" factor. In a society undergoing massive transformation, people cannot yet expect to feel good, but at least Russians might feel that the worst is behind them and conditions are getting better. But when VTsIOM asks people whether or not this is the case, very few think the worst is past (table 11.1). When VTsIOM first posed this question near the end of the Gorbachev era, 69 percent thought that the hardest times were ahead (Levada 1995, E5). The fall of the communist regime and the introduction of an independent Russian Federation led to 73 percent thinking the worst times were still

TABLE 11.1

WHAT RUSSIANS SEE AS NORMAL POLITICS

Q: How would you evaluate the general political situation in Russia?

	1993	1994	1995	1996
Favorable	1%	–	–	–
Calm	3	6%	3%	1%
Tense	61	62	57	57
Critical, explosive	27	23	35	35
Difficult to answer	8	9	6	6

NOTE: Mean for 10 monthly surveys in 1993; 8 in 1994; 6 in 1995.

Q: Do you think that we are living through the hardest times now, or they are behind us, or they are still ahead?

	1991	1992	1993	1994	1995	1996
Already behind us	4%	2%	5%	7%	5%	6%
Hardest time now	22	22	25	20	20	21
Still ahead	67	69	54	55	55	52
Difficult to answer	7	7	16	19	20	22

NOTE: Mean for 4 monthly surveys in 1991; 6 in 1992; 10 in 1993; 6 in 1994; 6 in 1995.

SOURCES: 1991–95: VTsIOM nationwide representative sample surveys with Ns ranging from 1,500 to 2,500; for details see Levada 1995, P4, E5. January 1996: New Russia Barometer V, a nationwide representative sample survey conducted by VTsIOM between 12 and 31 January with 2,340 respondents.

ahead in January 1992. Had these expectations been met immediately, the proportion now expecting the hardest times ahead would have fallen dramatically. In fact, recurring economic and political shocks have doubled the proportion of Russians so confused that they find it difficult to say when the hardest times will be.

At the time of the December 1995 election, the government had spectacularly failed to manufacture a "feel good" atmosphere, or even a "feel less bad than before" sentiment. VTsIOM surveys immediately before and after the election found 52 percent believing that the hardest times were still ahead, and 21 percent that they were here and now. That was the mood of the electorate on Sunday, 17 December 1995, the day of Russia's first "normal" election.

Consequences of Irrational Parties

Since fraud and manipulation were normal in Soviet elections, many politicians who had learned their politics in the old regime expected to see them in free elections too. Furthermore, charging the Central Electoral Commission with fraud offered a convenient scapegoat for the great majority of the contestants who suffered defeat. But independent observers found no substantial evidence to support allegations that the election had been stolen. Nor was it rational to believe that the Yeltsin administration would manipulate the count to produce a result in which government supporters were badly defeated. Russian politicians had to face the unpleasant fact that an outcome in which nine-tenths of parties failed to win any party-list seats was the logical consequence of their irrational behavior in refusing to form coalitions.

Heavy criticism of its handling of the 1993 election left a mark on staff at the Central Electoral Commission, which was visibly seeking to learn from past mistakes (S. Orttung 1995). The commission received significant technical assistance and was open in meeting foreign observers; it also had 60,000 observers from the parties monitoring its activities. The Organization for Security and Cooperation in Europe sent a large delegation of parliamentarians from 26 OSCE countries in Europe and North America (OSCE 1996). The European Parliament (1996) also monitored the election. Observers spread out across the country and met with representatives of losing and winning parties as well as with election officials. While their visits were brief, foreign observers provide evidence independent of the self-interest and suspicions of directly involved contestants.

In the new Russia, as in the old, public administration falls short of 100 percent accuracy or efficiency, and election administration is no exception. For example, the Central Electoral Commission informed some local commissions the night before the poll or on the morning of the vote about changes in the ballot paper, which had to be made by hand. The state budget allocated to the elections was insufficient. There was some voting before the polls were scheduled to open. There were too few officials and booths to handle surges of voters, which encouraged open voting rather than waiting in line for a voting booth to mark a ballot in private. Foreign observers noted the "evident physical exhaustion of some commission members" in meeting their punishing schedule and said fatigue led to minor errors at some counts (OSCE 1996, 17–19; European Parliament 1996, 7).

Russian voters had little experience of casting secret ballots, and in

Soviet days impersonation and fraud were more acceptable than a district reporting a low turnout of voters in favor of the communist regime. In the Duma contest there were reports of individuals casting ballots on behalf of other persons, usually relatives or friends, of entire families marking their ballots as a group, and of soldiers being marched to polling stations. The very large party-list ballot paper encouraged people to spread the ballot out on a table to read and mark, rather than go into the privacy of a cramped booth; this was formally a violation of the election law.

The OSCE delegation reported the morning after the election that Russia had "successfully carried out these second multiparty elections in an overall free and fair manner" (OSCE 1996, annex 1). The European Parliament delegation also told the press the morning after the election that the election had been "up to international standards," with "no serious irregularities." It found voting was "conducted everywhere in a calm and orderly manner," although there were some minor infringements that were the result of circumstances "of a practical nature, and not evidence of fraudulent intent." Subsequent published reports recommended minor changes in election law and in the administration and enforcement of laws. The stiffest criticism was made of the conduct of the campaign, including the collection of signatures on nomination papers, fund raising, and the role of the media. The overall conclusion was that the 1995 Duma election was a great improvement on the 1993 contest, making it the "first real democratic election" (European Parliament 1996, 8).

The election result immediately and dramatically revealed the irrationality of the vote-seeking efforts of politicians and parties. Fewer than one-tenth of the parties cleared the 5 percent threshold necessary for the award of party-list seats (table 11.2). With under a quarter of the list vote, the Communist Party came first. The Liberal Democratic Party of Vladimir Zhirinovsky claimed a "moral" victory because, after political commentators had written it off due to the emergence of competing nationalist parties, it finished second in the party-list vote. Its 11 percent vote, however, was half what it had won in 1993. Our Home Is Russia, led by Prime Minister Viktor Chernomyrdin, came third, but it won only a tenth of the vote. A reform party, Grigorii Yavlinsky's Yabloko, was the only other group to clear the proportional representation threshold, with just under 7 percent of the vote.

At least half a dozen parties paid the penalty of being "disagreeable" rather than coalescing, thus falling just below the 5 percent threshold needed to qualify for Duma seats. The vote for the hard-line

TABLE 11.2

ELECTION TO THE RUSSIAN DUMA, 1995

	PR party list			Single-member		Total seats	
	Vote	Seats					
	%	N	%	N	%	N	%
A. *Cleared 5 percent threshold* (4)							
Communist Party	22.3	99	44.0	58	25.8	157	34.9
Liberal Democrats	11.2	50	22.2	1	0.4	51	11.3
Our Home Is Russia	10.1	45	20.0	10	4.4	55	12.2
Yabloko	6.9	31	13.8	14	6.2	45	10.0
B. *Won single-member seats* (18)							
Agrarians	3.8			20	8.9	20	4.4
Power to the People!	1.6			9	4.0	9	2.0
Russia's Democratic Choice	3.9			9	4.0	9	2.0
Congress of Russian Communities—Lebed	4.3			5	2.2	5	1.1
Women of Russia	4.6			3	1.3	3	0.7
Forward, Russia!	1.9			3	1.3	3	0.7
Ivan Rybkin Bloc	1.1			3	1.3	3	0.7
Pamfilova-Gurov-Lysenko Bloc	1.6			2	0.9	2	0.4
Communists-Working Russia-For Soviet Union	4.5			1	0.4	1	0.2
Workers' Self-Government	4.0			1	0.4	1	0.2
Trade Union and Industrialists	1.6			1	0.4	1	0.2
S. Govorukhin Bloc	1.0			1	0.4	1	0.2
My Fatherland	0.7			1	0.4	1	0.2
Common Cause	0.7			1	0.4	1	0.2
Transformation of the Fatherland	0.7			1	0.4	1	0.2
Russian Unity and Accord	0.4			1	0.4	1	0.2
Economic Freedom	0.1			1	0.4	1	0.2
89 Regions of Russia	0.1			1	0.4	1	0.2
Independents				78	34.7	78	17.3
C. *Won votes but no seats* (21)							
Derzhava	2.57						
Ecologists-Cedar	1.39						
Beer Lovers' Party	0.62						
Muslim Social Move't Nur	0.57						
National-Republican Party of Russia	0.48						
Pre-election Bloc of Party Leaders[a]	0.47						
Association of Russian Advocates	0.35						

	PR party list			Single-member		Total seats	
	Vote	*Seats*					
	%	N	%	N	%	N	%
For the Motherland!	0.28						
Christian Democratic Union—							
Christians of Russia	0.28						
Pre-election Bloc of							
Party Leaders[b]	0.21						
Peoples' Union Party	0.19						
Tikhonov-Tupolev-							
Tikhonov	0.15						
Utility Workers of Russia	0.14						
Social Democrats	0.13						
Russian Popular Move't	0.12						
Federal-Democratic Move't	0.12						
Stable Russia	0.12						
Bloc of Independents	0.12						
Duma 96	0.08						
International Union	0.06						
Generations of the							
Boundary	0.06						
D. *Other ballots*							
Against all lists	2.8						
Invalid vote	1.9						
Totals		225	100	225	100	450	100

Registered electorate: 107,496,558.

Total vote: 69,204,819 (valid vote 67,884,200).

Turnout: all votes, 64.4 percent; valid vote, 62.5 percent; positive vote for parties on list, 59.7 percent.

SOURCE: Derived from *Vestnik Tsentralnoi izbiratelnoi komissii Rossiiskoi Federatsii*, no. 1 (21), 1996, 18–51.

a. Incorporating the following parties: Defense of Pensioners and Veterans, Eradication of Crime and for Law and Order, Defense of Health, Education, Science and Culture, Defense of Youth, Association of Free Trade Unions, Justice, and Defense of Nature.

b. Incorporating the following parties: Defense of Children, the Russian Women Party, the Orthodox Party, the People's Christian-Monarchist Party, Union of the Slavic Peoples, the Zemlya-Matushka Party of Rural Toilers, Defense of Invalids, and the Party of Victims and the Swindled.

Communists—Working Russia—for the Soviet Union fell half a percent below the threshold. Divisions among reformers left Russia's Democratic Choice, a big winner in the 1993 Duma election, without any party-list seats, 1.1 percent under the threshold. The division of the nationalist vote meant that Alexander Lebed's Congress of Russian Communities—KRO fell 0.7 percent below it. The party of the independently minded eye surgeon Svyatoslav Fedorov, Workers' Self-Government, was 1 percent below the barrier. One interest-group party, Women of Russia, failed to clear the barrier because they took less than one-tenth of the women's vote, and another, the Agrarians, failed to win party-list seats because they won less than a sixth of the rural vote.

To win a single-member district, a candidate needed less than 0.22 percent of the total vote cast in these constituencies. The local orientation of single-member seats meant that a candidate did not need a party label to be elected, and it could even be a handicap. The largest category of winners in the single-member seats were independents, taking seventy-eight seats. This was barely half the number of independents elected in 1993, reflecting the incentives to politicians to affiliate with a party bloc in the Duma. Some candidates presented themselves as "independents" when in fact they belonged to a party, and others claimed the backing of a party for which they were the only Duma representative.

A total of twenty-two parties won single-member seats, but only four won as many as ten. The Communist Party was the leader, more than trebling the single-member seats that it had won in 1993. This showed it had regained the organizational ability to field winning candidates in the regions. Once again, the Liberal Democrats, winning only one single-member seat, revealed their dependence upon a personality at the top of the party-list ticket, Vladimir Zhirinovsky. In spite of being the party of government patronage, Our Home Is Russia won only ten seats in single-member districts. Eighteen parties that failed to clear the party-list threshold each managed to win at least one single-member seat. The Agrarians won twenty seats, more than in 1993. Yegor Gaidar's Russia's Democratic Choice succeeded in taking nine single-member seats. Women of Russia won three single-member seats, but this was no compensation for losing all their party-list seats. Former General Alexander Lebed inadvertently revealed the limitations of a personality party. While he could not convert his personal following into 5 percent of the national party-list vote, he won a seat for himself in the single-member district of Tula. Other personality parties not winning seats on the party list also benefited their leaders; for example,

Ivan Rybkin's bloc took only 1.1 percent of the list vote, but its leader was elected for a single-member seat in the Voronezh region.

With almost two dozen parties, the new Duma represented a wide variety of opinions, but not the electorate as a whole. The irrational fragmentation of parties turned the 5 percent threshold into a mechanism for *dis*proportional representation. Almost half the vote went to parties that failed to clear the party-list threshold, and this effectively doubled the number of seats awarded the four parties that did clear the threshold. With 22 percent of the party-list vote, the Communists would have secured only fifty seats in a PR system without a minimum threshold; in the event, they won ninety-nine seats. Zhirinovsky's Liberal Democrats won 22 percent of the party-list seats with only 11 percent of the vote, and Our Home Is Russia and Yabloko similarly benefited.

To some degree all electoral systems are disproportional, for it is impossible to match the share of votes to the share of seats to the last tenth of a percent. Nor is it necessarily desirable: proponents of responsible party government endorse the first-past-the-post electoral system on the grounds that it encourages accountable party government by manufacturing a majority of seats for the party winning a plurality of votes, so voters know whom to reward or punish at the next election.

The 1995 Duma election produced the most disproportional election result of any free and fair proportional representation election (figure 11.1). The average West European PR system distributes seats within 6 percent of perfect proportionality, whereas the Duma result was 49 percentage points from this goal. The average first-past-the-post system in Anglo-American democracies falls 21 percentage points short of pure proportionality; the Duma result was more than twice as disproportional. The 1993 French parliamentary election was previously the most disproportional free election on record, but that was a mark of success, for the French had designed their system to exclude extreme parties of right and left. The extreme disproportionality of the outcome was not intended. Most parties in the Duma that had approved the election formula did not win any seats in the party-list ballot. The outcome was the collective result of the miscalculations of irrational politicians, determined to campaign in parties of their own rather than aggregate policies and personalities in order to win more seats in parliament.

Even though the Duma was freely and fairly elected, it did not represent the electorate as a whole. The turnout, 64.4 percent, was up almost 10 percentage points on 1993, but this meant that the big-

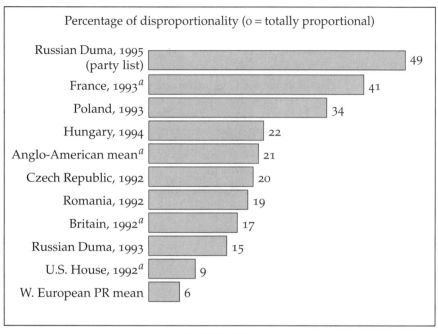

FIGURE 11.1

DISPROPORTIONALITY IN ELECTION RESULTS

SOURCE: Except for Russia, adapted from Richard Rose (1996c, table 8.3).

NOTE: The index is half the absolute value of the difference between a party's percentage of the total vote and its percentage of parliamentary seats.

a. First-past-the-post electoral system.

gest "party" in the electorate were nonvoters. The turnout included 2.8 percent who explicitly voted against all parties and another 1.9 percent who cast invalid ballots, reducing the number who cast valid votes to 59.3 percent of the electorate.

In effect, the electorate ended up being divided into three groups: those who cast no votes, those who cast a vote that was wasted because it favored a party that failed to cross the threshold for party-list seats, and those who voted for a party that won a share of list seats (figure 11.2). Voters for winning and losing parties in the list competition were almost equal in number. Those who voted for an unsuccessful party list could not be said to be represented by party members who won single-member seats elsewhere in the Russian Federation, for such Duma members represent a district, not a national party. Moreover, with a

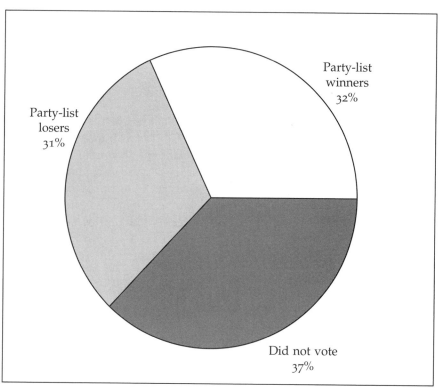

FIGURE 11.2

MOST ELECTORS NOT REPRESENTED IN THE DUMA

SOURCE: See table 11.1.

NOTE: "Did not vote" category includes invalid votes and those voting against all.

dozen or more candidates and no second-round runoff vote in single-member districts, the majority of votes in such districts were wasted, and a candidate could win a seat with less than a quarter of the district's vote.

Profiles of Party Voters

Describing Russians who chose to vote as "supporting" a party is a misleading projection of the assumptions of an established democracy. In the 1995 Duma election, the great majority of Russian voters did *not* support a party in the sense of identifying with it. As in 1993, the great majority were demobilized: they did not belong to a party, identify with a party, or trust politicians (see chapter 7; Rose 1995e). Even though Russians were willing to vote, the choices of many voters were votes *against*, some voting against the government and economic reform and some against the communist past. Among those who were not protest voters, apathy or lukewarm endorsement of a party was more likely than firm commitment.

In a normal system, parties enter each new election reasonably confident that they will retain the votes of those who have supported them previously, for party identification ensures substantial continuity. In the absence of party identification, however, Russian parties could not rely on their 1993 voters to support them again in 1995. Nor did party leaders want to stand pat, for only three parties had won as much as a tenth of the vote in that contest, and new parties, such as the party of the prime minister, Our Home Is Russia, had to compete with parties already in the field. The majority of voters entered the campaign without a firm commitment to any party; only 37 percent told the fifth New Russia Barometer that they had made up their minds about whom to vote for long before the start of the campaign (Rose 1996b, 63). Low commitment led to every party with a significant share of the vote in 1993 seeing it change substantially in 1995: the Communists doubled their vote, and Zhirinovsky's Liberal Democratic vote was halved, and this was also the fate of the Agrarians. The vote for Women of Russia fell by almost half, and for Russia's Democratic Choice by more than three-quarters.

Political attitudes were again the major determinants of party choice. Table 11.3 illustrates influences on the vote for nine parties that did relatively well (or least badly) in the competition for votes. Insofar as a particular issue is of no concern to a party, its voters will resemble a cross-section of the electorate. In the evaluation of old and new regimes, Communist voters were most distinctive; more than four-fifths approved the old regime while less than a fifth endorsed its successor. Voters for the Liberal Democrats and the Party of Workers' Self-Government also strongly tilted in favor of the past. The only group of voters strongly against the past favored Yegor Gaidar's Russia's Democratic Choice. Three-quarters rejected it; more than half of Yabloko voters did so too. No party, not even Our Home Is Russia, had a majority in favor of the new regime.

Attitudes toward authoritarianism also strongly distinguished two ideological blocs. Three-quarters of Russia's Democratic Choice and Yabloko voters rejected dictatorship by a strong leader, army rule, and a return to communist rule. A high percentage also did so among voters

TABLE 11.3
INFLUENCES ON PARTY CHOICE
(PERCENTAGE ENDORSING ANSWER)

	Total	Wom	OHR	Yab	RDC	Com	CRC	LDPR	Self-Govt	Agr
Political										
Pro old regime	63	56	52	45	25	82	50	65	67	71
Pro current regime	29	31	39	40	41	19	23	27	30	51
Return to Communist rule	43	31	19	12	12	88	32	45	23	26
Dictator needed	34	37	23	18	11	43	38	54	21	29
Blame Yeltsin	74	55	59	66	66	87	76	68	76	55
Blame Communists	34	36	41	43	57	18	50	33	40	37
Blame entrepreneurs	35	23	28	24	18	45	28	43	36	47
Trust parties	21	2	13	11	11	37	21	21	15	4
Trust Duma	15	3	14	12	10	19	28	18	9	12
Situation explosive	35	33	22	37	21	37	26	46	32	35
Worst times ahead	52	54	40	46	33	58	49	55	48	52
CPSU member in family	36	16	31	31	36	47	40	27	29	14
Economic										
Falling household living standard	59	59	49	49	36	66	52	69	70	39
Social structure										
Female	53	84	50	59	51	49	40	40	66	52
Villages	27	28	25	20	6	29	17	33	34	60
Age 60+	22	10	22	15	9	38	15	13	11	15

SOURCE: Centre for the Study of Public Policy, New Russia Barometer V (1996). For full details of questions, see Rose 1996b.

for Fedorov's Workers' Self-Government party, indicating that their endorsement of the old regime was due to its welfare policies rather than its authoritarianism. Among Communists, five-sixths endorsed at least one authoritarian alternative, as did two-thirds of Liberal Democrats. The only party with a majority of its voters endorsing a strong dictatorship was Zhirinovsky's party, and the only party with a majority endorsing a return to the communist regime was the Communist Party of the Russian Federation.

The unpopularity of Boris Yeltsin meant that a majority of voters for every party, including Our Home Is Russia, blamed the president for the country's economic problems. A third of voters blamed communists for Russia's economic problems; the only party with a majority of voters blaming the communists was Russia's Democratic Choice; half of General Lebed's voters also blamed communists. A third of all voters blamed entrepreneurs, and those doing so tended to be distributed widely among all parties. Anxiety was evident throughout the electorate. About half the voters for all parties except Russia's Democratic Choice feared that the worst times were still ahead, and there was widespread agreement that the political situation was threatening; the chief difference between partisans was whether the situation was tense or explosive.

Trust in parties is normally considered a civic virtue, but in the Russian context it most often characterizes Communist voters. Conversely, liberal reform voters are lowest in trust, because the party that most readily comes to their mind is the Communist Party of the Soviet Union. Trust in the Duma is above average among Communists and nationalists, a reflection of the Duma's leadership in opposing the Yeltsin administration.

Because a majority of Russians felt their household living standard had fallen since the abandonment of the command economy, this issue did not discriminate in the choice of an antigovernment party. Among the minority who had not been hurt by the change in economic regime, however, there was a tendency to favor Russia's Democratic Choice, the most outspoken advocate of the market economy. The most significant social structure influences on voting were very predictable: Women of Russia drew five-sixths of its vote from women, Agrarians drew the great bulk of their votes from people in the countryside, and Communist voters were disproportionately old (cf. Rose and Carnaghan 1995).

Russian parties differ not only in the influences that shape their vote but also in the degree to which they are distinctive, representing a bloc of voters with well-defined political and economic attitudes or social characteristics. With a multiplicity of parties differing on more than one dimension, the relative distinctiveness of each party can be determined by using discriminant function analysis (Klecka 1980). Here it predicts party choice on the basis of political, economic, and social structure data in the fifth New Russia Barometer survey, commencing in early January 1996, a few weeks after the Duma election (cf. Rose 1996b). With nine parties, a random assignment of respondents to parties might predict as few as 11 percent of cases correctly. Extracting five discriminant functions, each typically highlighting one or two political attitudes, correctly classifies 48 percent of voters, far better than chance (for details of the discriminant function analysis, see Rose, Tikhomirov, and Mishler 1996).

The Communist Party is by far the most distinctive party in Russia (figure 11.3; see also Budilova et al. 1996). Even though parties usually become "fuzzier" in their electoral profile when their vote increases, it is particularly striking that the Communist electorate remains distinctive even after doubling its vote from 1993. Four-fifths can be accurately predicted because Communist voters share distinctive political attitudes about the past and present. Russia's Democratic Choice ranks third in distinctiveness; 51 percent of its voters can be precisely predicted. To a substantial extent this party is a mirror image of Communist voters, endorsing economic reform and rejection of the communist legacy. The vote for Russia's Democratic Choice was much lower because more Russians prefer the past to reform. It drew a disproportionate amount of support from the young, the Communists from the old.

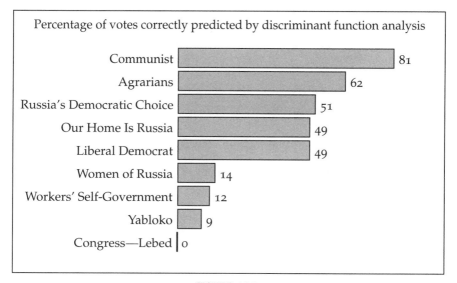

FIGURE 11.3
VARIABLE DISTINCTIVENESS OF PARTIES

SOURCE: Result of a discriminant function analysis of New Russia Barometer V (January 1996) using political, economic, and social structure variables; a total of 48 percent of voters correctly predicted.

NOTE: $N = 2,340$; 1,205 cases analyzed.

As the governing party, Our Home Is Russia appealed to all voters with an interest in power, an interest more likely to be material than ideological. Even though it was a newly founded party, its voters were relatively distinctive, being noteworthy for viewing the current situation as somewhat less explosive and threatening than did voters for other parties. They were also more tolerant of the policies of President Yeltsin. Yabloko, normally classified along with Russia's Democratic Choice as a liberal reform party, has a fuzzy focus; only 9 percent of its vote can be accurately predicted, and a larger portion of Yabloko voters are inclined to Communist attitudes than to the views of Russia's Democratic Choice. Yabloko used the appeal of its leader, Grigorii Yavlinsky, and its distance from both the Yeltsin administration and the communist past, to attract votes across the political spectrum. Fedorov's Party of Workers' Self-Government stands outside the reform bloc because its voters tend to agree with the Communists on social issues while differing in their evaluation of Communist rule.

If political attitudes toward the old and new regimes were the only determinants of voting, Communist strength would have increased by almost half. This did not happen because the Communists had competitors offering similar views about the two regimes but adding something extra. This was most obvious for Women of Russia and the Agrarians, who attracted many voters with attitudes similar to the Communists but who also were women or lived in the countryside. But nine-tenths of women did not vote for the party claiming to represent their interests.

The unique feature of the Liberal Democratic Party's appeal was the "in your face" rhetoric of its leader, Vladimir Zhirinovsky. While Zhirinovsky often made remarks that frightened Russian democrats, his one-liners constituted a kind of "shotgun" authoritarianism that produced an electoral appeal scattered across the Russian population. The Liberal Democratic vote had an ethnocentric appeal; it also drew a protest vote against the current regime. For this reason, a substantial minority of Liberal Democratic voters were similar in their attitudes to the Communists.

By December 1995 nationalist rhetoric, whether about re-creating the Soviet Union or about subduing Chechens, could be voiced in one or another form by many parties. The Congress of Russian Communities, led by former General Alexander Lebed, similarly had a broad appeal. Voters for Lebed's party were the hardest to predict of any of the nine parties: two-fifths appeared to have most attitudes in common with Communist voters—except for the personal appeal of the general.

Interpreting the Results

The immediate reaction of President Yeltsin to the election result was to claim that all was well: "We have no reason for concern or to regard the election as a tragedy. The majority of the new Duma consists of parties which follow and will follow the policy of democratization and observance of human rights and personal freedoms which Russia has started and which it will not give up' (*Moskovskaya pravda*, 21 December 1995, 1). Prime Minister Viktor Chernomyrdin claimed the results showed that "Russia's citizens have said that our reforms must be continued and improved," and he pledged no changes in government policies (*Segodnya*, 20 December 1995, 1). But Gennadii Zyuganov called the outcome a "political and moral referendum" in favor of those, like the Communists, who advocated a united state and social justice. He described the result as a crushing defeat for politicians such as Gaidar, who were seeking to "destroy the Russian state," and for the government, since Chernomyrdin's party gained the support of only one voter in ten (*Nezavisimaya gazeta*, 21 December 1995, 2).

Even though he had claimed victory, Yeltsin immediately changed the composition of the Russian government in order to signal a shift away from reform. A foreign minister conciliatory to the West, Andrei Kozyrev, was replaced by Evgenii Primakov, who had been in charge of counterespionage and had close associations with the Arab world. The last economic reformer, Anatolii Chubais, was sacked, and the reform-oriented head of the presidential administration, Sergei Filatov, was replaced by Nikolai Egorov, a former minister for nationality affairs.

The Red bloc of parties did best, for the Communist Party of the Russian Federation and allied parties took 33.8 percent of the valid popular vote for party lists (cf. table 11.2 and chapter 10). The "Brown" parties of nationalists collectively came second with 20 percent of the vote; the Liberal Democratic Party of Vladimir Zhirinovsky was strong, and Lebed's party was also in this bloc. Thus, the combined "Red-Brown" vote of Communists and nationalists was more than half the total, a figure that led to the outcome being reported as an endorsement of reaction. While the arithmetic was correct, the politics was oversimplified, for the Red-Brown vote was not cast for a common program but dispersed among eight different parties. Nonetheless, the group was sufficiently coordinated to elect Gennadii Seleznev, a Communist and former editor of *Pravda*, as the speaker of the new Duma, and to elect Yegor Stroev, a Communist and former Politburo and Party Secretariat member, as the new Speaker of the upper house, the Council of the Federation.

Eight parties of liberal reform, led by Yabloko, collectively took 16.3 percent of the vote, and six parties of social reform, headed by Svyatoslav Fedorov's Workers' Self-Government Party, claimed 9.1 percent of the vote. Thus, opposition parties supporting the constitution won a quarter of the vote. The government bloc, led by Our Home Is Russia, could claim only 16.9 percent of the vote. Altogether, the liberal reformers, social reformers, and voters for the government parties collected 42.3 percent of the vote, a substantial amount, albeit weakened in impact by being divided among more than sixteen different parties.

The failure of parties was revealing too. Theories seeking to apply conventional Western models of party systems to postcommunist politics imply support for a religious party; in Russia a party of Orthodox believers could also claim to be a nationalist party (cf. Evans and Whitefield 1993; Mair 1996). However, the Christian Democratic Union–Christians bloc secured less than 0.3 percent of the vote. The electoral law allowed ethnic parties to register, but because Russians constitute more than four-fifths of the Russian Federation's population and non-Russian nationalities are divided into many different ethnic groups and ethnic parties; the vote for ethnic parties (as distinct from Russian nationalist parties) was very low. A nominally Muslim party, Nur, took 0.6 percent of the vote. At the other end of the traditional/modernist spectrum, green or ecology parties have become established in Western Europe (see, e.g., Knutsen 1995; Rose 1996c, figure 6.4). Soviet industrialization caused huge ecological damage, affecting the health of individuals as well as the natural environment (see, e.g., Feshbach and Friendly 1992). But the ecology party, Cedar, won only 1.4 percent of the vote.

Many presidential hopefuls treated the parliamentary ballot as a chance to demonstrate their popular appeal. In the event, the vote demonstrated the limited attraction of personality parties. The "biggest" vote for an unambiguously presidential party was 11 percent for Zhirinovsky's Liberal Democrats; second came Grigorii Yavlinsky's Yabloko with 7 percent of the vote; and third, the Congress of Russian Communities, with only 4 percent of the vote. Alexander Rutskoi, a former vice-president of the Russian Republic who was arrested after the October 1993 confrontation, saw his Great Power Party, Derzhava, gain less than 3 percent of the vote. Insofar as Our Home Is Russia was a party for President Yeltsin's supporters, its 10 percent vote confirmed the unpopularity of the president (cf. chapter 8). The importance of political attitudes rather than personality was underscored by the Communist Party of the Russian Federation coming first in the Duma election, despite the lackluster personality of its leader, Gennadii Zyuganov.

At the start of 1996, the Yeltsin government could be described as echoing the intraelite politics of the Soviet Union, for it was conducted by "clan warfare," with different clans controlling different ministries and policies, yet united in their desire to cling to power (Graham 1995; cf. Skilling and Griffiths 1967; Roeder 1993). Of all the parties represented in the Duma that met in January 1996, the "oldest" was the Liberal Democrats, founded by Vladimir Zhirinovsky in 1990. The Communist Party of the Russian Federation had a longer pedigree, but was not the only party that descended from the old CPSU (see Sakwa 1996). All other parties were new. The fluidity of political allegiances was a reflection of a low demand from voters distrustful of politics, and the oversupply of parties by irrational politicians. The result was a "floating party system."

Instability is compounded as elected representatives find themselves members of a "floating Duma." Any politician who starts to think about the next election must wonder where that half of the vote that did not elect any members will go next time, and whether his or her current party or another would be better able to capture votes. Alternatively, in the inchoate state of Russia, Duma members may decide there is no point in worrying about what Russians may be thinking in the year 2000—assuming another election is held on schedule. Instead, they may concentrate on exploiting to maximum advantage their present position within the *Koltsevaya doroga,* the Moscow ring road that defines the "inside the beltway" politics of the Russian Federation.

When the second Duma met in January 1996, members immediately faced the need to choose or confirm their party labels. Some successful candidates had run as independents, some in the name of parties to which they did not belong; others were members of different parties than those under whose banners they ran, or even members of two parties. Moreover, two-thirds of the winners of single-member seats were either independents or belonged to parties that had failed to clear the 5 percent barrier and thus gain substantial blocs of Duma members.

The organization of the new Duma showed that many elected representatives were starting to drift away from the labels on which they had run for election (table 11.4). Necessity and invention were the spurs to change. Duma rules prescribed that to gain valued committee assignments within parliament and to gain office space and other facilities, individuals had to belong to a party faction with at least thirty-five members. Only four parties emerged from the December election with

TABLE 11.4

CHANGING PARTY AFFILIATIONS OF DUMA MEMBERS,
1995–96

	Duma seats		
	Won at election	Duma, Feb. 96	Change
Communist Party	157	147	−10
Our Home Is Russia	55	66	+11
Liberal Democrats	51	51	0
Yabloko	45	46	+1
Agrarians	20	37 [a]	+17
Russian Regions	–	42 [a]	+42
Power to the People!	9	38 [a]	+29
Fifteen other parties	35	–	−35
Independents	78	23	−55
	450	450	

SOURCE: 1995 Duma election: table 11.2; 1996 Duma membership: *Spisok deputatov Gosudarstvennoi Dumy (po sostoyaniyu na 16.02.96)* (Moscow: Gosudarstvennaya Duma, 1996, duplicated).

a. Deputies' groups formed principally by Duma members elected from single-member districts, supplemented by deputies elected by party list.

sufficient seats to qualify for a full set of Duma privileges; 142 Duma independents or members of eighteen parties were temporarily without official recognition as parties in parliament.

A total of 100 Duma members switched affiliations in the weeks between the announcement of the election result and the organization of parliament. Two large groups with a total of eighty-eight deputies were formed—Russian Regions and Power to the People—by independents and members of small parties making common cause to claim Duma privileges. The two groupings were not so much political parties as liaisons or marriages of convenience. The Agrarian Party managed to become recognized as a separate faction in the Duma by "borrowing" deputies from the Communist Party in order to meet the parliament's thirty-five-member requirement to qualify for Duma privileges. Our Home Is Russia, as the party of government, was able to pick up eleven deputies. Only the Liberal Democrats and Yabloko, each large enough to qualify as a Duma party in its own right, had their memberships remain virtually unchanged.

ships remain virtually unchanged.

In form the 1995 Duma election was democratic, but the outcome raised questions about the future of Russian government. Had the Duma election shown the commitment of Russia to democracy, because dozens of parties had competed for votes? Or was the vote in favor of Communists and nationalists a signal that Russia was moving back to its Soviet past? There was substantial evidence in support of each view.

⟪ 12 ⟫

Competition between Regimes:
Yeltsin vs. Zyuganov

In an established democracy, respect for the rules of the game is more important than holding power outside the law. Elections are about the choice of government within the constitution; the rule of law is taken for granted. Russia, however, has never been an established democracy. Those in government have not been committed to constitutional government; the end—gaining and holding political power—has justified the means. Boris Yeltsin rose to the top by challenging established authority and finally overturning it. After being elected president in 1991 as an antiregime candidate, Yeltsin became averse to the risk of elections. The spring 1993 referendum did not put his hold on power at stake; it simply asked the electorate to give him a blank check to carry on. In the October 1993 confrontation with parliament, Yeltsin demonstrated that when push came to shove, physical force was more important than the opinions of the courts.

The 1996 presidential election offered voters a choice between candidates offering competing regimes. President Boris Yeltsin was not so much the defender of the 1993 constitution as he was its author. As author, he reserved the privilege of interpreting the constitution as he wished, with or without rewriting it. His chief opponent, Communist Party leader Gennadii Zyuganov, was heir to the tradition in which the end justified the means; the party had created Soviet-style "socialist legality" in which millions of Russians had been killed or imprisoned in Siberia on political grounds.

The 1993 constitution called for a presidential election to be held in summer 1996 and every fourth year thereafter. Thus the first issue facing the government was whether or not to respect this requirement. The issue was controversial within the Yeltsin entourage. In the light of the December 1995 Duma election there were grounds to fear the president might lose if an election were held. Electoral defeat threatened Yeltsin's supporters with loss of privilege and financial gain; it also raised the risk that a successor might prosecute them for alleged economic or political "crimes." The debate about whether or not to hold an election continued until within two weeks of the decisive vote. There was a parallel debate about whether the president should leave office, even if defeated at the ballot box. Ominously, President Yeltsin vetoed a parliamentary bill on the orderly transfer of power from one president to another, claiming it had technical deficiencies. In any event, he added, it was not needed because he was certain to remain in office.

A Competitive but Not Consolidated Democracy

A new democracy is consolidated if and when the great majority of parties and major political institutions do not compete by offering authoritarian alternatives as a cure for the country's ills and the great majority of voters do not demand undemocratic alternatives (see Burton et al. 1992; Di Palma 1990). But, if electoral competition involves parties challenging the regime and they win a significant share of the vote, this is evidence that the regime is not consolidated, and it may even be the prelude to its repudiation. For example, in a free and fair election in Germany in the 1920s, Communists and Nazis together claimed half the vote and the Weimar Republic fell. The French Fourth Republic fell in 1958 after being under attack from antiregime parties on both the Gaullist right and the communist left.

The consolidation of democracy has been achieved in the majority of postcommunist countries in Central and Eastern Europe (Rose and Mishler 1996a). Few parties offer alternatives to democratic electoral competition, and those that do win few votes. Furthermore, the army, police, and other major institutions are not centers of intrigue against authority. The transfer of power between the old communist regime and leaders of new institutions in each of these countries was worked out in a series of negotiations in which the interests of different sides were accommodated (see, e.g., Crawford and Lijphart 1995, esp. 181ff.). The commitment of politicians to a democratic regime does not require a firm belief in democratic principles. Motives can include enjoyment of the fruits of winning office in a free election, personal ambition, and the prudential desire to avoid the penalties of an unsuccessful attempt to seize power unconstitutionally.

Consolidation necessarily involves incorporating in the new regime people who have served under an undemocratic regime. Given the scale of political mobilization in a Soviet-style system, to bar everyone associated with the Communist regime from participating in politics would create a large group of alienated politicians with a vested interest in bringing down the new regime. In Central and East European countries, the communist parties have been disbanded. Many members who joined those parties for nonideological opportunistic reasons, such as gaining promotion or material benefits, have either left politics or joined other parties. Public opinion surveys show that throughout Central and Eastern Europe the political attitudes of ex-communists are now much the same as those of noncommunists. Ex-communist politicians who have remained in politics have formed parties that explicitly reject the alien Soviet-dominated past and claim to be social democratic. In Poland, Hungary, Bulgaria, and Lithuania such parties have used the shortcomings of anticommunist governments to win power (see Rose 1996a; Kitschelt 1995).

In Russia, former Communist Party members are active in the new regime and in many parties. So varied are the political outlooks of ex-CPSU members that having been a member of that party is not a good predictor of political attitudes. President Boris Yeltsin spent most of his political career as a full-time CPSU apparatchik. Yegor Gaidar wrote for *Pravda* and was once a department head in *Kommunist,* the party's theoretical journal; his successor as prime minister, Viktor Chernomyrdin, was a member of the central committee of the CPSU. The liberal former mayor of St. Petersburg (and former Communist), Anatolii Sobchak, has argued: "To fear Communists does not make sense because we were all Communists. We had 20 million members" (quoted in Thornhill 1996a).

There has been no consensus between old and new Russian elites in support of a democratic regime, even though the failure of the August 1991 coup showed that it is easier to talk about a coup than to bring one about. Russian political elites often voice doubts about whether Russia can (or should) become democratic. In the months preceding the Duma election, calls to postpone the election came from such Yeltsin loyalists as Vladimir Shumeiko, then speaker of the Federation Council, and Gennadii Burbulis, a former presidential aide. General Alexander Lebed asserted that because of national history, it would take generations before Russia could become democratic. Others feared that a Communist election victory would lead to a coup, either by the Communists or by anticommunists seeking to deny them the fruits of electoral victory (see table 12.1).

TABLE 12.1

ELITE DOUBTS ABOUT DEMOCRACY IN RUSSIA

Democracy is a good word. But in order for it to become a reality in Russia, a colossal amount of work is required. It is still early to speak about it. We will achieve it in two or three generations. I won't live to see that time, and you won't either.

—General Alexander Lebed, leader, Congress of Russian Communities (R. Orttung 1995, 19)

I would very much like to live in a free country, but I very much fear that the path to freedom could kill us.

— Kakha Bendukidze, leading Russian business person (Freeland 1995a)

If the Communists came to power the vested interests they threaten would mount a coup in order to protect their property.

— Georgii Satarov, aide to President Yeltsin (Freeland 1995b)

When you hear talk of postponing elections in Russia, that can mean postponing them for centuries.

— Grigorii Yavlinsky, leader of Yabloko (Dempsey and Peel 1995)

Doubts of the Russian elite about the stability of democracy are echoed in public opinion. The fifth New Russia Barometer survey, conducted just after the Duma election, found that between the 1993 and the 1995 Duma elections the number of Russians saying they approved of the old Communist regime rose by 8 percentage points. Concurrently, those favoring the new regime fell by 7 percentage points. Fifty-nine percent of Russians were positive about the old regime, compared to 28 percent positive about the new regime (Rose 1996b, 49). Among the nine parties that won the most votes in the Duma contest, the supporters of eight were more likely to endorse the old Communist regime than the new; only Russia's Democratic Choice, the most committed of the liberal reform parties, had more voters in favor of the new regime than the old. Nevertheless, Communists were the sole group of partisans showing virtual unanimity in rejecting the new regime. Divisions within parties about the old and the new regime added to elite instability.

Nostalgia for a quiet political past is not the same as a demand for authoritarian rule. The authoritarianism scale measures endorsement of three undemocratic alternatives: dictatorship, army rule, or a return to Communist rule. The post-Duma election New Russia Barometer found that 45 percent of electors interviewed rejected all three authoritarian alternatives, and a majority of voters for six different parties did not endorse any authoritarian alternative (figure 12.1). Furthermore, replies showed that in Russian politics there is competition between undemocratic alternatives: five-sixths of Communist voters endorsed a return to the old Communist regime, and an absolute majority of Zhirinovsky's Liberal Democrats endorsed a strong dictatorship.

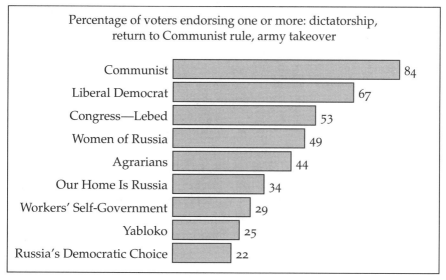

FIGURE 12.1

SUPPORT FOR AUTHORITARIAN ALTERNATIVES BY PARTY

SOURCE: Centre for the Study of Public Policy, New Russia Barometer V, 12–31 January 1996; for full details, see Rose 1996b, 57f.

A Polarizing Campaign

The election of a president is the opposite of the election of a Duma. Only one individual can be president, whereas a parliament represents the diversity of opinions and interests that divide the electorate. Duma representatives are free to say whatever they choose; collectively, the result is confusion, as many deputies voice conflicting demands. The president is expected to resolve debates by giving direction to government. While the Duma talks about what ministries ought to do, a president has the authority to tell ministries to act. The power of the Russian president is increased by the ability to issue decrees having the effect of law without approval by the Duma.

The two-ballot procedure for electing a Russian president is like that of France or like some elections in the American South. The first round is open to a large number of candidates. The wide choice of candidates increases the likelihood that a voter can cast a ballot for a candidate close to his or her own point of view. But the greater the number of candidates in the first round, the more likely it is that none will receive half the vote. If so, a second-round runoff is held between the two top candidates so that the winner gets more than half the vote. But the elimination of all but two alternatives means that for a significant fraction of voters the winner will be the second-best or "lesser evil" choice rather than a leader whom they trust.

A total of seventy-eight candidates registered an intention to run for the presidency, but by nomination day, 16 April 1996, only seventeen had collected the signatures needed for nomination. Whether nominated by a political party or, as in the case of Boris Yeltsin, by an independent initiative of voters, to appear on the ballot a candidate required a million signatures of electors, with no more than 7 percent coming from any one republic or region of the Russian Federation. The Central Electoral Commission rejected the registration of six candidates on the grounds that a substantial number of the nominating signatures had been forged, and the Supreme Court upheld the action against challenges. Of the rejected candidates—Galina Starovoitova, Democratic Russia; Lev Ubozhko, Conservative Party; Vladimir Podoprigora, Russian Compatriots' Assembly; and three businessmen, Sergei Mavrodi, Artem Tarasov, and Vyacheslav Ushakov of the Moscow Investment Fund—none was of political consequence.

The nature of the ballot made it easy to personalize the contest. Among the eleven candidates with their names on the ballot, two stood out: the incumbent president, Boris Yeltsin, and Gennadii Zyuganov, the leader of the Communist Party of the Russian Federation, which had come first in the December Duma election. As leader of a party that had never endorsed reform and never held office under Yeltsin, Zyuganov could claim to be the leading anti-Yeltsin candidate. Yeltsin's standing as a reformer had suffered as a result of twists and turns in economic policy and the war in Chechnya, leading one scholar to describe him as an "all thumbs democrat," well suited to "ram causes forward and brush aside obstacles" but not to the cultivation of support across the political spectrum that is "the stuff of a stable democracy" (Colton 1995, 50). Zyuganov was not a charismatic personality, but he represented a party that supported the bureaucratic "banality of evil" pioneered by Josef Stalin.

No candidate could hope to win by mobilizing only convinced supporters, for none was popular among as much as a quarter of the electorate, let alone the majority necessary for victory. At the start of the campaign, the largest bloc of voters were "don't knows." Among those expressing a preference, the largest group rejected both Yeltsin and Zyuganov, favoring a candidate not so closely identified with the past or the new regime (see Rose 1996b, 66ff.). The first task of the front-runners was to gain sufficient votes to qualify for the second-round runoff election. Zyuganov might hope to do this by appealing to a well-organized Communist minority. For Yeltsin, a president without a party, the target was the don't knows, who tended to be a cross-section of Russian public opinion. If successful in this, each candidate had to position himself to become the second choice of those favoring candidates eliminated after the first round, for they would be the voters deciding the outcome of the critical runoff ballot.

The revival of Yeltsin the campaigner. Although Boris Yeltsin rose to the top as a vigorous campaigner, after the establishment of the Russian Federation he become an increasingly remote figure, and his popularity suffered accordingly (see chapter 8). On 15 February, when Yeltsin announced (at Yekaterinburg, his home base in the Urals) that he would run for reelection, the opinion polls showed him far behind, and many of his staff thought he would lose. A senior Russian pollster briefing the president at the start of the campaign was amazed to find that Yeltsin thought he was the most popular politician in Russia; no one had shown him the mass of polling evidence registering his unpopularity.

None of Yeltsin's closest advisers had any experience of running a democratic election campaign. Initially, the campaign was headed by the first deputy prime minister, Oleg Soskovets, an ally of Alexander Korzhakov, who was nominally placed in charge of the campaign, and a campaign office was set up in the well-guarded President Hotel, formerly a select residence for the Central Committee of the CPSU. The electoral inadequacies of this group led Russian businessmen to propose the establishment, on another floor of the President Hotel, of a second campaign group headed by Anatolii Chubais, whom the president had just sacked as economics minister. Another businessman arranged for three professional campaign consultants from California to occupy other hotel rooms, from which they too could proffer advice. The multiplicity of advisers was in keeping with Yeltsin's habit of playing conflicting groups off against one another so that he could reserve strategic decisions for himself. To have someone coordinating activities who was undoubtedly loyal to his interests, the president brought in his daughter, Tatyana Dyachenko. While she had the advantages of unlimited access to the president and his trust, the thirty-six-year-old computer engineer lacked any political experience.

A staff cannot run a campaign without a candidate, and Boris Yeltsin was his staff's biggest problem. Two serious heart attacks in 1995 and bouts of heavy drinking had taken their toll on Yeltsin's health and on his public image. To many he appeared incapable of taking charge of government. Public appearances in which the president appeared enfeebled or incapacitated as a result of drink would be sure votelosers. Yeltsin had a history of appearing in public when he was unfit to do so or disappearing from sight when he was expected to appear. On a memorable occasion when the president's plane touched down at Shannon Airport, the prime minister of Ireland stood on the tarmac expecting to meet him, but Yeltsin did not leave his plane as planned.

A successful campaign required "bringing the president back from Ireland," that is, making sure he was psychologically and medically fit to campaign actively and publicly. This happened; as business backer Boris Berezovsky explained, "at key points in his life, Yeltsin wakes up" (quoted in Hockstader and Hoffman 1996, 1). During five months of campaigning Yeltsin made thirty-three trips outside Moscow to show himself to the electorate in carefully stage-managed appearances. On the campaign trail, he expressed surprise to find that conditions were not always satisfactory and promised crowds that he would spend money without restraint to set things right. Yeltsin's election manifesto admitted that transforming the economy was causing pain, and he admitted, "I have made mistakes." But Yeltsin then added confidently, "I know better than anyone else how to correct them," and he promised to improve welfare, reduce corruption, and encourage economic growth (*Rossiiskie vesti*, 1 June 1996, 1–16).

President Yeltsin could not run on his record, for the popular mood was dominated by a "feel bad" factor. At the start of 1996, 83 percent considered their families' economic situation unsatisfactory, according to the fifth New Russia Barometer. Furthermore, only 22 percent felt their living standards had risen since Yeltsin had entered office five years previously, whereas 58 percent said they had fallen, and only 25 percent considered their economic situation likely to improve in the next five years (Rose 1996b, 20f.). In the six months leading up to the vote, the official economy continued to contract and prices continued to rise. In late March the International Monetary Fund (IMF), acting under strong pressure from the American White House, granted a $10 billion loan to tide the Russian government over the election period. The strings attached to the loan, the adoption of strict economic policies after the election, were not publicized.

The war in Chechnya was another negative entry in the president's record, for it antagonized nationalists and Communists, who saw it as undermining the authority of the Russian state, and reformers, who saw it as undermining democratization. The mass of the electorate saw it as a "no win" war causing more than 30,000 deaths in the Russian Federation. Chechen leaders were ready to negotiate with President Yeltsin, believing he would make preelection concessions; they also feared that a Communist victory might cause an intensification of the conflict. A cease-fire in the seventeen-month battle was announced on 27 May in Moscow; the day afterward, Yeltsin paid a stage-managed flying visit to the area. The cease-fire kept Chechen troubles out of the news until after the election, which the Chechens boycotted. But the cease-fire was not a peace treaty; fighting resumed shortly after election day.

Given widespread public dissatisfaction with government, the primary theme of the campaign was negative: preventing the "greatest evil," a return to Communist Party control of government. Even though the Communist Party was the biggest party in the country, it was still a minority party, and even though Zyuganov was the front-runner in opinion polls, his support fell far short of the 50.1 percent necessary to become president. Campaigning against the Communists was intended to increase the polarization of the electorate, in the belief that the majority of undecided voters would choose Boris Yeltsin as a lesser evil. The American campaign advisers argued:

> Voters don't approve of the job Yeltsin is doing, don't think things will ever get any better and prefer the Communists' approach. There exists only one very simple strategy for winning: first, becoming the only alternative to the Communists; and second, making the people see that the Communists must be stopped at all costs. (quoted in Kramer 1996)

Such an argument was critical in leading the reform-minded former prime minister, Yegor Gaidar, to endorse Yeltsin. It was also used in an attempt to court the support of Alexander Lebed and Grigorii Yavlinsky in the second-round ballot.

Given that the Communists had governed Russia for more than seventy years, the Yeltsin campaigners had no difficulty in dredging up unpleasant facts from the past. Ten million copies of a full-color propaganda paper, *God Forbid,* threatened a return to the worst excesses of the Stalin era if Zyuganov had become president. Crude cartoon leaflets portrayed Communists as the cause of starvation, theft, oppression, and murder, and directly associated Zyuganov with Stalin, and even Hitler, with the punning headline, *Zyug Heil.* Another leaflet pictured Zyuganov and Zhirinovsky in front of portraits of Hitler and Stalin, and advised, "We all have our bones to pick with the Yeltsin-Chernomyrdin government. But does that mean that we should embrace the Communists and Zhirinovskyists? Can we really have forgotten everything?" A one-hour Yeltsin campaign video gave only fleeting glimpses of Yeltsin: it was primarily a catalogue of Communist crimes, starting with executions in the 1920s through the purges of Stalin to the death of Soviet soldiers in Afghanistan. (The war in Chechnya was not mentioned.) The video also highlighted ecological disasters, such as the drying up of the Aral Sea and the 1986 nuclear accident at the Chernobyl power station.

In electioneering, the Yeltsin campaign benefited from being the party in power, for it commanded the very substantial resources of the state. President Yeltsin had appointed regional officials and government ministers who wielded substantial influence over resources of concern to enterprises as well as local governments. The Russian political tradition, going back to the time of Tsar Ivan the Terrible, made subordinates hesitate to risk offending their superiors. It also encouraged politicians to think that governors and enterprise managers could dispose of blocs of votes in the way in which landowners could command their serfs. Control of state administration gave Yeltsin campaigners generous mass media coverage, the use of government telecommunications and travel facilities, and opportunities for stage-managed events.

The party of power had no trouble raising money. The transformation of the economy had produced a small number of Russian multimillionaires in banking, the media, and industry, who feared that their new properties and lifestyle would be forfeit in the event of a Communist victory. Although there was an official limit of little more than $3 million on campaign expenditure, businesses contributed at least $100 million to finance campaign efforts, and some estimates put the total as high as $500 million (Hockstader and Hoffman 1996, 1). In Russia, unlike most West European countries, paid political advertising on television was legal, within limits—although state officials did not act when these limits were exceeded. Business supporters were prepared to put their bankrolls where their mouths were. "Yeltsin benefited not from

Californians telling him to go anti-Red but rather rich Russians who would keep his campaign green" (Remnick 1996, 46).

The media were encouraged to give positive coverage to the president and to ignore or attack his opponents. The tactics were not those of deft-fingered "spin doctors" but the more insistent pressures of the "heavy squad." In January the popular Moscow mayor Yuri Luzhkov met editors to seek their support, arguing that, if they valued their freedom, journalists should do everything possible to secure Yeltsin's re-election, for their freedoms would be the first to be lost if the Communists won (Matlock 1996, 28). The director of the president's Department of Information and Propaganda, Valery Kucher, declared, "We are not going to give the Communists equal time or conditions. They don't deserve it. They are an anticonstitutional party" (European Institute for the Media 1996a, 1). To strengthen media support, the president appointed Igor Malashenko, head of Russia's only independent television station, NTV, as a member of his reelection campaign, and sacked Oleg Poptsov, who had directed the All-Russia State TV and Radio Company, because that channel had criticized the Chechen war.

Media owners were ready to volunteer support to Yeltsin because of their fear that a Communist victory threatened a return to an era in which the media were strictly controlled by the state. In a pun on the Russian names of the two leading Soviet papers, *Pravda* (in English, Truth) and *Izvestiya* (News), the saying was, "In *Pravda* there is no truth and in *Izvestiya* there is no news." A return to those days would deprive new media moguls of their editorial freedom and their chance to make money. Many Russian journalists did not welcome being the objects of intimidation and co-option, but some argued that there was no alternative. A liberal television commentator, Nikolai Svanidze, told a Western journalist, "I am not sure that people in the West understand that a political fight is going on here that has no rules. And if the Communists win, then the media will lose their independence. There is no choice" (quoted in De Waal 1996).

An independent tabulation of media coverage showed that the Yeltsin team was very successful in securing a lopsided picture of the campaign on television (European Institute for the Media 1996a). The three nationwide Russian television channels, ORT, RTR, and NTV, gave President Yeltsin 53 percent of all the prime-time television coverage between 6 May and 3 July. This was almost three times the 18 percent of coverage given Zyuganov, and almost five times the 11 percent given all other candidates combined. Equally important, there were 492 more positive than negative references to President Yeltsin, whereas there were 313 more negative than positive references in the coverage of Zyuganov. The variety of print media spread press attention across a range of candidates. Nonetheless, Yeltsin received more, and more favorable, coverage. The president's supporters, as well as Zyuganov's newspaper backers, ran news and comment together in ways that the European Institute for the Media (1996a, 10) described as "strident, harsh and one-sided." But ordinary Russians were unlikely to view their media through the same eyes as Western observers accustomed to strong, independent media. A third of the people read no newspaper regularly, and more turned to local papers than to the leading national papers (Rose 1996b, 41). Decades of being subject to Communist propaganda encouraged skepticism and distrust of what was said or shown on television as well as in the press. Insofar as harsh and one-sided anti-Communist propaganda rang false to Russians with memories of the past, it would have hurt Yeltsin's cause. But if the messages rang true, evoking the past would have strengthened Yeltsin's claim to be the "lesser evil."

The campaigners feared that even though Yeltsin was sure to qualify for the runoff ballot, he might finish second in the initial vote. Given the widening gulf between the Communists and the anti- (and ex-) Communist Yeltsin, there was no prospect of Communists converting to the Yeltsin cause. Yeltsin's chances of entering the runoff as the front-runner would be increased by nationalist competitors taking votes from Zyuganov, because nationalists could appeal to voters disaffected with the Yeltsin record yet unhappy about a return to Communist ways. Every vote taken from Zyuganov by a nationalist candidate made it that much easier for Yeltsin to finish first.

While the extreme behavior of Vladimir Zhirinovsky limited his appeal in a presidential race, the "above politics" position of a former general, Alexander Lebed, gave him an appeal to disaffected voters. Lebed put forward an "ideology of common sense," calling for Russia to have "dignity, pride in its history, respect for its labor and certainty in the future" (*Argumenty i fakty*, no. 22, 1996, 5). Lebed had come up the hard way through the military, where he made his name as a paratrooper in Afghanistan and also as a thorn in the side of the military hierarchy. At the breakup of the Soviet Union he was in charge of troops in a Russian enclave in the newly independent Republic of Moldova. He publicly rejected orders from Moscow to withdraw and responded to a similar suggestion from American UN representative Madeleine Albright with the blunt remark, "It's time all those uninvited advisers got a boot in the behind." In 1995 Lebed resigned from the army and was elected to the Duma in December. He praised achievements of other military leaders in politics, sometimes evoking de Gaulle and sometimes Augusto Pinochet, the Chilean leader who had boosted that country's economy while killing "no more than three thousand people." After the vote, Vladimir Zhirinovsky lamented to a reporter, "Lebed stole my act and he stole my votes. I should take him to court" (Remnick 1996, 52; see also Lebed 1995).

Before the first-round ballot, the president's team talked with many candidates about forming alliances. It appeared to do more than talk with Lebed: his campaign received an influx of money, and television coverage was often positive. The European Institute for the Media (1996b, 7) found that Lebed was the only candidate besides Boris Yeltsin who received more favorable than unfavorable coverage on television.

Boosting turnout was another strategy that the Yeltsin campaign used in an effort to finish ahead of Zyuganov. Survey data showed that Communist voters were strongly committed and thus most likely to vote even if there was a low turnout. There was also consistent evidence that young voters were least likely to support the Communists but were not always inclined to vote. Because a high turnout favored the president, the media were encouraged to run a "nonpartisan" get-out-the-vote campaign. The Yeltsin camp sought to boost the president's appeal to young voters by staging rock concerts and other events for youth; the president himself even appeared at one, and was shown on television dancing to rock music. In another step specially designed to appeal to the young, Yeltsin issued a decree abolishing conscription in the Russian army in four years' time. Military conscripts, worried about being used as "cannon meat," a slang term describing an assignment to Chechnya, were told that they would not be sent there without their own consent (*Izvestiya*, 18 May 1996, 1–2).

Since there could be no guarantee that Boris Yeltsin would be in first place after all the votes were cast, members of the Yeltsin entourage explored the possibility of canceling the election, either before or after the first-round ballot was held. American campaign advisers reported that when they met Deputy Prime Minister Soskovets on 27 February he told them, "One of your tasks is to advise us, a month from the election, about whether we should call it off if you determine that we're going to lose" (quoted in Kramer 1996). In the first several months of the campaign Yeltsin's support rose—but he remained behind Zyuganov. At the beginning of March, the Institute for the Study of Parliamentarianism, which had a reputation for having gotten the

Duma election right, showed 24 percent of the electorate favoring Zyuganov and only 8 percent favoring Yeltsin. At the beginning of May, it
showed Zyuganov still ahead of Yeltsin by a 10-percentage-point margin (*Argumenty i fakty*, no. 21, 1996, 3).

Anxiety about the election result led to an orchestrated series of
statements calling for the suspension of the election and the formation
of a government of national unity. The call came from an academic
group, led by Gennadii Osipov, president of the Russian Academy of
Sciences, and from thirteen business leaders (*Izvestiya*, 27 April 1996, 2).
Boris Berezovsky, head of a financial and industrial conglomerate, described the presidential ballot as a confrontation between competing
views of "the essential nature of our social and economic structure. A
question like this cannot be decided by voting; it is only decided by
civil war" (quoted in Freeland 1996a, 2). Colonel-General Leontin Kuznetsov, commander of the Moscow military district, ominously warned,
"Elections could lead to destabilization, which would stir up all Russia,
all Russian-speakers, including the military" (Hearst 1996a, 15).

A leader in discussions about canceling the election was the person closest to the president, at the office and as a tennis-playing and
late-night drinking companion, Alexander Korzhakov, a former KGB
official. Korzhakov was known as the leader of the "party of power" or,
after the conflict began in Chechnya, "the war party." Korzhakov preferred to issue orders rather than engage in reasoned discussion—and
he was also commander of a 20,000-strong presidential bodyguard. He
told Galina Starovoitova, a former Kremlin adviser and Duma deputy,
that elections were "too risky, they are just a Western idea," adding,
"why risk everything just to have some people put pieces of paper into
something called a ballot box" (Remnick 1996, 47). Decrees were
drafted for the dissolution of parliament, the banning of the Communist Party, and the cancellation of the election. Proposals to suspend the
election were put to Yeltsin in March, but he rejected them. Korzhakov
floated the idea again on May Day, when he told Western interviewers:

> A lot of influential people are in favor of postponing the election, and
> I'm in favor of it too, because we need stability. If we have elections
> there is no way of avoiding a fight. Society is split. Even families are
> split, some for Yeltsin, some for Zyuganov. Such a division of souls is
> dangerous. (*Izvestiya*, 6 May 1996, 1)

By this time Yeltsin was optimistic of winning the election, and he publicly rebuked Korzhakov.

There was continued speculation that, however people voted, Boris Yeltsin would remain president "one way or the other." It was suggested that the Yeltsin camp was trying to scare voters into giving it their support to prevent the president's staff from proclaiming a dictatorship rather than surrender office after a defeat at the polls. A popular joke was the head of the Central Electoral Commission informing the president after the second-round ballot that he had both bad news and good news: the bad news was that Zyuganov had got 55 percent of the vote; the good news was that Yeltsin had taken 65 percent! (*Izvestiya*, 11 June 1996, 3).

The Communist problem: too hard a core. Inspired by its good performance in the Duma election and by the return to power of ex-communists in other countries, the Communist Party entered the presidential election optimistic about its chances of victory. Its leader, Gennadii Zyuganov, stood for the presidency as the candidate of the National Patriotic Front, a name chosen to appeal to a broad spectrum of "Brown" nationalist voters as well as traditional Red supporters. Parties represented in the Front included the Agrarians, the Marxist-Leninist Working Russia party led by Viktor Anpilov, and former Vice-President Rutskoi's Derzhava party. The Red bloc had taken a third of the vote in the December Duma election, and the Brown parties a fifth of the vote. Thus, if Zyuganov could successfully appeal to both blocs, he had a good chance of emerging the winner in the second-round ballot. When cries were raised about suspending the election, the Communist leader came out for free and fair competition:

> We must guarantee the elections are carried out in a strictly democratic, honest and legal fashion, and at the same time sit around a table with all the parties and movements and sign an agreement that the outcome of the election, as expressed by voters, will be sacred. (Hearst 1996b)

The Communist leader faced great difficulties in seeking to appeal to every group from unreconstructed Marxist-Leninists to Western business leaders whose confidence he sought when addressing the World Economic Forum in Davos, Switzerland, in February 1996. There were no moderates within his coalition to balance the hardliners, for they had moved into other parties and for the most part were backing Yeltsin. The Communist Party of the Russian Federation had no intention of becoming a social democratic party along lines pioneered in Hungary. It drew much of its support from those who longed for the good old days before Mikhail Gorbachev. Zyuganov's election manifesto called for tighter state control of the economy and the "great" days of the Soviet Union, when that country was respected and feared around the world. It made no mention of Marx or Lenin but did include a reference to Franklin D. Roosevelt (*Pravda*, 28 May 1996, 1–2).

The strength of the Communist Party was also its weakness; consistently, it showed much more committed support than any other party, but its hard-core support was insufficient to win a straight runoff ballot. Attacking the shortcomings of the Yeltsin government was easy for Zyuganov to do, but it did not differentiate his candidacy from that of others in the field. Furthermore, many who supported anti-Yeltsin parties were also anti-Communist. For example, half the voters for Lebed's party in the Duma election did not approve of the old Communist regime, and a third of Zhirinovsky's voters felt the same (cf. table 11.3). Even many people nostalgic about the past did not necessarily want to return to a one-party state. In the fifth New Russia Barometer survey, 39 percent said they would welcome a return to a Communist regime, but this figure was well short of the magic 50.1 percent needed to win the presidency (Rose 1996b, 58).

In an attempt to counter anti-Communist propaganda emphasizing the crimes of Stalin and threatening civil war, Zyuganov brought forward moderate, conciliatory themes. He promised economic stability through greater state initiatives, but the details were left vague. A Communist spokesperson suggested the party had much in common with President Bill Clinton (*Nezavisimaya gazeta*, 29 May 1996, 2). Others in the Communist camp made more aggressive appeals. In the Duma the party successfully sponsored a resolution rescinding the agreement to break up the Soviet Union and give independence from Russia to Ukraine, Belarus, and other Soviet republics; this created anxieties among leaders in neighboring countries and in the West. Anatolii Lukyanov, the number-two man in the party and a prominent supporter of the failed 1991 coup, appeared to want the party to run against McDonalds. In the belief that there was widespread anti-Western sentiment in the Slav electorate, he told a British journalist, "the more advertising the West puts all over the streets of Moscow, the more the West pumps its films onto our television, the more the Russian people will oppose them" (Scott 1996).

Campaigners produced credible attacks on their opponents while making incredible promises to the voters. For example, in early April President Yeltsin signed a decree promising the prompt payment of pension arrears, even though the government did not have the cash in hand. In addition, pensions were raised significantly from 1 May, seven weeks before the first ballot. On the campaign trail Yeltsin claimed he could secure payment to workers whose employers were much behind in paying them. In early April he signed a decree instructing state financial institutions to create a program to restore private savings to the 70 million depositors who had lost savings as a result of inflation. If the promise were carried out, it would have cost up to $160 billion. Regional budgets received 33 trillion rubles from the State Bank (*Izvestiya*, 14 June 1996, 1). The sum actually spent on Yeltsin's giveaway campaign was calculated at $10 billion, almost exactly the amount that the IMF had loaned Russia with the expectation it would be invested in the economy and later repaid to the international institution (cf. *The Economist*, 1996, 41).

Gennadii Zyuganov was a long-time adherent of an atheist party that as recently as 1986 had committed itself to the "broad dissemination of a scientific materialist world outlook" and had rules obliging party members to "combat resolutely" any signs of "religious prejudice," that is, positive religious beliefs. Nonetheless, in 1996 he promised religious freedom and courted the votes of believers by appearing in photographs with Orthodox priests.

As the campaign progressed, public opinion surveys registered significant improvement in Boris Yeltsin's position. In the initial January poll, Yeltsin was named by only 8 percent of those who stated a preference for a candidate, far behind the 21 percent naming Zyuganov and marginally less than three other rivals, Zhirinovsky, Yavlinsky, and Lebed (figure 12.2). Such numbers frightened all members in Yeltsin's entourage, leading some to argue for a more positive campaign, and others to argue that the election should be canceled.

During the lengthy campaign, Yeltsin's support rose 28 percentage points. By the end of March, it was up to 18 percent, 7 points behind Zyuganov. By this time Yeltsin had widened the distance between himself and other candidates who offered a third alternative. By the end of April, Yeltsin's support stood at 21 percent, still trailing Zyuganov. But VTsIOM surveys also showed that the proportion thinking Yeltsin would win was changing dramatically: it was 13 percent in January and 41 percent by late April. Negative campaigning was also having an impact; the percentage saying that they would not like to see Zyuganov become president rose from 21 percent to 31 percent between February and late April, and by June it was higher than the rejection of Yeltsin as president. In March, more voters thought Zyuganov was likely to make things better, and more thought Yeltsin was likely to make things worse. By early June, 39 percent thought Zyuganov would make

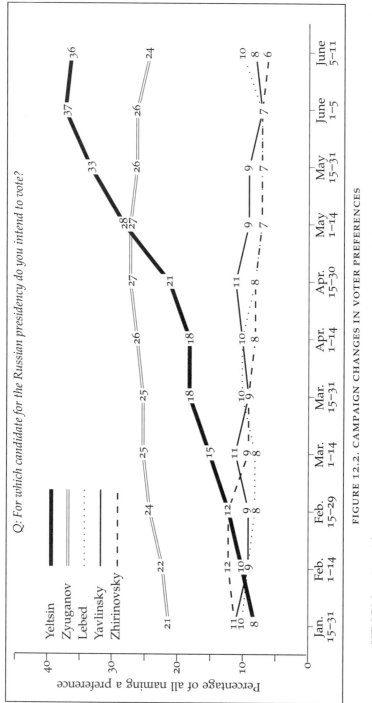

FIGURE 12.2. CAMPAIGN CHANGES IN VOTER PREFERENCES

SOURCE: VTsIOM nationwide representative sample surveys of the electorate, with about 1,600 respondents each, as reported in *Izvestiya*, 11 June 1996, 2, and 13 June 1996, 5.

conditions worse, compared to 21 percent with a similarly negative view of Yeltsin (Zorkaya 1996, 12; results of VTsIOM survey of 5–12 June 1996).

The VTsIOM polls showed Yeltsin catching up with Zyuganov in the first half of May, a finding confirmed by other surveys (*Argumenty i fakty*, no. 23, 1996, 2); by the end of May, Yeltsin appeared to be 7 percentage points ahead. The final published poll gave Yeltsin 36 percent of the overall vote, with Zyuganov second and Lebed third.

Finishing First — Barely

Just in case voters had not got the message of the president's campaign, on the night before the initial vote, the first channel of state television, ORT, showed the award-winning film *Burnt by the Sun*, set during the worst period of Stalin's purges. Its star, Nikita Mikhalkov, had been a leading name in the Duma list of Our Home Is Russia and was campaigning for Yeltsin's reelection.

Voting took place on Sunday, 16 June. Those who had spent the day at a country dacha had time to vote after returning home because the polls were open until 10:00 P.M. The turnout, 69.7 percent, was 5 percentage points higher than in the December Duma election (and more than 11 percentage points higher than the turnout in the 1992 U.S. presidential election). Moreover, the number of invalid votes and votes against all names on the list, two classic measures of disaffection, was 2.9 percent, down almost two-fifths from the Duma contest (cf. table 12.2 and table 11.2).

The aggressive campaign produced the result that Boris Yeltsin wanted: he finished ahead of Gennadii Zyuganov. The margin was narrow, 3.3 percentage points, but it was enough to establish Yeltsin as the frontrunner in the critical second-round ballot. Moreover, it registered a major comeback for Yeltsin from where he had stood in popular favor at the start of the year, and it was more than treble the share of the popular vote cast in the December Duma election for the government party, Our Home Is Russia. The big boost in Yeltsin's vote by comparison with that for the prime minister's party was not so much a reflection of the popular appeal of the president as it was a consequence of the smaller number of choices in the presidential race and the reduction of realistic alternatives for the presidency to two, a Communist or the anti-Communist Yeltsin. The president welcomed such a race, declaring, "After the first round the situation is different. The choice is simpler: either back to revolutions and upheavals or for-

TABLE 12.2

FIRST-ROUND 1996 PRESIDENTIAL ELECTION RESULT

16 June 1996: Registered electorate = 108,495,023

Candidates	Vote	
	Percentage	Number
Boris Yeltsin, Independent	35.3	26,665,495
Gennadii Zyuganov, Communist	32.0	24,211,686
Alexander Lebed, no party	14.5	10,974,736
Grigorii Yavlinsky, Yabloko	7.3	5,550,752
Vladimir Zhirinovsky, Liberal Democrat	5.7	4,311,479
Svyatoslav Fedorov, Workers' Self-Government	0.9	699,158
Mikhail Gorbachev, International Fund		
Socioeconomic and Political Research	0.5	386,069
Martin Shakkum, Socioeconomic Reform	0.4	277,068
Yuri Vlasov, National Patriotic Party	0.2	151,282
Vladimir Bryntsalov, Russian Socialist Party	0.2	123,065
Aman-Geldy Tuleev, Communist[a]	0.0	308
Against all candidates	1.5	1,163,921
Total valid vote	68.7	74,515,019
Invalid ballots	1.4	1,072,120
Total turnout	69.7	75,587,139

SOURCE: Central Electoral Commission communiqué published in *Rossiiskaya gazeta,* 22 June 1996, 1.

a. Withdrew from race at last minute in favor of Zyuganov.

ward to stability and prosperity" (*Rossiiskaya gazeta,* 18 June 1996, 1).

Nevertheless, Yeltsin's share of the vote, 35 percent, was far below what he had registered in each of his previous campaigns (figure 12.3). In the first competitive elections in the Soviet Union in 1989, Yeltsin's vote in his Moscow constituency was 89 percent, a record high. In June 1991 he had no difficulty in winning election outright on the first ballot in the contest for the presidency of the Russian Federation. He finished 41 percentage points ahead of his Communist-backed opponent and 51 points ahead of the third-place candidate, Vladimir Zhirinovsky (see table 2.3). In 1996 Yeltsin could run only a few percentage points ahead of a Communist, and his lead over Zhirinovsky was down by 30 percentage points.

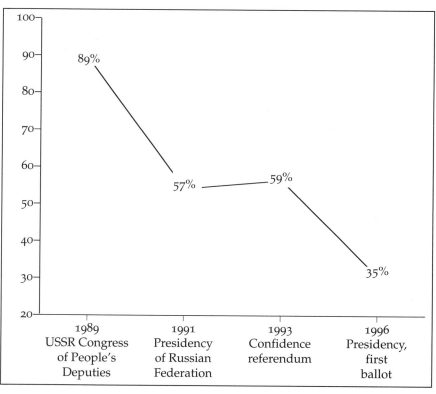

FIGURE 12.3
CHANGING FORTUNES OF BORIS YELTSIN

SOURCE: Data reported in chapters 2 and 4 and above.

The vote for Yeltsin was also much lower than the endorsements he had claimed in referendums only three years before. In April 1993 a referendum question asking for a vote of confidence in Yeltsin as president was endorsed by 59 percent, and a question asking voters to express their views about his economic and social policies was endorsed by 53 percent, figures one-half to two-thirds higher than the vote Yeltsin registered in the 1996 presidential race. Furthermore, the vote for Yeltsin as president was more than a third lower than the vote for the presidentialist constitution he had presented to the Russian people in the December 1993 referendum (cf. tables 4.2, 5.1).

Zyuganov's vote was up by almost half compared to the party-list vote for the Communist Party in the Duma election. Nevertheless, the vote was only 1.4 percent more than the total cast for the Communist and Agrarian lists at the Duma election. This indicated that while there was a consistent commitment to the Red cause, there was also a persisting ceiling. The Communists faced difficulties in gaining support from voters who recognized that Zyuganov was the only credible anti-Yeltsin candidate.

Alexander Lebed made a surprisingly strong showing, more than trebling the vote won by his party list in the Duma election. While 14.5 percent of the vote was less than Ross Perot claimed in the 1992 American presidential election, Lebed's supporters argued with some justification that his appeal to voters with Brown and Red inclinations had reduced Zyuganov's vote sufficiently to enable Yeltsin to finish ahead in the first round. Lebed also drew some votes from Vladimir Zhirinovsky, who finished fifth, with less than half the vote claimed by the Liberal Democratic list in the 1995 Duma vote and one-quarter the vote that the Liberal Democrats had gained in 1993, when it was the only nationalist party conducting a vigorous campaign. Zhirinovsky's decline was attributed to competition from Lebed and to many voters' unwillingness to endorse so outspoken a protest candidate for the serious office of the presidency. Grigorii Yavlinsky was the chief representative of economic reform, as Yegor Gaidar had not entered the race and reluctantly backed Yeltsin. During the campaign Yavlinsky engaged in extensive semipublic discussions with the Yeltsin camp but did not endorse him. Yavlinsky finished fourth, with a vote slightly up from Yabloko's Duma performance but with fewer votes than promised by his personal popularity at the start of the campaign.

Six candidates were very much also-rans, each winning far less than a million votes, the number of signatures necessary to get their names on the ballot in the first place. Mikhail Gorbachev, five years earlier the president of the Soviet Union, campaigned against a return of the Communists to power and against Yeltsin's policies. At one hostile rally he told the audience that they were partly to blame for the country's troubles because they had voted for Yeltsin in 1991. A heckler replied, "But you should have annulled the vote." Gorbachev finished seventh, with only 0.5 percent of the vote. Aman-Geldy Tuleev, a Communist miners' leader, dropped out of the race three days before polling day, pleading that it was a "civic duty" and asking his supporters to transfer their votes to Zyuganov. Ballot papers had already been printed and local election officials were instructed to delete his name manually. But because ballots had already been cast in some remote polling stations, he received 0.0004 percent of the vote.

A Forced Choice

Although the first-round ballot was a good result for Boris Yeltsin, it was not good enough to guarantee him victory in the crucial second round. Almost two-thirds of those who had turned out to vote had refused to endorse him, but the same was true of Gennadii Zyuganov. Thus the outcome of the runoff would be determined by the behavior of the 23 million voters who had rejected both Yeltsin and Zyuganov on the first ballot. Even though none of the also-ran candidates could deliver all of his or her support as a solid bloc, so large was the share of the vote up for grabs that relatively small advantages could be sufficient to tip the balance in the runoff. VTsIOM surveys indicated that by mid-April the second preferences of voters initially opposed to both front-runners were sufficiently pro-Yeltsin to give him a slim edge in the second-round ballot (Zorkaya 1996, table 9). But the lead was not large or firm enough to guarantee victory.

Fearful that their lead would not last, the Yeltsin camp decided to hold the second-round vote as soon as possible. The date chosen was Wednesday, 3 July, only seventeen days after the first-round ballot and less than two weeks after the official declaration of the first result. Believing that a high turnout would help Yeltsin because his supporters were less committed than Communists, a day in the middle of the week was selected, so that voters would not miss voting because they were away at weekend dachas. Election day was made a public holiday to give more people free time to vote.

Alexander Lebed's ability to win 10 million votes, sufficient to guarantee Yeltsin the presidency, made his position of intense interest to the Yeltsin camp, even though there was no guarantee that Lebed could deliver all his supporters to the president, as many had Red-Brown inclinations inimical to the Yeltsin cause. Nor was a large bloc of Lebed voters necessary to win, because Yeltsin was certain to pick up a significant shares of the vote from Yavlinsky and other anti-Communist candidates. Nonetheless, as a candidate who commanded sufficient votes to make Yeltsin president, Lebed's endorsement was courted aggressively by Yeltsin, and the groundwork for cooperation had already been established in the campaign for the first-round vote. Moreover, Lebed's emphasis on law and order complemented the Yeltsin campaign's emphasis on the "disorder" that would follow if the Communists won.

Even though he had recently described Boris Yeltsin as a sick former party boss while campaigning against him in the presidential race, Alexander Lebed was installed in the Kremlin as head of the Security Council. The council had no legislative authorization, making Lebed's

authority dependent on the goodwill of the president plus whatever independent political status he could carve out against competitors. Furthermore, the council had no explicit power of command and control
over ministries. The standing of Lebed was strengthened by the simultaneous sacking of Pavel Grachev as minister of defense. Grachev was
unpopular because of his support for the Chechen war and allegations
of corruption, giving him the nickname "Pasha Mercedes." As a former
army officer, albeit one who had previously held no more than a field
command, Lebed now had an opening to put into action his proclaimed goal of rooting out corruption in government.

Lebed's goals went far beyond the military, for he saw himself as a
man of destiny whose leadership might someday restore Russia's
greatness by means unspecified. He called for purging Russia of "foul
sects," such as Mormons, who were undermining the country's traditional religions, which he named as the Orthodox church, Islam, and
Buddhism, conspicuously omitting Judaism as part of Russia's tradition (Reeves 1996, 13). As a first step in expanding his power, Lebed announced that he should become vice-president, making him heir apparent in the event of Yeltsin's death or incapacity. But there was no
such post under the 1993 constitution. To create such a post would
place Lebed above Prime Minister Chernomyrdin in the official hierarchy. The prime minister resisted this move, as well as Lebed's attempt
to claim additional powers over economic and social affairs.

Within the Yeltsin camp, the first-round victory of the president
was a setback to members of his entourage who believed the best way
to retain power was to cancel the election. In a move that echoed Soviet
days, Korzhakov authorized the arrest of two media advisers on the
president's campaign team, Sergei Lisovsky and Arkadii Yevstafev, as
they were leaving the White House, the seat of the Yeltsin government,
at 5:00 P.M. on 19 June. Security officials alleged that their arrest was
made because they had $500,000 in cash; Lisovsky asserted that the
money had been planted by special agents of Korzhakov's Presidential Security Service. The two men were questioned about the election
campaign; their interrogators demanded incriminating evidence
against Chubais and Prime Minister Chernomyrdin, both enemies of
Korzhakov. The two men used their cellular phones to inform colleagues at the Yeltsin campaign headquarters what had happened. At
midnight the media were informed; their directors were allies of the
campaigners and opponents of Korzhakov. At 4:20 A.M. the newly appointed head of the security council, Alexander Lebed, declared on
television, "Attempts are being made to wreck the second round [of the

vote]. Those who want to throw the country into the abyss of bloody chaos deserve no mercy at all" (Thornhill and Freeland, 1996, 2).

Once news of the arrests was made public, President Yeltsin became the target of intensive lobbying from Chubais, Lebed, and others, who regarded the arrests as an attempt by Korzhakov to seize unchallenged authority in the circle of the president. At midday, Yeltsin announced that it was time for "fresh faces"; he sacked Korzhakov, security bureau chief Mikhail Barsukov, and their ally, First Deputy Prime Minister Oleg Soskovets. The explanation given was that "they were taking too much and giving back too little" (*Izvestiya*, 20 June 1996, 1; 21 June 1996, 1–2). The decision was not an easy one for the president; Yeltsin's wife told a television interviewer that getting rid of Korzhakov was one of the most painful acts in her husband's career, describing it as "like losing a limb." Anatolii Chubais declared, "This event marks the final stage of a long and arduous struggle, the struggle between that part of Yeltsin's administration which worked to ensure Yeltsin's victory in a democratic election and that part of Yeltsin's administration which preferred to use force" (Thornhill and Freeland 1996, 2). Just to be safe, Chubais decided that he had better travel around Moscow in a bullet-proof Mercedes protected by armed guards.

The final twist in the campaign was the disappearance of Yeltsin himself from public view one week before election day. The president's office issued a series of explanations, saying that he had a cold and had lost his voice as a result of campaigning; therefore, his doctor had prescribed rest. In an attempt to counter the belief that his absence was the result of another heart attack or heavy drinking, the president's office sought to portray him as actively in charge of government. In a procedure reminiscent of the Stalin era, just before polling day Yeltsin gave an interview consisting of written answers to written questions (*Rossiiskaya gazeta*, 1 July 1996, 3). A recorded two-minute television appeal by the president on 1 July did nothing to dispel rumors, for he appeared to be under heavy medication or to have suffered a stroke (*Nezavisimaya gazeta*, 2 July 1996, 1). "The man is a living corpse; we're just waiting for him to drop dead," commented Vladimir Zhirinovsky (Remnick 1996, 56).

On election day, the media waited at the polling station where Yeltsin was expected to cast his ballot, but the president did not appear. He voted at a polling station outside Moscow, Barvikha, where there was a health complex for treating the Kremlin elite. Only the official state television cameras were allowed to record what President Yeltsin looked like when he cast his ballot.

The Communists were boxed in by the actions of the Yeltsin campaign. They had hoped to put together a coalition of anti-Yeltsin nationalists and Communists to secure a majority in the runoff. The alliance between Yeltsin and Lebed destroyed this strategy, for it encouraged the largest block of nationalists to put anti-Communist sentiments ahead of their anti-Yeltsin views. Sensing that the party was becoming isolated, Zyuganov announced on 24 June that, if elected, he would lead a coalition government composed in equal parts of his own party, other Duma parties, and Chernomyrdin's ministers.

Communists were further handicapped as, "by one means or another," the Yeltsin camp put pressure on the media to minimize coverage of the Communist campaign. The Communist Party said it would not use paid political advertising because this was inappropriate in its ideal society. At the very end of the second round, however, the party bought time for a last-minute commercial, but it was never broadcast. The state-owned pro-Yeltsin channel, ORT, said technical reasons prevented it from being aired; the Communists alleged censorship (European Institute for the Media 1996b, 10). As the prospect of victory receded, Communists began to prepare an alibi. Even before the first-round vote, Viktor Ilyukhin, Communist head of the Duma's security commission, had declared, "I think the results of the election will, in simple terms, be falsified. Boris Yeltsin will be declared president although Gennadii Zyuganov will win" (*Izvestiya*, 25 May 1996, 1).

No Turning Back

The second-round ballot produced a clear-cut result, the defeat of Gennadii Zyuganov. The Communist leader won just 40 percent of the vote, trailing more than 10 million votes behind Boris Yeltsin, a margin so great that it could not be explained away by vote fraud (table 12.3). The vote reflected the Yeltsin campaign's success in creating fear of a Communist victory by recalling evils of the past and warning that if the Communists won, it would not lead to a democratic alternation of government—for reasons unspecified. Even though the elimination of nine candidates meant more than 22 million first-round voters had to act differently in the second-round, Zyuganov appeared to have hit a Red ceiling. He increased his support by fewer than 6 million votes.

Boris Yeltsin's victory was beyond challenge, for he finished more than 13 percentage points and 10 million votes ahead of Zyuganov. The coordinator of the observer team of the Organization for Security and Cooperation in Europe, Michael Meadowcroft, declared that the result

TABLE 12.3

SECOND-ROUND 1996 PRESIDENTIAL ELECTION RESULT

3 July 1996: Registered electorate = 108,600,730

Candidates	Vote	
	Percentage	*Number*
Boris Yeltsin, Independent	53.8	40,208,384
Gennadii Zyuganov, Communist	40.3	30,113,306
Against both candidates	4.8	3,604,550
Total valid vote	68.1	73,926,240
Invalid ballots	0.7	780,405
Total turnout	68.8	74,706,645

SOURCE: Central Electoral Commission communiqué published in *Rossiiskaya gazeta*, 10 July 1996, 1.

"accurately reflects the wishes of the Russian electorate," albeit agreeing with media observers that the campaign itself had not lived up to West European standards of fairness (Owen 1996). In the second-round ballot, Yeltsin's support increased by 13.5 million votes, which came from a multiplicity of sources. According to polls, about 7 million people who had voted for Lebed in the first-round swung to Yeltsin in the second ballot, as did more than 4 million who had voted for Yavlinsky. Among Lebed's original supporters, 63 percent supported Yeltsin in the second round, as did an estimated 75 percent of Yavlinsky's voters (see *Argumenty i fakty*, no. 28, 1996, 2). Alexander Lebed was widely (and incorrectly) credited with "delivering" victory to Yeltsin, although Yeltsin would still have emerged the winner if all of Lebed's voters had abstained.

Although he won more than half the popular vote, Boris Yeltsin could not claim to be the overwhelming choice of the Russian electorate. The limited base of his support is shown by the behavior of the electorate as a whole (figure 12.4). In an election in which all contestants claimed Russia's fate was at stake, nonvoters were the largest group; the first choice of 29 percent of the total electorate was not to vote. Just under one-quarter made Yeltsin their first choice; he owed re-election to the additional support he drew in the second round from the one-eighth of the electorate who had initially favored another can-

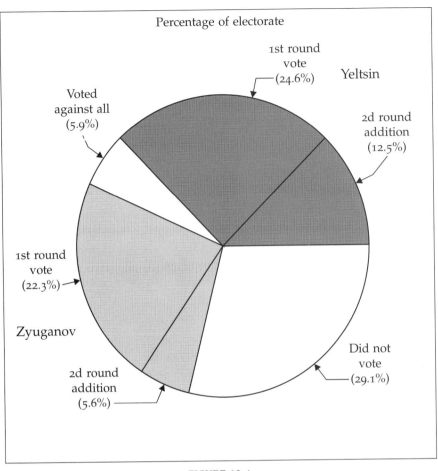

Percentage of electorate

1st round vote (24.6%) — Yeltsin

Voted against all (5.9%)

2d round addition (12.5%)

1st round vote (22.3%)

Zyuganov

Did not vote (29.1%)

2d round addition (5.6%)

FIGURE 12.4
DIVISION OF THE PRESIDENTIAL ELECTORATE

SOURCE: As in tables 12.2, 12.3.

didate. While the turnout was virtually the same in both rounds, in the second the proportion voting against both candidates trebled to almost 6 percent.

The day after the vote, the president made a recorded television announcement thanking the electorate for the vote of confidence and declaring that he wanted a government that would unite people of different views to work for the country's good. Yeltsin did not resume planned meetings with international leaders until 16 July, three weeks after he had disappeared from public view. Behind the scenes, he gave evidence of being at work by firing Nikolai Yegorov, an ally of Korzha-kov and advocate of war in Chechnya, and replacing him with Anatolii Chubais, the economic reformer he had sacked just after the December Duma election, but who returned to favor as the leader of the victori-ous campaign team. The appointment of Chubais created a counter-weight in the Yeltsin entourage to the influence of Alexander Lebed.

The media announced that its enlistment in the Yeltsin cause had been only for the duration of the presidential campaign. On 5 July the daily *Segodnya* said that while it had backed Yeltsin aggressively to se-cure political stability and the "victory of common sense over idiocy," the paper would now "return to where it belongs, in opposition to the authorities." By the end of the week, Moscow papers were headlining accounts of a parliamentary investigation into corruption in the de-fense ministry when it had been headed by the president's former ally, General Pavel Grachev. The media also began to criticize Yeltsin's pol-icy in Chechnya as the cease-fire there showed signs of breaking down.

The 1996 presidential election showed that in less than a decade *glasnost* ("openness") had been achieved far beyond Mikhail Gorba-chev's original intent. For the first time, the head of the Russian state was chosen in free and open competition. Yet democracy is not only about deciding who governs but also about how a country is governed. In the first Yeltsin administration a fundamental requirement for de-mocracy, the rule of law, was not established. Presidential authority was not accountable to the courts or to parliament. The struggle for control of government was conducted within the executive, and within the president's entourage, rather than in public. Critical decisions, such as the launching of a military offensive in Chechnya, were the result of Kremlin court politics. Everyday decisions tended to be produced by "clans," networks of ministry officials, interest groups in the public, private and "gray" sectors, and persons in the president's entourage. The power of such networks is an obstacle to democracy. In the words of a leaked memorandum by an American official in Moscow, "There are very few committed supporters of democracy in the clans. Demo-cratic procedures, including elections, are mostly seen as weapons in the struggle for power" (Graham 1995).

A democratic regime does not lodge power in an individual above the law but in a constitution. The political career of Boris Yeltsin has made a historic contribution to the democratization of Russia, but de-mocratization has not been the overriding goal of the party apparatchik from Sverdlovsk. In the words of Gennadii Burbulis, a close early ally of Yeltsin, he has "two hearts, two motors, two ideas," one favoring authoritarian methods and the other "purely situational" democratic principles invoked as and when they can be useful, as in challenging the power of Mikhail Gorbachev (quoted in Remnick 1996, 48). The process of democratization requires a constitution that is not just the vehicle for one man, Boris Yeltsin, but an impersonal source of authority. The 1993 Russian constitution can become something different from a "one man" constitution only as and when power is freely and fairly transferred from one incumbent to another.

For the moment, power rests with Boris Yeltsin. In Russia power is not a legal concept, as in the American Constitution, which confers powers on Congress as well as the president. In the United States the very act of invoking the Constitution to justify actions implies recognition of the rule of law; it also accepts that presidential actions can be challenged and even nullified in the courts. In Russia, by contrast, the word for political power, *vlast*, refers to domination by the powers that be. Yet democracy is not a system of domination; it is about taming power. In Russia, there is a need to tame *vlast* on a continental scale.

৶ Appendix A ৶

The Surveys

An extraordinarily rich body of literature is available about everyday life in communist Russia, based largely on insights and speculation illustrated by anecdotes and case studies plus a few small-scale surveys (see, e.g., Connor and Gitelman 1977; Shlapentokh 1989). In communist systems, private opinions were regarded by the state as potentially subversive. Individuals developed what Nadezhda Mandelshtam called "linguistic dualism," distinguishing between the "institutionalized hypocrisy" of state-approved opinions and the views that people expressed only in private to trusted friends (quoted in White 1979, 111).

The collapse of the Soviet regime means that it is now possible to examine public opinion through the normal social science method of nationwide sample surveys. But questionnaires used to measure public opinion do not write themselves; the questions asked depend on the interests of the researchers and what they regard as important. At least five different kinds of surveys can be identified (cf. Rose and Haerpfer 1994a).

1. *Current events* surveys, because they attract media coverage, are the most visible. By definition, topics of media concern are newsworthy. But many such surveys refer to ephemeral events, parties, or personalities or attempt to predict an election months or years before it happens (cf. Shlapentokh 1994; Miller et al. 1996). If surveys about current attitudes are frequently repeated, as is done by VTsIOM (the All-Russian Center for the Study of Public Opinion), it is then possible to turn replies into measures of political and economic trends (see Levada 1995).

2. A *sponsor model* asks questions of immediate utilitarian concern to the organization paying for the survey, whether Coca-Cola or the U.S. government. But what interests the sponsors may not interest ordinary Russians.

3. Many Western social scientists use a *destination model* to organize research in Russia. The starting point is a listing of the attributes of a democratic system or market economy as this is understood in OECD countries. Questions are put to Russians to see how they measure up to Western standards of democracy (see Miller et al. 1993; Gibson et al. 1992). Implicit in a destination model is the teleological assumption that Russians want to become "just like us" or at least "enough like us" to make Anglo-American market democracies an appropriate standard for evaluation. But this is not the case. When the third New Russia Barometer survey asked Russians whether their country should develop like Western Europe or according to its own traditions, 78 percent wanted to follow Russian traditions; only 22 percent favored a West European model.

4. It is both logically and empirically more realistic to start with an *origins model,* which specifies mass behavior and attitudes in what is now the *ancien régime* (for a review of that literature, see Welch 1987). Even though this regime has formally disappeared, it is an axiom of socialization research that many attitudes and patterns of behavior learned in the first decade or two of life persist subsequently.

5. Describing Russia as in transition raises the question Where is it coming from? Seventy years of rule by a party with a totalitarian vocation imposing the institutions of a nonmarket economy meant that at the start of 1992 Russia was a *stressful,* not a modern, society. In only one respect was the society modern: it was complex. In a modern society complex institutions operate rationally according to calculations based on observable and predictable cause-and-effect relations. A modern society is also a civil society, in which the state respects the rule of law, and economic and social institutions are independent of the state. Russia was not like that (see Rose 1994b). In a narrow sense, the institutions could be described as functional because they produced benefits for those in command of the system. But societies can function in many different ways. Experts have variously described the society as "pseudo-modern" (Winiecki 1988) or even "surreal" (Z 1990) because of the contrast between ideology and reality.

The New Russia Barometer (NRB) survey was conceived in 1991, when the Soviet Union was still in existence and Mikhail Gorbachev was its leader, as the outgrowth of a dialogue between Richard Rose and a group of reform-minded Russian social scientists (for the background, see Rose and Tikhomirov 1995, 11ff.). It has been conducted by the Centre for the Study of Public Policy in parallel with the New Democracies Barometer, an annual survey of ten countries of Central and Eastern Europe organized by the Paul Lazarsfeld Society, Vienna (Rose and Haerpfer 1994b; 1996).

The philosophy of the New Russia Barometer survey is to concentrate on activities of concern to ordinary people in their everyday lives; it thus follows the philosophy of the authors of *The American Voter* to design a questionnaire that is "in the main dependent on the point of view" of the respondent (Campbell et al. 1960, 27). In no sense, however, is the New Russia Barometer a conventional voting study. In a stable democracy ordinary people spend a small part of their waking hours concerned with politics; it is thus important to consider what ordinary people do when they are not voting. In Russia the politicization of everyday life under communism meant that people watched politics closely, but much of their interest was motivated by a desire to *avoid* being thought politically incorrect. Furthermore, every Russian knew that voting was *not* a way to influence the Soviet government. The transformation of Russian society has given people the chance to vote as they wish, but it has also created much more urgent needs and opportunities that individuals must deal with here and now. Individuals at the bottom of an "hourglass" society may prefer freedom from the state to dependence on it to resolve their problems (see Rose 1995g).

The New Russia Barometer surveys are concerned with how people are reacting to the political and economic transformations around them, of which free elections are but a part. The critical issue for ordinary Russians is not, Would you rather live like Swedes or Californians? but, What do you do to keep body and soul together here and now? Economic activity was conceived as occurring in a multiplicity of economies, official and unofficial, monetized and nonmonetized, all of which were readily capable of observation and measurement, for example, growing vegetables on a small allotment. In politics, the critical question concerns the change in regimes. The old communist regime was a fact that everyone had experienced; the new regime, whatever its character, can thus be compared with the old. The more negative the old appears, the more a change may be welcomed, if only as a lesser evil.

The first New Russia Barometer survey went into the field in January 1992, a few weeks after the dissolution of the Soviet Union. It concentrated on the most basic question of economic sociology: How are you surviving? (For results, see Boeva and Shironin 1992.) Political questions concentrated on reactions to the old and new regimes. Each subsequent New Russia Barometer has repeated trend questions and developed topics of special interest and relevance, ranging from privatization to elections (for a review of trend results from the first four surveys, see Rose and Tikhomirov 1995). The data analyzed in this book come from the second, third, and fifth New Russia Barometer surveys.

New Russia Barometer II

The New Russia Barometer II survey was organized by the Centre for the Study of Public Policy and Dr. Irina Boeva and Dr. Viacheslav Shironin, Centre for Economic Reform, Moscow. It was conducted by VTsIOM between 26 June and 22 July 1993 and was financed by a grant from the British Foreign Office Know-How Fund. The universe was the population of the Russian Federation aged sixteen and above; in this book respondents under the age of eighteen are excluded, since they are too young to vote. The Center first stratified the Russian Federation into fifteen regions. This geographical dispersion is particularly important, for many surveys cover only one city or a few major cities, even though Moscow and St. Petersburg together constitute less than 15 percent of the country's population. In this survey, 70 percent of respondents were from the European regions of Russia and 30 percent from Russia east of the Urals.

Each region was stratified into urban and rural areas, and the urban population was stratified proportionate to population into oblast and krai capitals, peripheral towns of oblasts and krais, capitals of autonomous regions, and peripheral towns of autonomous regions. Within this framework, towns were randomly selected with a probability equal to their share of the total population. A total of 85 urban and rural areas were selected, and 153 primary sampling units were drawn with a probability proportionate to the population. Within each primary sampling unit, households were listed by addresses; up to thirty addresses were drawn randomly. Within each household the person whose birthday was nearest the date of interview was selected as the respondent.

The field staff followed the normal practice of asking the respondent to complete the questionnaire in his or her handwriting while the interviewer waited to collect it. In 170 cases, the respondent was unable to complete the questionnaire in this way. In such cases the interviewer read the questions and recorded the responses. The length of interviews varied from 30 to 88 minutes; the mean length of interview was 55 minutes.

Face-to-face rather than telephone interviewing is especially important in Russia because fewer than half of Russians have a telephone and the distribution is skewed. Completed interviews were 78.2 percent of the total number of households in the sample, and refusals to participate 6.2 percent. After subtracting households where there were errors in addresses and other valid causes for not seeking an interview, five-sixths of all valid names drawn were interviewed (see table A.1). VTsIOM verified fieldwork by inspecting all questionnaires and making callbacks in person or telephoning 191 respondents.

TABLE A.1

NEW RUSSIA BAROMETER II SURVEY

1. Total number of households in sample	2,525
Less	
2. No contact because of errors in addresses, death, illness, respondent absent for a long period, or no one home after three calls back	−394
3. Respondent refused to participate	−156
4. Total interviews	1,975

The representativeness of respondents can be compared with a number of characteristics in the Russian census of 1989. The sample shows a good fit for gender, age, and urban/rural divisions. More educated people are overrepresented, a common feature of surveys in Russia as in many Western societies. Variations from the original sample design in four sampling points slightly altered spatial representativeness. Hence, a multiple regression analysis using gender, age, education, and town size was undertaken on a region-by-region basis to produce weights to reduce differences between census figures and sample responses. The regions were weighted to match the regional census population. Because of rounding error, the number of respondents in the weighted sample is 1,973. The effects of weighting are given in table A.2. The analyses reported in this book are restricted to respondents aged eighteen years and above. Full details of the questionnaire and responses can be found in Rose, Boeva, and Shironin (1993).

TABLE A.2

REPRESENTATIVENESS OF RESPONDENTS, NRB II

| | *Respondents* | | |
	Original	*Weighted*	*Census*
Women	57%	55%	55%
Men	43	45	45
Age 16–19	6	7	7
Age 20–24	10	9	9
Age 25–39	33	33	33
Age 40–54	27	23	12
Age 55+	24	28	28
Higher education	20	15	14
Secondary education	56	48	48
Without secondary education	24	37	38
Living in central cities	39	36	36
Living in other urban areas	36	37	37
Living in rural areas	25	27	27

New Russia Barometer III

The New Russia Barometer III survey was organized by the Paul Lazarsfeld Society, Vienna, and was financed by grants from the British
Foreign Office Know-How Fund; the Deutsche Paul Lazarsfeld Gesell-
schaft, Berlin; the Austrian Central Bank; the Austrian Kontrollbank;
the Creditanstalt-Bankverien, Vienna; and BAWAG, Vienna. Fieldwork
was undertaken by Mnenie Opinion Service, Moscow, under the direction of Dr. Grigory A. Pashkov. The questionnaire was piloted with 100
interviews in Rostov on Don and Petrozavodsk between 26 and 28 February 1994 and then refined. The results published here are based on
fieldwork undertaken between mid-March and early April 1994. The
universe for the sample was the population of the Russian Federation
aged eighteen and above. The Federation was first stratified into fourteen different regions and then further stratified on a proportionate-to-
population basis according to urban and rural divisions and differences
in the administrative structure of each region. Within each region seven
sampling points were selected, with the number of interviews proportionate to population. Interviewers then selected a sample of respondents on the basis of a quota set for each region by gender, age, education, and nationality.

The target number of responses was 3,500; in the event, 3,535 interviews were completed. The regional distribution of the respondents, compared to the 1990 recorded population, is shown in table A.3. The validity of the interviews was randomly spot-checked by Mnenie and by Ernst Gehmacher, director of the Institut für Empirische Sozialforschung, Vienna. Comparison of characteristics of survey respondents with census figures showed a good fit for the sample distribution by gender, age, education, and region; hence, no weighting has been used. Full details of the questionnaire and responses can be found in Rose and Haerpfer (1994c).

TABLE A.3

REGIONAL DISTRIBUTION OF RESPONDENTS, NRB III

| | Sample | | 1990 Census |
	N	%	%
Northern	138	4.0	4.1
North West	118	3.3	2.4
Moscow	226	6.4	6.1
Central	534	15.1	14.5
Volga-Vyatka	202	5.8	5.7
Central Black Soil	184	5.2	5.2
Volga	446	12.7	11.2
North Caucasuses	375	10.6	11.5
Urals	513	14.5	13.7
Western Siberia	335	9.4	10.2
Eastern Siberia	180	5.1	6.2
Far East	176	4.9	6.2

New Russia Barometer V

The fifth New Russia Barometer was organized by the Centre for the Study of Public Policy and conducted by VTsIOM between 12 and 31 January 1996. The universe of the sample was the population of the whole of the Russian Federation aged 16 and above. The figures in this text report only adults; respondents under 18, the age to qualify for voting, are excluded.

The survey was based on a multistage stratified random sample. VTsIOM first stratified the Russian Federation into eleven macroeconomic regions. Each region was further stratified into urban and rural areas, and the urban population stratified proportionate to population into oblast and krai capitals; peripheral towns of oblasts and krais; capitals of autonomous regions; and peripheral towns of autonomous regions. Within this framework, towns were randomly selected with a probability equal to their share of the total population. In all, 104 urban and rural places were selected. Within this framework primary sampling units were drawn with a probability proportionate to population. In each primary sampling unit households were listed by addresses, and an address was selected randomly as the starting point for interviewing. Interviewers were instructed to seek an interview at every nth house on the route. At each address the interviewer asked for the resident whose birthday was closest to the date of interview to complete the questionnaire. Face-to-face rather than telephone contact is especially important in Russia, since fewer than two-fifths of Russians have a telephone. Where respondents were old or infirm, the interviewer administered the questionnaire orally.

A total of 214 interviewers were involved. VTsIOM collected data on the voting preferences of its interviewers and they were widely dispersed across the political spectrum. In interviewer preferences, Yabloko was the only party favored by more than a tenth of interviewers; the Communist Party was second, and Our Home Is Russia third.

In all, 4,508 contacts were made and 2,426 persons were interviewed, a response rate of 53.8 percent. The fall in the response rate is partly due to an increased lack of interest in being interviewed, also evident in established democracies and partly due to this survey's detailed focus on political questions of less interest to many respondents than the economics of everyday life. Only in Moscow and in Bushkirksoe was the refusal rate above half. VTsIOM inspected all questionnaires, and verified 10 percent of interviews by making callbacks to individuals at their home or, where feasible, by telephone. The questionnaires were coded by VTsIOM in Moscow. The exclusion of 86 respondents under the age of 18 reduced the sample analyzed here to 2,340 persons, a number as large as or larger than the normal American or British nationwide election survey.

When the representativeness of respondents is compared with Goskomstat data for the Russian population in 1993, the sample shows a good fit for gender, age, and urban/rural divisions. Once again, better educated people are overrepresented, a common feature of surveys in Western societies, too. The data were weighted by VTsIOM to match the regional census population in terms of gender, age, education, town size and, because of the proximity to the general election, party preference. The effects of weights are shown in table A.4.

TABLE A.4
EFFECTS OF VTSIOM WEIGHTING, NRB V

	Respondents	
	Original sample	Weighted
Gender		
Women	57.1%	54.5%
Men	42.9	45.6
Age		
Age 18–19	2.0	2.1
Age 20–29	18.0	18.8
Age 30–39	24.0	25.3
Age 40–49	21.2	18.7
Age 50–59	16.3	15.2
Age 60–69	12.4	13.2
Age 70+	6.2	6.5
Education		
Higher education	27.8	14.0
Technical education	25.9	24.5
Secondary education	15.0	13.3
Vocational + secondary education	14.5	18.8
No complete secondary education	16.8	29.4
Party preference		
Communist	23.6	26.7
Yabloko	13.4	10.7
Our Home is Russia	10.6	9.9
Liberal Democratic Party	8.2	9.8
Russia's Choice	6.9	4.5
Others	37.3	38.4

⟪ Appendix B ⟫

Definitions of Variables

The questions used in the analyses from the NRB II and NRB III surveys are listed in the following paragraphs in the English-language translation prepared by Stephen White. The scoring of variables and details of the composition of scales are also included where appropriate. Table B.1 lists the variables, their scoring, means, and standard deviations. Scales based on questions that asked the respondents for a range of negative or positive responses, such as "strongly disagree" to "strongly agree" on a five-point scale, are scored from a negative value to a positive value, such as −2 to +2. Therefore, a value of 0 means the weight of opinion is evenly divided. When the questions asked for positive responses, such as level of international threat, the resulting multiple-item scale is scored on a positive scale (such as 0 to 4). Questions vary in the natural forms of response. The proportion of "don't know" responses varies between questions (see Carnaghan 1994). Where those replying "don't know" are a small percentage of the total and of little substantive significance, in statistical analyses they are coded to the mean value of the question, and as necessary rounded to the nearest whole number when used in an additive scale. The proportion of missing values is negligible; they have generally been excluded from the analyses when individual items are used or coded to the mean where multiple-item scales have been calculated.

Political Attitudes

Political regime evaluations are based on three questions asking the respondent to make political evaluations of the communist regime, the current regime, and the regime in the future (for details, see Rose 1992;

Rose and Mishler 1994). The questions were: "Here is a scale for evaluating how the political system works. The highest mark is 100, the lowest, minus 100. (1) Where on the scale would you place the system of government before perestroika [in NRB III: the former communist regime]? (2) Where would you place our present system of governing [in NRB III: our current system with free elections and a multiparty system]? (3) Where would you place our political system in five years' time?" Each scale is scored on a continuous scale in units of 10, from minus 100 (lowest evaluation) to plus 100 (highest evaluation).

Freedom is a multiple-item additive scale combining four questions concerning personal freedoms (for details, see Rose 1995d). The questions were these: "How about differences between the system of government before perestroika and our current system. For each of the following, would you say it is better than during the communist period, much the same, or worse? (1) Everybody has a right to say what they think. (2) One can join any organization one likes. (3) Each individual can decide whether or not to believe in God [in NRB III: Everyone has freedom of choice in religious matters]. (4) Everyone can decide individually whether or not to take an interest in politics." The items in the freedom scale were selected from a battery of eight questions[1] by factor analysis of NRB II and III, with a reliability coefficient (Cronbach's alpha) of .73 in NRB II and .68 in NRB III. The original items were scored −1 = worse, 0 = same or don't know, 1 = better. Combining the four items produces a scale running from −4 (most negative about freedom) to +4 (most positive about freedom).

Respondents were asked a series of five different questions about alternatives to the current regime (for details, see Rose and Mishler 1995). A factor analysis identified three items as constituting an *authoritarianism* scale.[2] The questions were as follows: "Our current political system is not the only possible one. Some people say that another would be better for us. What do you think? Here are some statements; please tell me to what extent you agree with each of them." The three statements were: "(1) It would be better to restore the former communist system. (2) The army should rule. (3) We do not need parliament or elections, but instead a strong leader who can make decisions and put them into effect fast." The items have an average interitem correlation of .25 and a reliability coefficient (Cronbach's alpha) of .49. The items were originally scored 0 = strongly disagree, 1 = disagree, 2 = don't know, 3 = agree, 4 = strongly agree; the three-item combined scale was rescored to run from −3 (least authoritarian) to 3 (most authoritarian). *Communist Party membership* is based on the question:

TABLE B.1

INDEPENDENT VARIABLES, SCORING, AND MEANS

Independent variables	Scoring	NRB II Mean	NRB II Std. dev.	NRB III Mean	NRB III Std. dev.
Political attitudes					
Political regime evaluations					
Communist	−100 to +100	19.0	57.0	4.0	58.0
Current	−100 to +100	−16.0	51.0	−13.0	51.0
Future	−100 to +100	10.0	53.0	15.0	48.0
Freedom	−4 to +4	2.3	1.8	2.8	1.4
Authoritarianism	−3 to +3	N.A.	N.A.	−1.0	1.5
Communist Party membership	0 = no; 1 = one or more family members but not self; 2 = self	N.A.	N.A.	.53	.73
Trust in institutions					
State	−5 to +5	N.A.	N.A.	−2.4	2.2
Workers' groups	−5 to +5	N.A.	N.A.	−2.7	2.0
Market	−5 to +5	N.A.	N.A.	−2.9	2.3
Traditional institutions	−5 to +5	N.A.	N.A.	0.0	2.6
International threats	0 to 4	1.0	1.3	1.2	1.3
Blame for economic problems					
Government	0 to 6	N.A.	N.A.	3.5	2.3
Capitalists	0 to 6	N.A.	N.A.	.8	1.5
Communists	0 to 6	N.A.	N.A.	3.0	2.1

Economic attitudes

Evaluations

	Scale				
Current family	−2 = very unsatisfied, −1 = not very satisfied, 0 = don't know, 1 = fairly satisfied, 2 = very satisfied	−0.6	1.1	−0.5	1.2
Retrospective family	−2 = much better now, −1 = somewhat better, 0 = the same, 1 = somewhat worse, 2 = much worse now	0.4	1.3	−0.7	1.3
Prospective family	−2 = much worse in five years, −1 = somewhat worse, 0 = the same, 1 = somewhat better, 2 = much better in five years	0.0	1.1	0.1	0.9
Destitution	0 (none) to 9 (highest)	2.1	1.9	2.1	1.6
Consumer goods	0 to 4	1.4	1.2	1.8	1.2
Economic regime evaluations					
Socialist economic system	−100 to +100	38.0	49.0	16.0	53.0
Current economic system	−100 to +100	−25.0	48.0	−46.0	46.0
Economic system in future	−100 to +100	8.0	53.0	1.0	54.0

Independent variables	Scoring	NRB II		NRB III	
		Mean	*Std. dev.*	*Mean*	*Std. dev.*
Social structure					
Gender	1 = female, 0 = male	.56	.50	.55	.50
Religious	0 = none, don't know, 1 = somewhat religious, 2 = religious	.7	.8	.9	.8
Age					
Young, 18–29	1 = yes, 0 = no	.22	.42	.23	.42
Old, 60 or more	1 = yes, 0 = no	.20	.40	.21	.41
Education	0 = elementary, 1 = secondary, 2 = technical, 3 = higher	1.4	1.0	1.4	1.0
Books in home	1 = yes, 0 = no	N.A.	N.A.	.49	.50
Ethnic Russian	1 = yes, 0 = other	.86	.43	.82	.38
Urbanization	0 = village, 1 = population less than 100,000, 2 = population 100,000 to 500,000, 3 = population more than 500,000, 4 = Moscow or St. Petersburg	1.7	1.3	1.7	1.3
Lives in Asiatic Russia	1 = yes, 0 = no	.32	.47	.24	.43

SOURCES: Centre for the Study of Public Policy, New Russia Barometer II (1993); Centre for the Study of Public Policy/Paul Lazarsfeld Society, New Russia Barometer III (1994).

"Were you or anyone in your family a member of the Communist Party of the Soviet Union?" It is scored 0 = no, 1 = one or more family members but not self, 2 = self.

Trust in institutions reflects a factor analysis of a battery of sixteen items; the factor loadings are shown in table B.2.[3] The four scales thus derived were scored from 0 (least trust) to 10 (most trust).

International threats combines four items concerning national security. The question in NRB II was: "Do you think any of the following

TABLE B.2

TRUST IN INSTITUTIONS

Q: *There are various public institutions in Russia such as legislative and executive bodies, courts, and the police. Please indicate your trust in them on this scale, where 1 denotes maximum distrust and 7 indicates maximum trust.*

	Factor loadings (decimals omitted)			
	I	II	III	IV
State				
Police	83	15	08	12
Courts	82	13	16	07
Civil servants, executive bodies	78	24	12	04
Workers' groups				
Old trade unions	13	79	−11	20
New trade unions	21	76	22	01
Patriotic associations	14	66	19	08
Market				
Foreign organizations, experts advising our government	14	06	85	07
Private enterprise	12	16	83	−01
Traditional institutions				
Church	−04	16	08	88
Army	43	09	−03	63
Eigenvalues	3.4	1.3	1.2	.9
Percentage variance explained	34.0	13.0	12.0	10.0

SOURCE: Centre for the Study of Public Policy/Paul Lazarsfeld Society, New Russia Barometer III (1994).

NOTE: Varimax rotated factor loadings from a principal components factor analysis with unities in the main diagonal. The reliability coefficients (Cronbach's alpha) for each scale are, respectively, .80, .67, .66, and .41.

pose a threat to peace and security in this society?" and in NRB III: "Could any of the following states pose a threat to our national security?" The four countries selected by factor analysis from a total of eight were China, Germany, the United States, and Iran (in NRB II "Islamic countries").[4] In NRB II and NRB III the four items have average interitem correlations of .39 and .34 and reliability coefficients (Cronbach's alpha) of .71 and .67, respectively. The items were scored 0 = no threat or don't know, 1 = some or big threat, and then combined to produce additive scales running from 0 (least threat) to 4 (most threat).

Blame for economic problems consists of three multiple-item scales blaming government, capitalists, or communists for the country's economic problems. The three scales were identified from an original battery of sixteen items by the factor analysis shown in table B.3.[5] The items were scored 0 = not at all, 1 = not much, 2 = somewhat, 3 = definitely. They were then combined and rescored from 0 (least blame) to 6 (most blame).[6]

Economic Attitudes

Microeconomic evaluations are represented by three questions about the family's economic situation in the present, the past, and the future. The *current microeconomic evaluation* question was: "How do you rate the economic situation of your family today?" The responses are scored −2 = very unsatisfied, −1 = not very satisfied, 0 = don't know, 1 = fairly satisfied, 2 = very satisfied. The *retrospective microeconomic evaluation* was: "How does the economic situation of your family compare with five years ago?" The responses are scored −2 = much better now, −1 = somewhat better now, 0 = the same, 1 = somewhat worse now, 2 = much worse now. The *prospective microeconomic evaluation* question was: "What do you think your family's economic situation will be in five years' time?" The responses are scored −2 = much worse in five years, −1 = somewhat worse in five years, 0 = the same, 1 = somewhat better in five years, 2 = much better in five years.

Destitution in NRB II is based on the question: "In the past year, has your household sometimes done without any of the following because of a shortage of goods or money?" and in NRB III: "Sometimes one has to do without things that are really necessary. How often during the last 12 months did you have to do without _____." The scale combines food, heating and electricity, and essential clothing; in NRB II each item is scored 0 = never, 1 = rarely, 2 = sometimes, 3 = often, and in NRB III 0 = never, 1 = sometimes, 2 = very often, 3 = constantly. The

TABLE B.3

BLAME FOR ECONOMIC PROBLEMS

Q: Who is to blame for our economic problems, and how much?

	Factor loadings (decimals omitted)		
	I	II	III
Government			
Russian president personally	88	14	01
Russian government	82	08	14
Yegor Gaidar	82	20	05
Capitalists			
Capitalists	20	86	−09
Foreign governments	22	86	−03
Jews	02	67	17
Communists			
Communists	−03	02	88
Nomenklatura	19	04	84
Eigenvalues	2.9	1.6	1.3
Percentage variance explained	37.0	20.0	17.0

SOURCE: Centre for the Study of Public Policy/Paul Lazarsfeld Society, New Russia Barometer III (1994).

NOTE: Varimax rotated factor loadings from a principal components factor analysis with unities in the main diagonal. The reliability coefficients (Cronbach's alpha) for each scale are, respectively, .84, .75, and .68.

resulting additive scale runs from 0 to 9. *Consumer goods* is an additive scale based on whether the household had a car, a telephone, a dacha in the country, or (in NRB III only) a color television.[7]

Economic regime evaluations are represented by three questions asking the respondent to make evaluations of the past system, the current system, and a future economic system. The questions were: "Here is a scale for evaluating how the economy works. The highest mark is 100, the lowest, minus 100. Where on the scale would you place the economic system before the start of perestroika [in NRB III: the socialist economy in 1989]? Where would you place the current economic system? Our economic system in five years' time?" Each scale is scored continuously in units of 10, from minus 100 (lowest evaluation) to plus 100 (highest evaluation).

Social Structure

Gender is scored 1 = female, 0 = male. *Religious* in NRB II is church attendance, scored 0 = agnostic or atheist, 1 = attends rarely, 2 = attends several times a year or more. In NRB III this item is a question asking how religious the respondent considered himself or herself to be and is scored 0 = none or don't know, 1 = somewhat religious, 2 = religious. Generations of Russians differ substantially in their experiences (see Rose and Carnaghan 1995); the youngest and oldest generations are especially likely to be distinctive. Hence, *age* is measured by two dummy variables: age 18 to 29 years, and age 60 years or more; those age 30 to 59 years are the excluded category.

Education is scored 0 = elementary, 1 = secondary (also including vocational), 2 = technical, and 3 = higher (combining higher incomplete, university, and scientific degree). *Books in home* is based on whether or not the respondents reported having 100 or more books at home and is scored 0 = no, 1 = yes. *Ethnic Russian* is scored 0 = other, 1= Russian. *Urbanization* is scored ordinally from rural areas to Moscow and St. Petersburg. *Lives in Asiatic Russia* includes the regions of Chelyabinsk, Omsk, Kemerovo, Novosibirsk, Chita, Krasnoyarsk, Magadan, and Sakhalinsk.

Notes

1. The four items not forming part of the factor solution in NRB II and NRB III were "One can travel or live anywhere one wants"; "People like me can have influence on government"; "One need not be afraid of illegal arrest"; and "Government treats everybody equally and fairly."
2. The two items not forming part of the factor solution in NRB III were "Experts, not parliament and government, should make the most important economic decisions"; and "The monarchy should be restored."
3. The six items not included in the scale were "President Yeltsin"; "Parties"; "Government"; "Mass media"; "Parliament"; and "Peasants' organizations."
4. The four countries not included in the scale were Japan, Poland, Belarus, and Ukraine.
5. The eight items not included in the scale were "Those who introduced reforms"; "The workers"; "Businessmen"; "Present Russian parliament"; "Local government authorities"; "Mafia"; "We Russians ourselves"; "Disintegration of the USSR."
6. For consistency, all three scales were given a score running from 0 to 6. In the cases of blaming the government and blaming foreigners, this involved

combining the following three pairs of responses: 0 and 1; 2 and 3; 8 and 9.
7. To ensure comparable scoring between the two survey measures, the three consumer goods in NRB II are scored 0 for none, 1.3 for one only, 2.6 for two, and 4 for three.

ᐊᐧᐁ Appendix C ᐁᐧᑯ

Methods

Several methods are used to analyze the NRB II and NRB III survey data. Factor analysis is used to derive attitude scales listed in appendix B. This statistical technique identifies any underlying structure that may exist among a range of separate items (see Kim and Mueller 1978). Each of the nine scales was constructed as described in appendix B.

The multivariate analyses primarily use ordinary least squares (OLS) regression techniques (Achen 1982; Lewis-Beck 1980). In each of the figures, the full range of independent variables defined in appendix B was regressed on the dependent variable; figures report the coefficients that were statistically significant at the 1 percent level or better, using a two-tailed test. Missing values were treated using the "pairwise present" procedure. The figures reported are standardized (β) regression coefficients; they show the relative weight of the particular independent variable in predicting the dependent variable. For example, in figure 4.1 the standardized coefficient of .14 for freedom suggests that it is about twice as important as gender in predicting support for the president and government, with a coefficient of .07. The variance explained is the adjusted R^2. Finally, where the analysis has been conducted on a subsample of the survey population (for example, being restricted to voters only), this is noted below the figure together with the number of respondents. In all other cases, the full sample of respondents aged eighteen or above is used.

Given the large number of independent variables in the regression models, multicollinearity was a potential problem. Taking a correlation of ±.70 as the rather conservative level at which multicollinearity may produce unreliable estimates in multivariate analyses, inspection of the correlation matrices for the two surveys revealed that the largest correlation in NRB II was .69 and in NRB III was .55. In NRB II there were three correlations of .60 or above, one correlation between .50 and .59, and four correlations between .40 and .49. In NRB III there were only three correlations of .50 or above and only two correlations between .40 and .49; the remainder were less than .40. In each survey the three strongest correlations involved political regime and economic regime evaluations (for a full discussion of their relationship, see Mishler and Rose 1996a): in NRB II, evaluation of communist regime and evaluation of socialist economic system ($r = .68$), evaluation of current regime and evaluation of current economic system ($r = .66$), and evaluation of future regime and evaluation of future economic system ($r = .69$); in NRB III, evaluation of communist regime and evaluation of socialist economic system ($r = .51$), evaluation of future regime and evaluation of future economic system ($r = .55$), and evaluation of current and future regimes ($r = .53$).

The dependent variables are scored as indicated in table C.1.

TABLE C.1

HOW DEPENDENT VARIABLES WERE SCORED

Figure 4.1	Support for president and government	3 = totally support, 2 = generally support, 1 = partly support, 0 = no support at all
Figure 5.2	Voted for the constitution	2 = voted in favor, 1 = don't remember, 0 = voted against
Figure 5.4	Supports strong presidency	2 = president, 1 = both president and parliament equal, 0 = parliament
Figure 7.2	Party identification	1 = identifies with party, 0 = does not identify with party
Figure 8.3	Trust in Yeltsin, 1993	7 = trust a lot, 4.6 = trust somewhat, 2.3 = not much trust, 1 = no trust

Ordinary least squares regression techniques produce unreliable estimates when the dependent variable is nominal or categorical. In these cases, logistic regression must be used (King 1989). In chapter 7, we have therefore used logistic regression to estimate the models predicting support for the seven political parties. The full logistic regression models are reported in table C.2. Two figures are given: the parameter estimate and the standard error. The parameter estimate summarizes the slope of the relationship between the independent and the dependent variables. The exact interpretation of this coefficient will depend on how the independent variable is scored (either dichotomous or continuous); it represents the change in the logit for a change of one unit in the independent variable. The standard error provides an estimate of the reliability of the coefficient.

TABLE C.2
LOGISTIC ANALYSIS RESULTS FOR PARTY SUPPORT

	Communist		Russia's Choice		Agrarian		Liberal Democrat		Women of Russia		Yabloko		Democratic Party	
	Est	(SE)	Est	(SE)	Est	(SE)	Est	(SE)	Est	(SE)	Est	(SE)	Est	(SE)
Political regime evaluations														
Communist	.01*	(.00)	.00*	(.00)	.01*	(.00)	.00	(.00)	.00	(.00)	.00	(.00)	.00	(.00)
Current	.00	(.00)	.00	(.00)	.00	(.00)	.00	(.00)	.00	(.00)	.00	(.00)	.00	(.00)
Future	.00	(.00)	.00	(.00)	.00	(.00)	.00	(.00)	.00	(.00)	.00	(.00)	.00	(.00)
Freedom	-.27*	(.07)	.11	(.07)	.08	(.08)	.01	(.06)	.09	(.08)	-.02	(.07)	.06	(.09)
Authoritarianism	.15	(.08)	-.08	(.07)	-.08	(.08)	.14*	(.06)	-.02	(.07)	-.13	(.08)	-.09	(.09)
Communist party membership	.72*	(.14)	.13	(.10)	.22	(.14)	-.53*	(.11)	-.05	(.13)	-.17	(.12)	.12	(.15)
Trust in institutions														
State	.15*	(.06)	.03	(.04)	.00	(.05)	-.07	(.04)	-.06	(.05)	.00	(.05)	-.01	(.06)
Workers' groups	.09	(.07)	-.17*	(.05)	.03	(.06)	-.02	(.04)	.04	(.05)	.01	(.05)	.01	(.07)
Market	-.10	(.07)	.08	(.04)	-.23*	(.07)	-.04	(.04)	-.02	(.05)	.11	(.04)	-.08	(.07)
Traditional institutions	-.23*	(.05)	.01	(.03)	.07	(.05)	.09*	(.03)	.01	(.04)	-.07	(.04)	.06	(.05)
International threats	-.12	(.08)	.08	(.06)	-.08	(.08)	.08	(.06)	-.09	(.07)	.07	(.07)	-.02	(.09)
Blame for economic problems														
Government	.23*	(.07)	-.30*	(.04)	.01	(.06)	.17*	(.05)	.03	(.05)	.08	(.05)	.11	(.06)
Capitalists	.08	(.06)	-.04	(.06)	-.15	(.08)	.08	(.05)	.02	(.06)	-.22	(.08)	-.05	(.08)
Communists	-.21*	(.07)	.19*	(.04)	.02	(.06)	-.13*	(.04)	-.13*	(.05)	.05	(.05)	-.01	(.06)
Household economic situation														
Retrospective family	-.01	(.08)	-.05	(.06)	.00	(.09)	.05	(.06)	.09	(.08)	-.02	(.07)	.03	(.09)
Current family	-.19	(.12)	-.05	(.08)	.32*	(.12)	.11	(.08)	.01	(.10)	-.06	(.09)	-.11	(.12)
Prospective family	-.33	(.14)	-.02	(.10)	.13	(.15)	.06	(.10)	.19	(.13)	.04	(.11)	-.14	(.15)

	Communist		Russia's Choice		Agrarian		Liberal Democrat		Women of Russia		Yabloko		Democratic Party	
	Est	(SE)	Est	(SE)	Est	(SE)	Est	(SE)	Est	(SE)	Est	(SE)	Est	(SE)
Economic regime evaluations														
Socialist economic system	.00	(.00)	.00	(.00)	.00	(.00)	.00	(.00)	.00	(.00)	.00	(.00)	.00	(.00)
Current economic system	.00	(.00)	.01*	(.00)	.00	(.00)	.00	(.00)	.00	(.00)	.01	(.00)	.00	(.00)
Economic system in future	.00	(.00)	.00	(.00)	.00	(.00)	.00	(.00)	.00	(.00)	.00	(.00)	.00	(.00)
Destitution	.04	(.08)	-.06	(.06)	.05	(.08)	-.04	(.06)	.03	(.07)	.08	(.06)	-.12	(.09)
Consumer goods	.02	(.11)	.06	(.07)	-.23	(.11)	-.10	(.08)	.04	(.09)	.03	(.08)	.07	(.11)
Female	-.37	(.22)	.42*	(.16)	-.13	(.22)	-.92	(.16)	2.02	(.25)	-.05	(.18)	-.31	(.23)
Religious	.02	(.15)	-.06	(.10)	-.03	(.14)	.02	(.10)	.02	(.12)	-.03	(.12)	-.14	(.16)
Young, 18-29	.14	(.36)	-.23	(.20)	.16	(.31)	.11	(.21)	.06	(.24)	-.26	(.24)	.13	(.30)
Old, 60 or more	.14	(.27)	.29	(.21)	.38	(.26)	-.41	(.21)	-.47	(.26)	-.02	(.25)	-.44	(.34)
Education	.03	(.11)	-.06	(.08)	-.10	(.12)	-.04	(.09)	-.07	(.10)	.10	(.09)	-.05	(.12)
Books in home	.97*	(.26)	-.07	(.17)	-.04	(.24)	-.26	(.17)	-.47	(.20)	.30	(.20)	.02	(.25)
Ethnic Russian	-.68*	(.27)	.33	(.20)	-.19	(.27)	.05	(.21)	.05	(.24)	.03	(.23)	-.11	(.28)
Urbanization	.08	(.09)	.06	(.06)	-.67*	(.11)	-.12	(.07)	.04	(.08)	.14	(.07)	.08	(.10)
Lives in Asiatic Russia	-.38	(.26)	.35	(.18)	-.11	(.26)	-.09	(.18)	.24	(.20)	-.26	(.21)	.33	(.24)
Constant	-3.14		-2.00		-2.03		-1.02		-3.60		-3.13		-3.19	
-2 log likelihood	972.9		1532.6		827.6		1369.7		1039.7		1063.8		696.7	

SOURCE: Centre for the Study of Public Policy/Paul Lazarsfeld Society, New Russia Barometer III (1994).

NOTES: Logistic regression analysis showing parameter estimates (Est) and standard errors (SE) predicting support for the political parties.

An asterisk denotes significance at $p < .01$, two-tailed. The analyses are restricted to voters ($N = 1,449$).

References

Achen, Christopher
   1982 *Interpreting and Using Regression.* Beverly Hills, Calif.: Sage.
Almond, Gabriel A., and Laura Roselle
   1989 "Model Fitting in Communism Studies." In *Politics and the Soviet System,* ed. Thomas F. Remington. London: Macmillan.
Almond, Gabriel A., and Sidney Verba
   1963 *The Civic Culture: Political Attitudes and Democracy in Five Nations.* Princeton: Princeton University Press.
Anderson, Eugene N., and Pauline R. Anderson
   1967 *Political Institutions and Social Change in Continental Europe in the Nineteenth Century.* Berkeley: University of California Press.
Anderson, John
   1994 *Religion, State and Politics in the Soviet Union and Successor States.* Cambridge: Cambridge University Press.
Anfinogenov, A., et al.
   1993 *Tri "da" Prezidentu.* Moscow: Moskovskii rabochii.
Anokhin, Pavel
   1994 "Solovetskie chudesa, ili kak 434 izbiratelya otdali 1604 golosa." *Rossiiskie vesti,* 3 March, 2.
Aslund, Anders
   1995 *How Russia Became a Market Economy.* Washington, D.C.: Brookings Institution.
Baitin, M.I.
   1965 "Referendum i demokratiya." *Sovetskoe gosudarstvo i pravo,* no. 2, 157–58.
Barabashev, G.V., and V.I. Vasil'ev
   1989 "Stanovlenie reformy." *Sovety narodnykh deputatov,* no. 5, 9–17.
Barnes, Catherine
   1994 "Post-Election Environment Poses New Challenges for Russian Central Election Commission." *Elections Today: News from the International Foundation for Electoral Systems* 4, no. 4: 6–7.

Baylis, Thomas A.
   1996   "Presidents versus Prime Ministers: Shaping Executive Authority in Eastern Europe." *World Politics* 48, no. 3 (April):297–323.
Beeston, Richard
   1996   "Yeltsin Aide Lifts the Curtain on Kremlin of Spies and Bullies." *The Times,* 6 February 1996, 13.
Belin, Laura
   1995   "Are the Communists Poised for Victory?" *Transition* 1, no. 22 (1 December):20–25.
Berezkin, A.V., et al.
   1989   "Geografiya vyborov narodnykh deputatov SSSR v 1989 g. (pervye itogi)." *Izvestiya Akademii Nauk SSSR: Seriya geograficheskaya,* no. 5:5–24.
Berlin, Isaiah
   1969   *Four Essays on Liberty.* London: Oxford University Press.
Bershidsky, Leonid
   1995   "Korzhakov: President to Declare in February." *Moscow Times,* no. 860 (16 December), 1.
Bialer, Seweryn
   1980   *Stalin's Successors: Leadership, Stability, and Change in the Soviet Union.* New York: Cambridge University Press.
Boeva, Irina, and Viacheslav Shironin
   1992   *Russians between State and Market: The Generations Compared.* Glasgow: University of Strathclyde Studies in Public Policy, no. 205.
Boldin, Valery
   1994   *Ten Years That Shook the World.* New York: Basic Books.
Bremmer, Ian, and Ray Taras, eds.
   1996   *New States, New Politics: Building the Post-Soviet Nations.* Cambridge: Cambridge University Press.
Breslauer, George W.
   1978   "On the Adaptability of Soviet Welfare-State Authoritarianism." In *Soviet Society and the Communist Party,* ed. Karl W. Ryavec, 3–25. Amherst: University of Massachusetts Press.
Brezhnev, L.I.
   1978   *Leninskim kursom.* Vol. 6. Moscow: Izdatel'stvo politicheskoi literatury.
Brovkin, Vladimir
   1990   "The Making of Elections to the Congress of People's Deputies (CPD) in March 1989." *Russian Review* 49:417–42.
Brown, Archie
   1996   *The Gorbachev Factor.* Oxford: Oxford University Press.
Brunner, Georg
   1990   "Elections in the Soviet Union." In *Elections in Socialist States,* ed. Robert K. Furtak. Hemel Hempstead, Herts.: Harvester Wheatsheaf.
Brym, Robert J., and Andrei Degtyarev
   1993   "Anti-Semitism in Moscow: Results of an October 1992 Survey," *Slavic Review* 52:1–12.

Budilova, Elena, Leonid Gordon, and Alexei Terekhin
 1996 "Elektoraty veduyushchikh partii i dvizhenii na vyborakh 1995 g.
        (Mnogomerno-statisticheskii analiz)." *Ekonomicheskie i sotsial'nye
        peremeny: monitoring obshchestvennogo mneniya*, no. 2, 18–24.
Budte s nami
 1995 Moscow: Kongress russkikh obshchin.
Burton, Michael, John Higley, and Richard Gunther
 1992 "Elite Transformations and Democratic Regimes." In *Elites and
        Democratic Consolidation in Latin America and Southern Europe*, ed.
        John Higley and Richard Gunther, 1–37. New York: Cambridge
        University Press.
Butler, David, and Austin Ranney, eds.
 1994 *Referendums around the World*. London: Macmillan.
Butler, David, and Donald Stokes
 1969 *Political Change in Britain: Forces Shaping Electoral Choice*. London: Mac-
        millan.
Byulleten': see *Vestnik*
Campbell, Angus, Philip E. Converse, Warren Miller, and Donald E. Stokes
 1960 *The American Voter*. New York: Wiley.
Carnaghan, Ellen
 1994 *Alienation, Apathy or Ambivalence? "Don't Knows" and Democracy in
        Russia*. Glasgow: University of Strathclyde Studies in Public Pol-
        icy, no. 237.
Center for the Preservation of Contemporary Documentation, Moscow
 1985 Fond 89, perechen' 36, document 16.
 1991a Fond 89, perechen' 22, document 24.
 1991b Fond 89, perechen' 22, document 59.
 1991c Fond 89, perechen' 22, document 63.
 1991d Fond 89, perechen' 22, document 65.
 1991e Fond 89, perechen' 22, document 81.
Chervertyi S"ezd narodnykh deputatov SSSR 17–27 dekabrya 1990 g.
 1991 *Stenograficheskii otchet*. 4 vols. Moscow: Izdanie Verkhovnogo Soveta
        SSSR.
Chinn, Jeff, and Robert K. Kaiser, eds.
 1996 *Russians as the New Minority: Ethnicity and Nationalism in the Soviet Suc-
        cessor States*. Boulder, Colo.: Westview.
Colton, Timothy J.
 1979 *Commissars, Commanders, and Civilian Authority: The Structure of Soviet
        Military Politics*. Cambridge, Mass.: Harvard University Press.
 1995 "Boris Yeltsin: Russia's All-thumbs Democrat." In *Patterns in Post-
        Soviet Leadership*, ed. Timothy J. Colton and Robert C. Tucker,
        49–74. Boulder, Colo.: Westview.
Commission on Security and Cooperation in Europe
 1990 *Elections in the Baltic States and Soviet Republics*. Washington, D.C.:
        Government Printing Office.

Connor, Walter D., and Zvi Y. Gitelman, eds.
　1977　*Public Opinion in European Socialist Systems*. New York: Praeger.
Converse, Philip E., and Georges Dupeux
　1966　"Politicization of the Electorate in France and the United States." In
　　　Elections and the Political Order, ed. Angus Campbell et al. New
　　　York: Wiley.
Cook, Linda J.
　1993　*The Soviet Social Contract and Why It Failed*. Cambridge, Mass.: Har-
　　　vard University Press.
Cox, Gary W., and Samuel Kernell, eds.
　1991　*Divided Government*. Boulder, Colo.: Westview.
Crawford, Beverly, and Arend Lijphart, eds.
　1995　"Post-Communist Transformation in Eastern Europe." *Comparative
　　　Political Studies* 28, no. 2, 171–314.
Crewe, Ivor
　1994　"Voters, Parties and Leaders Thirty Years On." In *Developing Democ-
　　　racy*, ed. Ian Budge and David McKay, 56–78. London: Sage.
Dalton, Russell J.
　1996　*Citizen Politics: Public Opinion and Political Parties in Advanced Western
　　　Democracies*. 2d ed. Chatham, N.J.: Chatham House.
Davydov, A.A.
　1991　"Vsesoyuznyi referendum—vzglyad sotsiologa." *Sotsiologicheskie
　　　issledovaniya* no. 8, 154.
*XIX Vsesoyuznaya konferentsiya Kommunisticheskoi partii Sovetskogo Soyuza 28
iyunya–1 iyulya 1988 goda.*
　1988　*Stenograficheskii otchet*. 2 vols. Moscow: Politizdat.
Deklaratsiya Obshchestvennogo ob'edineniya "Yabloko"
　1995　Moscow. Mimeographed.
Dempsey, Judy, and Quentin Peel
　1995　"Yavlinsky Warns of Poll Delay Dangers," *Financial Times*, 13
　　　November, 2.
De Waal, Thomas
　1996　"Yeltsin Trails Badly in Russia's Biggest Opinion Poll So Far." *The
　　　Times* (London), 1 May, 12.
DiFranceisco, Wayne, and Zvi Gitelman
　1984　"Soviet Political Culture and 'Covert Participation' in Policy Imple-
　　　mentation." *American Political Science Review* 78:603–21.
Di Palma, Giuseppe
　1990　*To Craft Democracies: An Essay on Democratic Transitions*. Berkeley: Uni-
　　　versity of California Press.
Dmitriev, A.V., and Zh. T. Toshchenko
　1994　"Sotsiologicheskii opros i politika." *Sotsiologicheskie issledovaniya*, no. 5,
　　　42–51.
Duchacek, Ivo
　1973　*Power Maps: The Comparative Politics of Constitutions*. Santa Barbara,
　　　Calif.: ABC Clio.

The Economist
    1996   "Russia's Daunting Future." 6 July, 41–42.

Edwards, George C. III, with Alec M. Gallup
    1990   *Presidential Approval: A Sourcebook.* Baltimore: Johns Hopkins University Press.

Eliseev, B.
    1992   *Institut Prezidenta Rossiiskoi Federatsii.* Moscow: Yuridicheskaya literatura.

Emmons, Terence
    1983   *The Formation of Political Parties and the First National Elections in Russia.* Cambridge, Mass.: Harvard University Press.

European Bank for Reconstruction and Development (EBRD)
    1995   *Transition Report 1995.* London: EBRD.

European Institute for the Media
    1996a *Media and the Russian Presidential Elections: Preliminary Report.* Düsseldorf: European Institute for the Media.
    1996b *Monitoring the Media Coverage of the 1995 Russian Parliamentary Elections: Final Report.* Düsseldorf: European Institute for the Media.

European Parliament
    1996   *Report on the Observation of the Legislative Elections in Russia of 17 December 1995.* Brussels: European Parliament Delegation for Relations with Russia. Duplicated.

Evans, Geoffrey, and Stephen Whitefield
    1993   "Identifying the Bases of Party Competition in Eastern Europe." *British Journal of Political Science* 23, no. 4:521–48.

Fedorov, Boris
    1995   *Vpered, Rossiya!* Moscow: Dvizhenie "Vpered, Rossiya!"

Feshbach, Murray, and Alfred Friendly
    1992   *Ecocide in the USSR: Health and Nature under Siege.* New York: Basic Books.

Filatov, Sergei
    1995   *Na puti k demokratii.* Moscow: Moskovskii rabochii.

Finer, S.E., Vernon Bogdanor, and Bernard Rudden, eds.
    1995   *Comparing Constitutions.* Oxford: Clarendon Press.

Fiorina, Morris P.
    1981   *Retrospective Voting in American National Elections.* New Haven: Yale University Press.

Fish, Steven
    1995   *Democracy from Scratch: Opposition and Regime in the New Russian Revolution.* Princeton: Princeton University Press.

Frazer, Graham, and George Lancelle
    1994   *Zhirinovsky: The Little Black Book.* Harmondsworth, Middlesex: Penguin.

Freedom House
    1994   "The Comparative Survey of Freedom: 1994." *Freedom Review* 25:4–21.

Freeland, Chrystia
     1995a "Democracy Indicted in the Name of Reform." *Financial Times*, 7 November, 2.
     1995b "Turn against the Crimson Tide." *Financial Times*, 11 November, 2.
     1996a "Draped in the Enemy Flag." *Financial Times*, 11 May, 2.
     1996b "Russian Reform on Ice." *Financial Times*, 20 January, 2.
Freeland, Chrystia, and John Lloyd
     1996 "Russia's Communists Cry Foul." *Financial Times*, 23 May, 2.
Friedgut, T.H.
     1979 *Political Participation in the USSR*. Princeton: Princeton University Press.
Gallagher, Michael, and Pier Vincenzo Uleri, eds.
     1996 *The Referendum Experience in Europe*. London: Macmillan.
Garton Ash, Timothy
     1990 "Eastern Europe: Après le Déluge, Nous." *New York Review of Books* 37 (16 August):51–57.
Gessen, Masha
     1995 "Cross Purposes." *New Statesman and Society*, 22 September, 22–23.
Gibson, James L.
     1994a "Survey Research in the Past and Future USSR: Reflections on the Methodology of Mass Opinion Surveys." *Research in Micropolitics* 4:87–114.
     1994b "Understanding Anti-Semitism in Russia: An Analysis of the Politics of Anti-Jewish Attitudes." *Slavic Review* 53:796–806.
Gibson, James L., Raymond M. Duch, and Kent L. Tedin
     1992 "Democratic Values and the Transformation of the Soviet Union." *Journal of Politics* 54:329–71.
Gilison, Jerome M.
     1968 "Soviet Elections as a Measure of Dissent: The Missing One Percent." *American Political Science Review* 62:814–26.
Gorbachev, Mikhail
     1987a *Izbrannye rechi i stat'i*. Vol. 2. Moscow: Izdatel'stvo politicheskoi literatury.
     1987b *Izbrannye rechi i stat'i*. Vol. 3. Moscow: Izdatel'stvo politicheskoi literatury.
     1987c *Izbrannye rechi i stat'i*. Vol. 4. Moscow: Izdatel'stvo politicheskoi literatury.
     1987d *Perestroika*. London: Collins.
     1989 *Izbrannye rechi i stat'i*. Vol. 5. Moscow: Izdatel'stvo politicheskoi literatury.
Gorbacheva, Raisa
     1991 *Ya nadeyus'*. Moscow: Novosti.
Goskomstat
     1993 *Rossiiskaya Federatsiya v 1992 godu. Statisticheskii ezhegodnik*. Respublikanskii informatsionno-izdatel'skii tsentr.

Graham, Thomas
1995 "Novyi rossiiskii rezhim." *Nezavisimaya gazeta,* 23 November, 5.
Gregory, Paul R.
1990 *Restructuring the Soviet Economic Bureaucracy.* New York: Cambridge University Press.
Grossman, Gregory
1977 "The 'Second Economy' of the USSR." *Problems of Communism* 26:25–40.
Grushin, B.A.
1967 *Mneniya o mire i mir mnenii.* Moscow: Izdatel'stvo politicheskoi literatury.
Grushin, B.A., and L.A. Onikov
1980 *Massovaya informatsiya v sovetskom promyshlennom gorode.* Moscow: Politizdat.
Grushin, Boris
1994 "Fiasko sotsial'noi mysli." *Mir mnenii i mneniya o mire,* no. 5, 9–11.
Haas, Silja, Robert W. Orttung, and Ondrej Soukup
1995 "A Demographic Who's Who of the Candidates from the 12 Leading Parties." *Transition* 1, no. 22 (1 December), 11–13.
Hahn, Jeffrey
1988 "An Experiment in Competition: The 1987 Elections to the Local Soviets." *Slavic Review* 47:434–47.
Hall, Peter, Jack Hayward, and Howard Machin, eds.
1994 *Developments in French Politics,* Rev. ed. London: Macmillan.
Halligan, Liam, and Boris Mozdoukhov
1995 *A Guide to Russia's Parliamentary Elections.* London: Centre for Transition Economics Briefing, no. 1. Mimeographed.
Hankiss, Elemer
1990 *East European Alternatives.* Oxford: Clarendon Press.
Hayes, Bernadette C., and Clive S. Bean
1993 "Political Efficacy: A Comparative Study of the United States, West Germany, Great Britain, and Australia." *European Journal of Political Research* 23:261–80.
Hayward, Jack, ed.
1993 *De Gaulle to Mitterrand: Presidential Power in France.* London: Hurst.
Hazareesingh, Sudhir
1994 *Political Traditions in Modern France.* Oxford: Oxford University Press.
Hearst, David
1996a "Election 'Could Split Army and Country.'" *The Guardian,* 8 May, 15.
1996b "Yeltsin Promises Poll Will Go Ahead." *The Guardian,* 7 May, 7.
Hearst, David, and Martin Walker
1996 "Fears Grow That Nervous Yeltsin May Delay Ballot." *The Guardian,* 6 May, 2.

Hedlund, Stefan, and Niclas Sundstrøm

    1996   "Does Palermo Represent the Future for Moscow?" *Journal of Public Policy* 16, no. 2: forthcoming.

Hermet, Guy, Richard Rose, and Alain Rouquié, eds.

    1978   *Elections without Choice.* London: Macmillan.

Higley, John, and Richard Gunther, eds.

    1992   *Elites and Democratic Consolidation in Latin America and Southern Europe.* New York: Cambridge University Press.

Hill, Ronald J.

    1976   "The CPSU in a Soviet Election Campaign." *Soviet Studies* 28:590–98.

    1980   *Soviet Politics, Political Science and Reform.* Oxford: Martin Robertson.

Hockstader, Lee, and David Hoffman

    1996   "From Tears to Triumph: How Yeltsin Came Back." *International Herald Tribune,* 8 July, 1.

Holzmann, Robert, Janos Gacs, and George Winckler, eds.

    1995   *Output Decline in Eastern Europe.* Dordrecht, Netherlands: Kluwer.

Hough, Jerry F.

    1994   "The Russian Elections of 1993: Public Attitudes toward Economic Reform and Democratization." *Post-Soviet Affairs* 10, no. 1 (January–March):1–37.

Howard, A.E., ed.

    1993   *Constitution Making in Eastern Europe.* Baltimore: Johns Hopkins University Press.

Hughes, James

    1994   "The 'Americanization' of Russian Politics: Russia's First Television Election, December 1993." *Journal of Communist Studies and Transition Politics* 10, no. 2 (June):125–50.

Huntington, Samuel P.

    1991   *The Third Wave: Democratization in the Late Twentieth Century.* Norman: University of Oklahoma Press.

Huskey, Eugene

    1995a "The Rise of Contested Politics in Central Asia: Elections in Kyrgyzstan, 1989–90." *Europe-Asia Studies* 47:813–33.

    1995b "Weak Russian State Expanding Exponentially." *Kennan Institute for Advanced Russian Studies Meeting Report* 12, no. 18.

Il'ichev, L.F., ed.

    1983   *Filosofskii entsiklopedicheskii slovar'.* Moscow: Sovetskaya entsiklopediya.

Inglehart, Ronald

    1977   *The Silent Revolution: Changing Values and Political Styles among Western Publics.* Princeton: Princeton University Press.

International Foundation for Electoral Systems (IFES)

    1995   Russian National Survey. Washington, D.C.: IFES. Mimeographed.

International Institute for Democracy, ed.

    1995   *The Rebirth of Democracy: 12 Constitutions of Central and Eastern Europe.* Strasbourg: Council of Europe Press.

Ishiyama, John T.

1996 "Red Phoenix? The Communist Party in Post-Soviet Russian Politics."
      Party Politics 2:147–75.

"Izbiratel'nye bloki: kto est' kto"

1993 *Rossiiskie vesti,* 11 December, 2.

Jones, Charles O.

1994 *The Presidency in a Separated System.* Washington D.C.: Brookings
      Institution.

Kagarlitsky, Boris

1995 *Restoration in Russia.* London: Verso.

*Kalendarnyi plan meropriyatii po podgotovke i provedeniyu vyborov deputatov
Gosudarstvennoi Dumy Federal'nogo Sobraniya Rossiiskoi Federatsii*

1995 Moscow: Tsentral'naya izbiratel'naya komissiya Rossiiskoi Federatsii.

Karklins, Rasma

1986 "Soviet Elections Revisited: Voter Abstention in Noncompetitive Vot-
      ing." *American Political Science Review* 80:449–69.

Katsenelinboigen, Aron

1978 *Studies in Soviet Economic Planning.* White Plains, N.Y.: Sharpe.

Keeler, John T.S., and Martin Schain

1996 "Presidents, Premiers and Models of Democracy in France." In
      Chirac's Challenge, ed. Keeler and Schain. New York: St. Martin's.

Khakamada, Irina

1995 *Obshchee delo: prosto o slozhnom.* Moscow: Rektor komm'yunikeishnz.

Kiewiet, D.R.

1983 *Macroeconomics and Micropolitics.* Chicago: University of Chicago Press.

Kim, Jae-On, and Charles W. Mueller

1978 *Factor Analysis: Statistical Methods and Practical Issues.* Beverly Hills,
      Calif.: Sage.

Kinder, Donald, and D.R. Kiewiet

1979 "Economic Discontent and Political Behavior." *American Journal of Po-
      litical Science* 23:495–527.

1981 "Sociotropic Politics: The American Case." *British Journal of Political
      Science* 11:129–61.

King, Gary C.

1989 *Unifying Political Methodology.* Cambridge: Cambridge University
      Press.

Kitschelt, Herbert

1995 *Party Systems in East Central Europe: Consolidation or Fluidity?* Glasgow:
      University of Strathclyde Studies in Public Policy, no. 241.

Klecka, William

1980 *Discriminant Analysis.* Beverly Hills, Calif.: Sage Series in Quantitative
      Applications in the Social Sciences, 07-001.

Klyamkin, Igor

1993 "Do i posle parlamentskikh vyborov." *Polis,* no. 6, 39–53.

Knutsen, Oddbjorn
    1995 "The Impact of Old Politics and New Politics Value Orientations on Party Choice." *Journal of Public Policy* 15, no. 1, 1–64.
Kolkowicz, Roman
    1967 *The Soviet Military and the Communist Party.* Princeton: Princeton University Press.
Kolosov, V.A., et al.
    1990 *Vesna 89. Geografiya i anatomiya parlamentskikh vyborov.* Moscow: Progress.
Komarovsky, V.S., ed.
    1989 *Vremya vybora.* Moscow: Politizdat.
Komarovsky, V., and E. Dugin
    1989 "Otsenka izbiratelei." *Sovety narodnykh deputatov,* no. 11, 63–67.
Konstitutsii Rossiiskoi Federatsii (al'ternativnye proekty)
    1993 2 vols. Moscow: Obozrevatel'.
Konstitutsionnyi vestnik
    1990–94 17 numbers. Moscow: Konstitutsionnaya komissiya RSFSR.
Kornai, Janos
    1992 *The Socialist System: The Political Economy of Communism.* Princeton: Princeton University Press.
Kornberg, Allan, and Harold Clarke
    1992 *Citizens and Community: Political Support in a Representative Democracy.* Cambridge: Cambridge University Press.
Kostikov, Vyacheslav
    1996 "Rasstavanie s Prezidentom." *Argumenty i fakty,* no. 3, 3, and no. 5, 3.
Kostyukov, Anatolii
    1994 "Provokatsiya po neostorozhnosti." *Obshchaya gazeta,* no. 19, 8.
Kotok, Viktor F.
    1964 *Referendum v sisteme sotsialisticheskoi demokratii.* Moscow: Nauka.
Kowalewski, David
    1980 "Human Rights Potential in the USSR: Statistical Trends for 1965–1978." *Universal Human Rights* 2:5–29.
Kramer, Michael
    1996 "Rescuing Boris." *Time,* 15 July, 18–28.
Kryshtanovskaya, Olga, and Stephen White
    1993 "Public Attitudes to the KGB." *Europe-Asia Studies* 45:169–76.
Kuznetsov, E.L.
    1996 "Iz istorii sozdaniya instituta Prezidenta SSSR." *Gosudarstvo i pravo,* no. 5, 95–104.
Lange, Bernd-Peter
    1994 *The Russian Parliamentary Elections: Monitoring of the Election Coverage in the Russian Mass Media.* Düsseldorf: European Institute for the Media.
Lazarev, B.M.
    1990 "Prezident SSSR." *Sovetskoe gosudarstvo i pravo,* no. 7, 3–14.

1991 "Ob izmeneniyakh v pravovom statuse Prezidenta SSSR." *Sovetskoe gosudarstvo i pravo,* no. 8, 32–44.

Lazarsfeld, Paul, Bernard Berelson, and Hazel Gaudet
1944 *The People's Choice.* New York: Duell, Sloan and Pearce.

Lebed', Alexander
1995 *Za derzhavu obidno . . .* Moscow: Moskovskaya pravda.

Leitzel, Jim
1995 *Russian Economic Reform.* London and New York: Routledge.

Lentini, Peter
1991 "Reforming the Electoral System: The 1989 Elections to the USSR Congress of People's Deputies." *Journal of Communist Studies* 7, no. 1 (March):69–94.

1994a "Elections and Political Order in Russia: The 1993 Elections to the Russian State Duma." *Journal of Communist Studies and Transition Politics* 10, no. 2 (June):151–92.

1994b "Electoral Associations in the 1993 Elections to the Russian State Duma." *Journal of Communist Studies and Transition Politics* 10, no. 4 (December):1–36.

————, ed.
1995 *Elections and Political Order in Russia.* Budapest: Central European University Press.

Lentini, Peter, and Troy McGrath
1994 "The Rise of the Liberal Democrats and the 1993 Elections." *Harriman Institute Forum* 7, no. 6 (February).

L'Etang, Hugh
1995 *Ailing Leaders in Power 1914–1995.* London: Royal Society of Medicine.

Levada, Yuri
1995 *Democratic Disorder and Russian Public Opinion: Trends in VCIOM Surveys 1991–95.* Glasgow: University of Strathclyde Studies in Public Policy, no. 255.

1996 "Vybory: peisazh posle bitvy i pered nei." *Izvestiya,* 11 January, 2.

Levansky, V.A., et al.
1989 "Izbiratel'naya kampaniya po vyboram narodnykh deputatov SSSR 1989 g. (Opyt sotsiologicheskogo issledovaniya)." *Sovetskoe gosudarstvo i pravo,* no. 7, 12–25.

Lewis-Beck, Michael S.
1980 *Applied Regression: An Introduction.* Beverly Hills, Calif.: Sage.

1988 *Economics and Elections: The Major Western Democracies.* Ann Arbor: University of Michigan Press.

Liberal'nyi plan dlya Rossii
1995 2d ed. Moscow: Dvizhenie "Vpered, Rossiya!"

Ligachev, Ye. K.
1992 *Zagadka Gorbacheva.* Novosibirsk: Interbuk.

Lijphart, Arend, ed.
1992 *Parliamentary versus Presidential Government.* Oxford: Oxford University Press.

Linz, Juan J.
　　1978　"Non-Competitive Elections in Europe." In *Elections without Choice,*
　　　　　ed. Guy Hermet, Richard Rose, and Alain Rouquié. London: Mac-
　　　　　millan.
Linz, Juan J., and Arturo Valenzuela, eds.
　　1994　*The Failure of Presidential Democracy: Comparative Perspectives.* Balti-
　　　　　more: Johns Hopkins University Press.
Lipset, S.M.
　　1960　*Political Man.* New York: Doubleday.
Lipset, S.M., and Stein Rokkan, eds.
　　1967　*Party Systems and Voter Alignments.* New York: Free Press.
Lysenko, V.
　　1995　"Evolyutsiya post-kommunisticheskikh organizatsii." *Svobodnaya
　　　　　mysl',* no. 5, 66–74.
Lyubarsky, Kronid
　　1994a　"Fal'sifikatsiya." *Novoe vremya,* no. 7, 8–12.
　　1994b　"Fal'sifikatsiya-2." *Novoe vremya,* no. 9, 10–13.
McAllister, Ian, and Robert Darcy
　　1992　"Sources of Split-Ticket Voting in the 1988 American Elections." *Politi-
　　　　　cal Studies* 40, 695–712.
McAllister, Ian, and Stephen White
　　1995a　"Democracy, Parties, and Party Formation in Postcommunist Russia."
　　　　　Party Politics 1, 49–72.
　　1995b　"The Legacy of the Nomenklatura: Economic Privilege in
　　　　　Postcommunist Russia." *Coexistence* 32, 217–39.
McFaul, Michael, and Nikolai Petrov, eds.
　　1995　*Previewing Russia's 1995 Parliamentary Elections.* Washington, D.C.:
　　　　　Carnegie Endowment.
MacKuen, Michael B., Robert S. Erickson, and James A. Stimson
　　1992　"Peasants or Bankers? The American Electorate and the U.S. Econ-
　　　　　omy." *American Political Science Review* 86, 597–611.
Mair, Peter
　　1996　*What Is Different about Communist Party Systems?* Glasgow: University
　　　　　of Strathclyde Studies in Public Policy, no. 259.
Markov, Sergei
　　1995　"Izbiratel'nye ob'edineniya v Rossii v preddverii parlamentskikh
　　　　　vyborov 1995 goda." In Igor' Klyamkin et al., *Analiz elektorata
　　　　　politicheskikh sil Rossii.* Moscow: Komtekh, 62–91.
Materialy plenuma Tsentral'nogo komiteta KPSS 5–7 fevralya 1990 goda
　　1990　Moscow: Politizdat.
Matlock, Jack F. Jr.
　　1996　"The Struggle for the Kremlin." *New York Review of Books* 43, no. 13 (8
　　　　　August):28–34.
Maynard, John
　　1942　*The Russian Peasant.* 2 vols. London: Gollancz.

Medvedev, Roy
1975 *On Socialist Democracy.* London: Macmillan.
1979 *How I Ran for Election and How I Lost.* Nottingham: Spokesman.
Mendras, Marie
1993 "Les trois Russie. Analyse du référendum du 25 avril 1993." *Revue Française de Science Politique* 43: 897–939.
Mickiewicz, Ellen
1981 *Media and the Russian Public.* New York: Praeger.
Mikhaleva, N.A., and L.A. Morozova
1990 "Reforma respublikanskogo izbiratel'nogo zakonodatel'stva," *Sovetskoe gosudarstvo i pravo,* no. 6, 29–39.
Miller, Arthur H., William M. Reisinger, and Vicki L. Hesli, eds.
1993 *Public Opinion and Regime Change: The New Politics of Post-Soviet Societies.* Boulder, Colo.: Westview.
Miller, John
1993 *Mikhail Gorbachev and the End of Soviet Power.* London: Macmillan.
Miller, William L., Stephen White, and Paul Heywood
1996 "Twenty-five Days to Go: Measuring and Interpreting the Trends in Public Opinion during the 1993 Russian Election Campaign." *Public Opinion Quarterly* 60, 106–27.
Mishin, A.A.
1987 "Referendum." In *Yuridicheskii entsiklopedicheskii slovar'.* 2d ed., ed. A. Ya. Sukharev, 410. Moscow: Sovetskaya entsiklopediya.
Mishler, William, and Richard Rose
1996a "Trajectories of Hope and Fear." *Comparative Political Studies* 28:553–81.
1996b "Trust, Distrust and Scepticism in Post-Communist Societies." *Journal of Politics,* forthcoming.
Moore, Rita
1995 "The Path to the New Russian Constitution." *Demokratizatsiya* 3:44–60.
Morrison, John
1991 *Boris Yeltsin: From Bolshevik to Democrat.* Harmondsworth, Middlesex: Penguin.
Narodnoe khozyaistvo SSSR v 1982 g. Statisticheskii Sbornik
1983 Moscow: Finansy i statistika.
Nelson, Lynn D., and Irina Y. Kuzes
1995 *Radical Reform in Yeltsin's Russia: Political, Economic, and Social Dimensions.* Armonk, N.Y.: Sharpe.
Nenashev, N.F.
1993 *Poslednee pravitel'stvo SSSR.* Moscow: Krom.
Neumann, Iver B.
1996 *Russia and the Idea of Europe.* London: Routledge.
Neustadt, Richard E.
1960 *Presidential Power.* New York: Wiley.
Niemi, Richard, and Herbert Weisberg
1984 *Controversies in Voting Behavior.* Washington, D.C.: CQ Press.

Noelle-Neumann, Elisabeth

1993   *The Spiral of Silence: Public Opinion—Our Social Skin.* 2d ed. Chicago: University of Chicago Press.

Ob obshchikh printsipakh organizatsii mestnogo samoupravleniya v Rossiiskoi Federatsii

1995   Moscow: Yuridicheskaya literatura.

Ob osnovnykh garantiyakh izbiratel'nykh prav grazhdan Rossiiskoi Federatsii

1995   Moscow: Yuridicheskaya literatura.

Obshchestvennoe mnenie v tsifrakh

1989   No. 2, September.

O'Donnell, Guillermo

1993   "On the State, Democratization and Some Conceptual Problems: A Latin American View with Glances at Some Postcommunist Countries." *World Development* 21, no. 8:1355–69.

1994   "Delegative Democracy." *Journal of Democracy* 5:55–69.

O'Donnell, Guillermo, and Philippe C. Schmitter, eds.

1986   *Transitions from Authoritarian Rule: Tentative Conclusions about Uncertain Democracies.* Baltimore: Johns Hopkins University Press.

OECD

1995   *Economic Survey: The Russian Federation.* Paris: OECD.

Okun'kov, L.A.

1996   *Prezident Rossiiskoi Federatsii. Konstitutsiya i politicheskaya praktika.* Moscow: Infra M/Norma.

Onikov, L.A., and N.V. Shishlin, compilers

1978   *Kratkii politicheskii slovar'.* Moscow: Izdatel'stvo politicheskoi literatury.

1989   *Kratkii politicheskii slovar'.* 6th ed. Moscow: Izdatel'stvo politicheskoi literatury.

O referendume Rossiiskoi Federatsii

1995   Moscow: Yuridicheskaya literatura.

Orttung, Robert W.

1995   "Yeltsin's Most Dangerous Rival: A Profile of Aleksandr Lebed." *Transition* 1, no. 22: 17–19.

Orttung, Susan Kennedy

1995   "Will the Duma Elections Be Fair?" *Transition* 1, no. 22 (1 December), 40–42.

OSCE

1996   *Report on the Elections to the State Duma in the Russian Federation 17 December 1995.* Copenhagen: OSCE International Secretariat.

Osnovnye polozheniya programmy bloka "Profsoyuzy i promyshlenniki Rossii—Soyuz truda"

1995   Moscow. Mimeographed.

O vyborakh deputatov Gosudarstvennoi Dumy Federal'nogo Sobraniya Rossiiskoi Federatsii

1995   Moscow: Yuridicheskaya literatura.

O vyborakh Prezidenta Rossiiskoi Federatsii

1995   Moscow: Yuridicheskaya literatura.

Owen, Elizabeth
1996 "Vote Called Fair in General, Biased in Parts." *Moscow Times,* 6 July, 4.
Pervyi S"ezd narodnykh deputatov SSSR 25 maya–9 iyunya 1989 g.
1989 *Stenograficheskii otchet.* 6 vols. Moscow: Izvestiya, vol. 1.
Pestrukhina, Elena
1994 "Bednye pereigrali bogatykh." *Moskovskie novosti,* no. 18, 7A.
Platforma izbiratel'nogo ob"edineniya "Pamfilova-Gurov-Lysenko" (Respublikanskaya partiya Rossiiskoi Federatsii).
1995 Moscow: Institut sovremennoi politiki.
Polozhenie o vyborakh deputatov Gosudarstvennoi Dumy v 1993 godu
1993 Moscow: Izvestiya.
Ponomarev, B.N., ed.
1982 *Konstitutsiya SSSR. Politiko-pravovoi kommentarii.* Moscow: Izdatel'stvo politicheskoi literatury.
Post, Jerrold M., and Robert S. Robins
1993 *When Illness Strikes the Leader.* New Haven: Yale University Press.
Potichnyj, Peter J.
1992 "Elections in the Ukraine, 1990." In *The Politics of Nationality and the Erosion of the USSR,* ed. Zvi Gitelman. London: Macmillan.
Pravda, Alex
1986 "Elections in Communist Party States." In *Communist Politics: A Reader,* ed. Stephen White and Daniel Nelson. New York: New York University Press.
Predvaritel'nye itogi
1993 A set of results of elections to the Federation Council and State Duma produced under the auspices of the president and government. Duplicated.
Predvybornaya platforma [bloka Ivan Rybkina]
1995 Moscow: Realisty.
Predvybornaya pozitsiya izbiratelnogo bloka 'Kommunisty-Trudovaya Rossiya—Za Sovetskii Soyuz.'
1995 Moscow. Mimeographed.
Pribylovsky, Vladimir
1995 *43 linii spektra. Kratkoe opisanie vsekh predvybornykh blokov.* Moscow: Panorama.
Proekt konstitutsii Rossiiskoi Federatsii. Sbornik materialov
1992 Moscow: Respublika.
Programma vserossiiskogo obshchestvenno-politicheskogo dvizheniya "Nash dom—Rossiya"
1995a Moscow: NDR.
Programma politicheskogo dvizheniya "Zhenshchiny Rossii"
1995b Moscow: Zhenshchiny Rossii.
Programma. Ustav Agrarnoi partii Rossii.
1995c Moscow: APR.

Pugacheva, M.G.
1994   "Institut konkretnykh sotsiologicheskikh issledovanii Akademii nauk
       SSSR, 1968–1972 gody." *Sotsiologicheskii zhurnal* 1, no. 2:158–72.
Putnam, Robert D., with Robert Leonardi and Raffaella Y. Nanetti
1993   *Making Democracy Work.* Princeton: Princeton University Press.
Radio Liberty
1991   *Radio Liberty Report on the USSR* 3 (29 March):13.
Radkey, Oliver Henry
1950   *The Election of the Russian Constituent Assembly of 1917.* Cambridge,
       Mass.: Harvard University Press.
Raina, Peter, ed.
1995   *The Constitutions of New Democracies in Europe.* London: Merlin.
Razmustov, Vladimir
1995   "Istoriya prinyatiya zakona o vyborakh v Dumu." *Nezavisimaya gazeta,*
       29 November, 1, 5.
Reeves, Phil
1996   "Yeltsin's New Ally Reveals His Darker Side." *Independent* (London),
       28 June, 13.
Remington, Thomas F., and Steven S. Smith
1995   "The Development of Parliamentary Parties in Russia." *Legislative
       Studies Quarterly* 22:457–89.
Remnick, David
1996   "The War for the Kremlin." *New Yorker,* 22 July, 40–57.
Rigby, T.H.
1964   "Crypto-politics." *Survey* 50:183–94.
Rodin, Ivan
1993   "Poka do vyborov dopushchen 21 izbiratel'nykh blokov."
       Nezavisimaya gazeta, 9 November 1993, 1.
Roeder, Philip G.
1989   "Electoral Avoidance in the Soviet Union." *Soviet Studies* 41:462–83.
1993   *Red Sunset: The Failure of Soviet Politics.* Princeton: Princeton
       University Press.
1994   "Varieties of Post-Soviet Authoritarian Regimes." *Post-Soviet Affairs*
       10, no. 1:61–101.
Rokkan, Stein
1970   *Citizens, Elections, Parties.* Oslo: Universitetsforlaget.
Rose, Richard
1991   *The Postmodern President.* 2d ed. Chatham, N.J.: Chatham House.
1992   "Escaping from Absolute Dissatisfaction: A Trial-and-Error Model of
       Change in Eastern Europe." *Journal of Theoretical Politics* 4, no. 4
       (October):371–94.
1993   "Contradictions between Micro and Macro-Economic Goals in Post-
       Communist Societies." *Europe-Asia Studies* 45:419–44.
1994a "Getting by without Government: Everyday Life in Russia." *Daedalus*
       123:41–62.

1994b "Postcommunism and the Problem of Trust." *Journal of Democracy* 5:18–30.

1995a "Adaptation, Resilience, Destitution: Alternative Responses to Transition in Ukraine." *Problems of Post-Communism* 42:52–61.

1995b "Beware Opinion Polls: There Are Too Many Parties to Pick the Winner." *Transition* 1, no. 22 (1 December):6–10.

1995c "A Crisis of Confidence in British Party Leaders?" *Contemporary Record* 9, no. 2, 273–93.

1995d "Freedom as a Fundamental Value." *International Social Science Journal,* no. 145, 457–71.

1995e "Mobilizing Demobilized Voters in Post-Communist Societies." *Party Politics* 1:549–63.

1995f *New Russia Barometer IV: Survey Results.* Glasgow: University of Strathclyde Studies in Public Policy, no. 250.

1995g "Russia as an Hour-Glass Society: A Constitution without Citizens." *East European Constitutional Review* 4:34–42.

1996a "Ex-Communists in Post-Communist Societies." *Political Quarterly,* 67:14–25.

1996b *New Russia Barometer V: Between the Elections.* Glasgow: University of Strathclyde Studies in Public Policy, no. 260.

1996c *What Is Europe?* New York: Longman.

Rose, Richard, Irina Boeva, and Viacheslav Shironin

1993 *How Russians Are Coping with Transition: New Russia Barometer II.* Glasgow: University of Strathclyde Studies in Public Policy, no. 216.

Rose, Richard, and Ellen Carnaghan

1995 "Generational Effects on Attitudes to Communist Regimes: A Comparative Analysis." *Post-Soviet Affairs* 11:28–56.

Rose, Richard, and Christian Haerpfer

1994a "Mass Response to Transformation in Post-Communist Societies." *Europe-Asia Studies* 46:3–28.

1994b *New Democracies Barometer III.* Glasgow: University of Strathclyde Studies in Public Policy, no. 230.

1994c *New Russia Barometer III: The Results.* Glasgow: University of Strathclyde Studies in Public Policy, no. 228.

1996 *New Democracies Barometer IV.* Glasgow: University of Strathclyde Studies in Public Policy, no. 262.

Rose, Richard, and Ian McAllister

1996 "Is Money the Measure of Welfare in Russia?" *Review of Income and Wealth* 42, no. 1:75–91.

Rose, Richard, and William Mishler

1994 "Mass Reaction to Regime Change in Eastern Europe: Polarization or Leaders and Laggards?" *British Journal of Political Science* 24, no. 2:159–82.

1995   *What Are the Alternatives to Democracy in Post-Communist Societies?* Glasgow: University of Strathclyde Studies in Public Policy, no. 248.

1996a   "Representation and Leadership in Post-Communist Political Systems." *Journal of Communist Studies and Transition Politics* 12, no. 2:224–46.

1996b   "Testing the Churchill Hypothesis: Support for Democracy and Its Alternatives." *Journal of Public Policy* 16, no. 7:29–58.

Rose, Richard, and Evgeny Tikhomirov

1995   *Trends in the New Russia Barometer, 1992–1995.* Glasgow: University of Strathclyde Studies in Public Policy, no. 256.

Rose, Richard, Evgeny Tikhomirov, and William Mishler

1996   *Understanding Multi-Party Choice: The 1995 Duma Election.* Glasgow: University of Strathclyde Studies in Public Policy, no. 271.

Rossiiskaya Federatsiya v 1992 godu. Statisticheskii ezhegodnik

1993   Moscow: Respublikanskii informatsionno-izdatel'skii tsentr.

Rossiiskii statisticheskii ezhegodnik. 1994. Statisticheskii sbornik

1995   Moscow: Goskomstat Rossii.

Ryabov, Nikolai

1993   "Nam est' iz kogo vybirat'." *Rossiiskaya gazeta,* 11 December 1993, 1.

Rybkin, I.P., ed.

1994   *Pyataya Gosudarstvennaya Duma.* Moscow: Izvestiya.

Safarov, R.A.

1963   "Institut referenduma v usloviyakh obshche-narodnogo gosudar-stva." *Sovetskoe gosudarstvo i pravo* no. 6, 15–25.

1975   *Obshchestvennoe mnenie i gosudarstvennoe upravlenie.* Moscow:

Sakharov, N.Áuridicheskaya literatura.

1994   *Institut prezidentstva v sovremennom mire.* Moscow: Yuridicheskaya literatura.

Sakwa, Richard

1990   *Gorbachev and His Reforms, 1985–1990.* Hemel Hempstead, Herts: Philip Allan.

1993a   "Parties and the Multiparty System in Russia." *Radio Free Europe/Radio Liberty (RFE/RL) Research Report* 2 (30 July):7–15.

1993b   *Russian Politics and Society.* London: Routledge.

1995   "The Russian Elections of December 1993." *Europe-Asia Studies* 47, no. 2 (March):195–227.

1996   *The Communist Party of the Russian Federation and the Electoral Process.* Glasgow: University of Strathclyde Studies in Public Policy, no. 265.

Sartori, Giovanni

1994   *Comparative Constitutional Engineering.* London: Macmillan.

Sbornik normativnykh aktov o referendume Rossiiskoi Federatsii, 16 oktyabrya 1990–14 yanvarya 1993 g.

1993   Moscow: Izvestiya.

Schmidt, Josephine
   1996   "In the Court of Tsar Boris." *Transition* 2, no. 5 (8 March), 62.
Schneider, Eberhard
   1996   "Duma-Wahlen 1995." *Ost-Europa* 46:126–33, 225–36, 430–48.
Schumpeter, Joseph A.
   1952   *Capitalism, Socialism and Democracy.* 4th ed. London: George Allen &
          Unwin.
Scott, Carey
   1996   "Lenin's Heirs Plot Second Red Revolution." *Sunday Times* (London),
          31 March, sec. 1, 15.
Sedov, L.A.
   1994   "Politicheskii analiz. Nakanune i posle vyborov." *Ekonomicheskie i
          sotsial'nye peremeny: monitoring obshchestvennogo mneniya,* no. 2,
          28–30.
Seymour, Charles, and Donald Paige Frary
   1918   *How the World Votes: The Story of Democratic Development in Elections.* 2
          vols. Springfield, Mass.: C.A. Nichols.
Shakhnazarov, Georgii
   1993   *Tsena svobody. Reformatsiya Gorbacheva glazami ego pomoshchnika.* Mos-
          cow: Rossika/Zevs.
Shlapentokh, Vladimir
   1987   *The Politics of Sociology in the Soviet Union.* Boulder, Colo.: Westview.
   1989   *The Public and Private Life of the Soviet People: Changing Values in Post-
          Stalin Russia.* New York: Oxford University Press.
   1994   "The 1993 Russian Election Polls." *Public Opinion Quarterly* 58, no. 4
          (Winter):579–602.
Shlapentokh, Vladimir, et al.
   1994   *The New Russian Diaspora: Russian Minorities in the Former Soviet Repub-
          lics.* Armonk, N.Y.: Sharpe.
Shokarev, V. Yu., and A.G. Levinson
   1994   "Elektorat Zhirinovskogo." *Ekonomicheskie i sotsial'nye peremeny: moni-
          toring obshchestvennogo mneniya,* no. 2, 30–33.
Shugart, Matthew Soberg, and John M. Carey
   1992   *Presidents and Assemblies: Constitutional Design and Electoral Dynamics.*
          New York: Cambridge University Press.
Skilling, H. Gordon, and Franklyn Griffiths, eds.
   1967   *Interest Groups in Soviet Politics.* Princeton: Princeton University Press.
Slater, Wendy
   1994   "Russia's Plebiscite on a New Constitution." *Radio Free Europe/Radio
          Liberty Research Report* 3 (21 January):1–7.
Slider, Darrell
   1990   "The Soviet Union." *Electoral Studies* 9:295–302.
Slider, Darrell, Vladimir Gimpel'son, and Sergei Chugrov
   1994   "Political Tendencies in Russia's Regions: Evidence from the 1993 Par-
          liamentary Elections." *Slavic Review* 53, no. 3 (Fall), 711–32.

Sobchak, Anatolii
    1991   *Khozhdenie vo vlast'*. Moscow: Novosti.
Solzhenitsyn, Alexander
    1968   *V kruge pervom*. London: Collins.
Stalin, I.V.
    1967   *Sochineniya*. Vol. 1. Stanford, Calif.: Hoover Institution.
Stanley, Harold W., and Richard G. Niemi
    1994   *Vital Statistics on American Politics*. 4th ed. Washington, D.C.: CQ Press.
Steele, Jonathan
    1996   "Television Tsar." *The Guardian* (London), 1 July, sec. 2, 15.
Sud'bu strany reshaet kazhdyi (O pervom referendume SSSR)
    1991   Moscow: Izvestiya.
Suksi, Markku
    1993   *Bringing in the People: A Comparison of the Constitutional Forms and Practices of the Referendum*. Dordrecht: Nijhoff.
Taagepera, Rein
    1990   "Baltic Elections, February–April 1990." *Electoral Studies* 9:303–11.
Taagepera, R., and M.S. Shugart
    1989   *Seats and Votes: The Effects and Determinants of Electoral Systems*. New Haven: Yale University Press.
Taras, Ray
    1993   "Leaderships and Executives." In *Developments in East European Politics*, ed. Stephen White, Judy Batt, and Paul Lewis. Durham: Duke University Press.
Taylor, Charles L., and David A. Jodice
    1983   *World Handbook of Political and Social Indicators*. Vol. 1. New Haven: Yale University Press.
Thornhill, John
    1996a "Russian Communists: Same but Different," *Financial Times*, 14 January, 2.
    1996b "Russia's Second Round Already Under Way." *Financial Times*, 18 July, 2.
Thornhill, John, and Chrystia Freeland
    1996   "Showdown in the Kremlin Dark." *Financial Times*, 21 June, 2.
Thurber, James A.
    1991   *Divided Democracy: Cooperation and Conflict between the President and Congress*. Washington D.C.: CQ Press.
Tolz, Vera
    1993   "Drafting the New Russian Constitution." *Radio Free Europe/Radio Liberty Research Report* 2:1–12.
Tolz, Vera, and Julia Wishnevsky
    1994   "Election Queries Make Russians Doubt Democratic Process." *Radio Free Europe/Radio Liberty Research Report* 3, no. 13 (1 April): 1–6.
Towster, Julian
    1948   *Political Power in the USSR 1917–1947*. New York: Oxford University Press.

Transition
1995   "Russia Prepares to Vote." *Transition* 1, no. 22:6–43.

Treivish, Andrei
1993   "Izbiratel'naya raznogolitsa." *Segodnya*, 23 October, 3.

Tretii [III] S"ezd Kommunisticheskoi partii Rossiiskoi Federatsii (materialy i dokumenty)
1995   Moscow: Informpechat'.

Ulc, Otto
1982   "Legislative Politics in Czechoslovakia." In *Legislatures in Comparative Perspective*, ed. Daniel N. Nelson and Stephen White. Albany, N.Y.: SUNY Press.

Unger, Aryeh
1981   "Political Participation in the USSR: YCL and CPSU." *Soviet Studies* 33:107–24.

Urban, Michael E.
1992   "Boris El'tsin, Democratic Russia and the Campaign for the Russian Presidency." *Soviet Studies* 44:187–208.

Vasil'ev, V.I., and A.E. Postnikov, eds.
1995   *Vybory v Gosudarstennuyu Dumu. Pravovye problemy.* Moscow: Bek.

Vedomosti
1938–93   Title varies: to 1989, *Vedomosti Verkhovnogo Soveta SSSR;* in 1989–91, *Vedomosti S"ezda narodnykh deputatov SSSR i Verkhovnogo Soveta SSSR;* in 1992–93 in the Russian Federation, *Vedomosti S"ezda narodnykh deputatov Rossiiskoi Federatsii i Verkhovnogo Soveta Rossiiskoi Federatsii.* Moscow, weekly.

Vestnik
1993–   [to 1995, *Byulleten'*] *Tsentral'noi izbiratel'noi komissii Rossiiskoi Federatsii.* Moscow, irregular.

Vneocherednoi tretii S"ezd narodnykh deputatov SSSR, 12–15 marta 1990 g.
1990   *Stenograficheskii otchet.* 3 vols. Moscow: Izdanie Verkhovnogo Soveta SSSR.

Vorotnikov, V.I.
1995   *A bylo eto tak . . . Iz dnevnika chlena Politbyuro TsK KPSS.* Moscow: Sovet veteranov knigoizdaniya.

Vybory deputatov Gosudarstvennoi Dumy. 1995. Elektoral'naya statistika.
1996   Moscow: Ves' mir.

Vychub, G.S.
1980   *Pis'ma trudyashchikhsya v sisteme massovoi raboty gazety.* Moscow: Izdatel'stvo Moskovskogo universiteta.

Vyzhutovich, Valerii
1994   "Tsentrizbirkom prevrashchaetsya v politicheskoe vedomstvo." *Izvestiya*, 4 May, 4.

Weaver, R. Kent, and Bert A. Rockman, eds.
1993   *Do Institutions Matter? Government Capabilities in the United States and Abroad.* Washington, D.C.: Brookings Institution.

Welch, Stephen
 1987 "Issues in the Study of Political Culture: The Example of Communist
   Party States." *British Journal of Political Science* 17:479–500.
White, Stephen
 1979 *Political Culture and Soviet Politics.* London: Macmillan.
 1983 "Political Communications in the USSR: Letters to Party, State and
   Press." *Political Studies* 31:43–60.
 1985 "Noncompetitive Elections and National Politics: The USSR Supreme
   Soviet Elections of 1984." *Electoral Studies* 4:215–29.
 1988 "Reforming the Electoral System." *Journal of Communist Studies* 4:1–17.
 1991 "The Soviet Elections of 1989: From Acclamation to Limited Choice."
   Coexistence 28:513–39.
 1994 *After Gorbachev.* 4th rev. ed. Cambridge: Cambridge University Press.
 1995 "Public Opinion and Political Science in Postcommunist Russia."
   European Journal of Political Research 27:507–26.
———, ed.
 1990 "Elections in Eastern Europe." *Electoral Studies* 9, no. 4: 275–366.
   Special issue.
White, Stephen, Graeme Gill, and Darrell Slider
 1993 *The Politics of Transition: Shaping a Post-Soviet Future.* Cambridge: Cambridge University Press.
White, Stephen, and Ian McAllister
 1996 "The CPSU and Its Members: Between Communism and
   Postcommunism." *British Journal of Political Science* 26, no.
   1:105–22.
White, Stephen, Ian McAllister, and Olga Kryshtanovskaya
 1994a "El'tsin and His Voters: Popular Support in the 1991 Russian Presidential Elections and After." *Europe-Asia Studies* 46:285–303.
 1994b "Religion and Politics in Postcommunist Russia." *Religion, State and
   Society* 22:75–88.
Wimberg, Ellen
 1992 "Socialism, Democratism and Criticism: The Soviet Press and the National Discussion of the 1936 Draft Constitution." *Soviet Studies*
   44:313–32.
Winiecki, Jan
 1988 *The Distorted World of Soviet-Type Economics.* London: Routledge.
Wyman, Matthew, Bill Miller, Stephen White, and Paul Heywood
 1994 "The Russian Elections of December 1993." *Electoral Studies* 13, no. 3
   (September):254–71.
Wyman, Matthew, Stephen White, Bill Miller, and Paul Heywood
 1995 "Public Opinion, Parties and Voters in the December 1993 Russian
   Elections." *Europe-Asia Studies* 47, no. 4 (June):591–614.
Yegorova, Yekaterina
 1995 "Selling Gray Candidates," *Moscow Times,* 15 December, 2.

Yeltsin [El'tsin], Boris

1990   *Ispoved' na zadannuyu temu.* Leningrad: Sovetskii pisatel'.

1994   *Zapiski Prezidenta.* Moscow: Ogonek.

Z

1990   "To the Stalin Mausoleum." *Daedalus* 119, no. 1 (Winter):295–344.

Za blagopoluchie cheloveka. Predvybornaya platforma Partii samoupravleniya trudyashchikhsya, sozdannoi i rukovodimoi Svyatoslavom Fedorovym.

1995   Moscow. Duplicated.

Za nashu Sovetskuyu rodinu! Predvybornaya platforma Kommunisticheskoi partii Rossiiskoi Federatsii.

1995   Moscow: Informpechat'.

Zaslavsky, Victor, and Robert J. Brym

1978   "The Functions of Elections in the USSR." *Soviet Studies* 30:362–71.

Zhirinovsky, Vladimir

1993   *Poslednii brosok na yug.* Moscow: LDP.

1995   *Programmnyi manifest Liberal'no-demokraticheskoi partii Rossii.* Moscow: LDP.

Zlatopol'sky, D.L.

1982   *Verkhovnyi Sovet SSSR—Vyrazitel' voli sovetskogo naroda.* Moscow: Yuridicheskaya literatura.

Zlobin, Nikolai

1994   "From the archives." *Demokratizatsiya* 2, no. 2 (Spring), 316–31.

Zlokazov, G.I.

1990   "Konstitutsiya 1977 goda. 'Nesvoevremennye' mysli sovremennikov." *Voprosy istorii KPSS*, no. 10, 72–85.

Zorkaya, N.A.

1996   "Prezidentskie vybory: elektoral'nye ustanovki rossiyan v aprele 1996 g." *Ekonomicheskie i sotsial'nye peremeny: monitoring obshchestvennogo mneniya*, no. 3, 11–16.

Index of Names

Index of Subjects

About the Authors

Stephen White is professor of politics and a member of the Institute of Russian and East European Studies at the University of Glasgow. He is also president of the British Association for Slavonic and East European Studies. His publications include *Political Culture and Soviet Politics*, *The Bolshevik Poster*, *After Gorbachev*, and *Russia Goes Dry*.

Richard Rose is director of the Centre for the Study of Public Policy, University of Strathclyde, and international adviser to the Paul Lazarsfeld Society, Vienna, with which he has been conducting surveys of more than fifteen postcommunist countries since 1991. Rose is internationally known for his writings on the quantitative aspects of comparative politics; he has given seminars and lectures in thirty-five countries, and his writings have been published in sixteen languages and *samizdat*.

Ian McAllister is professor of government and chair of the Department of Government at the University of Manchester. He has previously held appointments at the University of New South Wales and the University of Strathclyde. From mid-1997 he will be director of the Research School of Social Sciences at the Australian National University. He is the author of *Political Behavior* and coauthor of *Dimensions of Australian Society* and *The Australian Political System*. His research interests are in the areas of comparative political behavior, political parties, and voters and electoral systems.